The Voiding of Being

Studies in Philosophy and the History of Philosophy

General Editor: John C. McCarthy

Volume 61

The Voiding of Being

The Doing and Undoing of Metaphysics in Modernity

William Desmond

The Catholic University of America Press
Washington, D.C.

Copyright © 2020
The Catholic University of America Press
All rights reserved

Library of Congress Cataloging-in-Publication Data
Names: Desmond, William, 1951– author.
Title: The voiding of being : the doing and undoing of metaphysics in modernity / William Desmond.
Description: Washington, D.C. : The Catholic University of America Press, 2020. | Series: Studies in philosophy and the history of philosophy; Volume 61 | Includes bibliographical references and index. | Summary: "The author amplifies important themes in the unfolding of modern metaphysics, exploring diverse aspects of current skepticism and offering a defense in terms of his metaxological metaphysics. Along the way he engages both the long tradition and more modern writers, such as Heidegger and Marion"— Provided by publisher.
Identifiers: LCCN 2019037733 | ISBN 9780813232485 (cloth) | ISBN 9780813232492 (ebook)
Subjects: LCSH: Metaphysics.
Classification: LCC BD111 .D444 2020S | DDC 110—dc23
LC record available at https://lccn.loc.gov/2019037733

τὸ ὂν λέγεται πολλαχῶς
Aristotle, *Metaphysics* 1003b5

∞

For Conor, Liam, and James
Godsends, Grandchildren:
May they be good guests at the feast of creation

Contents

Acknowledgments   xi

Introduction   1

1. The Voiding of Being: On the Doing and Undoing of Metaphysics in Modernity   17

    The Plurivocity of Being and Modern Metaphysics   17
    The Doubling of Being and Metaphysics   19
    The Devaluation of Being: Between Autonomous Thought and Religion   23
    Rationalist and Empiricist Voidings: Dianoetic and Aesthetic Univocity   27
    Voiding Being and Transcendental Positing: The Kantian Equivocation   30
    Being Nothing and the Whole: Hegel's Speculative Completion   37
    The Overdeterminacy of Being and Transdialectical Metaphysics   41

2. Analogy and the Fate of Reason   49

    Analogy, Plurivocity, and the Fate of Reason   49
    Analogy, Reason, and Religious Figuring   53
    Modern Reason, Geometrical Figuring, Weakening Analogy   56
    Analogy, Univocity, and Correspondence   62
    Moralizing Analogy: The "as if" of Kantian Practical Reason   69
    Sublating Analogy Speculatively: The Hegelian "Is"   74
    Analogy and Reason's De-sublation: Post-Hegelian Postulations   78
    Reason's Plurivocal Promise, Revolt, and Aesthetic Analogy   83
    The Vocation of Transdialectical Reason: Analogy on the
        Verge of the Hyperbolic   88

3. The Dearth of Astonishment: On Curiosity, Scientism, and Thinking as Negativity   96

    Curiosity and Scientism   96
    Between Indeterminacy and Overdeterminacy   102
    Ontological Astonishment and Hegelian Negativity   104
    Being Overdeterminate: Wonder as Astonishment   106

Being Indeterminate: Wonder as Perplexity   112
Being Determinate: Wonder as Curiosity   116
The Idolatry of Contracted Curiosity and Its Limitless Self-Expansion   120

4. Are We All Scholastics Now? On Analytic, Dialectical, and Transdialectical Thinking   126

Schooling Philosophy   126
Hermeneutic and Technical Scholasticism   129
Analytic Thinking   133
Dialectical Thinking   142
Transdialectical Thinking   148
Deschooling Dialectic: Wittgenstein or Hegel Again?   154
School Days Over: Back to *Skolē*   158

5. Between System and Poetics: On the Practices of Philosophy   160

Vocation   160
Betweens   161
Metaxology   163
System   165
Antisystem   167
Being Systematic   170
Finesse   173
Poetics   176
Singing Thought   179
Religious Porosity   184
Beyond the Solitudes of Immanence   188

6. Saturated Phenomena and the Hyperboles of Being: On Marion's Postmetaphysical Thought   193

Opening Metaphysics: Not Quite a Has-been   193
General Contrast of Saturated Phenomena and the Hyperboles of Being   195
The Idiocy of Being and Vanity   203
The Aesthetics of Happening, Icons, Idols   207
The Erotics of Selving and the Erotic Phenomenon   211
The Agapeics of Community: Does Marion Redeem the Promise?   219

7. Being True to Mystery and Metaxological Metaphysics   226

Opening   226
Being True, Metaphysics, and Mystery   230
Being True to Mystery: Between Determinability and the Overdeterminate   235
Univocity, Equivocity, Being True to Mystery   237
Dialectic and Being True to Mystery   243
Metaxology and Being True to Mystery   246

8. Flux-Gibberish: For and against Heraclitus 252
    Opening 252
    Aristotle's Irritation 254
    Wording Flux and Gibberish 259
    Heraclitus and Saturated Equivocity 262
    Companions of Heraclitus: Hegel and Nietzsche 266
    Hegel's Endorsement of Heraclitus and Aristotle 270
    The Overdeterminacy of Being and the Fluent Cosmos 274
    Listening to Wording the Between 280

Selected Bibliography 285

Index 291

Acknowledgments

A slightly shorter version of chapter 1 appeared as "The Metaphysics of Modernity" in *Oxford Handbook in Theology and Modern European Thought*, edited by Nicholas Adams, Graham Ward, and George Pattison (Oxford: Oxford University Press, 2013), 543–63. A shorter version of chapter 2, "Analogy and the Fate of Reason," appeared in the *Oxford Handbook of Catholic Theology*, edited by Lewis Ayres (Oxford: Oxford University Press, 2019), 72–93. In chapter 3 I made use of some pages from "Overdeterminacy, Affirming Indeterminacy and the Dearth of Ontological Astonishment" that appeared in *The Significance of Indeterminacy: Perspectives from Asian and Continental Philosophy*, edited by Robert Scott and Gregory Moss (New York: Routledge, 2018), 51–66. Chapter 4 appeared in an earlier version as "Are We All Scholastics Now? On Analytic, Dialectical and Post-dialectical Thinking" in *Yearbook of the Irish Philosophical Society* (2010–11): 1–24. A version of chapter 5 appeared as "Between System and Poetics: On the Practices of Philosophy" in *Between System and Poetics: William Desmond and Philosophy after Dialectics*, edited by Thomas Kelly (Aldershot: Ashgate, 2007), 13–36. A version of chapter 8 appeared as "Flux-gibberish: For and Against Heraclitus," *Review of Metaphysics* 70 (March 2017): 473–505. I thank the publishers and editors for permission to make use of these materials.

For their generous openness to my work, I would like to warmly thank John Martino, philosophy and theology acquisitions editor at the Catholic University of America Press, as well as John McCarthy, general editor of the series in which this book appears. My gratitude to Theresa Walker for seeing the book through to publication. Finally, I am appreciative of the help of Paul Higgins and Ryan Duns in the copy-editing and proofing stages of the production of the book.

The Voiding of Being

Introduction

In contemporary philosophy the status and indeed the very viability of metaphysics is a much contested issue. One need only take cognizance of the following: the prevalence of contemporary claims about the overcoming (*Überwindung*) of metaphysics (Heidegger); or the project of the destruction (*Destruktion*) of the history of metaphysics (Heidegger again); or the scientist repudiation of metaphysics (positivism, overt or covert); or the deconstruction of metaphysics (Derrida); or confident claims that our epoch is to be one of postmetaphysical thinking (Habermas, for instance); or of Marion's categorical claim that phenomenology now replaces metaphysics as first philosophy. To many concerned with metaphysics, Aristotle might be seen to offer something like an inaugural definition of metaphysics in terms of a threefold task, namely, as first philosophy (*protē philosophia*) treating of first causes (*aitiai*) or principles (*archai*), then as the science of being *qua* being, and finally as the science of the highest being, *ho theos*, the divine. One calls to mind also the later more Scholastic systematization of metaphysics in terms of *metaphysica generalis* and *metaphysica specialis*, the first dealing with being as *ens commune*, the second dealing with God, the soul, and the world. Such an approach of Scholastic rationalism is at work in Kant's critique of metaphysics, and also in Hegel's post-Kantian science of logic (his "objective logic," he claims revealingly, takes the place of *metaphysica generalis* or "ontology").[1] It may well be that both the Aristotelian and Scholastic-rationalist definitions and practices of metaphysics do not fully answer thought, both extensively and intensively. Perhaps they do not fully answer thought even with regard to the unavoidable questions they themselves pose. This, one has to add, may be true of all philosophizing.

---

1. See G. W. F. Hegel, *Science of Logic*, trans. A. V. Miller (New York: Humanities Press, 1969), 63–64.

That said, one might still argue that such approaches do not exhaust the plurality of possible practices of metaphysical thinking, even within the so-called tradition of metaphysics itself. If I were to settle on a canonical saying of Aristotle which still has the power to release us to this plurality, it would be less his statement on the threefold task, just cited, as his claim that being is said in many senses: *to on legetai pollachōs* (τὸ ὂν λέγεται πολλαχῶς, *Metaphysics* 1003b5; see also 1028a10). This claim is immensely suggestive. I have tried to develop it in the direction of a metaxological metaphysics.[2]

Concerns of such a metaphysics will recur in explorations to come, but given Aristotle's saying I propose that there is no overcoming of metaphysics as such, for there is no univocal essence of metaphysics to be overcome. In fact, there are *many practices* of metaphysics, Platonic, Aristotelian, Thomistic, rationalistic, transcendental, idealistic, realistic, analytic, process, and so on. Metaphysical thinking is, so to say, monstrous and not a little unlike a hydra: chop off one head and another grows. I do not mean this as a criticism—for the very act of chopping off heads is itself a head of this incorrigible hydra. It too is "metaphysics." Best to get one's head straight, so to say, and do good metaphysics. To address this plurality as if it were some univocal essence is too reductive. One worries that a hidden univocalization of "metaphyiscs" is effective in much of the rhetoric claiming that we are now "postmetaphysical," even as that same rhetoric scourges the univocity of "metaphysics."

One might speak of metaphysics as first philosophy (*protē philosophia*) insofar as it involves mindful reflection of the meaning(s) of the "to be"—on the plurivocity of meanings to the "to be." Where postmodern thinkers often take plurivocity as a mortal strike against metaphysics, I take it rather as its lifeblood. I take the invocation of the Aristotelian adage as importantly shifting the stress on the different tasks assigned by Aristotle to metaphysics. While each of these tasks, or an adaption, might be defensible in its own way as absolutely fundamental, in an important manner they are secondary to how we understand the many senses of the "to be." The tasks will be addressed differently if, for instance, a univocal

---

2. On this different take on metaphysics, see especially William Desmond, *Being and the Between* (Albany: State University of New York Press, 1995). See also William Desmond, *The Intimate Strangeness of Being: Metaphysics after Dialectic* (Washington, D.C.: The Catholic University of America Press, 2012).

sense of being is to the fore, or an equivocal. Nor need we take as canonical something like the rationalist Scholastic scheme of general and special metaphysics. It may have hugely defined what the practice of metaphysical thinking and its systematization meant for many centuries but it does not exhaust the originating sources, nor the plurivocity of practices of metaphysical thinking. All of our efforts to be true, all our stabs at the intelligibility of beings and processes, are subtended by different senses of being, though mostly we are unmindful of these as such. We need to be awoken to these senses and their wide-ranging significance. Those who claim to be postmetaphysical are as much in the debt of these senses, indeed embody them diversely, as the metaphysicians they claim to overcome. Seen thus, there is no overcoming of metaphysics—overcoming metaphysics is itself metaphysics.

While the matter at stake here has a historical and systematic dimension, the systematic point is crucial. Human beings can think and live intelligently and in openness to the intelligibility of things without an explicit metaphysics, but to be a philosopher who engages with first philosophy, one must search for some more explicit mindfulness, attentive to the enabling sources of such intelligence and intelligibility. This means to bring more explicitly a developed habit of mindfulness to bear on what is at play in being, first with regard to the many senses of the "to be," and then especially with regard to the basic presuppositions, sources, and orientations toward the "to be" that mark our being in the midst of things. Each being, every process or becoming, every event, every action, even every possibility (for a possibility is not nothing) participates in one way or other in the sourcing powers of the "to be." We human beings exist as more or less mindful, and this is not only because we exist from these sources but because we are enabled to think about and possibly comprehend something of their enabling powers. To be enabled to such mindfulness, to be called to it, makes the human being the *animale metaphysicum* (as Schopenhauer put it).

Even when we claim to be postmetaphysicians we are this *animale metaphysicum*. Postmetaphysicians may not be the best of metaphysicians, but willy-nilly some implicit metaphysics or set of metaphysical presuppositions are at work. This is not to say that metaphysics in this explicitly philosophical sense is everything, for we can understand things without philosophical reflection about the enabling sources of being and minding. But trying to be mindful of these sources is essential to the task of first philosophy. This does not make metaphysics a first grounding science on the foundation of which other sciences are then built. This is not a good way to put the point. In fact, metaphysics as first philosophy is always secondary, in the sense that it presupposes the enabling of these sources, either in an ontological or epistemic sense. We wake up in the midst of things and this enabling is already effective, and it is only when our waking up turns in a certain direction to what is at play in the between that metaphysics as a more reflective mindfulness begins to take shape. This is not a matter of *a priori* dictation to the between, as the "midst," but of a certain fidelity to it, to the wording of the between.[3] Metaphysical presuppositions about the "to be" are at play mostly unacknowledged, in common sense, in politics, in ethics, in art, in science, in religion, in philosophy, indeed in "postmetaphysical" philosophy itself. We are called to fidelity to be true in understanding what is thus at play in the wording of the between.

Perhaps certain ways of doing metaphysics may have to be criticized, and perhaps this is part of what being "postmetaphysical" implies. If I am not mistaken a version of Platonism, in the form of the Nietzschean cartoon, is often the kind of ("transcendent") metaphysics criticized. Criticized also might be a kind of Scholastic rationalism with its effort to systematize logically the perplexities at stake, and so to domesticate the metaphysical astonishment that gives rise to the perplexities in the first place. But Platonism, Aristotelianism, Scholastic rationalism, you name it, none of these exhausts the possible practices of metaphysical thinking.

Putting aside the systematic concern, the postmetaphysicians often present their point in epochal terms: there is an unfolding from ancient, through medieval, to modern, and now we arrive at postmodern conditions of thought. This unfolding is sometimes presented teleologically, and even when the teleological import comes under criticism an ineluctable orientation to our postmodern present still reigns. I am tempted to think of a postmodern resurrection of a kind of Comtean teleology: religion for the infants, metaphysics for the adolescents, and now positive science, or its diverse successors, for fully arrived and matured hu-

---

3. See my essay "Wording the Between," in *The William Desmond Reader*, ed. Christopher Simpson (Albany: State University of New York Press, 2012), 195–227.

manity. And then, almost like postmodern Comtean priests, prominent thinkers announce the arrival of the new era of the postmetaphysical. Nevertheless, if the question is more crucially systematic than historical, it is also more elemental than epochal. The perplexities are ancient, and yet not ancient: they are archaic in bearing on what originates all determinate questions, and so they abide with us still, and are as new as the day after tomorrow—always behind us, always before us, perhaps because always deeper than us, and always above us too. Indeed, in relation to the archaic perplexities—and Plato and Aristotle already gave admirable expression to them—there is never an absolutely final settlement, as if these perplexities were determinate problems that could be solved once and for all, and so dissolved and put behind us.

This point holds for the premodern, the modern, or the postmodern. "Postmetaphysical" thinking hinders rather than helps us if it impedes the living memory of these archaic perplexities. There is, for us, no univocal final settlement of the deepest metaphysical questions. They arise from primal astonishment, itself elemental rather than epochal. They give expression to perplexities beyond any one determinate settlement, perplexities that belong to no epoch, but mark us as what we are: mindful beings astonishingly awoken to the intimate strangeness of being. These perplexities return to us again and again, and again and again we must turn to them. Postmetaphysicians risk turning away from the return, and thus risk missing the turn, again and again.

Does what I call metaxological metaphysics have a kind of likeness to the "step back" (*der Schritt zurück*) out of metaphysics enjoined by Heidegger? Yes, in one sense, though in a sense different to the one intended by him. The metaxological "step back" is from "metaphysics" understood as a determinate practice of metaphysical thinking, in this way or that. Like the many senses of being, there are many more or less determinate practices of metaphysics, and not all of them stay true to their own originating sources. Some practices of metaphysical thinking betray their enabling sources in the act of claiming to complete or realize them. Aristotle's reminder that being is worded in many ways can be taken to heart in a new and renewing way by means of a kind of metaxological "step back."

I make the point in a manner that applies not only to the "to be" but also to the "to be" as good. Though I will in due course speak of the voiding of being in modernity, this voiding has an intimate relation to the tendency to divorce being and good, a divorce affecting how we practice ethical reflection also. This kind of "step back" has an analogous relevance to ethics, and the potencies of the ethical.[4] We need to "step back" out of different, determinate ethical systems to understand the ethos of being as hospitable, or not, to good, as manifesting, or not, the good of the "to be." We need to "step back" also to understand the potencies of our being ethical that are sources of different ethical formations, or determinate systems. Understanding the different ethical potencies allows us to understand better the enabling powers of being ethical, different minglings of which, or particular dominances of which, go into the formation of determinate ethical outlooks, such as Platonism or Christianity, or Kantianism or Nietzscheanism, to name an important few. Analogously in metaphysics, there are ontological-metaphysical potencies which enable the practices of a determinate form of metaphysics and which can enter into a plurality of formations with each other, but which are never exhausted by any particular practice. These ontological potencies enable us to configure the primal ethos of being, and we live in the reconfigured ethos, often forgetting the more primally given ethos of being.

Part of the task of the metaxological "step back" is to come to some mindfulness of this primal ethos, in light of the many ways being is worded, and the already operative potencies of being at work there that enable the different determinate formations of our thinking. This "step back" is not a step outside the between. We are determined out of the primal ethos and enabled to be relatively self-determining, but we participate in it as more than all determinations and our self-determination. In it, we cross through it, pass along it, we come to it again by passage in and through the determinate and the self-determining, and through the informing senses of the "to be," through univocity, equivocity, dialectic, and metaxology. The primal ethos and the enabling potencies cannot be deconstructed because they enable both construction and deconstruction and are prior to and beyond both. They are at work even when we claim to be postmetaphysical, which is never being postmetaphysical in

---

4. See the introduction to William Desmond, *Ethics and the Between* (Albany: State University of New York Press, 2001); for a brief summary, see William Desmond, "The Potencies of the Ethical," in *An Ethics of/for the Future*, ed. Mary Shanahan (Cambridge: Cambridge Scholars Publishing, 2014), 62–75.

fact, but is a condition more or less sleeping to what enables it as a determinate practice of antimetaphysical thinking. And so even to be antimetaphysical is again to be metaphysical.

∽

In the reflections that I offer in this work, I explore further diverse aspects of the contested status of metaphysics and a metaxological response to it. In other works, perhaps most fully in *Being and the Between*, I have tried to develop this metaxological metaphysics in response to what I understand are different skeptical, if not hostile approaches to metaphysics quite common in our time. While the fuller systematic dimensions of this metaxological metaphysics are outlined elsewhere, here I offer a set of studies which amplify important themes in the unfolding of modern metaphysics, while adding nuance here and there to what is involved in the more systematic articulation of a metaxological metaphysics. These nuances call forth also a philosophical finesse for the trans-systematic.

The particular reflections here were originally developed in response to different queries and invitations, but certain recurrent considerations keep coming back, considerations embodied in the themes here explored. In developing a metaxological metaphysics, a *logos* of the *metaxu*, a wording of the between is asked of us, but this calls forth a kind of *ruminative* recurrence to persistent perplexities that abide with us, despite the contested status of metaphysics. Ruminative recurrence might sometimes look like repetition, especially given the diverse occasions of the original composition of these reflections, but I have tried to avoid this as much as possible. This book gathers together some of these ruminative reflections under the heading of the voiding of being. While the voiding of being might conjure up too negative associations, the aim of the thoughts gathered here is not at all negative. While attempting to understand that voiding, our appreciation of the promise of metaphysical thinking can also be renewed and indeed extended—extended beyond skepticism and hostility to metaphysics, in an ethos of philosophical thought claiming to be "postmetaphysical." This remains to be seen in the body of the work, but a brief outline of the different chapters will give a foretaste of what is to come.

I open in chapter 1 with the voiding of being, suggesting that the doing of metaphysics in modernity has tended to the undoing of metaphysics, with religious and theological repercussions. A major source of this

I find in the unrelenting stress on the univocal determinability of being which yields the inverse result, namely, an equivocal indeterminacy verging on the voiding of being. I think one can defend the view that the sources of metaphysical thinking are in an original astonishment before being in its being there at all. There is something "too much" about this being there; it is overdeterminate in the sense of exceeding our determination. As such it arouses our perplexity, a troubled and indeterminate restlessness of mind seeking to make intelligible sense of it. Perplexity yields to a curiosity when it is focused on more determinate beings and determinable happenings. Metaphysics in modernity has focused very strongly on the determinability of being, and with bringing being from a perplexing and equivocal indeterminacy toward more and more univocal determination. Curiosity looks to conquer conceptually the original overdeterminacy, and with this too to overcome the original metaphysical astonishment. The given ethos of being is overtaken with a variety of univocalizing figurations such that the end of metaphysics seems to lie in the absolute determinability of being. What follows is the dispelling of the original astonishment: the doing of metaphysics becomes its undoing. I look at key episodes in this voiding of being, leading up to to Kant and Hegel as hugely significant for metaphysics in modernity, and for what comes after modernity.

My approach is both historical and systematic: historical in touching on some major thinkers in modernity; systematic in that how metaphysics has been understood itself reflects a constellation of senses of being which are not always laid out with systematic clarity. Given that the plural nature of the practices of metaphysical thinking is important, I argue against any univocal totalization of "metaphysics"; we should do justice both to the plurivocity of being, beyond all totalization, and the plurality of practices of metaphysics. The fateful divorce of the "to be" and the "to be" as good (or in an older language, the divorce of being and good as transcendentals) is not to be forgotten. After Kant and Hegel metaphysics seems fated to fall back into a post-idealist, post-rationalist equivocity. This condition is still with us. In all of this I ask about a certain dearth of ontological astonishment and a kind of evacuation of the overdeterminacy of being, its "too muchness" for univocal determination, and its excess to self-determining thought. My purpose is not to end with the voiding but to pose the question as to whether there is a transdialectical metaphysics wherein fidelity to ontological astonishment lives on. If so, perhaps it also sows the seeds of new thought with implications extending beyond metaphysics, for perhaps our aesthetic understanding, for perhaps our ethical orientations, for perhaps our religious and theological understanding.

In chapter 2 I respond to a question posed to me about analogy and the fate of reason. I explore how analogy and reason have hugely defined the traditions of reflection on the most ultimate issues in philosophy and theology. I explore a certain plurivocity in the meaning(s) of reason and analogy, and do not propose that there is a fate of reason quite but rather a *vocation* to redeem this plurivocal promise. The nature of reason is at issue here too. Reason is understood differently depending on which sense of being is in the ascendant. If univocity is in the ascendant, as in modern rationalism, a philosophical and theological feel for what analogy might mean tends to be weakened. If equivocity comes back, as it inevitably does, reason goes to school with finesse and is more attentive to figurations of being that elude precise determinations and are more hospitable to the analogical way. I will indicate how the oscillation between univocity and equivocity can be understood dialectically, but also how modern dialectical reason, because it is too much under the sovereignty of a reason that would be self-determining, fails to do justice to what is of the essence in true analogy, namely, the superlative difference of the divine, beyond determination and self-determination. This is in no way to slight the fact that analogical likening is also a dynamic relating, and hence the affirmation of "being different" is not set in opposition to "being in relation." I explore analogy in modern rationalism and empiricism, in Kant's critical reason, in Hegel's speculative reason, and in a number of postdialectical forms of thought. I want to suggest that the promise of the postdialectical is to open up the transdialectical. The end again is to come into a space where the promise of a metaxological metaphysics is not killed in the womb. I will suggest that there is something metaxological about analogy in trying to be true to the between-space of communication between the finite and the infinite, and the dynamic intermediating of likening and unlikening eventuating there. I will also ask if a certain metaxological finesse for analogy has something to offer within the postmodern ethos which stresses the aesthetics of happening—understood not in an aestheticist manner but with robust ontological stress.

In chapter 3 I focus on the dearth of ontological astonishment, which I find in what, on the surface, look like two very disparate forms, namely Hegel's determinate negation and the scientistic orientation to being. Hegelian negativity has had many successor forms, though they might not describe themselves as such. But both prior to Hegel and after him a widely present view is that to be intelligible is to be determinate; indeed to be, properly speaking, is to be determinate. The status of determinacy and determination is at issue. I understand the scientistic orientation as a formation of curiosity taken over by a desire for the relentless univocal determination of being, in both theoretical and practical senses. One must ask, however: how comes the determinate to be determinate? How does it come about that being as determinate is determinable by thought and hence rendered intelligible? The issue of a *becoming* determinate is at stake here, not just some entirely static sense of being. Hegel's stress on determinate negation, or more generally on subjectivity as self-relating negativity, responds to such questions. What is simply given to be is not intelligible as such; it is a mere immediacy until rendered intelligible, either through its own becoming intelligible, or through being made intelligible by thinking. Thinking as negativity moves us from the simple givenness of the "to be" to the more determinately intelligible; but the former (the "to be") is no more than an indeterminacy, and hence deficient in true intelligibility, until this further development—determination—has been made by thinking as negativity. A central complexity in Hegel's view is that thinking as determinate negation is crucially in process toward knowing itself as a process of self-determining. Hence his more complex description: self-relating negativity. The operation of negation is not only a determination of what is other to the thinking, it is the coming to itself of the thinking process. In that sense the return of thinking to itself, in the process of determining what is other, is not just making determinate, it is *self-determining*. The determining power of thinking in negativity is hence inseparable from how we understand the meaning of *freedom*. An overall logic governs the movement of thinking as negativity: from indeterminacy to determination to self-determination.

I see an analogous process in the scientistic form of curiosity, itself a contraction of wonder now zoned on the determinate. The dearth of ontological astonishment in Hegel sees being as the most indigent of the categories that is all but nothing, until thought understands that it has already passed over into becoming. Instead of being as the marvel of the "too much," it is an indigence of all but nothing. In scientistic curiosity we find a contraction of this sense of the given marvel of being. I distinguish between different modalities of wonder: first, a more primal ontological astonishment that seeds metaphysical mindfulness; second, a restless perplexity in which thinking seeks to transcend initial indeterminacy toward more and more determinate outcomes; third, a more determinate curiosity in which the initiating openness of wonder is dispelled in a determinate solution to a determinate problem. Such determining thought can be correlated with a powerful curiosity that renders intelligible the given, rather than with a primal astonishment before the marvel of the "to be" as given.

The given "to be" shows a fullness impossible to describe in the language of negativity, though indeed in a certain sense it is no thing. The overdeterminacy of being asks of us a different *logos*, a different sense of being, a different sense of nothing—not the nothing defining a determinate process of becoming, or a determining nothing defining a self-becoming: a nothing out of which a coming to be arises, a coming to be that is more primal than becoming. Becoming and self-becoming presuppose this other sense of coming to be. A sense of this is communicated in the happening of a primal astonishment before the happening of the "to be." This is an overdeterminacy rather than just an indigent indeterminacy. In light of it, the processes of determination and self-determination are secretly accompanied by what they cannot entirely accommodate on their own terms. All of this has implications for a kind of counterfeit infinity that can be generated by the limitless self-expansion of the contracted curiosity we find in scientistic orientations. These, no less than Hegel's claim to a self-sublating infinity, cause one to question whether we are really dealing with a *counterfeit double of the true infinite* as overdeterminate rather than self-determining. The defection from metaphysical wonder in the mode of primal astonishment also has implications for the rampant will to univocalize all life, whether in a theoretical or practical sense.

In chapter 4 I explore the appropriateness of certain forms of thinking for metaphysics, whether they are analytic, dialectical, or transdialectical, via the question: are we all Scholastics now? It would appear that

Scholasticism has mostly vanished from the philosophical scene, but I am made to wonder if we are all Scholastics now. Looking at the two supposedly main camps of contemporary philosophy, the continental and the analytic, what do we see? On the one side, the hermeneutical Scholasticism of the text; on the other side, the Scholasticism of the technical or quasi-technical analysis. I first offer some thoughts on this matter in connection with the professional schooling of philosophy. There are more systematic considerations at stake, asking us to look at three forms of thinking: analytic, dialectical, and transdialectical. In analysis we find an oscillation between equivocity and univocity; in dialectic we find a self-mediation of univocity and equivocity and the constitution of a more embracing perspective, inclusive of the opposite sides of a question; in transdialectical thinking we find an intermediation of equivocity beyond univocity and dialectic, with metaxological finesse for nuances of otherness, not appreciated in univocity, and not properly minded in dialectic. Analytic thinking is driven by curiosity, dialectical thinking by perplexity, transdialectical thinking by the resurrection of originary astonishment which itself is more primordial than curiosity and perplexity, and hence more original than analysis and dialectic. The genealogies of both analytic and continental philosophy evidence important relations to dialectical thinking, and I will remark on this matter in respect of the promise of postdialectical thinking. Once again my more affirmative aim is not simply critique, but to offer some suggestions in connection with what I call the "deschooling of dialectic," and the recuperation of genuine philosophical *skolē*.

The *relation between system and poetics* is relevant here, and to this I turn in chapter 5. The relation between the philosopher and the poet is riddled with controversy since the beginnings of philosophy, but the matter is no less urgent today, when the dialogue between philosophy and its others is sometimes posed in a fertile way with respect to the power of the poetic to speak to thought, in Heidegger most obviously. I look at the fruitfulness of the notion of the *metaxu*, and how differently it can help us in this dialogue. The "between" is plurivocal, and this is relevant to the space between system and poetics. "Between" system and poetics might mean less a tension or agon between these two, and more an opening to something *beyond* system. Into that space between system and something beyond, the poetic inserts itself. We need to understand the nature and significance of system, but there are also philosophical occasions when system no longer seems relevant and appropriate. Something beyond systematic encapsulation calls forth a different response at the limit. The most well-known instance might be in Plato: when discursive reason reaches a certain limit, there is a resort to more poetic, and crucially, more mythic ways of speaking. This space of the beyond of system requires a different voice, but this is not necessarily an abjuration of philosophical reason but a response called forth from philosophical reason at the limit, or at the utmost reach of its explicitly discursive powers. That space beyond also signals something to which I do not find adequate either the sublationary infinitism of Hegelian idealism or the postulatory finitism of the deconstructors of idealism. Both end in their own version of self-circling immanence. To be true to the space between system and poetics calls us to the practice of philosophy on the porous threshold between immanence and transcendence. This is a philosophy of finitude not postulatory and a philosophy of infinitude not sublationary. If a metaxological philosophy is properly mindful of the space *between* system and poetics, this means that a transdialectical practice of philosophy can be systematic without claiming to be *the* system, can be porous to the poetic and the religious, even when it is systematic. In this chapter I try to exemplify something of this "being between."

Chapter 6 is an exploration of Jean-Luc Marion's notion of the saturated phenomenon and what I call the hyperboles of being, and all this in the context of his claims about "postmetaphysical" philosophy. The aesthetic and religious dimensions of the matter are also not to be lost from view. Marion's notion of the saturated phenomenon has been widely discussed, and not least in relation to how philosophy might approach religion. I want to reflect on the nature of the saturated phenomenon, especially in respect to how it overlaps with and diverges from the hyperboles of being that I have developed in *God and the Between*.[5] The hyperboles of being are happenings within immanence that yet cannot be entirely determined in the terms of immanence. Finite immanence, I suggest, is best described as a *metaxu*, articulated by a creative pluralization of happenings, beings, and processes, held together and sustained in differentiations by proliferating networks of relation. And yet it is impossible to

---

5. William Desmond, *God and the Between* (Oxford: Blackwell, 2008), esp. chap. 6.

close all this into one single totality, because within the between of finite immanence the boundaries we encounter again and again prove porous. The between itself is porous to what is itself impossible to finitize fully. I would say our being religious is the most intimate and ultimate testimony to this constitutive porosity, always and everywhere on the verge of mystery beyond finitization, even when communicated in finitude. There are important overlaps between saturated phenomena and the hyperboles of being but there are also significant divergences. These throw light on the relation of phenomenology to religion, and the unavoidability of metaphysics, understood metaxologically, and not at all in terms of the Heideggerian critique of ontotheology.

My concerns in chapter 7 extend some of the considerations of the previous chapter by looking at what it means to be true to mystery in light of the fourfold sense of being developed in *Being and the Between*. To that end I draw some connections between this understanding of "being true," mystery, and the fourfold sense of being. The univocal understanding correlates with a more *determinable* sense of the true, the equivocal with a *more indeterminate* sense, the dialectical with a more *self-determining* sense, the metaxological with an *overdeterminate* sense of being and truth. This overdeterminacy exceeds determinability and self-determination, and is not just a matter of a lacking indeterminacy. But what then of "mystery"? "Mystery" is often a null category for philosophers, being seen as a defection from the quest for the determinability of truth. Particularly for the more rationalist philosopher, it is a canonization of our lack of knowledge, an evasion of the demand to know, and a curb on reason's project of more and more complete self-determination. By contrast, I would correlate a surplus sense of mystery with being true to the overdeterminate, and not to be construed simply in terms of univocal determinacy, equivocal indetermination, or dialectical self-determination. There is a being true to mystery which comes to know itself in the spirit of truthfulness which knows that it does not know. Being true is not just in thought thinking itself but is called on to thought that is more than, other to thought at home with itself.

There is an ontological-metaphysical side to this in the granting of an agnostic between where nonpossession of absolute truth is inseparable from truthful fidelity to truth beyond one. What this means is that the modern ideal of philosophy as autonomous knowing comes to be untrue to this being true to mystery. It means also that the familial relation between religion and philosophy need not be repudiated. Rather it opens a between space where the overdeterminacy of given being and a surplus sense of mystery call forth a being truthful, itself called to fidelity to the true as other to our determination or self-determination. The hyperboles of being and Marion's saturated phenomena can be seen as engaged with a being true to mystery in this space of the between.

In chapter 8 I offer a companioning reflection on Heraclitus. Heidegger recurs to the pre-Socratic thinkers as offering us a release from the debilitating effects of the forgetfulness of being, said to be set in motion by Plato. My reflection on and with Heraclitus is carried out with very different intentions, and not at all concerned to frame "the tradition" with any totalizing characterization such as "ontotheology." We need a differently released orientation to thinkers like Heraclitus. I find Heraclitus a companion in wording the between, in being metaxologically in the midst of things, while struggling for the best words, the best *logoi*, to articulate its significance. The companioning power of the thought of Heraclitus is full of promise for wording the between. My thoughts here are occasioned by an impression of irritation on Aristotle's part when speaking of the Heracliteans. The term "flux-gibberish" is my way of putting a word on this irritation. My thoughts are not primarily in the mode of a scholarly or philological study but as inspired by, companioned by Heraclitus. With Heraclitus such a companioning approach has not been uncommon, as he seems to be just the kind of thinker that inspiringly calls forth such a companioning response. Of course, I worry that companioning becomes ventriloquizing, and that Heraclitus's words serve too much like a Rorschach blot onto which we project ourselves. I worry that Heidegger sometimes does this. I will spend more time with the respective interpretations of Hegel and Nietzsche. Perhaps it is not entirely avoidable that we find in Heraclitus what we bring to him, yet there is something resistant in his mode of articulation that makes one diffident in (pro)claiming that now at last I am the privileged one to understand him. Heraclitus offers us striking thoughts that strike one into thought—that open up philosophical porosity to the deepest perplexities. In coining the term flux-gibberish I am interested how flux connects with the determinacy and constancy of intelligibility. If some pervading sense of the flow of becoming must be granted, how does this bear on the constancy of intelligibility? How can we think the flow and the constancy together? My reflections try to indicate that return to this inspiring "pre-Socratic" thinker has much to offer in renewing metaphysical perplexity in a contemporary and metaxological mode. The voiding of being is not the first word for metaphysics, and not the last.

1 ∽ The Voiding of Being

On the Doing and Undoing of Metaphysics in Modernity

THE PLURIVOCITY OF BEING AND MODERN METAPHYSICS

The sources of metaphysical thinking are in an original astonishment before being in its being there at all. There is something "too much" about this being there; it is overdeterminate in the sense of exceeding our determination. As such it arouses our perplexity, a troubled and indeterminate restlessness of mind seeking to make intelligible sense of it. Perplexity, in turn, yields to a curiosity that is zoned on more determinate beings, and the determinable dimensions of happenings. I would like to suggest that metaphysics in modernity has focused very strongly on the determinability of being, and with bringing being from a perplexing and equivocal indeterminacy toward more and more univocal determination. We look to overtake conceptually the original overdeterminacy, and to that degree the project is also the overcoming of metaphysical astonishment. To this end we reconfigure the given ethos of being in a variety of univocalization figurations. The end of metaphysics seems to lie in the absolute determinability of being, and with this the dissolution of the original astonishment. The doing of metaphysics is its undoing.

Is there more to be said? Recalcitrant equivocities keep coming back, something with which we are only too familiar in postmodernity. I want to look at how an unrelenting stress on determinability yields the inverse result, namely, an indeterminacy verging on the voiding of being. We

---

A first version of this study appeared under the title "The Metaphysics of Modernity," chap. 25, in *Oxford Handbook of Theology and Modern European Thought*, ed. Nicholas Adams, George Pattison, and Graham Ward (Oxford: Oxford University Press, 2013). I revert to the original title.

encounter a paradoxical coupling of determinable fixing and indeterminate voiding. My reflections here will lead to Kant and Hegel as hugely significant for metaphysics in modernity, and indeed for what comes after modernity. But Kant and Hegel are as much inheritors of older patterns of thinking already in train in modernity as well as initiators of newer patterns whose implications still challenge us. A certain dialectic of univocal fixations and equivocal recalcitrances reaches a high point in Hegel's speculative philosophy, after which modern metaphysics seems fated to fall back into a deeper post-idealist, post-rationalist equivocity in which we still seek orientation. In all of this there is a certain dearth of ontological astonishment and a kind of evacuation of the overdeterminacy of being. The question this poses for us is whether there is a post-dialectical or transdialectical metaphysics wherein fidelity to ontological astonishment lives on and seeds new thought.

My approach will be both historical and systematic: historical in touching on some major thinkers in modernity; systematic in that how metaphysics has been understood itself reflects a constellation of senses of being which are not always laid out with systematic clarity. It is important to bear in mind the plural nature of the practices of metaphysical thinking. Sometimes the critique of metaphysics is done in a shadow of Scholasticism, in Heidegger even, and those influenced by him. Modern rationalism is not devoid of connection to the earlier Scholasticism, while the reactions of Kant and Hegel to rationalism are important. In the twentieth century Heidegger has had a huge influence and is to be honored for trying to resurrect the question of being. One worries about a second forgetfulness of being, as many of those indebted to him speak more about him than about being. Rather than a univocal totalization of "metaphysics," we should focus both on the plurivocity of being, beyond all totalization, and the plurality of practices of metaphysics.[1]

---

1. We should not forget thinkers such as A. N. Whitehead, *Process and Reality: An Essay in Cosmology*, ed. D. R. Griffin and D. W. Sherburne (New York: The Free Press, 1978); Karl Jaspers, *Philosophy*, 3 vols., trans. E. B. Ashton (Chicago: University of Chicago Press, 1969–71); and Gabriel Marcel, *The Mystery of Being*, 2 vols., trans. G. S. Fraser (London: Harvill Press, 1951), and in the United States, figures like Paul Weiss, *Being and Other Realities* (Chicago: Open Court, 1995), and others who do not fit into the divide between continental and analytic philosophy. There is a tradition of thinkers variously indebted to Aquinas, whether these be more traditional Thomists, transcendental Thomists, or others again like Jacques Maritain, *A Preface to Metaphysics* (New York: Sheed and Ward, 1948). One remembers also Edith Stein, *Finite and*

THE DOUBLING OF BEING AND METAPHYSICS

In the popular mind metaphysics has to do with what lies beyond our ordinary experience, with things of a higher and perhaps spiritual nature, such as the soul and God. It often seems defined by certain binary conceptions such as appearance and reality, the sensible and the spiritual, the visible and the intelligible. The result is said to be a doubling of being, a two-world picture: the "here and now" and the "beyond," the aesthetic and the noetic, time and eternity. Metaphysics has something to do with moving to the second set of terms from the first, a move that perhaps is motivated by the first, but that is fulfilled by the second, and that seems to condemn the first to a derivative, or negative, even degenerate status. Of course, the serving maid has her laugh at the expense of Thales, and speculative thought will be confirmed in its bad name—at least in the eyes of serving maids. We find the basis for this binary conception in many practices of philosophy, not least in Plato, and not a few modern conceptions seem to side more with the servant maid than Thales.

This concept of metaphysics has especially been attacked at the latter end of modernity, not least by Nietzsche.[2] Metaphysics avoids life here and now, voids immanent being as aesthetic happening. There is something at work overall in modernity that can be taken to end here and I will return to this. We are dealing with still living questions. If we have been touched by Nietzsche we will also be tender to the claimed connection of metaphysics and religion: Christianity is Platonism for the people, he famously said, though Schopenhauer all but said as much in his earlier essay on our need for metaphysics.[3] The issue of divine transcen-

---

Eternal Being, trans. K. F. Reinhardt (Washington, D.C.: ICS Publications, 2002), and her attempted dialogue between phenomenology and medieval thought. Latterly in continental philosophy figures like Gilles Deleuze (with Felix Guattari), *What Is Philosophy?*, trans. H. Tomlinson and G. Burchell (New York: Columbia University Press, 1994), and Alain Badiou, *Being and Event*, trans. O. Feltham (London: Continuum, 2005) remind us of metaphysics as a living option. There is much fresh openness to metaphysics coexisting with much talk about our being "postmetaphysical." It would require another study to address analytic metaphysics which thrives largely out of the shadows of the perplexing equivocities that continental metaphysics has undergone since Kant and Hegel. Analytic metaphysics is driven to seek a kind of dianoetic univocity, exploring and negotiating its diverse possibilities.

2. Friedrich Nietzsche, *Twilight of the Idols and the Anti-Christ*, trans. R. J. Hollingdale (Harmondsworth: Penguin, 1968).

3. Arthur Schopenhauer, *The World as Will and Representation*, trans. E. F. J. Payne (New York: Dover, 1966), vol. 2, chap. XVII.

dence is often taken to be closely aligned with this binary conception. I will touch on this issue, since there is more at stake with transcendence, religious or metaphysical, than allowed for by binary ways of thinking.

It would be misleading, however, to fixate on this binary conception. In the ancient world what came to be called metaphysics was simply called "first philosophy" and first philosophy claimed to deal with the most ultimate sources of intelligibility, the most original sense(s) of being, and not necessarily in separation from concern with different domains of beings wherein in life we find ourselves diversely. Plato draws our attention to our renewed perplexity about the "to be" in the *Sophist* (244a), and Heidegger recalls this perplexity at the beginning of *Being and Time*.[4] But one might think of Aristotle, in the work that historically came to be known as the metaphysics, who explicitly posed the question of first philosophy as bound up with the idea that being is said in many senses (*Metaphysics* 1003b5).

I would formulate this as the question: what does "to be" mean, what is it "to be," what is the sense, what are the senses of the "to be"? The first nature of this has to do with the fact that all beings, events, processes are, or happen to be. That they are at all is something that exceeds what they are. What they are may have a certain universality specific to this or that kind of event or process or being, but the "that it is at all" of their being what they are is something more universally shared. If so, it is not abstract at all, but the most intimate thing to all beings insofar as they are. There seems to be a universality that is more than a mere generality, more than a specific universality, a kind of hyper-universality—"transcendental" is the traditional word for this. While we might think of this as merely abstract and indeterminate—for it is not anything in particular, nor is it any kind of being or process—it might be said to be intimate to all beings and processes as such. I would call it an intimate universal. We should bear this in mind when later we see the tendency in modernity to render being as an empty indeterminacy, hence not only weakening or losing the concrete universality, but also the intimacy. We will come to this emptying out or voiding of being.

We can take Aristotle's view of the plurivocity of being as fruitful for

---

4. Martin Heidegger, *Being and Time*, trans. Joan Stambaugh, revised by D. J. Schmidt (Albany: State University of New York Press, 2010).

our purposes. The senses of being he outlines, and Aquinas concurs, are the univocal, equivocal, and the analogical.[5] Very generally, the univocal sense puts the stress on sameness; the equivocal puts the stress on difference, a difference sometimes dissimulated by our ways of speaking; while the analogical somehow mixes the same and the different, being partly one and partly the other, and with reference to the relation of the sameness and difference to something shared by both. Aristotle, it is true, talks of a primary sense of being, which is *ousia* (sometimes translated as substance), and difficulties with what is called a substance metaphysics are part of the controversies of modern thought. The question of the highest being, *ho theos*, in Aristotle's conception of first philosophy, is also replete with questions—not only whether God is to be described as the highest being (*ens supremum*) but whether there is something to God not to be confined to the terms of metaphysics, a God beyond metaphysics, and beyond, just because God is God, and nothing but God is God. What I have called the intimate universality of being is very suggestive about the being of the divine as no being, in one sense no-thing at all and yet enigmatically intimate to all things as their always companioning enabling source of being. These issues continue to haunt metaphysical perplexity.

This plurivocity can be helpful for getting a hold of crucial dimensions of modern metaphysics. I suggest a quest for supreme univocity, with a recurrent oscillation with equivocity. On one side, this leads to the weakening of the analogical sense of being, and on the other, to the emergence of a more dialectical sense, which tries to mediate univocity and equivocity. Nevertheless, the quest for univocity still persists and equivocations in modern dialectic inevitably raise questions about a postdialectical or transdialectical way of philosophizing. In the aftermath of idealistic dialectic, metaphysics has often been condemned in terms of a postdialectical equivocity, but one might ask if something more is possible. My suggestion is that at the end of modernity we need to reformulate the plurivocity in a fourfold way, adding to univocity, equivocity, and dialectic what I term the metaxological sense of being. Like dialectic, this also deals with the interplay of univocal sameness and equivocal differ-

---

5. Thomas Aquinas, *Commentary on Aristotle's Metaphysics*, rev. ed., trans. John P. Rowan (South Bend, Ind.: Dumb Ox Press, 1995).

ence, identity and otherness, but with a sense of the openness of the between space of finite being, where it is not always to the point to mediate a more inclusive whole but rather to dwell with the rich ambiguities of the middle, especially trying to grant what brings us to the limit of inclusion in the immanence of a dialectical whole.

What of the analogical sense? The metaxological might be aligned with the analogous in this regard—an analogy is always *between* one thing and an other. The nature of that between or *metaxu* is at issue for metaphysical thinking. I will say more about analogy in the next chapter. I think this fourfold sense of being can both take us back behind modernity, back even behind premodernity, and point us forward to postmodernity and beyond. If there is a metaxological metaphysics, it cannot be slotted simply into a contrast of the premodern and the modern. That said, we must be willing to bring a more generous hermeneutic to premodern metaphysics. At the same time, the fourfold sense of being can help us see some of the major episodes of modern metaphysics in an illuminating light.

Metaphysics as *meta ta physika* has been taken to mean the things beyond the physical, and the word seems to direct us away from the "here and now."[6] But there is a significant double sense to the word *meta*: *meta* can mean both "in the midst" but also "over and above," "beyond." This double sense defines something of what metaphysics might mean: thought concerning both the immanent and the transcendent, thought immanently self-surpassing, yet thought surpassed by what is not determined purely immanently. The *metaxu* as immanence is a given porosity of being, already in relation to what is beyond itself. This means that it is impossible to fixate univocally an immanent side and a transcendent side, a "here and now" and a "beyond." There is thinking that passes between them on an ontological boundary that we cannot absolutely fix.

I suggest that this double sense of "meta" can be taken to correspond to the difference of *ontology* and *metaphysics*. Ontology (as a *logos* of *to on*) can be taken as an exploration of given being as immanent; metaphysics can be seen as opening a self-surpassing movement of thought that points us to the porous boundary between immanence and what

---

6. It has been suggested that the word derives from the classification of an Alexandrian librarian: the texts lying next to the texts dealing with *ta phusika*, the physical things.

cannot be determined entirely in immanent terms. Premodern metaphysics is sometimes taken to opt for the "meta" as "above," while modern philosophy generally has opted for the "meta" as immanent. In modernity any such doubleness tends to be seen as an equivocity to be overcome or replaced by a more immanently inclusive univocity. This turn away from the "meta" as "above" stretches from the beginnings of modernity to significant currents that proclaim themselves to be postmodern and postmetaphysical. If the doubleness of the "meta" suggests a porous boundary between immanence and what is not determined entirely in immanent terms, we will have to demur in the face of modern and postmodern efforts to postulate finite immanence as the absolute horizon of significance, greater than which none can be thought.

THE DEVALUATION OF BEING: BETWEEN AUTONOMOUS THOUGHT AND RELIGION

Here it is relevant to recall a "between space" connected with this doubleness of the "meta," that is, the space between philosophy and religion. One might connect a reconfiguration of this "between space" with the devaluation or voiding of being. Being religious is perhaps our most ultimate way of addressing the ultimate equivocities of being, and indeed of our being addressed by the ultimate mystery itself. In premodern metaphysics what seems evident is a certain porosity of religion and philosophy. In modernity the hegemony of theology is progressively eschewed, as the autonomy of philosophy is more and more asserted. It is still possible in such a development for the ethos of being to be religiously inflected, and for the practice of philosophy to be either secretly or overtly porous to what the religious communicates. One could suggest, however, that in modern metaphysics this relation to theology is haunted by equivocity, going in hand with a certain mutation in religious porosity. Some might attribute this to the legacy of an univocalization of being and the divine in the late Middle Ages—and there is something to this—but if this is so, what is perhaps more significant is the emergence of an orientation of mind that would univocalize all being in a more immanently active sense. I am thinking of modernity, early modernity especially, as marked by a kind of epistemic irritability with the equivocity of being. This equivocity is a perplexing ambiguity in things whose significance often eludes us. Of this we are tempted to think we ought to be master. The drive to be the determining measure and a kind of ontological irritation and impatience go hand in hand. We must construct modes of knowing and active interventions that make us the measure of what is other to us, especially as so elusively equivocal.

One thinks of the modern mathematization of nature and the hope of empowering technological interventions. One thinks of how in the scientific objectification of nature, externality is stripped of all its qualitative textures, these being consigned to mere secondary qualities—bare being is little more than a devalued thereness. Also the uncoupling of autonomous thinking from religion is connected with a loss of the good of the "to be." Every "to be" is just there neutrally, and not marked with a worth that is both endowed and inherent to it. In the modern frame there is a repudiation of the Aristotelian fourfold causality. Ends or final causes will always be marked by some equivocity; there is no mathematical univocity about them. But their exclusion from the scheme of intelligibility yields a *purposeless process*, ongoing from nothing to nothing. There is an evaporation of the sense of the good as defining the teleology of being. The good of the whole is no longer there, and in its place we find ontologically devalued thereness.

Here the premodern hospitality of being and good, signaled in the old doctrine of the transcendental concepts, is replaced by the divorce of being and good. The worth of being is not for itself. It is for us to determine what it is. There is a reconfiguration of the ethos of being in terms of valueless objectivity and a subjectivity said to be source of all value. There is not an ontological porosity between being and us, a porosity, moreover, marked by the texture of qualitative value, understood first in an ontological and not moral sense. Irritation with equivocity also goes with a lessened appreciation for the figurative, for the fact that we figure our sense of being. One might argue that the analogical sense allowed a figuration of the world replete with signs of the divine, which allowed a feel for the intimate strangeness of being, and a poised living with equivocity. A dominating univocity loses this poise. The poise of finesse for the figurative now yields to a different figuring power, the determining power of geometry.

The devaluation of being goes with a diminution of our original receptivity to being, and the substitution of doubt for wonder. What we doubt we no longer love with a native ontological affirmation. We retract from that, we retract it, and given being appears as a valueless other over against us—an ob-ject—something thrown over against us. If being religious helps in keeping open porosity between human and divine, our original mindfulness to being as other is a porosity in rapport with that is there, in wonder and astonishment. With doubt that porosity mutates into a suspicion of the other, and a suspicion of ourselves as unable to know that other. True, this can be a productive suspicion in that it breeds a new endeavor to be in which we project our determining power over the whole of the otherwise valueless thereness.

We see this relative to science and technology as reductive of the equivocal otherness to objects that are to be subject to the measure of a univocalizing science. We see this also as relative to philosophy, now proclaiming itself as autonomous knowing. One thinks of Descartes and hydra-like doubt—doubt about historical traditions, expressed in cautious diffidence in relation to theological authority, methodical doubt diversely expressed in the practice of a philosophy half in and half out of older forms—half in terms of the older Scholastic concepts, half out in plotting the new science. The canonical concepts of old are redeployed to underwrite an epistemic certification of the new, certification that will grant licence to a science whose practical benefits will allow us to become the masters and possessors of nature. This is a pretence to the overcoming of equivocation but it introduces a kind of equivocation into the practice of thought. If this is absolutely autonomous the relation to what is other to thought is shrouded in a new equivocity.

Is the autonomous philosopher a friend or a foe of metaphysics and the divine? Is there a metaphysics recessed here which in the long run proves to be godless? Doubts about the "meta" as "above" lead toward the latter in the long term. Because our inhabitation of the ethos of being is configured according to a religious sense of things, it is not surprising that the practice of philosophy would reflect this. This is not just a matter of theology having a certain intellectual hegemony, as in medieval times. I am thinking more of how the forms of life are inflected in the ethos of being with a porosity to that middle space between the human and the divine. Theology is a reflection on this middle space in light of claims to revelation by the divine itself. Theology adds to the reconfiguration of the religious ethos, but it does not fundamentally alter the giveness of our primal porosity as religious—unless there are forms of theology that clog access to the divine communication, instead of enabling its deeper appreciation and understanding.

For we can so emphasize autonomy that we inevitably have metaphysical cramps in dealing with anything heteronomous. If it is in the nature of metaphysics to be "meta," it always has to come to terms with the heteronomous. But the autonomization of thinking goes with a reconfiguration of the ethos of being, because in the light of a *nomos* of *to auto*, *to heteron* is less to be immediately denied as mediately reconfigured. Added to the devaluation of given being as other, the structural effect of this reconfiguration in the patterns of thinking is that the previous premodern porosity to the religious must be closed off. One could claim that religion is porous to the most radical of heteronomies, and this not necessarily in the mode of binary opposition mentioned earlier, but even in the very richness of immanence itself. The richest sense of the "to be" tells us of what cannot be delimited to immanence only. But this autonomy, whether affirmed in rational form, or deconstructed into more irrational energies, is shadowed by an ontological allergy to the "above."

What about the release of immanent transcending beyond immanence? If autonomy is in the ascendant, this immanent transcending bends back to itself, that is, to immanence again. If there is a porosity of metaphysics to religion in premodern thinkers, modernity is the epoch in which this porosity is at best viewed as equivocal in light of a more conceptual univocity. At worst it is closed off entirely, because anything communicated through that porosity not only reeks of equivocity but threatens to mutilate the self-proclaimed autonomy of immanent thought. This passage in the porosity cannot be let be.

And yet we must ask again: is modernity, in the configuration at issue, an *interim* from which we are now emerging? There are signs that this may be the case, but these signs are themselves equivocal and need discernment in terms other than autonomous immanence. If this is true, part of what comes after modernity—and if metaphysics is to continue—is a new porosity to the religious.

RATIONALIST AND EMPIRICIST VOIDINGS:
DIANOETIC AND AESTHETIC UNIVOCITY

Turning back to an earlier phase of modernity, I want briefly to call to mind two dominant pursuits of the determinability of being, namely, rationalism and empiricism, both of which have contributed to the voiding of being and the undoing of metaphysics. These represent opposite but complementary efforts to reconfigure the ethos of being in accord with, in one case, a kind of dianoetic univocity, and in the other case, a kind of aesthetic univocity. Both search for a kind of univocity that is never entirely attained. While empiricism sought aesthetic univocity in grounding sense-impressions, rationalism was in search of a dianoetic univocity. By the latter I mean to recall the quasi-mathematical kind of thinking of *dianoia* we find on the third level of Plato's Divided Line. In modernity this can be connected with what Pascal calls *l'esprit de géométrie*. Rationalism is bound up the self-assertion of autonomous thinking and its uncoupling from the equivocities of the religious.

I take what is at play here to feed into a modern apotheosis of reason in the form of rationalism, fighting off any contamination by philosophy's others, and claiming absoluteness for itself. Reason turns to itself as its own and only standard, claiming to be sufficient for itself. It turns toward given creation as to be reconceptualized in the univocities of scientific and mathematical exactitudes. It turns to the human being as its own measure of self-determination, uncoupled from any mysterious God who cannot be quite univocally factored in any equation of immanent autonomy. Overall reigns the conviction that purely on the basis of *a priori* reasoning we can have certain and universal knowing of the most ultimate things. It is not coincidental that the Gods produced by this way of thinking should be what elsewhere I describe as the Gods of geometry.[7] This is most evident in figures like Spinoza and Leibniz. *L'esprit de finesse* risks being replaced by *l'esprit de géométrie*. Pascal already suspected this in relation to Descartes, realizing that without finesse, there is no religion, and perhaps also no true metaphysics.[8] The

---

7. *God and the Between*, chap. 3.
8. Granted Pascal is not a systematic philosopher, yet he helps us pose a question for metaphysics: What happens when metaphysics is identified with reason too closely modeled on the spirit of geometry? Do we often get the systematic dogmatists of rationalism? What would

Gods of geometry seem to produce rational certainty about the ultimate but they rouse skepticism as to their compatibility with the living God of religion. Geometry without life itself dies, for there is more to life than geometry—and a God of geometry alone, without finesse, is not far from the death of God later proclaimed with existential pathos. That proclamation comes out of a kind of finesse, but in the world reconfigured according to geometry, it is a finesse for what is not there, rather for the God who is—regardless of the geometrical reconfiguration. Finesse itself suffers from the hegemony of geometry. How to bring the two together in proper poise is a great question.

The ascendant professorial rationalists of the eighteenth century are not now widely studied but thinkers like Wolff and Baumgarten were importantly to shape the mind of Kant, with consequences for the succeeding practices of metaphysics. Eighteenth-century rationalism is not unconnected with the heritage of Scholasticism. One thinks of how the scheme of general and special metaphysics was to shape the pedagogy of the schools for centuries, general metaphysics dealing with *ens*, special metaphysics with the soul, God, and the world. This Scholastic, rationalistic scheme lies in the background of Kant, and it is a shadow behind Hegel. Indeed it has continued to influence Scholastic philosophy claiming a debt to Thomas Aquinas right into the twenty-first century. It is a shadow that also lies at the back of the Heideggerian critique of "metaphysics." The quest of dianoetic univocity puts me in mind of Badiou's claim that ontology is mathematics, though significantly from the present point of view he claims that "the void" is "the proper name of being."[9]

The dianoetic univocity we are dealing with here leads to an evacuation of being, not unrelated to the previously mentioned devaluation of being. We are certainly not talking about the "too muchness" of being in its given overdeterminacy. Being becomes little more than the most indeterminate of universal concepts, and because it is indeterminate it is empty of the determinate contents that we know from the ordinary engagements of the world in everyday experience. With rationalism we overhear the confidence in reason purring at its own claim to establish truth from itself alone. If one were Jonathan Swift, one might worry that

---

metaphysics look like if it incarnated the *esprit de finesse*? Would it look metaxological in a plurivocal, transdialectical manner?

9. Badiou, *Being and Event*, 52–59.

one had stumbled on a lost Laputan island of perfect metaphysics where purely on the basis of thought alone its inhabitants can claim certain universal knowledge of the ultimate things.

As we know from the history books, the twin of rationalism is said to be empiricism, as the twin of the *a priori* is the *a posteriori*. It is not surprising that with empiricism the search for determinable univocity is aesthetic, in the sense of deriving from the senses and sensible being. The world is as appearing to our senses, and in this appearance we find the point of true contact with concrete being. The search for grounding impressions is at the origin of determination and determinability. These are supposed stable points of given reference, back to which we must appeal to supply the requisite (ontological) warrant of our knowing. Being is aesthetic univocity. I would say that the stress on the aesthetics of happening can open a very rich conception, and we find such a one in some phenomenological accounts, such as Merleau-Ponty's notion of the flesh of the world. This is a transdialectical response, but here aesthetic univocity is meant to fill up the empty universality of being as a dianoetic univocity. Do either aesthetic or dianoetic univocity help us escape the flying island of Laputa? Do impressions put us back on the earth where we encounter what is in the flesh? Do we need to see the ontological intimacy of "impressions" with the aesthetics of happening? Or is our ploy here to reconfigure this happening in entirely immanent, and at times even mechanical terms: immanent as being due to something in here in us receiving the input from what is out there; mechanical in being processed as determinate by the determining mechanisms of the psyche? This is not the fundamental ontological porosity of being. Again it rather presupposes it. It is shaped by a configuration which is still framed by a dualism of "in-here" and "out-there."

In important respects, there is no aesthetic univocity as such. This is brought home to us by the unfolding of the implications of empiricism. From the search for grounding impressions, we pass to phenomenalism, and further by the way of ideas to something closer to a subjective idealism, and indeed thence also to the vanishing of even the fixed "self" on which the aesthetic univocities are to be impressed. I would rather connect the aesthetic univocity of empiricism with the fundamental porosity of the human being to what gives itself in the aesthetic happening of being. But of this porosity no absolute univocalization is possible, since every univocalization presupposes it. Without the porosity the receptivity of metaphysical mindfulness to being makes no sense, but while this porosity is presupposed by all determinate cognitive activities, it is easily misunderstood or distorted. Our sensuousness, our incarnate being, our flesh is itself an ontological porosity, but it is not free of the saturated equivocity from which to escape or overcome is part of the project of modernity. To dwell in this saturated equivocity of the flesh asks for finesse, not just geometry, and without the finesse the metaphysical significance of the flesh itself is not going to be understood. (Merleau-Ponty had finesse in this equivocal matter of flesh.) The empiricists tend to be the twins of the rationalists, but just as there is no self-contained dianoetic univocity, there is also no such aesthetic univocity. All univocities taken as yielding certainty and universality seem to be dissolved by Hume. We end here with the skeptical inversion of the certitudes of the rationalists. This is not much help to metaphysics, and contributes to its undoing, especially of the rationalistic sort, nor indeed to any kind of cognitive claim, even as the world goes on and Hume can enjoy backgammon and a glass of claret. How to bring geometry and finesse together in proper poise continues to be a great question for modern metaphysics.

VOIDING BEING AND TRANSCENDENTAL POSITING: THE KANTIAN EQUIVOCATION

We reach one of the watersheds of metaphysics in modernity—namely, the work of Kant. He was called the "all-destroyer" by Mendelssohn (*der alles zermalmende Kant*), and many see him as a revolutionary turning point in modern thought. Without denying his importance, in truth he is the inheritor of a certain reconfiguration of the ethos of being in train since the onset of modernity, and to a degree he is asleep to some of the deeper metaphysical presuppositions of this reconfiguration, even while he expressed something of their essence, and imposed on them a modified reconfiguration. In some ways, he is more an end than a beginning—an end that begins something which, in due course, will call the frame of modernity into account.

Adapting one of Kant's famous sayings, dianoetic concepts without aesthetic intuitions are empty, aesthetic intuitions without dianoetic concepts are blind. His way between these two and beyond them he calls transcendental. Philosophy as transcendental is contrasted with traditional metaphysics which is transcendent, that is, dealing with realities beyond the boundaries of experience. Kant is still driven by a fundamental commitment to univocity in the determination of being. This is evident in his acceptance of Newtonian science and its world picture, in his architectonic ambitions in philosophy, in his desire to put metaphysics on the secure path of science, in his stress on rational necessity and universality as the only marks of true scientific cognition. He is heir of the dualism of modernity in this sense: we are not to try to bridge the dualism of subject and object in a naïve realist or purely objective manner, but must take the transcendental turn which supposes that we think objects as conforming to our knowing rather than our knowing conforming to objects. "Transcendental" in his usage refers to the conditions of the possibility of knowing, not as with the premodern usage referring to the (hyper)universality of being, truth, one, good, universals applicable to all being, beyond the generic universals applicable to kinds of being. In addition, Kant's transcendental ego might be seen as pointing toward a kind of metaphysics of subjectivity. Transcendental subjectivity is the most necessary principle of unity redefining the space between subject and object, reconfiguring their relation through its immanent synthesising power.

Kant speaks of a Copernican revolution, and one takes Copernicanism to be *heliocentric*. But where or what is the sun in Kant's way of thinking, if the knowing subject stands at the center of the constellation of intelligibilities? Plato is heliocentric, one might say. In his figuring, the sun refers us away from ourselves to the Good as transcendent. Because "transcendental" for Kant is not "transcendent," we are referred back to one side of the "meta," namely, the immanent side, understood in terms of the transcendental ego, the ultimate point of unity in the synthetic activity of knowing. We might talk even about a transcendental univocity. The point is that it is not being as being that interests Kant but our knowing of beings. Being is nothing for itself, being does not stun mindfulness with the "too muchness" of the overdeterminate. Being as determinable must be referred to transcendental positing, with a little supplementary help from the otherwise formless flux of aesthetic happening.

Kant presents us with a contrast between dogmatism and skepticism. He rejects the dogmatic metaphysicians, and sometimes this is taken to be a rejection *tout court* of all precritical metaphysics. But who are the dogmatic metaphysicians? Plato or Aristotle? Surely not. For Kant they are the rationalists of which he himself was earlier one. Kant was in revolt against his own Scholastic rationalism, though he produces a transcendental version of Scholastic rationalism. What of the skeptics? Kant was their opponent, though he confesses to being awakened from his own dogmatic slumbers by Hume and his skepticism. But his version of "critique" is rather like a Trojan horse from this standpoint. There may be a more insidious skepticism hidden in the thing, and it is brought into the center of all knowing under the seemingly respectable name of "critique." "Our age is an age of critique" he tells us, and we suspect he is advertising an epistemic superiority over the naïve realists. This self-congratulation might well be one of the bewitchments of the age. In the name of reason, critique itself becomes a new idol of skepticism that cannot see the beam in its own eye for all its rooting out of the specks in the old eyes of traditional philosophy, morality, and religion. The secret complicity of skepticism and critique returns in dialectic in its negative form, and also in more deconstructive thinking.

We should be hesitant about acceding to Kant's insinuation that the whole of traditional metaphysics is dogmatic.[10] Of course, the skeptic seems to win at least an indirect victory, because it turns out for Kant that we are incapable of knowing the thing itself. We are urged to dare to know, but what starts with a hortatory bang ends with an epistemic whimper, since we cannot know anything in itself. While this whimper is disheartening for metaphysics as a theoretical discipline, metaphysics can be heartened again if we shift to practical reason and the moral sphere.[11] This our relocation to a noncognitive space can seem hugely liberating. Indeed one might applaud it for enriching the sense of what it is to be—unknowingly. Nevertheless, it produces a downgrading of the claims of philosophical reason in the long run. It opens the gates to the others of theoretical reason, but this turn to morality as other will be fol-

---

10. Does the seed of a great simplification lie here? The seed of a totalizing of traditions of thought, a univocalizing of a plurivocity—a temptation to which many have yielded after Kant, when autonomy, critique, and so on make their own importance by downgrading in diverse and devious ways what has preceded them? A temptation not absent in the uses to which Heidegger's critique of metaphysics as "ontotheology" has been put?

11. *Critique of Practical Reason*, ed. and trans. Mary Gregor (Cambridge: Cambridge University Press, 1997).

lowed by more irrational others as time goes on. Kant would not approve of the latter, of course, but he does contribute to a flattening of the doubleness of the "meta." Our epistemic confinement to what is immanent in the domain of experience becomes a principle of immanence which rejects knowledge of the transcendent. This is equivocal, since there is a kind of beyondness to his moral God. It is questionable if Kant maintains a poise between immanent ontological reflection and metaphysical thinking about what is more than immanent.

What are some theological or religious consequences to which one might pay attention? There is especially what I describe as the antinomy of autonomy and transcendence as other. Kant's philosophy is one of autonomy, but where does transcendence have a place? The transcendence of nature is hard to distinguish from the valueless mechanism of Newtonianism. This is the deterministic nature of the *Critique of Pure Reason*,[12] though in his *Critique of the Power of Judgment* he tries to restore something of its life as "purposive."[13] This is an "as if" restoration, and still framed transcendentally. Going with the weakened "is" we are allowed to look at nature "as if" it were purposive. We cannot say: it *is*. The transcendence of the human being is reconfigured as moral autonomy set in opposition to heteronomy. God is the greatest of heteronomies, and hence we must defend morality without religion. God has to be brought back by Kant to deal with the antinomy of pure practical reason, in reconciling virtue and happiness. The suspicion is aroused that this is a moral *usage* of God, echoing an epistemic usage we find in Descartes. God allows us to deal with an antinomy in the immanent system of moral autonomy, but that is it really. We think we close a gap but we do not, of course. If God entails a transcendence greater than which none can be conceived, Kant has no way to handle the living God. God is folded back into morality, and we seem to have protected immanence from any intrusion from what is beyond itself.

In his style of thinking Kant is still quite Scholastic and his sense of being is quite anorexic. His withered sense of ontological astonishment is typically rationalist, even though he is tortured by worries that he might

---

12. *Critique of Pure Reason*, ed. and trans. Paul Guyer et al. (Cambridge: Cambridge University Press, 1989).
13. *Critique of the Power of Judgment*, ed. Paul Guyer, trans. Eric Matthews (Cambridge: Cambridge University Press, 2000).

be overshooting the mark in his trust in *ratio*. His moral philosophy is at the center. It is the only place where a kind of metaphysics might come to be, as we see from the title of one of his most famous books, *Groundwork of a Metaphysics of Morals*.[14] Only morality reveals something unconditional, and hence here there is some opening possible to the ultimate metaphysical perplexities. Interestingly, while there are little touches of a more ontological porosity in Kant's *Critique of the Power of Judgment*, in the final accounting he reiterates his rejection of all theology, and explicitly natural theology, except for a moral theology. In the end this is just morality, and not a lot of theology. You might as well drop the word "theology." Admittedly, Kant had a bit of a bad conscience, since there are troubling antinomies within moral autonomy which autonomy does not seem quite able to handle. A "supplementary" appeal to a moral God is not entirely closed off. We see this not only in Kant's dealing with happiness which moral virtue cannot guarantee, but also in radical evil which shows an inner debility, even perversion, in the root of our moral being.

Overall then dianoetic univocity gives way to transcendental univocity which gives way to moral autonomy, even as the Gods of geometry are replaced by the moral God. There is something metaphysical about this in reference to the doubleness of the "meta," since we move from the immanence of autonomy to the "beyond" of the moral God. Of course, this "beyond" was said by some not to be able to hold its ground. Already in Kant there is the equivocity as to whether it compromised the immanent autonomy he would absolutize, were it possible. But those who were to come were much less polite with any "beyond," and in the name of immanent autonomy, or indeed the autonomy of the immanent. The first sense of the "meta," the sense of being "in the midst"—closes itself off from the second sense as referring to the "beyond," and the result is the changing of the nature of metaphysics entirely in the direction of an immanent ontology.

Much lies hidden in all of this which will come more to expression in those who see themselves as inheriting Kant's emphasis. What comes to the fore is not necessarily the living consummation of Kant as the dissolution of his struggle for a calibrated equilibrium between aesthetic and

---

14. *Groundwork of a Metaphysics of Morals*, ed. and trans. Mary Gregor (Cambridge: Cambridge University Press, 1997).

dianoetic univocity. His transcendental univocity hides multiple equivocities, and these return in due course to wreck the self-satisfaction of his critical rationalism. One notes that his transcendental approach is originally a supposition: *ein Versuch*, an attempt. In due course, its suppositional or postulatory character falls out of attention, and it is taken with more apodictic certitude than at the starting point. It is an experiment but having reconfigured the ethos of being according to its postulations, it forgets that it is an experiment. Its postulations risk becoming dogmatic about its own claims, while the claims of others are treated with skepticism. All of this is at the origin of postulatory finitism, something hugely shaping philosophical approaches to metaphysics after Kant.

Kant is less truly a metaxological thinker as tending to an oscillation of univocity and equivocity. He equivocates both in terms of immanence as well as transcendence. Hegel tries to produce a dialectical response to that oscillation. Kant has a tendency to think that making a distinction constitutes a solution to an equivocal problem, though then one distinction generates another problem, and then another distinction is made, and so on and on. By the end, so many distinctions are made that one has pretty much forgotten the original problem, or it has been so enfeebled by the cuts of a thousand distinctions that one is tired and gives up on the putative disambiguation of the equivocity. Kant struggled against the smug apriorism of Scholastic rationalism but he remained entangled in the legacy of its characteristic practices. Perhaps such oscillating equivocity suggested to Heidegger that he might ventriloquise through Kant his own problems of fundamental ontology. Supposing this were true, it would say something about Heidegger. Heidegger does not seem to have benefited from the strong sense of moral unconditionality at the center of Kant's entire practice of philosophy.

Today we think of Heidegger when we hear the term "ontotheology," and he uses it to describe a certain way in which philosophy brings God into thought. A charge is directed at the *causa sui* of Spinoza or Hegel, and the charge sometimes seeps beyond these two toward the entire tradition of metaphysics. We should remember the term is Kant's from the *Critique of Pure Reason* (A632/B660), and mentioned in connection with the ontological argument. This is the proof of God by *a priori* reason, indicating that reason through itself alone can establish the existence of God. Kant is famous for his reputed demolition of the argument, and in that sense he is a foe of ontotheology. The demolition is resisted by reserves of complexity and nuance on less simplistic interpretations of the argument. But that aside, the purported demolition is a sign of the loss of faith in the strategies of a rationalistic metaphysics. Moreover, one can see more perspicuously some of the issues at stake if we grant this connection with Kant *vis-à-vis* ontotheology. Uttering the word "ontotheology" as a charge should be resisted. We need more discrimination. Remember indeed that in Kant there is a critique of rationalist metaphysics. There is a critique of approaches to the ultimate questions by *a priori* reason, understood in a theoretical sense. Nevertheless, a metaphysics of morals is possible which does allow us to think the ultimate things like God and the soul. And there abides the legacy of a kind of "beyond." The quest for transcendental univocity is qualified in how assertive we can be about the warranted results we can proclaim: almost nothing theoretically, and what is morally justified is qualified by an "as if" which weakens the sense of the "is." Not least, the matter reveals how hesitant we should be in letting this term "ontotheology" be a weapon against the entire tradition of metaphysics. If we connect ontotheology with the ontological argument, clearly Aquinas has already criticized that as a way to God. And even in the Anselmian version, and the prefiguration of it in Augustine, there is the porosity of religion and thought which insists again and again that *Deus semper maior*. It is a question whether this is just a way of bringing God into philosophy. It could rather be seen as an opening in immanent thought that explodes the pretension of immanent thought to close in on itself entirely. That is to say, the hyperbolic nature of God beyond all conceptualization is at issue when we think the thought of that greater than which none can be thought. This is not at all ontotheology in the bad sense, and indeed it overlaps with Kant's own mission against the conceptual idols of the uncritical rationalists.

I said there was an anorexic quality to the ontological attunement of Kant. This dearth of ontological astonishment is not greatly overcome in his metaphysics of morals. The starry skies above could be the opening to robust ontological astonishment in the aesthetics of happening but there is not more than a flash, even at that an "as if" flash, and then the devalued thereness reigns again. Even with the moral law, Kant drags his feet with anything "more," and we feel that he has not been taken beyond a cramped rationalism by these hyperbolic happenings. He is always trying to rein in the native self-transcending of the human spirit, confining us to the cramped little island of his truth, surrounded by the ocean of error and its deceitful mist banks and shifting shapes (*Critique of Pure Reason*, A235/B294–95). Confined to the island of his truth, the rest of being is full of threat and anxiety and even terror. We fear a quasi-Pascalian terror in hiding from itself, holding in check its ontological alarm in the architectonic structures of transcendental Scholasticism.

BEING NOTHING AND THE WHOLE: HEGEL'S SPECULATIVE COMPLETION

Hegel like Kant is a hugely influential thinker in connection with modern metaphysics and the voiding of being. Kant's transcendental response goes with an evacuation of the overdeterminacy of being, an anorexia of metaphysics whose yet undying impulse he still tries to nourish morally. Metaphysics clings to life, fed by a separation of theoretical and practical reason, hard to disentangle from a kind of laming of reason's confidence, paradoxically twinned with a mutation of the skeptical impulse in critique tempted to a hubris in its own debunking powers. Hegel rejected that debility of reason. In his thought one can discover much of a recapitulation of modernity and its reconfiguration. He was attuned to how the modern struggle with the duplicity of equivocity produces in univocity its own doubleness, evident in the form of binary thinking: object versus subject, determinism versus freedom, the dianoetic versus the aesthetic, rationalism versus empiricism, Enlightenment versus faith. Such binary thinking divides the whole, though it presupposes the whole. Hegel, by contrast, insists on the unity of reason in a speculative philosophy claiming to transcend such binary thinking, and their unexpurgated contamination of Kantian dualisms. The dualistic mode of thinking is the problem rather than the solution. To think the separation we must presuppose the togetherness. Hegel draws our attention to the self-surpassing character of thinking which cannot be separated from being. How being and thinking are together is the question.

There is a continuation and critique of Kant and a claim to complete him. Even though Hegel's speculative confidence is not now fashionable and something of Kant's critical caution is more to contemporary tastes, the fact is that Hegel asked many of the right questions about Kant, even if perhaps his answers still raise our eyebrows. Metaphysics seems finished after Kant, or theoretical metaphysics anyway. Hegel agrees: something revolutionary happens in Kant, but he and Schelling claimed to complete the revolution. They felt that Kantian critique was not thorough enough. There was too much of simply accepting as given the already laid out tablet of categories, more or less taken over from traditional Aristotelian Scholasticism.

Notice the stress on categories. There is a turn to the immanences of thought, yes, but the question of the priority of thought or being is important. If our primary stress is on categories, then we take knowing to be the measure of being, not being the measure of knowing. This stress on the categories is continuous with a turn to the immanence of thought, and the belief that a fuller unfolding of that immanence will yet yield the systematic completeness that Kant held to as a desideratum, even if the realization was not always what was desired. The immanence of thought can be seen as in agreement with Kant's prioritizing of the transcendental ego, even if this get reinterpreted in directions Kant would not approve. It provides philosophy with access to the source whence are generated the diversity of fundamental categories we need for the making intelligible of being. A determining source is required of the diverse categories needed for the determinability of being and the determination of its intelligibility. Accounting for this determining source will show it ultimately, for Hegel, to be self-determining. The doubleness of the "meta" will be collapsed into the immanence of self-determining thought. Logic and metaphysics will be the same in a post-transcendental ontology of the categories: Hegel's own *Science of Logic*.[15]

For Hegel there is a *determination process* more ultimate than *determinate products*. The dynamism of thinking is self-transcending and more than a series of fixed determinations, more than even the formal rules governing their connections. More than a formal logic we need a new logic, a logic that reveals as much a dialectic of being as of thought, because being and thought cannot be fixed as determinacies on two sides of a dualism. Dialectic deconstructs the dualism, overcoming the limits of binary thinking of the older metaphysics. Thus Hegel claimed that Kant's understanding of the antinomic character of reason is ripe with a

---

15. G. W. F. Hegel, *Science of Logic*, trans. A. V. Miller (New York: Humanities Press, 1969).

speculative significance we now need to harvest. What looks like an impasse for reason rather opens a space for a true speculative deployment of reason as ultimately *self-determining*. Hegel is still Kantian in taking over and speculatively transforming Kant's transcendental unity of apperception, and thus continues the modern stress on the self-determination of thinking rather than on being as such. Worth recalling, however, is the manner in which Hegel puts the ontological argument to his own speculative uses: against Kant's so-called demolition, he embraces it again for ontotheological purposes and to close immanent thought in on itself.

All of being—nature, history, God—will be said to be dialectically determinable in accord with reason's self-determination. Speculative dialectic will claim to offer the self-determining *logos* of the whole. We are to move beyond the fixed univocal determinacies of the analytic understanding, beyond the equivocities of the merely indeterminate, and this in order to complete metaphysics in a logic that shows thought to be immanently self-determining. Take note of how in this grand project, the overdeterminacy of being is evacuated from the outset in the direction of the most indeterminate, that is, empty concept, which is all but nothing, and must give way via becoming to more determinate being. One could see in all this a continuation of the voiding of being in the direction of an empty indeterminacy.

Consider the question: how does being come to be determinately intelligible? Hegel connects thinking with determinate negation, or more generally with subjectivity as self-relating negativity. What is simply given to be is not intelligible as such; it is a mere immediacy until rendered intelligible, either through its own becoming intelligible, or through being made intelligible by thinking. Thinking as negativity moves us from the simple givenness of the "to be" to the more determinately intelligible. The "to be" is no more than an indeterminacy, and hence deficient in true intelligibility, until this further development of determination has been made by thinking as negativity. Thinking as a process of negation is in process toward knowing itself as a process of self-determining. There is a logic overall that governs the movement: from indeterminacy to determination to self-determination. There is no overdeterminacy of being. Given being can barely be said to be, and even less can it be said to be intelligible until rendered so by determining thinking. Hence being becomes the most indigent of the categories that is all but nothing, until thought understands that it has already passed over into becoming. If we refer to the famous opening of Hegel's *Logic*, one could suggest, among other things, that Hegelian negativity, via a logic of self-determining thought, is born of and leads to a dearth of ontological astonishment. Instead of mindful porosity to being as the marvel of the "too much," we find rather the "nothing" of an empty indeterminacy.

There is here a certain apotheosis of the previously mentioned immanence of thought. The older metaphysics is criticized by a post-transcendental ontology of categories, all governed by the immanence of autonomous thought whose consummation Hegel's logical unfolding seeks to accomplish. I mention this connection with rationalism: in his *Encyclopaedia*, in treating of different attitudes of thought to objectivity, Hegel first directs himself to "metaphysics," by which he means, in fact, the rationalism of the eighteenth century, noted earlier in connection with Kant.[16] Hegel is not simply hostile but rather endorses the philosophical thinking of the things of reason, though now we must meet the standard Kantian requirement of subjecting the categories to critical reflection. Hegel sought a rethinking of these same matters in a post-Kantian perspective. The spirit of genuine speculative philosophy has not been "demolished" by the critique of Kant. Hegel's logic reminds us of a dialectical Wolffian rationalism set in dialectical motion; the static categories of rationalism are reorganized and set in motion, all on the way to the complete system of categories of his *Science of Logic*.

While the resources of dialectical thinking are rich, paradoxically Hegel's efforts to "complete" metaphysics may have done more to "demolish" it than Kant's more Scholastically cautious critique and his more overt intent to put metaphysics in its place. Once again surfaces the worry about a dearth of ontological astonishment about such a system. Our ontological attunement to the mystery of being is weakened. Being is both strange and intimate, and rationalism might be too callow to address it, but a dialectically dynamized transformation of rationalism might also be lacking in metaphysical finesse for it. The consummation of metaphysics in speculative dialectic, sometimes attributed to Hegel, wherein is developed a post-transcendental identity of being and

---

16. G. W. Hegel, *The Encyclopaedia Logic: Part 1 of the Encyclopaedia of Philosophical Science with the Zusätze*, trans. T. F. Geraets, W. A. Suchting, and H. S. Harris (Indianapolis, Ind.: Hackett, 1991), §§26–83.

thinking, may well contribute more to the sickening of the metaphysical impulse. The doubleness of the *meta* is collapsed into the univocity of immanence. One major theological consequence is the claim to speculatively surpass the transcendence of God. God too is made entirely immanent, and religious seeds are sown that in post-Hegelian thought will spring up and bloom as atheist darnel.

THE OVERDETERMINACY OF BEING AND TRANSDIALECTICAL METAPHYSICS

In a final reflection I want to say that since Hegel we can see a continuing wrestling with the voiding of being, often accompanied by the belief that "metaphysics" is behind us. I would say that perhaps certain practices of metaphysics are behind us but that metaphysics as concerned with the fundamental senses of the "to be" is not and can never be behind us. Sometimes the voiding of being takes on somber colors, not only in more nihilistic currents, but even in a darkening of devalued being into a kind of evil of being (such as we find with Schopenhauer and Nietzsche). In focusing on postdialectic metaphysics, I will be concerned to stress the move from the voiding of being to a rethinking of the recessed overdeterminacy of being. This is the "too muchness" of being for thought that thinks thought alone, that is, thought defining itself by the immanence of its own autonomy.

Hegel's speculative high noon was seen by some as the consummation of metaphysics but its aftermath was, paradoxically, less jubilation in mission accomplished as a malaise with rational philosophy itself, and the outbreak of a rash of antimetaphysical tics. To many, Hegel's confidence in speculative reason appeared as an overconfidence, producing a kind of metaphysical bubble, the deflation of which seems more true to immanence. Instead of the absolutely self-sublating univocity of Hegel, we must de-sublate the absolute and bring it more truly back to the human source, said to be its *incognito* producer. In Feuerbach, Marx, and others the God-man becomes the man-God. While this signals a hyperbolic self-assertion on the part of humanity, by contrast, speculative reason is stripped of its metaphysical pretensions, loses its self-confidence, and turns the negating power of thinking even against philosophy itself. The de-sublation of idealistic metaphysics can also be infiltrated by a recessed belief in the evil of being and in the face of this the modern subject can become the abject nonself of some postmodern expurgations. The hubris of the ascendant subject and the dejection of the abject nonself vie with each other, but for both the "big other" of traditional metaphysics and religion is dead.

It is worth noting that the question of the end of metaphysics is not a first for twentieth-century thought but is seeded in Hegel and extensively shaping those coming after him, such as Kierkegaard, Marx, Schopenhauer, or Nietzsche. The "overcoming of metaphysics" with Heidegger, or the excoriation of meaningless metaphysics with more positivistically-inclined philosophy (Comte, Carnap, and others), or the deconstruction of metaphysics with Derridean thought, all seem to lie along the line of this deflation of confidence in philosophical reason that we have diversely witnessed since Kant's critique of pure reason, and Hegel's reconfiguration of transcendental philosophy in terms of speculative dialectics. One could argue, however, that Hegel's system is not at all the consummation of metaphysics but the systematic completion of a project of being as determinability, culminating in a self-determining process, which in the beginning and in the end hides the overdeterminacy of being. This overdeterminacy is not the indeterminate, and exceeds determination and self-determination, and always calls for thought—thought in which some form of metaphysics is not only necessary but unavoidable.

Could one say that Hegel practiced an *equivocal dialectic*? I mean: what he took as a speculative unity of opposites seems to transcend the opposition (say, of immanence and transcendence), but the sleight of logic that seems to ceaselessly pass between them hides an abiding otherness, dissimulated because all power of unification is now on the side of immanence, and there is no true transcendence as genuinely other for itself. The equivocity of this dialectical unity is perhaps a reason why it soon splits in terms of the rival demands of the right and the left Hegelians. There is an internal instability already there in Hegel's speculative unity distributed between sameness and otherness—an equivocation on difference, a prioritizing of sameness. Some instability is impossible to avoid, because at issue is the *movement between* identity and difference. The movement can be tilted to one side or the other rather than be properly poised between them. The "trans" of the movement means return to the ethos of that between of sameness and otherness, identity and difference: the *metaxu*. And there we must search in thought for that philosophical poise—poise that perhaps allows our being thrown beyond closed immanence. We must question the self-determining form of the dialectic and recover the promise of transcendence as other, at work even in this form of dialectic but kept out of view, recessed, repressed, whited out. Why? Were its wording to be heeded, claims to closure and completeness—and to complete immanence—must be revisited and revised.

Might we here speak of a *transdialectical metaphysics*? The word "post" is perhaps too much of a temporal qualifier and there is here a *systematic issue* at stake as well as an historical. Historically, post-Hegelian philosophy has huge investments in trying to revolt against, or outlive, or modify that Hegelian practice of dialectic. This is true of both continental philosophy as well as analytic. Merleau-Ponty suggests that many strands of contemporary philosophy have incurred a debt to Hegel—he mentions Marx, Nietzsche, phenomenology, existentialism, and psychoanalysis.[17] Likewise, the historical narrative that plots the identity of analytic philosophy starts with Moore and Russell and is hugely defined by their turn against idealism and Hegelianism generally.[18] Systematically, transdialectical thinking better expresses the point in terms of the philosophical issues at stake. "Trans" indicates a beyond or a going beyond, and the question is whether dialectic does justice to both the going beyond of thinking as well as the beyond of thinking. It is important to note these two, because there *is* a going beyond of thinking in Hegel, but it is an immanent one, and hence there is, in the end, no beyond in a sense other to, or more robust than, an immanent transcending, the immanent transcending of thinking. There is no stronger sense of otherness and transcendence that finally does not submit without remainder to the appropriating power of immanent dialectical thought, as Hegel conceives this. Once again we return to the doubleness of the *meta*: in the midst and yet also beyond. Can these two be held together? How can we hold them together? Are we somewhere between these two?

To speak of the "trans" might remind some more of a Platonic dialectic than a Hegelian in respect of keeping open the porosity of philosoph-

---

17. Maurice Merleau-Ponty, *Signs*, trans. H. and P. Dreyfus (Evanston, Ill.: Northwestern University Press, 1964), 63.
18. Peter Hylton, *Russell, Idealism, and the Origins of Analytical Philosophy* (Oxford: Clarendon Press, 1990).

ical eros to transcendence as other. Interestingly, many anti-Hegelian post-Hegelians are often deeply in agreement with Hegel on this score. They are anti-Platonic, in claiming to be entirely immanent in their view or in their practice of philosophy. They may deconstruct the Hegelian totality but they share with Hegel the finally non-negotiable commitment to immanence as such. Deleuze is a clear example of this. Loud critic of Hegel though he is from a Nietzschean point of view, yet he is in complete agreement with Hegel as a philosopher of immanence—and not surprisingly, because for Hegel, as much for Nietzsche and Deleuze, Spinoza is the founding father, if not heroic figure of modern philosophy: the "Christ of philosophers," Deleuze puts it.[19] The impulse to absolutize a certain univocity of immanence can take different forms, other to the immanence of Hegel's self-determining system.

I think of the immanence of a postulatory finitism such as informs the fundamental ontology of Heidegger; or the immanence of the scientistic univocity informing many projects of science and technology in the will to overcome all the equivocities of given being and subject creation to the homogeneity of a projected human measure. I think of other forms: moral, through the immanence of absolute autonomy in Kantianism and its revisions; calculative, in the homogeneous reckoning of hedonistic bliss or mass happiness in utilitarianism; speculative and political, in the dialectical immanence of Hegelianism and its state; dialectical and revolutionary, in the political immanence of post-Hegelian totalitarianisms, be they Marxist or fascist; anti-dialectical and Dionysian, in the rhapsodic form that tries to break out of all form in the immanent Nietzschean world that is "will to power and nothing else besides," and we ourselves also "will to power and nothing else besides"[20]; or naturalizing and pragmatic, devoid of any suggestion of mystery at the heart of the intimate strangeness of given being.

Thought thinking itself reaches a kind of acme in Hegel's idealistic form of dialectic, but what emerges at this high noon is the need for thought thinking *the other of thought thinking itself.* We can see this in many figures—Marx, Kierkegaard, Schopenhauer, Nietzsche, Heidegger,

---

19. Gilles Deleuze and Felix Guattari, *What Is Philosophy?*, trans. H. Tomlinson and G. Burchell (New York: Columbia University Press, 1994), 60.

20. *The Will to Power*, ed. W. Kaufmann, trans. W. Kaufmann and R. J. Hollingdale (New York: Random House, 1967), 550; *Der Wille zur Macht* (Leipzig: Kröner Verlag, 1930), 697.

and well into the twentieth century. This other to thought thinking itself is at issue in many thinkers in the line of inheritance from post-Hegelian dialectic. Of course, there is nothing that entirely escapes controversy here. Moreover, one might suspect that not a few proposed candidates for this otherness are far from being postdialectical, and even less transdialectical, insofar as they embodying a recurrence of deep equivocity, or an oscillation of univocity and equivocity. (One could see analytic philosophy in a similar light.) It is interesting on this score to see something of a revival of the study of Schelling among postmodern thinkers. The other to thought thinking itself is at stake. Schelling sought to offer a positive philosophy (dealing with the "that" of existence) to balance and complete the negative philosophy (dealing with the "what" of things) whose impulse he shared with Hegel.[21] That his search already occurs from *within* idealism I take a sign of the "trans" as there hidden in, or covered over by the immanent practices of idealistic dialectic. These signs may indicate what kind of mindfulness is to be sought to think the "trans" better or more truly. Some recent commentators make Schelling much more non-Hegelian than he is; after all, Hegel was himself a Schellingian and the two cannot be so simply uncoupled from each other. One of the things binding them still is the canonical status of Spinoza. They both are in love with an immanent God—even if there is more darkness and recalcitrance and otherness to Schelling's version of that immanent God.[22]

There is a "trans" of thinking in the middle, a passage in the between, but in intermediation with what is other to thought thinking itself. The "trans" opens a plurivocal intermediation with the other to thought thinking itself. It opens up metaxological metaphysics, in answer to the "after" of Hegel, both in the sense of the "post" and in the sense of the "trans." Nevertheless, the "trans" is more important than the "post," and indeed in metaxological form it is able to rejoin earlier practices of philosophical dialectic, where finesse for the "more" of the beyond is less domesticated than in the immanent categories of a modern rationalis-

---

21. F. W. J. Schelling, *The Grounding of Positive Philosophy: The Berlin Lectures*, trans. Bruce Matthews (Albany: State University of New York Press, 2008).
22. Paul Higgins has helpfully drawn my attention to the fact that Kant in the *Opus Postumum* had concluded that the early Schelling was a Spinozist. See Kant, *Opus Postumum*, trans. E. Förster and M. Rosen (New York: Cambridge University Press, 1993), 147–48 and 274–75.

tic system. Beyond the geometrical God, beyond the moralized God, beyond the immanent God of the whole, beyond the new pagan gods of Nietzsche and Heidegger, there is the God of the *metaxu*.

Heidegger is not wrong to talk about a forgetfulness of being, even if one hesitates at his epochal framing of such a claim and its own univocalizing of the plurivocal practices of metaphysical thinking. One wonders about his implication in the voiding of being insofar as he ontologically privileges anxiety before the nothing. One wonders about his later gesture of crossing out being, a gesture saturated with equivocities asking further thought. Yet he does offer, among other things, important reflections on truth as *alētheia*, understood as more primordial than determinate truths that can be given more univocal propositional form. There is an interplay between determinacy and something more indeterminate. While an origin that is self-concealing in its revealing is not quite the voiding of being, it is in hearing distance of it, especially if we strongly stress the withholding, even retracting nature of the self-concealing revealing. The nonbeing of the no-thing of the self-concealing origin is hard to disentangle from being as nothing. If truth has to be wrested from the hiddenness, this is not the self-giving, gracious self-communication of the true. The voiding here would be a self-withholding indetermination. By contrast, if one were to speak of the origin as a fertile void, understood as kenotic, because agapeic, the fullness of being as overdeterminate would call for thought.

While not lacking ontological suggestions of the overdeterminate in later invocations of *Gelassenheit*, one worries if the shadow of the modern devaluation of being falls over Heidegger's thought, insofar as we seem to have being without the good, just as with Levinas we seem to have the good without being.[23] Beyond the voiding of being, metaphysical finesse asks new thought on the togetherness of the "to be" and the "to be good." One might think of the earlier Marion trying to escape

---

23. Emmanuel Levinas, *Totality and Infinity*, trans. A. Lingis (Pittsburgh, Penn.: Duquesne University Press, 1968), 103: "The Place of the Good above every essence is the most profound teaching, the definitive teaching, not of theology, but of philosophy." The good beyond being may be intended in a post-Heideggerian sense but what when existence without existents becomes the evil of being, *la mal de l'être?*, as it does in Emmanuel Levinas, *De l'existence à l'existant* (Paris: Fontaine, 1947), 19; *Existence and Existents*, trans. A. Lingis (The Hague: Nijhoff, 1978), 19.

the vice of Heideggerian being with a God without being.[24] But does this escape the devaluation if it means ending with being without God? In the later Marion we have the "saturated phenomenon," and while this is suggestive for something beyond the voiding of being, the stress seems more on the inverse of transcendental positing.[25] It remains in the frame of phenomenology rather than in the transdialectical *metaxu*. This *metaxu* is more fully an ontological-metaphysical space wherein we meet what I name as the *hyperboles of being*.

One could say that the forgetfulness of being is as much elemental as epochal. It is our nature to forget being in determining its overdeterminacy, as we reconfigure our constitutive participation in the intimate strangeness of being. We determine its overdeterminacy in pursuit of a cognitive mastery that just in its mode of knowing produces an unknowing of being as always more than us, as endowing and enabling us, even as we try to overtake it. A metaxological metaphysics can be seen as a systematic and trans-systematic response to this recurrent slippage into loss of mindfulness of being, into even a second forgetfulness of being. The overdeterminacy is not univocal determinability, not equivocal indetermination, not dialectical self-determination. It calls for an opening of thought to the other of thought thinking itself, and in companionship with some post-Hegelian signs that have been noted.

The voiding of being, while not devoid of nihilistic implications, indeed dangers, might also be said to lead to a kind of "return to zero" in which a new interface with the overdeterminacy of being becomes possible. The original porosity to being we see in ontological astonishment may open metaphysically to an effort to think anew the overdeterminacy of being. There is here something like a paradoxical conjunction of seeming opposites in bringing together this porosity and overdeterminacy: the first looks like "almost nothing," the second like something "all but too much." And yet this doubleness is truer to being and void: an original porosity of philosophy to being as given, undergone in the ontological astonishment that finds itself in receipt of communication from the overdeterminacy of being. This doubleness is also truer to the two-

---

24. Jean-Luc Marion, *God without Being*, trans. Thomas A. Carlson (Chicago: University of Chicago Press, 1991).

25. *In Excess: Studies of Saturated Phenomena*, trans. R. Horner and V. Berraud (New York: Fordham University Press, 2002).

fold "meta" of metaphysics. The excessive self-confidence of modern rationalism and idealism is over; the studied overcaution of analytic ordinariness is not fully true to the robust eros of philosophical mindfulness; the postulatory finitude of much recent continental philosophy is too self-insistently immanent; the abjection of postmodern antirationalism saws the branch of being on which it is unhappily sitting. One might speak of a new, endowed poverty of philosophy in which fresh porosity to the overdeterminacy of being can be opened. In a field long lying fallow, in the midst even of the darnel, new shoots of promise can show in, can grow out of postmodern perplexity.

2 ∽ Analogy and the Fate of Reason

ANALOGY, PLURIVOCITY, AND THE FATE OF REASON

Analogy and reason (*logos*) have hugely defined the traditions of reflection on the most ultimate issues in philosophy and theology. What reason means is not always univocally clear. Indeed, a certain plurivocity in its meaning is inseparable from the meaning(s) of analogy. In the philosophical tradition, to give a *logos* (*logon didonai*) is central to the task of philosophy. In the monotheistic tradition in its Christian form, *logos* is identified with God, overtly with the second person of the Trinity. The familial relation of both philosophical and religious *logos* has been applauded in some instances (recently and notably by Pope Benedict XVI). In other instances, interpretation of divine *logos*, understood religiously, is seen as too dominated by the Greek *logos*—the voice of Athenian *logos* speaks over the voice of Jerusalem, muffling it, garbling it. To voice something is to offer a *logos*, and we cannot avoid asking whether there is one voice or many voices, or one voice that voices itself in many voices.

Thus we find ourselves revisiting the classical position, expressed in Aristotle's famous saying: *to on legetai pollachōs* (*Metaphysics* 1003b5), being is voiced in many senses. Aquinas echoes Aristotle and concurs: *ens dicitur multipliciter*. This plurivocity bears on the univocal, equivocal, and analogical senses of being. Very generally put, the univocal sense of being puts the stress on sameness; the equivocal sense puts the stress on difference, a difference sometimes dissimulated by our ways of speaking; the analogical sense somehow mixes the same and the different, being partly one and partly the other, and with reference to the relation of the sameness and difference to something shared by both. Aristotle's distinction between the univocal, equivocal, and analogical senses of being is taken up by Aquinas and put to work, though what he himself says explicitly is not extensive. Admirers and commentators have devoted much attention to what his remarks might entail, for they reflect something woven into the texture of his thought, especially bearing on the divine difference. Is the plurivocity of being itself, or simply of our ways of talking about being? Some commentators have underplayed any metaphysical dimensions to the matter,[1] while others have developed metaphysical implications in ways more explicated than in Aquinas himself.[2] In any event, voicing happens in a space of betweenness, a space of relationality. Analogy is concerned not only about a middle way between univocity and equivocity, but about this very between of relationality. Analogy is itself a kind of between, and communicates a between.

In this between the plurivocity of being is to be taken seriously, both with respect to the pluralism of immanent creation, and with respect to the relation between creation and God. We are dealing with a certain communication and communicability beyond dualism. Perplexity keeps returning about the *likeness and unlikeness between* God and the finite creation. A crucial concern is the proper way to voice being, or the proper way(s) being voices itself in regard to the divine likeness and unlikeness: whether being voices itself plurally; whether, if plurally, there is no reducing of the many voices to one; whether only apparently plurally, while in truth it is always only one sense of itself that being voices; or whether irreducibly plural, though in the plurality of voices, differences of ultimate importance must be granted, and a singularly exceptional difference, if God is the one of which there is one and one only.

Traditional discussion has also focused on different kinds of analogy: analogy of proportion, of proper proportionality, of attribution. It is worth remembering that analogy has roots also in *mathematical* proportion or *ratio*, roots not unconnected with the fate of reason. There is also what one might call analogy of origination bearing on the likeness of a source and its issue. I will return to how Aquinas speaks of an analogical agent (*agens analogicum*). Important overall in analogy is the play of same and other, the intermediating between likeness and unlikeness.

---

1. Ralph McInerny, *The Logic of Analogy* (The Hague: Martinus Nijhoff, 1961); David Burrell, *Analogy and Philosophical Language* (New Haven, Conn.: Yale University Press, 1973).

2. Norris Clarke, *Explorations in Metaphysics* (Notre Dame, Ind.: University of Notre Dame Press, 1994); Erich Przywara, *Analogia Entis: Metaphysics: Original Structure and Universal Rhythm*, trans. John R. Betz and David Bentley Hart (Grand Rapids, Mich.: Eerdmans, 2014).

The intermediating itself is a dynamic relating rather than a static structure. A dynamic interplay can always be threatened by loss of equilibrium of same and other, likeness and unlikeness. The loss of equilibrium would tilt, on the one side, to pure univocity, on the other, to pure equivocity. But these are limiting cases of abstraction. Pure univocity would be unintelligible, for one could mark no difference in it, or between pure univocal being and something other. Instead of a voicing of being, one would end with Parmenidean silence at best. Pure equivocity would also threaten intelligibility, for we could mark nothing definite or determinate in it, or relate one difference to another. For to relate a difference to another difference must mean that the differences are invested with some identity, identity ruled out *ex hypothesi*. Pure equivocity is as unintelligible as absolute difference without any determinate difference and hence seems indistinguishable from pure univocity. These impossible extremities are the unintelligible limits between which analogical thinking, at its best, is poised, a between wherein a rich interweaving of sameness and difference is effected.

What of analogy and the fate of reason?[3] Fate brings to mind the ancient notion of *moira*, the ineluctable necessity above even the gods and Zeus. In the monotheistic religions nothing at all can be above God and a mindful providence is affirmed rather than an impersonal fate. There have been strands in the philosophical tradition for which reason is analogous to fate, that is, as ultimately an impersonal power determined inexorably by and to universal necessity. God may be a more personalized being suitable for the many, while reason offers the more ultimate principle suitable for the few. Shestov inveighs against this impersonal necessity and the "self-evidences" of reason and sets the personal God of Jerusalem over against the impersonal fate of Athens. Clearly Catholic theology

---

3. The original writing of this exploration reflects the fact that I was commissioned to write on "Analogy and the Fate of Reason." References to *fate* should be seen in this context, and indeed my suggested alternative to fate, namely, *vocation*. There are significant amplifications in this present version of my reflections. Of course, in the background is the pervasive sense of a crisis of reason after Hegel, and reference might have been made to Husserl's sense of crisis, in addition to Heidegger, and more generally to a lack of confidence in the postmoderns by contrast with the overconfidence of rationalistic Enlightenment. Postmodern philosophies of difference such as we find in Adorno, Deleuze, or Derrida are not coincident with a more analogical metaxology. After the overconfidence of rationalistic Enlightenment, they are often tied to the dialectic of univocity and equivocity, but not as embracing integrative dialectic, and none is fully metaxological.

must reject this view of the personal God as merely a convenience for the believing many, with impersonal reason for the philosophical few. The same holds for any final opposition of Athens and Jerusalem. Nevertheless, there are analogous universal claims made for Catholic thought. An important question is whether there is a univocal universal or a plurivocal, or perhaps an analogical universality in which the putative disjunction between the Gods of religion and philosophy is mediated rather than entrenched. I would speak rather of an intimate universal.

Modern Enlightenment and, in particular, Hegel's historicized version of Christian providence, suggests that reason is fated to surpass religion and all its figures, including its analogical figurations. Currently, post-Hegelians and anti-Hegelian thinkers resist any overt suggestion of providence, either religious or secularized. A more likely default position is an improvident economy of chance and necessity. The providence of Hegelian reason claims to sublate and thereby complete the equivocity of religious figuration, but this claim comes riddled with its own equivocity. The fated fulfillment is followed by a rash of revolts against speculative reason, ranging from positivistic claims to scientistic enlightenment to existential rebellion against systematic reason as such. Heidegger, of course, claims that such a putative fulfillment just totalized a falling away from an original unconcealing of being. The Hegelian and Heideggerian fatalities of reason yield two opposed forms of historicist univocity: reason as fated to teleological completion in immanence, and reason as in the secret services of the fated oblivion of being, cybernetically completed. Analogy does not fit into these extremes. It cannot be included in positivistic univocity, in existential equivocity, in any self-contained speculative system, and yet it is not completely outside all reasonable systematics.

We must ask if there is a plurivocal promise in reason itself. In what follows, I will not propose a fate of reason quite but rather a *vocation* to redeem this plurivocal promise. I will explore how reason understands itself differently depending on which sense of being is in the ascendant. If univocity is in the ascendant, as it tends to be in modern rationalism, a philosophical and theological feel for what analogy might mean tends to be weakened. If equivocity comes back, as it inevitably does, reason goes to school with finesse and is more attentive to figurations of being that elude precise determinations and are more hospitable to the analogical way. I will indicate how the oscillation between univocity and equivocity can be understood dialectically, but also how modern dialectical reason, because too much under the sovereignty of a reason that would be self-determining, fails to do justice to what is of the essence in true analogy, namely, the superlative difference of the divine, beyond determination and self-determination. Finally, I will suggest that there is something metaxological about analogy in trying to be true to the between-space of communication between the finite and the divine, and the dynamic intermediating of likening and unlikening eventuating there.[4] Philosophical and theological reason requires of us such a metaxological mindfulness. I will ask if a certain finesse for the analogy of origination has something to offer within the postmodern ethos which stresses the aesthetics of happening, understood not in an aestheticist manner but with robust ontological stress.

ANALOGY, REASON, AND RELIGIOUS FIGURING

Though associated with the senses of being in classical metaphysics, analogy is theologically connected with how we might intelligibly speak about the divine, especially given, in the monotheistic tradition, God's transcendence to finite categories. How we figure the divine is not self-evident, nor indeed is what we mean by reason. Analogy is a way of figuring, in light of being itself as open to figuration. There is a given ethos of being in which we participate, but which we figure and also can reconfigure.

---

4. There are different kinds of likeness/unlikeness and their interplay. Metaphor stresses the similar in the dissimilar (the king is a lion); while in the play of like and unlike, analogy gives a different stress to the unlikeness, hence its appropriateness *vis-à-vis* defending divine transcendence and difference. Aristotle speaks of the great power of metaphor of the poetic genius who sees the similar in dissimilars. But in analogy about God, even seeing the likeness, one finds the likeness always exceeded by the unlikeness or difference. David Tracy tends to assimilate analogy to metaphor, at least in one crucial passage—*The Analogical Imagination* (New York: Cross Roads, 1981), 410—he quotes Aristotle, and endorses a "similarity-in-difference" model. But this is not adequate to the difference. See S. McFague, *Metaphorical Theology* (Minneapolis, Minn.: Fortress Press, 1997), 198. David Burrell, *Analogy and Philosophical Language*, 161, also seems to endorse the priority of metaphor to analogy; he cites Coleridge and the great poets, who prophetically leap outside the ordinary and "part company with those travelling the securer and steadier road of analogical comparison." But properly understood, the greater difference, essential to analogy, always opens a door into the always greater darkness of the divine—the most insecure for the human measure, and shaking our most domestic steadinesses.

Figures, I suggest, need not necessarily be "merely" figurative, though fidelity to the ethos of being is asked of us. Figures can aesthetically word the between, the *metaxu* of being. Like being, figuring itself is plurivocal, hence always neighbors on the possibility of the equivocal. Important in the fate of reason is the way that a more rigid rational sense of figuring may well think it must uncouple itself from any taint of equivocity. Important will be the tension between a rational figuration as tempted to determinative univocal fixation and analogical figuration as opening to what exceeds such univocal determination.

Though often associated with Catholicism, analogy has pagan roots in the philosophies of Plato and Aristotle. Analogy in Thomas Aquinas entails a balance of identity and difference, continuity and discontinuity, with a tilt toward hyperbolic difference in the case of God's uniqueness, a difference always bordering on a kind of equivocity that cannot be completely immanently mediated, though the divine might mediate the equivocity. We are familiar with the theological placing of analogy on the Protestant index by Karl Barth when he refers to the analogy of being as "the invention of the Anti-Christ."[5] We are also familiar with how the ex-Catholic Heidegger dismissed analogy as bound up with the "system of Catholicism," a moldy relic of ontotheology.[6] And yet the rootedness and continuity with the philosophical tradition might be counted as a point in its favor—if theologically one thinks differently to Barth (as for instance, Erich Przywara does),[7] or philosophically to Heidegger (as for instance, Edith Stein does).[8]

The figurative dimension of analogy is most fruitful where our perplexity exceeds univocal determination. God is not a determinate being, but how can one think what is not finitely determinable or is as transdeterminate? God is not a being, not a creature. Moreover as infinite, God is not just the dialectical other of the finite, but infinitely other than the finite. And yet God is in intimate relation to the finite, its most intimate ontological companion as giving all finite being to be, even granting a

---

5. Karl Barth, *Church Dogmatics* I/1, rev. ed. (Edinburgh: T and T Clark, 1975), xiii.
6. See Martin Heidegger, *Schelling's Treatise on the Essence of Human Freedom*, trans. J. Stambaugh (Athens: Ohio University Press, 1985), 38, 186–87, 192.
7. Erich Przywara, *Analogia Entis*, in *Schriften*, vol. 3 (Einsiedeln: Johannes Verlag, 1962). See Philip Gonzales, *Reimagining the Analogia Entis: The Future of Erich Przywara's Christian Vision* (Grand Rapids, Mich.: Eerdmans, 2019).
8. Edith Stein, *Finite and Eternal Being*.

mysterious and hyperbolic asymmetry of the divine. This is not a matter of some dialectical mutuality of sameness and otherness in which likeness and unlikeness are on an equal footing, and so can be held together as moments of a more inclusive whole. The similitude is always exceeded by the dissimilitude. Augustine: *Si comprehendis non est Deus*. Aquinas: *Deus semper maior*. Analogy need not be deaf to postmodern concerns with difference *qua* difference. Barth and Heidegger to the contrary, the safeguarding of God's transcendence and being's otherness is very much in sight. On this score philosophy and theology are siblings in the same family.

Worth noting here is a certain plurivocity in how reason itself has been understood. Recall how, for instance, the sameness or difference of *theoretical* and *practical reason* is an important issue in both ancient and modern thought. Their sameness or difference will dictate different tasks of a philosophical and theological nature. What is meant by reason in modernity is not quite what the ancients meant by *theōria* and its contemplative regard of what is, simply as it is. Is there a univocity subtending theoretical and practical reason, or is their difference irreducible? The different sense of *theōria* in the ancient world has implication for both the analogical sense of being as well as the fate of reason. In the ancient and medieval view, *theōria* was not just a matter of our construction but more originally one of our reception. It was not a matter of a projection of our cognitive power but of a noetic porosity to the ultimate things. We are first recipients of gifts, not producers of products. We might be the latter in regard to practical reason, yet there is an other orientation which opens us more primordially to what is beyond us. This other porosity is not unrelated to the analogical sense of being and orientation to the divine.

In modernity, theoretical reason is tied up with hypothetical constructs, themselves projects of the human being. And while there is a speculative side to projective conjecture, there is a recessed practical project at work here. The other porosity, just mentioned, tends to be recessed by this practical project. The modern slogan is: We know what we construct. And hence the known is as much a reflection of us as of the things themselves—maybe more a reflection of us than what is other. The essential form of reason must then be self-reflective. Theoretical reason is itself a project, and hence in it is recessed a pragmatic relation of things *for us*.

Many moderns have welcomed this, rejoiced in it. Reason becomes more practical than ever in the broad sense of serving human desire. It is useful, or is to be useful, and "use" always implies some relation of being for us, to us. The shadow of an instrumentalization of being appears here, because it is not the otherness of what is known that is important but its relation to us and its being of service to this relation. If analogical thinking persists, we will think of our others on the analogy of ourselves and our self-relation. Analogy will not be a porous between-space of relationality; it will be a self-mediating space between us and ourselves, via a postulated or hypothesized other. We will only be able to think what is other on the analogy of ourselves. Analogy will also be projective of our power rather than participant in a more primal porosity between us and what is other. If there is a different stress on our porosity to the transhuman in premodernity, modern pragmatics risks clogging this and making essential relation finally into relation for us. This makes it hard to enter more intimately into an analogical inscape of things and God.

MODERN REASON, GEOMETRICAL FIGURING, WEAKENING ANALOGY

Finesse for the figurative tends to be overtaken in modernity by a more dominating stress on rational univocity. Such finesse meets with an epistemic irritation with the equivocity of things, and is overtaken by a more aggressive univocal reconfiguration of the ethos of being. The analogical sense of being, poised in the play of likeness and unlikeness, hospitable to communications suggestive of mystery rather than fixed on unambiguous assertions, loses footing in this reconfiguration. Figures can aesthetically be incarnations of what is noetic. The figure is the body of communication. *La bella figura*: an incarnation of being that aesthetically delights. Religiously one might think of the sacramental world as divinely figured: real presence in the elemental things granting sustenance, consummately communicated in consecrated bread and wine. Finesse for this tends to weaken in the modern univocalization that we find in the thoroughgoing mathematicization of nature, the objectivizing reduction of given being to a valueless thereness, and the singular elevation of the autonomous human being into the univocal exemplification of immanent freedom.

Thus we are not surprised by a diminution of finesse for the question of God among philosophers in modernity, from Descartes onward. Forgetfulness of the protocols going with analogy is coupled with either a more direct claim to move univocally from the finite to the divine, or with the absence of any such motion, if an equivocal skepticism about cognition paralyzes every move to what is more than the finite. That said, worth noting is the sense of analogy with origins in mathematical proportion (A:B::C:D). Mathematical ratio is a rational figure. This is not just a relation, but a relation of relations—a relation on one side of the equation is like a relation on the other side. Of course, if the "term" on one side of the ratio is God, it is impossible to fix the terms, or even the entire structure of the proportion with exact univocity. In connection with the divine, analogy is witness to and bounded by mystery. Nevertheless, the relation of analogy to mathematical proportion is significant, as mathematics is a formation of rational thinking which pursues the highest exactitude possible in its sphere of operation. Exactitude here is defined by the measure of a fixed univocity. That is, the terms at issue must have all ambiguity excluded. Such a desideratum influences our understanding of what is essential to the figures of reason. Not surprisingly, mathematical thinking has been taken, in ancient as well as modern times, as the paradigm for rational thinking. Reason becomes associated with the ideal of unambiguous univocity. Equivocation *per se* is understood as a problem, threatening of the unreasonable and to be overcome.

Recall how Plato was attracted to the precisions of geometry, and above the Academy's entrance reportedly hung: "Let no one enter who has not studied geometry." Of course, there is also a thinking higher than the dianoetics of geometry, an opening of the soul which is noetically receptive and which Plato associates with dialectic. Obviously modern rationalism was very much defined by the mathematical ideal, and one thinks in particular of Spinoza's way of philosophizing *more geometrico*. Here is one of the sources of the occlusion and the eventual eclipse of the God of analogy. Spinoza serves as one exemplary instance, on this score, with many descendants sharing his commitment to a certain univocity of being, understood also in an entirely immanent or horizontal sense. I think on that score of Deleuze, and recall one more time his dictum that Spinoza is the "Christ of philosophers." The time of immanence has come or is coming into its completion. Huge swathes of German idealism are bred from seeds of Spinoza, Kant, and Fichte, coupled with a widespread repudiation of the asymmetrical superior transcendence of the God beyond the whole, so beloved of earlier analogical thinkers. These seeds have themselves many post-Kantian mutants.

Perplexities about the divine may strike us which open thought beyond what can be made exact in terms of precise determinations. The signs of the divine may communicate to us in a manner which looks equivocal. In Pascal's terms we require then *l'esprit de finesse* rather than *l'esprit de géométrie*. Diminution of finesse for the signs of the divine accompanies the growing ascendancy of geometry in modernity. One might say that the modern weakening of analogy has much to do with a certain reconfiguration of the ethos of being. The "too muchness" of the given ethos of being, its overdeterminacy, is seen as too elusive, as even an intolerably equivocal milieu that must be reconfigured by a determining univocity which will overcome all given ambiguities. And the reconfiguration will be theoretical and practical: theoretical in the mathematicization of nature, practical in the invention of machines and technologies which will further our power over given creation in its otherness. The project of being "master and possessor of nature" (Descartes) reforms our way of figuring things in the direction of mathematical science with technological instrumentality serving us as the end of all things. Given creation is stripped of its ambiguous and qualitative textures, and reduced to rational, mathematicizable structure which gets at the primary qualities. But stripped of such qualitative textures creation as nature seems to communicate fewer and fewer of the signs of the divine. It is just a bare objective thereness, twinned with a subjectivity framing the void givenness in terms of its projective power. The deeper seeds of an analogical dwelling in being wither.

It might seem, then, that it is the fate of analogy itself to weaken, if not to disappear, in the more modern forms of reason. In premodern reason there was more finesse for the plurivocal significance of the analogical interplay of likeness and unlikeness, and not least because there was more porosity between religion and philosophy. In the modern ideal of autonomous thinking, reason is self-determining, hence not in service to something exceeding its own self-determination. One might call it self-serving reason, but if so, its porosity to what exceeds reason's own immanent terms is in tension with its aim to be fully self-determining.

Sometimes the porosity is entirely closed off. Sometimes a protocol of border patrols is negotiated in the conflict of the faculties.[9] Sometimes the closure of the border is conceived in quite the opposite manner, namely, as the sovereignty of reason over the immanent whole, and no space is to remain for religious faith as a genuine other with which reason is in familial dialogue.

If we look at some episodes of this self-serving reason, it will be hard to avoid a connection with the loss of the analogical, or at least its diminished appreciation in the practices of modern reason. It has been said that Scotus is the real grandfather of modernity insofar as the univocity of being is proposed and defended in his entire way of thinking. I understand that Scotus was engaged with the safeguarding of divine transcendence, but the univocity can seem to amount to a sameness which overarches the difference of the human and the divine. Whatever one thinks of Scotus himself, such a way of thinking harbors the always-present danger of making God one part or moment of a larger univocal totality of being of which finite created being is another moment. Such a way of thinking is brought to dialectical consummation in the Hegelian version of reason. Finite and infinite never stand on their own or in the difference, but both are moments of a more fully self-mediating totality. If "God" is anything, "God" is not a true self-determining concept but a religious representation of that whole more absolutely conceived in self-serving reason. This is to the diminishment of the (theistic) God beyond the whole, and consistent with the promotion of univocity, dialectically defined or not, and with the weakening of the sense that the dissimilitude is always greater than the similitude. Univocal thinking lives in dread of a dissimulating God. It cannot live patiently with the equivocity of divine mystery. The hyperbolic dissimilitude of the God beyond the whole is extruded out of the rational discourse of the immanent univocity of being as a whole. I will return to these themes.

There is no doubt that, in an entirely immanent sense, univocity enjoys sovereignty in the modern conception of reason. The root of analogical thinking in the mathematical ratio comes to the fore in a manner which leads to the accentuation of precise univocity and its fixation

---

9. "The Conflict of the Faculties (1796)," in *Religion and Rational Theology*, ed. and trans. A. W. Wood and G. Di Giovanni (Cambridge: Cambridge University Press, 1996).

to the diminishment of the analogical interplay between others that are both like and unlike. It is no accident that a *mathēsis* of nature should be the first desideratum of the modern rationalization of the givenness of being. More deeply, the claim of reason is to be seen as a *project* for the univocalization of all being. A project: it is not that the equivocal is not recognized—quite the opposite—rather, there is quite a feel for equivocities but these are essentially problems to be confronted and surmounted. The problem carries the anticipation of its own solution when it is properly formulated, that is to say, univocally articulated, and the solution will be the dispelling of the equivocity as entirely as possible. The project itself extends to the whole—where there is equivocity, there shall be univocity, and formulated in the most precise mathematical form possible. Where these precisions are not now forthcoming, this still remains the goal, and the project will work toward its attainment in all the areas of investigation. The pursuit of autonomy goes hand in hand with this project of univocal reason. The univocity of human self-serving is twinned with the self-service of univocal reason, and their sovereignties are to be extended over all being as other.

The *mathēsis* of nature, under the aegis of univocity, does not yield quite the univocity desired—it never does, in fact. The equivocal keeps coming back, in many forms. I invoke Whitehead. Whitehead was one of the heroes of modern logical univocity, someone whose first academic career was as a professor of mathematics; but at the end of his second career as a speculative metaphysician, and as a different kind of hero, he importantly said: "the exactness is a fake."[10] He also indicated something of the soft ground on which modern scientistic univocity stood, all the while believing it was close to hitting bottom level: the fallacy of simple location.[11] Analogical thinking entails a mindfulness beyond *l'esprit de géométrie*, but the geometrical mind can well be included in the finessed analogical mind, insofar as it too has a root in mathematical *ratio*. Can the *ratio* be given univocal exactitude? The answer is sometimes "yes," sometimes "no." This means there is a *ratio* beyond rationality in the geometrical mode. More generally: there is analogical reason beyond

---

10. "Immortality," in *The Philosophy of Alfred North Whitehead*, 2nd ed., ed. P. A. Schilpp (New York: Tudor, 1951), §XIX (700).

11. A. N. Whitehead, *Science and the Modern World* (New York: Macmillan, 1925), 49–51, 58, 63.

the mathematicization of reason we find in modern science. If the latter is hot in pursuit of the acme of univocity, the former has to be open to the return to the equivocal, the return of the equivocal, and with the aim of a mindful mediating of what it communicates.

That the fate of modern reason is not just univocally its Enlightenment version is suggested by the fact that the Enlightenment is shadowed by its twin, Romanticism. Modern reason is haunted by what it rejects as other to it. This other, as its shadow, is its intimate other. In broad strokes, the twinning of Enlightenment and Romanticism reflects an analogous twinning of *l'esprit de géométrie* and *l'esprit de finesse*. The latter tries to recuperate a sense of the analogically appropriate, though if there is a root of analogy in mathematical proportion, analogy has its connection with Enlightenment reason also. Consider, for example, the resort to analogy in the argument from design, formulated paradigmatically on the analogy of the watch. The analogy: as watch to watchmaker, so creation to God. This argument was much discussed in the eighteenth century when a combination of rationalism and empiricism, dianoetic and aesthetic univocity was in the ascendant. The aesthetic univocity of creation as a machine could be the basis of an analogical argument offering a dianoetic univocity to reason in connection with the machine-maker God. If this is an argument from analogy, based on a more or less univocalized picture of nature as a machine, it does not escape the equivocity it flees. Because the likeness is in interplay with unlikeness diverse possibilities are allowed. There is an openness in the analogical inference that cannot be dispelled. There is nothing absolutely univocal about the aesthetic givenness of the world.

Hume exploits this to increase skepticism about metaphysical and theological claims. Alternatively, a theological/metaphysical finesse might be required to read the signs of the divine communicated in the openness of that between space, a space in which immanence and transcendence are plurivocally intermediated but never reduced simply to one totality. One could say that for analogical thinking the plurivocity of signs is of positive significance. It is not a bad equivocity and a failure of univocal precision. It is worth noting that what we take as the most significant of signs tends to depend on what dominates in our efforts to configure the ethos of given being. Thus in the mechanistic world picture, the likeness of the watch dominates in Paley's version of the argument from design: our mechanisms are taken as a sign of a divine machine-maker. The entirety of creation is taken in under the *"as if" sign* of the machine. God is thought analogically under this determinate, that is, univocalizing "as if" sign. The fixed precision of satisfied univocity is never reached. The equivocity of the "as if" can be turned in a skeptical direction, as it was by Hume, simply by noting features of the immanent world that tell against a direct, univocal inference to the God of monotheism. If nothing else, perplexity about evil troubles the "as if" in relation to the inference to the goodness of God. Perhaps the play of likeness and unlikeness might form the basis for the inference to an apprentice god, or something other. In any case, some equivocity returns in the "as if."

There can be something deeper about the Romantic reaction to Enlightenment insofar as the immanent whole is more likened to an organism than to a machine. The immanent pantheistic divinity that goes with it brings its own new equivocities, not least about immanent evil. And though there is a secret employment of analogical thinking, it is not necessarily hospitable to the insuperable sense of divine difference we find in the older form of analogy. Pan(en)theism offers us a more immanent rhapsodic divinity, a dancer who cannot be told from the dance, with saturated aesthetic resonances which cannot quite be univocalized, and also with (quasi-) ethical resonances of an immanent self-determination of humanity. These resonances continue to resound into our own time. But overall we see, in a plurivocal way, how even in the immanences of a more thoroughgoing univocalization of creation, and of the spaces between creation and the divine, signs of transcendence keep coming back. Though there is an equivocity to these signs, they do ask us if they necessitate something like a renewal of analogical thinking. In the pursuit of univocal sameness, whether scientistic or aesthetic, equivocal differences keep reappearing—testament to the recurrent rhythm of likening and unlikening in the unfolding of things.

ANALOGY, UNIVOCITY, AND CORRESPONDENCE

Let me dwell on some of these themes a bit more, with an eye to seeing connections between analogy, univocity, and truth understood as correspondence. Truth understood as the mind's correspondence, or adequation to the things has been perhaps the most recurrent view of truth in the philosophical tradition. Granting many dimensions to this view, relevant for us is the conviction that human knowing corresponds more truly to the things the more it moves beyond the ambiguities of analogical thinking. It has sometimes been proposed that in the childhood of the human race analogies were needed, but these are more or less childish representations that a more mature reason, a more sovereign univocal reason, will overcome. The theme of autonomy goes hand in hand with this project of univocal reason. Human self-serving is joined to the self-service of univocal reason. Their sovereignty over all being as other is their project. This univocalizing project is present in the *mathēsis* of nature, present in the project of method in Descartes, and more explicit in the *characteristica universalis* of Leibniz. The modern sense of correspondence is ruled by a univocity that insists on a one-to-one correlation between the thoughts or representation we have "in the head or mind" with facts or states of affairs holding determinately in the real world "outside the mind." Correspondence putatively bridges the gap between our mental representations and such states of affairs. Thinking offers a representation which putatively must correspond one-to-one with some such external original or originals.

How close does this come to the interplay of likeness and unlikeness we find in analogical thinking? It tends to retreat from this double play to something more precisely univocal. Consider, by way of illustration, the way in aesthetics that the idea of *imitation* has become a much less rich notion in the modern version. It is often no more than a facile copying or reproduction. It is as if some geometrical mapping of univocal sameness would give us the exact replica of the original. Needless to say, a creative emergence in imitation itself tends to be stifled on this understanding. Creative participation in a plurivocal between space counts for less than fixing this between as a precisely enumerable set of determinate beings or events. But this quest of exact univocity in imitation generates the paradox that an exact replica would be no different from the original and hence either be the original itself or a new original for itself. In either case, the exact replica would not be at all the exact replica it claims to be. Such exact replication is self-subverting. It is subject to the nemesis of a new equivocity, destructive of its own claim to have overcome all equivocity.

With the mind of univocity in the ascendant, we can find the reduction of reason itself to some mechanical process, mirroring a world itself imaged as a machine. Again the equivocal rears its head. If reason were entirely mechanical in its replications it would not be reason, for as not other to mechanical reduplication, it would not know itself or its other. There would be no knowing of the machine, properly speaking. What knows, who knows, in the project of self-serving reason, would not know itself, and hence be incapable of truly serving itself (and it goes without saying, anything other than itself also). We should not forget that machines do not and cannot construct philosophical theories about themselves as machines. One hears the rejoinder that more complex machines can do so, will do so, if not now, then someday. This is a promissory note on a *metabasis eis allo genos*, conveniently deferred into a virtual space of (im)possibility, somewhere over the rainbow. Whether here or there, such machines would no longer be machines. Not only would they not be machines, but the vaunted autonomy nested at the heart of the project of univocity would itself not cease to generate new equivocities.

By contrast, one could claim that "correspondence" can be interpreted to have something of the analogical built into it—I mean again the interplay of likeness and unlikeness. Think of a correspondence between two people. There is a communication from one, and an answer from the other, and there is communication of reciprocation in the addressing and answering of the one and the other. If the address is not first a univocal proposition, or set of propositions, the answer is never a univocal repetition of what exactly was communicated in the first correspondence. To answer in that exact sense, would be like sending the same letter back to the sender, and hence more in the nature of a precise echo of sameness rather than a genuine correspondence of communication. It would be like writing letters to oneself—self-serving correspondence, hence not really correspondence with or to an other but part of a project of self-coherence.

Human reason would be self-communicating rather than primarily being in communication with being, as intimately in relation to it but not reducible to it. The communication of true correspondence opens up a between space and hence opens up a freedom of difference—but this freedom of difference is not autonomous self-determination. This latter comes from a one-sided contraction of the freedom of difference into a self-serving identity—an identity which is false precisely because it closes off the communication of the other, even while originally it was itself enabled to be itself by it, by just that opening of the between. An answer would be both to the original communication of the other, and yet also the initiation of something new in response, something different—that is, something unlike the original communication. There is necessarily likeness and unlikeness and necessarily an interplay between them. There is something analogical about it that can never be reduced to univocity. Or to equivocity, for after all, a communication is taking place, even if it cannot be pinned down with entirely unambiguous precision.

A skeptical equivocalism might bar one with the cognitive view that nothing can be known of the divine. More extremely, there is nothing to be known of that to which we are entirely unrelated. The collapse of difference produces a scientistic literalism. Creationism is the same as scientism in univocalizing the difference of a religious narrative and a scientific theory, as if they were homogenously on the same scale of cognitive determination. The assertion of unmitigated equivocal difference produces a silent autism concerning that with which we have no relation; and so without some relation, we collapse back into a univocity of immanence. There is nothing beyond. To a univocal literalism we add the supplement of an equivocal fictionalism that, in the long run, comes to the same. Univocity capsizes into equivocity or vice versa—a dialectical *peripéteia*.

Theologically, it should be evident that this univocity of modern reason must be hostile to analogy as understood Thomistically. There is, relative to reason, no opening to the hyperbolic transcendence of the divine. There is not only a *mathēsis* of the mechanical world, but also a claim to clarity and distinctness that is absolutely immanent to reason and that regards a world of entire immanence. Immanence itself becomes that greater than which none can be conceived. Univocal reason thinks the immanent whole greater than which none can be thought. We are on the way either to speculative sublations or anti-speculative deconstructions, self-sublating infinitism or postulatory finitisms—all under the aegis of a univocal totalism of immanence.

There is another aspect here of the fate of modern reason in its more Enlightenment versions to be shadowed by its Romantic twin. I am thinking here of the role of the figurative in the dominion of univocity, in terms of the *double* evaluation of imagination in terms of its contrast with reason. There is imagination for those who pride themselves on being champions of *l'esprit de géométrie*: source of error, say, in Hobbes and Spinoza. There is imagination for those intent on the restoration of some version of *l'esprit de finesse*: source of a deeper truth or higher revelation, as in the Romantics and after. In this dialectic of Enlightenment and Romanticism, it is notable how as the self-understanding of science itself matures into an appreciation of the role of the image, the role of the model, the epistemic contribution of imagination generally comes to be more positively appreciated. This might be seen as a concession to something closer to analogical thinking. It is as if in reaction to the aesthetic univocities of empiricism, and the dianoetic univocities of rationalism, something more is needed for a reason undernourished for more speculative forays, for adventures in self-transcending that carry it to the verge of conceptual comprehensibility.

If Enlightenment reflects *l'esprit de géométrie*, and Romanticism is recuperative of *l'esprit de finesse*, appreciation of analogy is cousin to the second, though if there is a root of analogy in mathematical proportion, analogy has its family connection with Enlightenment reason also. The upsurgence of stress on the imagination is perhaps compensatory for the recession of analogy by Enlightenment reason, and especially the recession of the excess of transcendence as other in the rationalistic configuration of being. If we think of Romanticism it brings many things to mind, some too like the apotheosis of autonomy, but others recalling us to the receptivity to what exceeds rational self-determination. There is something in excesses to self-determination; there are excesses in creation as other, for instance, in the aesthetic happening of the sublime. These excesses might be connected to the excess of dissimilitude that is the most essential side of the analogical unlikeness regarding divine transcendence. This is not an absolute other without any communication. It is paradoxically an absolute other that yet enters into relation and communication—into likenesses. One can see the Romantics as recuperating the aesthetic dimensions of the revelations of transcendence, more proximately through human self-transcendence, but also in the too-muchness of given nature as other, and both of these not necessarily to the exclusion of transcendence as other in an even more superlative sense.

We do find a resort to analogical argument in the regime/constellation of aesthetic and dianoetic univocity with empiricism and rationalism, but there can be something deeper about the Romantic reaction to Enlightenment. I refer again to the argument from design, formulated paradigmatically on the analogy of the watch: as watch to watchmaker, so creation to God. But because the likeness is in interplay with unlikeness diverse possibilities are allowed. There is an openness in the analogical inference that cannot be dispelled. If there is nothing absolutely univocal about the aesthetic givenness of the world, there is no absolutely univocal reason to plump for one absolutely certain conclusion. If the work/watch is not perfect, then why not infer a maker not also perfect or an apprentice in a learning curve, as Hume seems to suggest. There is no absolute escape from skepticism in this between space of analogical likeness and unlikeness. This is not to deny that perhaps this space calls for the cultivation of a metaphysical finesse rather than a reductive or mocking skepticism. Perhaps there are uses of skepticism with their own finesse, as chastising reason for overconfidence in itself not warranted by the finiteness of human cognition.

We can be inclined to take creation under a different analogical sign than the machine, as the Romantics did with the analogy of the organism. The organism is an analogical sign of a divinity that is not extrinsic like the clockmaker but immanent as a principle of life or becoming is immanent in an organism. An organism is an ordered whole that exhibits a kind of purposiveness, even though we find it hard to fix a designated designer. The dynamic of an organism is not a fixed univocal structure imposed by extrinsic divine geometry on an indifferent materiality, otherwise just there as formless. Organic design is dynamic and hence not a static purposed imposition of form on matter but a purposive unfolding of a fuller forming of itself. Thus one can see a governing analogy, an "as if" organicism guiding the Romantic reconfiguration of the ethos of being in a pantheistic, perhaps pan(en)theistic direction.

There are more "Platonically" oriented thinkers who are inclined to take mathematical form itself as the sign: the intelligible dianoetics of the aesthetics of happening suggests an analogical sign of transcendence as other, in addition to the mechanical and the organic sign. In this possibility there is a challenging interinvolvement of geometry and finesse in the appropriate analogical thinking of transcendence as other. Further again, one could also ask if *the human being*, beyond mechanism and organism and mathematical form, the human being as free, might also be designated as an analogical sign: a being both finite and yet infinitely restless, a determinate being and yet opening indeterminately to what is other, a sign of something hyperbolic to immanence in immanence itself. The human being would be as if a self-transcending sign pointing to a divine transcendence as more ultimate than itself. Better again: suppose we take a community of agapeic service as the incarnate sign of the living God—as the life of God on earth.

Of course, there is something about the classical theological configuration of analogy that would deny that we "project" the likeness to this divinity. I take the point, especially if we recall that the porosity of being and the *passio essendi* are ontologically prior to any "projection," itself a derived configuration of the *conatus essendi*. The likeness in interplay with unlikeness is already incarnated in the finite being; and if we can project at all it is only because that incarnation empowers a transcendence of self that is not produced by self alone or only a projection of self. Recalling the *passio essendi* and the porosity of being recalls us also to this more original derivation of our being given to be at all. We have to say that God is not analogous to us, but we are analogous to God. An asymmetry in dissimilitude is always present in this analogical way of thinking. The "as" between us and God is not just our "as if" projected into the heavens. Our projections thus are always, at least in part, idolatrous.

Overall then, we see in a plurivocal way how even in the immanences of a more thoroughgoing univocalization of creation, and of the spaces between creation and the divine, signs of transcendence keep coming back. And though there is an equivocity to these signs, they do ask us if they necessitate the question of whether a renewal of analogical thinking is called for even here. In the pursuit of univocal sameness, equivocal differences keep reappearing—testament to the recurrent rhythm of likening and unlikening in the unfolding of things. The interplay of likeness and unlikeness is not only between likeness and unlikeness but is itself an embodiment of the two together—the interplay incarnates the togetherness of likeness and unlikeness and also the absolution of likeness and unlikeness. This is so redoubled that it is not even an ordinary equivocation that a more powerful logicist univocity can overcome. There is a constitutive knot not merely of ambiguity but of mystery in this redoubled equivocity that is not merely equivocal. Idolatries are bewitched by untrue analogies, perhaps by the untruth of analogy.

MORALIZING ANALOGY: THE "AS IF" OF KANTIAN PRACTICAL REASON

If something of the fate of reason in modernity is bound up with the interplay of rationalism and empiricism, this is no less true of the mongrel transcendental form of Kant who tries to breed critical reason from a mingling of the two. Kant ends up with an "as if" mode of postulating God, and this "as if" is related to analogy, though it involves a weakening of any cognitive claim we might make in a speculative or theoretical manner. When Kant speaks of a transcendental philosophy this is not the traditional Aristotelian-Thomist way of speaking of the transcendentals as dealing with transcategorial universality bearing on being, one, true, good, perhaps beauty. Transcendentals are hypercategorial, for beyond the more usual sense of the universals dealing with kinds of beings, they have a bearing on being as such and all being. Kant's sense of transcendental reason (in the *Critique of Pure Reason*) has to do with our cognitive powers rather than directly with being itself. The transcendental is not to be defined either by the aesthetic sensibility of empiricism or the *ratio* of the rationalist but with what enables and holds together both as epistemic powers. Ultimately there is the transcendental subject, ground of all our knowing, ultimate point of unity or synthesis, making experience intelligible by the imposition of the categories of the understanding on the flux of the sensuous given.

Kant held that reason was the faculty of the unconditioned, and is marked by an impulse to transcend experience, even though it can make no justified theoretical claims about the ultimate, about God. Of interest for our purposes are not Kant's dealing with the analogies of experience in the *Critique of Pure Reason* but what might be interpreted as an analogical component to *practical* reason in the *Critique of Practical Reason*. Though he attacked the arguments of theoretical reason for God, on moral grounds we must think of God as if he does exist. This we must do to make sense of our moral being as under duty to an unconditionally obligating law. If there is here an analogical "as," it is in the form of a practical, moral "as if." Kant often thinks of God rather deistically, that is, in terms of an immanent mechanism defined over against a God beyond the mechanism. Still on moral grounds we must think *as if* God existed. There is no absolute rational univocity about this "as if," and rather, I think, more a kind of persisting equivocity. God is like a regulative ideal we must postulate—a *projected* transcendence as other. We cannot theoretically affirm such a God to be, but must think morally "as if" a moral God were. There is always a rationalistic cautiousness about Kant when venturing beyond (sense) experience. He tells us we must dare to know, but then he constructs an impressive conceptual edifice to convince us we can know nothing in itself. His is a philosophy of limits, but now he seems to transcend the limits, even transgress his own orders, and now just as quickly he reins in any outreaching to the unconditioned. Reason is torn between immanence and transcendence, though wherever possible Kant wants to make reason at home with itself in immanence.

In a number of places where Kant does talk about analogy, he repeatedly stresses a form of the analogy of proportion. For instance, in *Prolegomena to Any Future Metaphysics*, in connection with our "as if" knowledge of God, if we use, say, the analogy of the watch to a watchmaker, this "does not signify (as is commonly understood) an imperfect similarity of two things but a perfect similarity between two quite dissimilar things."[12] In the *Critique of Judgment* he briefly talks about analogy in connection with beauty as a symbol of the moral good.[13] Analogy falls under the symbol as an indirect exhibition of a concept. Again, his example connects with a form of the analogy of proportionality, namely, between a despotic state and a handmill: "For though there is no similarity between a despotic state and a hand mill, there certainly is one between the rules by which we reflect on the two and on how they operate [*Kausalität*]." We find something similar in *Religion within the Boundaries of Mere Reason*.[14] In his *Lectures on the Philosophical Doctrine of Religion*, he talks of "the noble way of analogy"[15] and again it is a form of the analogy of proportion that he identifies.[16] Yet all things considered, it is the way of the moral "as if" that is at the center of his approach to God.

If the Kantian "as if" evidences a kind of analogical thinking such

---

12. Immanuel Kant, *Prolegomena to Any Future Metaphysics*, trans. Paul Carus (Indianapolis, Ind.: Hackett, 1977), §§57–58.

13. *Critique of the Power of Judgment*, §59.

14. *Religion and Rational Theology*, ed. and trans. A. W. Wood and G. Di Giovanni (Cambridge: Cambridge University Press, 1996), 107.

15. Ibid., 366.

16. Ibid., 366–67; also 385–87.

that our moral nature impels us to think of the whole on the likeness of its being governed by a morally just God, there is a kind of transcendence being granted which seems to make less secure Kant's central project of making autonomous morality absolutely sufficient through itself alone. His successors were not content with this concession to transcendence. Perhaps Kant was reluctant to make the concession himself but found he was unable to avoid it. He was haunted by the heteronomy of God. His idealist successors wanted to exorcise this heteronomy more thoroughly.

One could see this exorcism as wanting to dispel the *dissimilitude* granted by Aquinas in analogy. If there is an "is" in the analogical likeness of Aquinas it is not Kant's "as if," nor, as we shall see, Hegel's "is." Remember that for Kant the "as if" is seen in light of a regulative ideal that we postulate or project into the "beyond." Aquinas holds we cannot avoid an affirmation of the "is" in cognitive judgment, but the meaning of the analogical "is" differs between the created and the creator. At the same time, the "is" of Aquinas is not the same as Hegel's concept of being in his *Science of Logic*, namely, the most indigent of categories, an indeterminate thought that immediately passes into nothing. For Aquinas there is something indeterminate about being, but not because it passes into nothing, but because, in the language I would use, it is overdeterminate: more than every determination, it is in excess of determinacy, hence not at all indeterminate but too much for our determination, even though every determinate being participates in the gift of being. This is something analogically like to God, which means also unlike, insofar as the "too muchness" of immanent being can never be taken to exhaust the super-plus overabundance of God. *Deus semper maior.* What is always more to God is more even than the overdeterminacy of given being in the prodigious plenitude of all finite creation. His metaphysical and theological finesse for the exceeding difference of the divine means that Aquinas is at home with an "as" that is not a univocal "is" in the rationalistic sense nor a speculative "is" in the idealistic sense, nor yet a transcendentally equivocal "as if" in the Kantian sense.

Before turning to Hegel, I offer this final thought on the significance of the differentiation between theoretical and practical reason. Kant is often admired as providing a balance between modern science and morality by his differentiation of theoretical and practical reason, and his use of the latter to recuperate the metaphysical themes of freedom, the soul, and God. But the matter has wider implications. Worries about theoretical and practical reason not being sufficiently differentiated are voiced against Plato's putative dictation to politics in theoretical terms alone. No doubt with Aristotle the two are differentiated: theoretical reason bears on what is always the same, which we can contemplate but cannot construct; practical reason bears on what could be other than it now is, hence also bears on what lies (relatively) within our power to effect. There is a difference between the orientation of reason to what always is, and the orientation of reason to what lies within our power to effect. The reason of *phronēsis* is not univocally the same as *nous theōretikos*.

Why is this important for our theme? If God always is, theoretical reason seems the privileged path. But supposing the being of God is not impersonal necessity, and that it communicates an intimate ethical call to the individual, would there not be an unavoidable practical dimension to our considerations? Is there a space beyond any divide of the theoretical and practical? Prior to it? The ancient sense of *theōria* did have a certain contemplative, admiring resonance, not unrelated to participation in a religious festival. Beholding and being engaged are responses that are held together. In Pascalian terms: geometry might be pursued in light of the tender sisterly pedagogy of finesse. What then to make of the modern slogan: We know what we construct?[17] This makes it hard to enter more intimately into an analogical view of things and God, if this entails a relation mingling likeness and unlikeness, a relation entailing a participant interplay, even in its contemplative registers. We can see here also an important source of changes in how many have come to conceive of the divine—seen simply also as our projection.

One might argue that practical reason, not theoretical, more truly opens us to God, and invoke Kant's moral way to God. But bear in mind the following equivocation. With Kant we might say that we must postulate the divine on the basis of *our moral being*, on whose basis we are warranted to think as if God exists. This "as if" is bound up with analogical thinking, in that we might postulate the "as if" God on the analogy of the moral judge. That it is *pure* practical reason that is central in all of this means that reason here is *not instrumental* (or technical or calcula-

---

17. Vico: *verum et factum convertuntur*; repeated by Marx, but now devoid of God's making of the true.

tive in Kant's way of talking). And yet pure practical reason does risk instrumentalizing the moral God to solve a dialectical problem at the heart of Kant's morality of autonomy, namely, to guarantee the unity of virtue and happiness which immanent practical reason cannot itself do. There is an equivocation in the "as if" concerning the relation of the God postulated to us and for us. We the postulators seem to define the terms of the other postulated.

The question then about the nature of this moral "as if": is it just a projective postulation, or is it truly porous to what exceeds us? Is the "as if" only seeded in our projective imagination, whose transcending finally regards only our immanent powers, or is there an "as" here shaping the analogical nature of given being: given "as" finite with the signature of the creator on creation as its work of art? This latter "as" would be an ontological feature of the art being received in being, and of its being open to the source beyond it that gives it to be itself at all. If this art work is viewed as work, it is not our work simply. Immanent works are "as" always already the ontological communications of the origin. A purely projective "as if" flattens the often equivocal space between the human and the divine, and remakes it more univocally as a construction of human power (even if hitherto not known to itself as such, or even thinking of itself as impotent).

We might conclude for now: perhaps there is something equivocal about modern practical reason—very often its claim to projective power, even in the guise of an analogical "as if," hides or celebrates human will to power. Kant seems to be an exception to this in trying to assert the purity of practical reason *qua* reason. Its "as if" is his only possible way to God. It is noncognitive: theoretical reason is viewed skeptically, while practical reason, viewed morally, offers the "as if" way of the ethical theology. His theoretical skepticism does lend a certain internal instability to the entire structure which pure practical reason cannot always stabilize, and practical reason succumbs to less pure forms of itself, that is to say, forms in which reason is more rampantly instrumentalized. Out of this equivocality of reason (between *theōria* and *praxis*, so understood) can spring a more univocal assertion of projective reason, and the loss of the analogical between. It may well be also that there are noncognitive "as ifs" that are not moral in Kant's sense and not strictly theoretical in the ancient speculative sense, but that are bound up with religious porosity to the divine, kept open in prayer and liturgy. The recession of such noncognitive "as ifs" has repercussions for the appreciation of analogical thinking.

SUBLATING ANALOGY SPECULATIVELY: THE HEGELIAN "IS"

The Kantian "as if" keeps open a space of difference between immanence and divine transcendence, but we might interpret Hegel to claim that there is an equivocation in that difference that reason can speculatively sublate. The Kantian equivocation lies in plotting the limits of reason, and proving by that plotting to be beyond the limits plotted. Kant must be on two sides of the limit to plot the limit. Hegel takes this as the fate of reason, namely, that reason cannot be limited, or rather that it posits its own limits and in that act transcends them. As self-limiting, reason is self-surpassing and self-transcending, and hence there is no finite limit to it. Reason is self-serving, and part of its serving is to determine itself, that is, on one side to make itself limited, and on the other side, because this limit is self-limitation, it is no limit, and hence there is an infinity to reason on which Kantian finitude equivocates.[18]

How does Hegelian reason relate to analogical thinking? In the main, there is no engagement with the issue as formulated in the Aristotelian-Thomist idiom. Nevertheless, one could argue that the place of analogy in later modernity is deeply affected by Hegel's efforts to develop to completion the power of dialectical-speculative reason. In a sense, this is a continuation of Spinozistic univocity and immanence. This entails a rejection of the signs of the God beyond the whole—there is no such God. The analogical argument from design, mentioned above, can have no meaning if there is no "over-there" toward which to aim, and if there is no going from "here" to "there." In the rejection of any form of irreducible transcendence, there remains only the "here." Not surprisingly, we find a coarsening of finesse for the meaning of divine dissimilitude. Hegel's criticism and transformation of the transcendentally equivocal reason of Kant is hugely significant for the fate of reason in modernity. There is a speculative reconfiguration of divine transcendence as other,

---

18. See Hegel, *The Encyclopaedia Logic*, §§40–60.

even as reason moves from a regulative to a constitutive role regarding the unconditioned. This might seem to be the consummation of reason. In fact, it is the consummation of the self-determining reason of modernity. This is self-serving reason, not reason in the services of truth not consummated by philosophy's own self-determination, a service such as we find in the premodern porosity of reason and faith.

Hegelian reason would see *equivocation* in the interplay of likeness and unlikeness of analogical thinking. This interplay cannot be completely determined and resists complete self-determination. This must follow from the hyperbolic dissimilitude of the divine. This is rejected as unreasonable for self-determining reason. What cannot be made determinate suggests a lack of intelligibility, suggests something more like an empty indeterminacy. Moreover, the divine dissimilitude is incompatible with the proclaimed autonomy of reason—it cannot be articulated on a logic of self-determining reason. The Hegelian critique of Kantian limits kicks in again, and the rational unacceptability of a "beyond" as such is reiterated. Of course, one could ask analogically if the relation on two sides of a limit is exactly the same, or rather a mixture of likeness and unlikeness. For instance, the move from finite to infinite might not be symmetrical with the movement from infinite to finite. For Hegel between these there is dialectically consummated symmetry—they are the same movement in the end, and hence a more ultimate speculative univocity comes to rule. For analogical thinking, the movement from finite to infinite is not the same as from infinite to finite. Hence they can never be just moments of one symmetrical self-mediating whole, nor of a totality defined by reciprocal determination of one side by the other.

Theologically, the move from creatures to God is not the same as the movement from God to creatures, and yet there is an analogical relation. It is not a finitely determinate relation, nor yet something determined by the autonomous power of self-determining reason. Creation itself testifies to a singular event of such asymmetrical movement. So also does redemption: the ultimate surprise of the divine gift of unconditional goodness, given for no reason humans can finally determine and yet not at all unreasonable in the sense of invidiously absurd.

From the standpoint of analogical thinking, Hegel's speculative dialectic of God is oriented to a univocity higher than the Spinozistic univocity, but it hides a dialectical equivocity bearing on the exceeding and asymmetrical difference when it comes to the dissimilitude of the divine. Hegelian reason offers a dialectical sublation of analogy, claiming to answer equivocities in the analogical relation between God and humans, or religion and philosophy. The effect, however, is to mask *new equivocations* in its claim to reconcile the seeming opposites. Divine transcendence is granted as a figurative way religious people talk, but this is just representational, not truly conceptual. We need a conceptual reconfiguration of the figurative meaning of religious representation, wherein all transcendence is relativized within a new comprehensive immanence. Hegel does not like the postulated character of Kant's God, but he is in the business of a secret postulation: the speculative project of reconstructing the God of transcendence, in constructing a "God" who in absolutely appearing in immanence also finally disappears as God.[19] God disappears as the transcendent God but reappears as historical man—immanent man who, posthumously to Hegel, appears more honestly down to earth, not at all as the God-man, but as the man-God.

Think of this as *not* bringing *pros hen* equivocation into the neighborhood of analogy but of transforming equivocation into a speculative univocity in which the One is defined entirely by the self-determination of immanent reason. Divine dissimilitude is a mere *Jenseits* to be overcome by that immanent self-determination. Religious representations equivocally fix the divine "beyond" in an imaginative figure that keeps the divine away in transcendence. That "away" is to be conceptually overcome in a speculative-dialectical univocity that does not reduce differences to a simple sameness but sublates them in an inclusive unity, including even the difference of divine transcendence. There is an equivocal sting to this too. For who is the One: the God-man or the man-God?

A final point on the fate of reason in terms of Hegel's claim to offer the reconciliation of logical necessity and existential self-determination. Fate is impersonal or transpersonal. Yet *moira*, in the ancient notion, is not a merely neutral necessity, since it cannot be dissevered from the idea of justice, *dikē*, even if that justice is beyond the measure of the human. This is a not unimportant idea if we want to consider the relation of reason and the divine. If there is a fate of reason, must the gods then and even God be subordinated to something more ultimate than them? This

---

19. See Desmond, *Hegel's God: A Counterfeit Double?* (Aldershot: Ashgate, 2003).

is clearly repudiated in the monotheistic religions. Nothing at all can be above God. Moreover, even if God is transpersonal in the human sense, God is not an impersonal power but deals most intimately with what touches human personhood in what is most deep in it. Is there a reason analogous to fate, reason in the sense of being ultimately an impersonal or transpersonal power determined inexorably by and to necessity? This, as thus stated, would be repudiated within the monotheistic religions. There have been many strands in the philosophical tradition that have thought of reason thus and as, in a certain sense, more ultimate than God. The idea: God may be the more personalistic form suitable for the many, while reason offers the more ultimately enlightened form, suitable for the few. And yet within the monontheistic religions universal claims are made for that are of an analogous order to the universal claims traditionally made by philosophical reason. One of the issues of importance here is whether there is a univocal universal or a plurivocal, or better put, an analogical universality in which the putative disjunction between the Gods of religion and philosophy is mediated rather than entrenched. In what I mean by the intimate universal something like an analogical universality is suggested.

There is no fate of reason if we think of fate as just mindless necessity. Reason would be fated then to emerge out of something nonreasonable and to end in something irrational. Bounded by two irrationalities, reason in its middle course would be so relativized by two irrationalities that any claim of ultimacy made on its behalf would be voided. Suppose then we replace mindless necessity with providence? Providence is fate mediated by mind. Of course, there is the Hegelian version of this which is not now widely accepted. If there is a fate of reason, it is to participate in this dialectical providence. What happens when reason tries to surpass such providence as religiously figured? Efforts in this direction are to be found in Kant's rational reconfiguration of biblical religion, as well as Hegel's rationalized version of Christian providence which ultimately humanizes and secularizes the divine spirit. Such a view of reason is fated to surpass religion and all its figures, including its analogical figurations. The fatality or providence of reason in the Hegelian system cannot be disconnected from the claim to sublate the figurative form of religion. This is a claim to completion but its speculative univocity is riddled with equivocity: the fulfillment it is followed by diverse revolts against (speculative) reason or apostasies from its claim to ultimacy. This can range from the extremes of positivistic arrogations of scientist enlightenment to existential rebellion against systematic reason as such. Currently, post-Hegelians and anti-Hegelian thinkers offer for consideration no providence at all, either religious or secularized. The story is more likely to be of an improvident evolution or an economy of chance and necessity.

ANALOGY AND REASON'S DE-SUBLATION: POST-HEGELIAN POSTULATIONS

What of analogy and the fate of reason in post-Hegelian thought? Hegel would relativize the figurative dimension, seeing analogy to be a representation (*Vorstellung*) which fixed the divine in a beyond. And one might argue that it is important to avoid thinking of the analogical figure as defined by a dualistic grid, with a static and quasi-mimetic fixation of the terms in relation. Nevertheless, metaxologically speaking, one might grant dynamic doubling, redoubling, on both sides of the relation of relations: the divine in relation to creation, creation in relation to the divine, the agapeics of the one meeting the groaning of the other, in a metaxological intermediation which allows the analogical avoidance of dualism, monism, and the indeterminate.

That said, one widespread development in post-Hegelian thought is the *de-sublation* of rationalistic postulations, and a reconfiguration of analogies of the divine along more humanistic lines. Divine transcendence blanked out, and we seem to need a new project: not the postulated projection of a moral God *à la* Kant, not the speculative sublation of divine difference in an immanent self-serving totality, but a *human project* of entirely immanent self-determination, not diffident about showing the face of atheism. There is something thought-provoking in the way Hegel's speculative reconciliation of man and God *reverses* into the aggressive humanistic atheism so prevalent in his left-Hegelian inheritors (Feuerbach and Marx are only two obvious instances). Hegel himself envisaged a postreligious humanism reconciled with its religious prehistory, but now his speculative sublation is de-sublimated, so to say. Reason passes back into a virulent negative dialectic, and more radically still into an atheistic critique and deconstruction of all religion. Instead of the balance of likeness and unlikeness, knowing and not-knowing in analogical thinking, instead of Hegel's absolute knowing which claims the immanent point of a *coincidentia oppositorum*, now there is no knowing of God because there is no God to know. Hegel's absolute knowing generates a humanistic double of God. Its hatred of all "beyonds" inverts into atheistic critique in search of pure immanence without God, hyperbolically proclaiming itself as the end of history, beyond which nothing greater can be thought.

We move from the cautions of Kant's critical reason, through the overconfidence of Hegel's speculative reason, to a post-Hegelian lack of confidence in reason. The workings of analogy are not to the fore, but just in this absence, it is the case that univocity, equivocity, and their dialectic here engender a *crisis of reason*, just at the moment of its claimed consummation. There is diffidence about the reach of the univocities of reason in Kant, there is overconfidence in the dialectical reach of reason in Hegel's speculative unity, there is the loss of confidence in reason after Hegel when unity itself because more and more a source of suspicion. The suspicion is that while reason is self-serving in one sense, the self served may not be quite the rational sovereign erstwhile sitting on the throne. Something more darkly equivocal is the power behind the throne. The fate of reason, already there in Kant, is to call itself into question, and not find itself in its own free self-service, but doing the *incognito* bidding of an other power that reason serves—will, economic exploitation, will to power, the unconscious, the libido, impersonal structure, difference itself, whatever. Modern reason's autonomy is threatened, threatens itself with an ominous heteronomy. Something different, not always with a benign difference, insinuates itself into the confidences of the interplay of likening and unlikening. The confidence of analogical interplay seems played out.

Post-Hegelian reason reveals a reversed sublation, a de-sublation that de-sublimates. Sublation negates, preserves, and lifts up, but a reverse sublation is a negation that negates but does not lift up and rather brings down. It transcends downward—not from man to God as ascent but from God to man as a descent that, by negating God above and beyond, is said to restore (alienated) man to his own power. So the story goes. De-sublation in the services of human restoration is the self-service of human power. I find recessed analogy in this, a new "as if." Here we find a form of postulatory finitism—we must hold onto the finite "as if" it were the ultimate horizon of meaning, beyond which no greater is to be thought.[20] This new postulatory "as if" initially seeds further postulates that, in turn, issue in the formation of new projects. The asymmetrical transcendence, and hence the dissimilitude of God is pushed out of the way again and again, and humans have appropriated for themselves the ultimate power. If there is piety in post-Hegelian impiety it shares with Hegelian piety a devotion to self-serving immanence. Both are renegade to the twofold order of immanence and transcendence present in the older analogy.

After the de-sublation of divine power follows the sublation of (divine) otherness into human power, but after this follows a *second de-sublation*. Behind the game of peek-a-boo of immanent transcendence in this postulatory project, reason seems fated to front for some nonrational other, say, the machinations of the will to power. The first de-sublation promises ultimate power to us, the second de-sublation descends into what is below reason. There is a theme of depth here, but it reverses the Platonic analogy of the sun which draws us beyond the Cave toward the transcendence of the Good. In the Cave we are underground men, but now the analogy suggests a de-sublating directionality, pointing down and down into a more original darkness. We are digging below the Cave to pits where the sun seems not to penetrate. (Of course, on this view, not even on the surface of the earth does the sun ever shine.) This turn away from higher transcendence and the penetration of our transcending into the lower underground is something we find with Schopenhauer, Dostoevsky, Nietzsche, and many others right into our own time—Bataille, for instance. There is dissimilitude here but it emerges from below. It is the abyss, the dark origin, it is the inhuman. The fate of reason is to be revealed to itself as not reasonable. The inhuman is the immanent other of the human.

Schopenhauer used the following analogy to explain his metaphysics in which will is more primordial than reason: it is not that the human is a microcosmos but that the world is like a *macro-anthropos*.[21] The an-

---

20. For instance in *Is There a Sabbath for Thought? Between Religion and Philosophy* (New York: Fordham University Press, 2005).

21. *The World as Will and Representation*, 2:642: "Ich habe den Satz umgekert und die Welt als Makranthropos nachgewiesen; sofern Wille under Vorstellung ihr wie sein Wesen erschöpft. Offenbar aber ist es richtiger, die Welt aus dem Menschen verstehn zu lehren als den

thropos is the one like to which, *pros hen*, the world is to be understood; the anthropos is not to be understood from the world. The world is to be likened to the human self writ large. There are traces of a similar likeness in Nietzsche also, though it is often dissimulated: the world is to be, in Zarathustra's words, the humanly thinkable world. [22] There is a kind of *pros hen* equivocation, for the One relative to which all analogies tend is will to power. Interestingly, the macro-anthropic position tends to its own inversion insofar as the human will comes now to be understood in terms of the dark underground of all-pervasive will to power. If we dig down into ourselves as caves we come across in ourselves the other of self, and are faced with the inhuman in the human, or the transhuman. This is an immanent otherness not fully subject to our own self-determination. This immanent otherness has much to do with the religious, though it may be pursued as a way into the darkness of more infernal caves, rather than the tunnel of the purification of our porosity that, as with Dante, leads from the underground of Hell up to the mountain of purgatory.

Post-Hegelian de-sublation leads to the self-deconstruction of reason rather than the self-sublation. Interestingly, it is the sublime that serves as the sign of this de-sublimation of reason with some of the postmoderns, even those using Kant, such as Lyotard. Opposites meet. The sublime is monstrous. The human subject is abject. You might say Nietzsche already understood this impossible condition when he said that we need art to save us from the truth. We need the "as if" truths of art to protect us from *the* truth, for *the* truth finally is horror. But if we know the truth that the truth of art is only an "as if" truth, then we know it is not true,

---

Menschen aus der Welt." *Sämtliche Werke*, ed. Wolfgang von Lohneysen (Darmstadt: Wissenschaftliche Buchgesellschaft, 1968), 2:824–25.

22. Friedrich Nietzsche, *Thus Spoke Zarathustra*, trans. R. J. Hollingdale (Harmondsworth: Penguin, 1961), "On the Blissful Islands," 110: "Could you conceive a god? – But may the will to truth mean this to you: that everything shall be transformed into the humanly conceivable, the humanly evident, the humanly palpable! You should follow your own senses to the end! And you yourself should create what you have hitherto called the World: the World should be formed in your image by your reason, your will, and your love! And truly, it will be to your happiness, you enlightened men! And how should you endure life without this hope, you enlightened men? Neither in the incomprehensible nor in the irrational can you be at home. But to reveal my heart entirely to you, my friends: *if* there were gods, how could I endure not to be a god! *Therefore* there are no gods." I have commented more on this discourse of Zarathustra in connection with postulatory finitism in *Is There a Sabbath for Thought?*, 38–42.

and horror should come back, if we refuse to deceive ourselves or act in aesthetic bad faith.

If this is the fate of reason, it is clear that any robust sense of analogy in the classical sense is impossible. And yet invocations of analogy are appropriate, insofar as post-Hegelian relations to reason are very much tempted by *aesthetic saving*. We are figuring things once again. In every aesthetic response, Nietzsche's included, there is something that might border on the possibility of something more open to the analogical.[23] The figurative is unavoidable, but how to figure? How to reconfigure the ethos of being in fidelity to its truth? These are some of the questions facing postmodern analogy. On the whole, the fate of reason in postmodernism reflects many dimensions of Nietzsche where the aesthetic has replaced the religious.[24] Instead of the old porosity of faith and reason, religion and philosophy, it is the new faith in an "as if" salvation by art. The postmoderns are more comfortable with the aesthetic play of possibility. Often, one suspects an *incognito* insinuation of the sacred is post-Enlightenment secular art. At best, secretly it is a wooing of the sacred; at worst, it is the outrage trying to provoke the sacred into showing its hand—execrating it when it retains its silent mystery. This is a complex story of the displacement of religious transcendence into art.[25] Its hiding there is part of the fate of post-Kantian reason. We need to come clean on the religious. In our recent reconfiguration of the ancient quarrel of the poet and philosopher, the philosopher is caricatured as the henchman of univocity, the poet honoured as the gay troubadour of plurivocity. Spare a thought for the religious witness who is sent packing, even before she or he arrives, as the decrepit retainer of a repressive transcendence.

---

23. See John Betz, "Beyond the Sublime: The Aesthetics of the Analogy of Being (Part One)," *Modern Theology* 21, no. 3 (July 2005): 367–411; "Beyond the Sublime: The Aesthetics of the Analogy of Being (Part Two)," *Modern Theology* 22, no. 1 (January 2006): 1–50.

24. See David Bentley Hart, *The Beauty of the Infinite: The Aesthetics of Christian Truth* (Grand Rapids, Mich.: Eerdmans, 2003).

25. See Desmond, *Art, Origins, Otherness: Between Art and Philosophy* (Albany: State University of New York Press, 2003).

REASON'S PLURIVOCAL PROMISE, REVOLT, AND AESTHETIC ANALOGY

If there a plurivocal promise in reason itself, is this promise one in which manifold freedoms are let, even unto a revolt against the norms of reason itself? If reason can let be its others, can it allow dissidence to itself to the extreme of insubordination? If Kant's reason was rather overcautious in its quasi-theism or moral deism; if Hegel's speculative reason was rather overconfident in its pan(en)theistic holism; if humanistic atheism, hubristically overconfident, hyperbolically proclaims itself as the end of history, beyond which nothing greater can be thought; do posthumanism or transhumanism significantly alter the picture? The post-Hegelian afflatus, many times deflated, but as many times reinflated, might be read as a sign of still not properly addressed equivocations in modern reason. If we are advocating a transhumanism, the issue of transcendence as a going beyond or being beyond does not itself go away. Are we dealing with a "trans" that still is the immanent self-transcendence of the human, or is there a different "trans," such as the transcendence as other often taken to name the divine? Need we close off from this transcendence the play of likeness and unlikeness in the way of analogy? We might speak of difference: always difference but the difference of what? The difference of nothing? What difference does that difference make? No difference. Things remain the same, absolutely the same, then, in the epoch of absolute difference. Would a new confidence bring back something of the original porosity of what is prior to reason and unreason, between reason and what is transrational? Must we consider a vertical analogical thinking rather than one defined by horizontal analogies?

Vertical might mean down as well as up. I think of Dostoevsky's underground man who hates the sovereignty of reason which he would rather shackle in the Cave than let build its crystal palace above ground. Reason is no longer to be self-serving; it is and must be the slave of the passions. Servile, it is not an ancilla of the divine. It is the toy of the will, a living tool, in Aristotle's word for the slave. Rather than a resurrection of analogical thinking, horizontally we might be tempted by the critique of instrumental reason by negative dialectic. In the name of what? Liberation. Suppose we are freed in the Cave, why should we turn up rather than down? Why should we turn down rather than up? What gives us direction? And to what are we directed? Is it not our love that directs us—our love of the light? Why then do we turn into the darkness? If it is only we ourselves self-directing, are we any less likely than now to end up again only circling around ourselves? But self-encirclement, though it calls itself a higher autonomy, is self-imprisoned. Instead of release to analogical being, we bring on the furious return of equivocity in the vice-like reign of univocal reason. The latter itself is in chains it does not want to recognize. The critique of one-dimensional man is the fury of the self-serving that cannot escape itself as self-circled. There is nothing beyond its totalized immanence. It can only writhe in its weariness with the flatness of the univocal whole. Its boredom with sameness is relieved by self-inflicted bloodletting. The "great refusal" finally creates nothing. There is nothing explicitly analogical about this fury of equivocation, though there are mimicries of release, simulacra of liberation.

You might wonder, however, if the fate of reason finds itself in a horizon where a kind of saturated equivocity reigns, and where the play of likeness and unlikeness comes back. Saturated equivocity reminds us of Jean-Luc Marion's saturated phenomenon, and I will speak of this in a later reflection, but there are saturated equivocities that belong more to the idol rather than the icon.[26] An extreme celebration of equivocity makes one wonder if the balance is now lost in favor of unlikeness. But again unlikeness to what? We recall *pros hen* equivocation but what now is the One? Is it the divine One? Or *das Ding*? Or difference as difference? Are we again dealing with an immanent god, even when "God" is the first word banned and the last word always side-stepped and never pronounced. Despite many postmodern movements repeatedly crucifying the human, there are as many movements where the human is openly or secretly resurrected. We are still the One, even when we dream of becoming transhuman or cyborgs or whatever science fiction allows to flash and vanish in our fevered souls. First we were the rational self-determining One, and then in univocal continuity we have become the equivocal self that is no self, that lacerates its own autonomy, and yet that knows no true beyond of itself, perhaps also it does not know itself, be-

---

26. If the earlier Marion is more insistent on the dissimilitude of the divine, does the later Marion come closer to the intimacy? By the earlier Marion I refer to works like *God without Being*; by the later Marion, I refer to works like *In Excess: Studies of Saturated Phenomena*, trans. R. Horner and V. Berraud (New York: Fordham University Press, 2002).

cause there is nothing of itself to know. Its "beyonds" are crystallized like virtual particles by unnatural experiments in which otherwise nonexistent entities of nature would not be at all. The violence of these experiments is analogous to splitting the atom: splitting the self, without God. What is not is more real than what is. "Nothing is but what is not" (Macbeth). But this too is a project, this violence on the self by the self. The unlikeness of the "not" is the project of nihilism, the postulation of what is not as higher than what is. Does this project hide a secret hatred of being as given?

Strangely nihilism makes strangely astonishing the light that should not be there at all. In the darkness of the dark origin there should be no light, and yet we "see" the dark origin, by virtue of the illumination of a light that we should not take at all with ultimate seriousness, if the dark origin is the ultimate. This is the perverse turn around in which the truth of nihilism is only "seeable" when it is "seen" in the light of truth. This light indicates that nihilism itself cannot be the ultimate truth. The truth of nihilism means truth is more ultimate than nihilism, and hence nihilism cannot be true. The truth of nihilism is its untruth.

You might say Nietzsche saw through this and hence says that there is no truth only truths, or indeed only my truth. Art saves us from the truth. The truth is horror, so we need the "as if" truth of art to protect us from the truth. But if we know the truth that the truth of art is only an "as if" truth, then we know it is not true, and horror should come back, if we refuse to deceive ourselves or act in bad faith. Nietzsche's aesthetic theodicy requires such bad faith, all the while parasitical on a truer truth without which his compassionate recommendation of the "as if" truth of art itself makes no sense. Nietzsche's aesthetic consolation is tragic in this sense, a form of philosophical pity in face of the horror of the truth. But once we wake up to the untruth of the "as if" truth, then we can no longer accept this theodicy. Nothing can be saved. Nothing is saved, except our self-deception about the "as if" truth of saving art. Nietzsche's theodicy is incredible. His god is only believable if we grant that there is nothing really believable. He claimed the Christian God died or was killed out of truthfulness. I see no way his god can escape a similar fate. In fact, the old God is more believable than his post-Christian Dionysus—a saving god who can save nothing. All of this is still only a disguised continuation of the same imprisonment of reason in the underground where the Minotaur always waits to devour the virgins of post-Christian faith. Nietzsche talked himself up as beyond virginity, as if he were all knowing, but he was a virgin too, eaten up by this Minotaur. He was twisted in the same perversity noted above: to see the untruth of truth one must see it by the light of truth, and hence there is something more always than untruth. What that "more" is remains to be truthfully explored, and one suspects that a truer way brings us back closer to older, wiser ways.

Art saves us from the truth of the dark origin, Nietzsche seems to suggest, but to see this, on his terms, we have to have one eye open, one eye shut. We have to, as it were, live the equivocation. We cannot do it entirely. We have to be untruthful if we want to be so saved—and we cannot be untruthful. Nor could Nietzsche, even given his honorable sense of the horror of truth.

The Nietzschean saving from nihilism by means of an aesthetic theodicy recalls for us the argument from design discussed above as an analogical argument. There is no such argument in Nietzsche, of course. There is a call for a new aesthetic dwelling and this as communicated in supreme form through tragic art.[27] Tragic art is sacred. It can never be univocal. Perhaps it is not *merely* equivocal, yet is it not dialectical either in Hegel's sense (a point beloved by postmoderns). There is suffering, there is breakdown, there is the sacrifice of autonomous univocity, there are sacrificial multiplicities that greatly are held together in a worldlike art work. All of this does put us in mind of the plurivocity of analogy. The saving of the human will be by means of something analogous to a new yet old sacred art. The fate of modern reason unfolds in the direction of the disenchantment of the world, but this is nihilism and a danger to humanity's future if the fate of reason does not give way to an aesthetic re-enchantment of the world: aesthetic theodicy. The dialectical twinning of Enlightenment (geometry) and Romanticism (finesse) finds a new contemporary form in pagan immanent mode here. "World—a work of art giving birth to itself!"[28] If there is an aesthetic "as" here, it continues the Spinozistic, Hegelian line of immanence and nothing but immanence. The analogical dissimilitude of the God beyond the whole is

---

27. Heidegger's call for a poetic dwelling on the earth is a recalling of Hölderlin's plea, and Nietzsche is a card-carrying member of Hölderlin's fan club.

28. *The Will to Power*, 419; *Der Wille zur Macht*, 533.

rejected in terms of a rhapsodic vision of the whole. Secretly the circle is being closed to keep out this God.[29]

The world as self-birthing work of art reminds one of the analogy of the self-organizing organism. There seems to be no external hand shaping it, no external purpose driving it or drawing it. It is its own purpose—and so it is without a why—beyond itself. This is a common attitude we find in philosophies of finitude: existence without a why, beyond itself. But can we simply accept the idiotic givenness as such without asking further about its why? If it is its own why or has no why, the new immanent "God" is like the old God who is ultimately its own why, and without any why, if by this we mean a finite be-cause. The art world of Nietzsche offers something analogous to an immanent pantheistic God, a form of religiosity expressly left open by Nietzsche. The analogy at work: not the world likened to a machine, not to an organism simply, but the world likened to a self-circling work of art, engendering itself, differentiating itself, bringing itself back from its multiplicities to unities, broadcasting itself again into new multiplicities and transient unities. In an immanent aesthetic whole, both prerational and post-rational, Nietzsche would complete a pantheistic Trinity, with the geometrical God of Spinoza as Father, the dialectical God of Hegel as spiritual Son, and his own Dionysian God as the dithyrambic (disseminating) Spirit—beyond which nothing more is needed, and in whose rhapsody we are to dance.

Even despite the Nietschean aestheticization, there is something notable in the return of the ethical. "Kant" keeps coming back, as allowing more than an aesthetic "as if" in the moral sphere, now in Levinasian form. I find this remarkable in a postmodern context. It is not that reason is rehabilitated; for reason is still also too often seen as the retainer of a repressive univocity or totality; and thus the ethicization shares something with the aestheticization. But it is really noteworthy that postmodernism has mutated into an ethical form in which the excess of transcendence has strangely become renewed. The leopard has changed its spots. "Rome versus Judea," Nietzsche forthrightly puts this contrast to us. This is pagan aesthetics versus monotheistic revelation, whether Jewish or Christian or Muslim. But now Judea has replaced Rome in the rankings of the ethical postmodern. Rome has become Judea in some of

---

29. See *God and the Between*, 132.

the post-Levinasian ethicists and they have no explanation for this transition, though not in doubt is their hyperbolic moral sincerity about the other.

"Rome versus Judea": both of these are present in the thinking of analogy, though if one were to think of these as "cities of words" (Cavell's phrase for Plato's *Republic*), the home names would be Athens and Jerusalem. In Aquinas's doctrine of analogy already the porosity of the two is met with fidelity to the asymmetrically superior, without the renegade freedom of self-serving reason. There is relation and communication between the two, qualified by the hyperbolic transcendence of the divine.

One might say that the self-organizing organic art is transcended by human art. But the aesthetic working of analogy brings us back to Plato's demiurge, or in the case of theism, a stress on creation which is impossible to model either on an organic becoming or a human self-becoming, or human making. Unlike Nietzsche there is a more explicit reference to the dissimilitude of the origin in the latter. There is also a more beneficent attitude to reason and its confidences. God the artist makes way for a kind of aesthetic theology in analogical thinking also.

THE VOCATION OF TRANSDIALECTICAL REASON: ANALOGY ON THE VERGE OF THE HYPERBOLIC

Is the fate of reason then the liquidation of analogy? Or is there a transdialectical sense of reason? I would say yes to the latter: reason allows the dialectical play of univocity and equivocity, and yet is more than self-determining dialectic. Reason is not simply self-serving but is opened to what is more than human reason at home with itself. Such reason I would call metaxological, because it is concerned with a *logos* of the *metaxu*, with wording the between. We might look anew at analogical thinking relative to this between, and especially in connection with a sense of superior transcendence. Such an approach would bring the analogical closer to the verge of the hyperbolic: the unlikeness of what is like and beyond all likeness. The analogical "as" opens to a hyperbolic "above" (*huper*).[30] Nor need a metaxological reconsideration of analogy be a ret-

---

30. I speak of the "is" of metaphor, the "as" of analogy, the "with" of symbol, and the "above" of hyperbole in *Being and the Between*, 207–22, and in *God and the Between*, 122–28.

rospective wistfulness for a supposedly exhausted tradition. It may harbor promise for renewed thinking of divine difference, after Hegelian reason and its post-idealist deconstruction. Between the overconfidence of idealist reason and the abjectness of anti-idealistic nonreason, there is a metaxological intermediation of divine intimacy and divine dissimilitude.

Involved in this metaxological intermediation, there is a doubling, though not necessarily a dualism of terms. Relating itself seems to require two terms at least; this is true even of self-relation, as the self has to be both itself and other to itself to be in relation to itself. By contrast, a relation of relations requires two doublets, or at least two self-doubling terms. This is significant in itself in that it seems to require at least a quadruplicity of terms (again this is so even if some of the terms entail a kind of self-doubling). Aristotle said that the smallest number properly speaking is two (*Physics* 220a27). One could ask if we have to count to two to count to one. But if we have to count to two to count to one, do we have to count to four to count to two? This may seem idle intellectual playfulness, but there are theological consequences. Consider a theological difference that is not a dialectically self-doubling one, as in Hegel. Hegel counts to two, counts to three—and this seems very Trinitarian, but the second is one self-doubled, and the third is the self-return of the first in the second. In the end, there is no counting beyond one. We end with a self-relating unity in relation to which all differentiation is internal. With a quadruplicity, or a genuine double or two genuinely self-doubling ones, the fourth is not the self-redoubling of the one. Beyond the self-mediating unity of Hegel, there is the One that creates a true other, a fourth that is not the immanent self-mediation of the original One. An original other is given to be in its otherness. This openness of difference then is not just a matter of dialectical self-return. The opening of this difference of the fourth is essential to making sense of analogical doubleness, one that keeps open a genuinely between space.

Our reason reveals a *metaxu*: between ignorance and wisdom; between finitude and infinity; between our being truthful and the truth. Analogical thinking can offer a fidelity to this between: truthful without being the truth; being truthful in being both like and unlike the truth. What about the relation to superior transcendence? Sometimes one wonders about a kind of *horizontal* analogy on the plane of immanence.

Consider, for instance, Deleuze's interest in the baroque. The baroque itself presents us with something like a threshold between the aesthetic and religious, at times a kind of religious aestheticism playing with faith. It playfully reveals a believing and a not quite believing, a playing with transcendence above it but without univocal sureness. There are exfoliations of immanence, mimicries of a more vertical transcendence, mimicries tempted to remain a still immanent transcendence. The playful equivocities are delighted to tease the now perhaps controvertible otherness of the vertical transcendence that perplexes and nonplusses our aesthetic playfulness.

Given the postmodern stress on otherness more or less recalcitrant to immanent autonomy, given the aesthetic stress in its figuration of things, perhaps the *analogy of origination* might be reinvoked, not in view of the religious as the threshold of the aesthetic, but of the aesthetic as the threshold of the religious. Analogy is not the constructing of a quasi-mathematical system or science, is not "merely" figurative, but calls for aesthetic finesse for figures with metaphysical and religious weight.[31] There is a receptive side to this finesse, it is not constructive simply. Metaxological reason, as transdialectical, suggests a *vertical* analogy exceeding the plane of immanence, though manifested in the hyperbolic figures of that plane. Might one say: such analogical figures can be graced, and graced because created? If wording the between were in a divine language, would we find ourselves speaking in tongues? For there is a patience of being (*passio essendi*) more original than our endeavor to be (*conatus essendi*). It calls for a certain reversal of projective aesthetics.

---

31. The plurivocity of figures is notable. One might invoke fictions, or speak of *la bella figura* and beauty, or of trying to figure things out, or of having a head for figures (meaning here numbers). There is a telling of numbers, and there are monetary tellings where we fumble in the greasy till. What does the figure tell us? We go figure, we configure, we reconfigure. The figurative is not merely figurative. All being is told in figures and we are told by the figures. Being told, we do not tell. We make up the figures, but there is something not made up. The figures offer an accounting and we must account for the figures. We tend to see reason as a thinking of the figures, in figures, and hence it need not be opposed to figurative telling. We think of counting and reckoning: this counts as one, this as two. There are fixations of the determinate unity of univocity, but this is in the figuring, not only fixed figures. The passing from figure to figure may be the true (ac)counting of things. This passing between might tell of reason as an analogical passing between (consult Aristotle). We figure we can place univocal figuring versus figurative figuring, as we might set geometry versus finesse, but figuring is actually on both side of the versus, though it is on both sides because it is passing between.

We are not creative first, but created. There is first given form and figure, and our enabled figuration entails a power first received rather than projected. Received power allows an elevation (*huper-ballein*: to throw or be thrown above) that is not a dialectical sublation because the creature is what it is, from the origin, as endowed. Likewise, the issue is more than the post-idealistic de-sublation, as after all *we receive ourselves* in being elevated beyond ourselves, before we can ever try to elevate ourselves. A transcendence other than our self-transcendence is already intimately enabling of our immanent self-transcending.

Aquinas's *agens analogicum* is steeped in a sense of given being as a creation.[32] Everything created communicates of the divine origin. The point is not "aesthetic theodicy" in, say, Nietzsche's sense, but the opening of a divine aesthetics in a more richly ontological and metaphysical register.[33] Figuring is not closed to trans-figuring. Take this example of horizontal analogy suggestive of metaxological intermediation with what exceeds the horizontal: the analogies of being between generations in becoming. Think of generational analogies in the *familial inheritance*, say, of facial features. Behold here in the face of the living child the uncanny likeness of the dead grandfather in that faded photo there. Family resemblances recur over generations and reveal an interplay of like and unlike, the presence of one in the other.[34] And yet there is more than mere equivocity, granting that there is much equivocity. The pluralism is a plurivocity, if there is interplay of like and unlike. The analogy of family generation shows plurivocity that is not simply univocal or equivocal, that is both and yet neither. Nor is it dialectical in the Hegelian sense explained above. If family resemblance were to be called analogical, it might be given a metaxological twist. In the image of the parent(s), or the ancestors, we can fix no first One on the horizontal plane. This plane is an open between. But the openness of the between is not just a being flanked by two forms of indefiniteness—the indefiniteness of the original and the end. A merely indefinite beginning begets nothing. A merely in-

---

32. See Josef Pieper, *The Silence of St. Thomas: Three Essays*, 3rd ed., trans. John Murray and Daniel O'Connor (South Bend, Ind.: St. Augustine's Press, 1999).

33. See Hans Urs von Balthasar, *The Glory of the Lord: A Theological Aesthetics, Volume One: Seeing the Form*, trans. E. Leivà-Merikakis (San Francisco, Calif.: Ignatius Press, 1982).

34. On the generational analogy of family resemblances, see *The Intimate Strangeness of Being*, 257–59. Wittgenstein's critique of the so-called essentialist fallacy is really a critique of a misleading fixation on univocity.

definite end completes nothing. And yet there is a mysterious love that is in passage between the generations: in each, beyond each, between each, and never just in one alone. Something of a surplus of secret goodness, an *incognito* generosity, is figured, is incarnated in the spread of finite generations. Do we perhaps have to ponder an origin that is overdeterminate: more than the univocity of the determinate, more the equivocity of the indefinite, and more the self-determining of immanent dialectic? On the boundary of the hyperbolic, does the porosity of the between point to this?

Art gets great play in postmodernism but religion seems to be the orphan without a proper name, or the grieving widow of a great one. Alert to porosity between religion and philosophy, transdialectical reason takes the desolate widow and orphan into new care. At issue is not just the aesthetic play of possibility, nor just the return of ethical self-determination. We need to transcend the oscillation of determinacy and indeterminacy; transcend not toward the ethical confined to our terms of self-determination but rather to the religious between. The religious between communicates something of the overdeterminacy of given being and its giving source that is even yet more hyperbolic than given being—*semper maior*. This is not to reinstate a dualism of immanence and transcendence but to ask if there are hyperboles of being in immanence that cannot be accounted for in entirely immanent terms and that raise mindfulness of what transcends immanence. In this middle space between the hyperbolic in immanence and the eminence of the divine superior lies the hyperbolic dissimilitude par excellence. The hyperboles of being are ontological "places" which call out for a renewal of analogical thinking in a metaxological mode. Granting the analogies of the immanent plane, there is no reason why analogical thinking might not wonder about likeness and unlikeness on the vertical plane.

Perhaps, then, it is the *vocation* of reason rather than the fate to verge on the hyperbolic in being, and in the metaxological space between philosophy and religion. I conclude with a pagan example and a Christian. To the pagan: consider how Plato speaks both of the sun as an analogy with the Good, and also the relation of the source and its offspring. The issue here is not one of a finite being or causality, but with the bringing to be of the determinately finite and intelligible, and indeed good. Witness this striking togetherness of the analogy of origination and something hyperbolic.[35] Socrates refuses to give a direct univocal account of the Good in itself and offers the figure of the offspring of the Good (*ekgonos te tou agathou*). The offspring is one most nearly made in the likeness of the Good (506e). He refers to the story of the father (*patēr*) but postpones this to another occasion (506e).[36] Generational analogy is invoked: the offspring of the Good stands in analogy (*analogon*, 508c) with the Good itself. The nonidentity in likeness is stressed (508ab, 509a) reminding us of the excessive difference of the Good itself, the famous *epekeina tēs ousias* (509b9). Glaucon exclaims in response (509c1–2): "By Apollo, a daimonic hyperbole [*daimonias huperbolēs*]!" What is daimonic refers us to a between space, a *metaxu* between mortals and divinity. Plato leads us upward and into the *metaxu* between mortals and divinities, there ventures boldly an iconic saying about the ultimate, but this iconic saying relativizes the ultimacy of our saying without relativizing the ultimate. This is very true to what one might call the creative equivocity of true analogical thinking.

The Christian example: if Aquinas's *agens analogicum* helps us some way to thinking the togetherness of transcendence and immanence, analogical agency is more than our merely linguistic attribution. It is not that God is an agent on analogy with some finite cause. Something about the be-causing of God is analogical, issuing in analogical likeness and unlikeness in an ontological sense. Be-causing is a causing to be. The creation of the different is here named, but with a difference that is not a dualistic opposition, but in some community between itself and the endowing origin. By contrast, a univocal cause would give rise to an effect the same as itself. God's causing would be the same again, a kind of ontological cloning. The concept of *causa sui* belongs in this conceptual space. That *causa sui* was very important for Spinoza and Hegel is not unconnected with the diverse workings of the univocal sense in their thinking. This might not be immediately evident with Hegel. Nevertheless, Hegel's God in creating gives rise to God again—not unlike a univocal cause, creation is God's self-creation. Hegel's God is self-cloning.

---

35. I draw on one or two ideas formulated in my Aquinas Lecture, "Analogy, Dialectic and Divine Transcendence: Between St. Thomas and Hegel," *Ramify* 1, no. 1 (Spring 2010): 4–26, revised in *The Intimate Strangeness of Being*, chap. 9.

36. In his *Metaphysics* 1021a15–27, Aristotle discusses three types of relation, one of which is producer/product. The father/son is the paradigm of this relation (1021a24–25).

(Thought-provoking is the fact that self-procreation was once called *generatio aequivoca*.) Hidden in these divine dialectics is the speculative autism of the spirit. Analogical causation might be said, by contrast, to create the finite other not as a self-othering, but through the interplay of likeness and unlikeness it releases the created other into its own being for itself, a being which is yet also in relation to God, as ultimate origin of all relations of communication between creation and Godself.

How would analogical causation differ from equivocal causation, if divine unlikeness is always more and obviates any reduction to sameness? One could say that equivocal causation would be the production of the different as effect which had *no relation* to the effecting cause. But without any such relation, this would mean that the effect would be no effect. Thus a sheerly equivocal causation seems to lack intelligibility insofar as it connects nothing with nothing, and something could not come to be. There would be no relation of source and outcome, and hence no outcome. If nothing would connect, there would be nothing, hence no creation, and no causing to be. The ultimate "outcome" is no outcome in such equivocal causation; it would not be the world of flux but an inversion into an absolutely unintelligible univocity, that is to say, a frozen motionless sameness impossible to distinguish from nothing.

Of course, "causation" in modern thought has become so univocalized as to be robbed of the ontological resonances of original creating. This is another reason why I prefer to speak of analogical origination. Original creating would be the effecting of what is both same and other, always granting an irreducible transcendence to God as the origin. Creation is a giving to be, a bringing to be by divine art in which what is brought to be is other to the giving source. And yet the finite creation is in being as related to the giving source, and shows some likeness to it, insofar as it is at all. The likeness has something to do with the "why" of the creating, its be-cause, namely, to communicate the good of "to be." What is the be-cause of bringing to be? No more in Aquinas than in Plato can we avoid invoking the *hyperbolic goodness* of the ultimate origin. One thinks of how, analogous to being at all through generational inheritance, there is a secret love of being that is passed from generation to generation. No finite generation possesses this love of the "to be," and yet all diversely participate in it. The reason of coming to be is nothing more than the good of the original and ultimate be-cause, nothing more than that it is good to be. This good of the "to be" is what both the origin and the created share, because the origin shares it by the releasing giving that is creating. The created is given a share in, participates in this ultimate good of the "to be."

God, in this view, is not an erotic absolute (like Hegel's) but an agapeic origin, in giving being to be out of the surplus plenitude of self-exceeding generosity. There is a divine fullness always already more than all finite realizations, a fullness that gives finiteness from this agapeic surplus that creatively endows finite beings other than itself. One recalls Paul's great hymn to love, *agapē*, along whose hyperbolic way (ὑπερβολὴν ὁδὸν, 1 Cor 12:31) we are enjoined to go, beyond the best of other great gifts, and even now as we see things in enigma (ἐν αἰνίγματι, 13:12). In thinking about analogy metaxologically, the erotics of generation is exceeded by the agapeics of divine origination. Perhaps the vocation of reason is to ponder this exceeding. Perhaps it is to grant anew the porosity of philosophy and religion, closed in the interim of univocalizing modernity, now itself coming to a close. In the interim of new time, the secret enigma of being, the mysterious love of the divine, passes beyond that closure.

3 ~ The Dearth of Astonishment
On Curiosity, Scientism, and Thinking as Negativity

CURIOSITY AND SCIENTISM

What looks like an insatiable curiosity seems to drive the scientific enterprise. In principle no question seems barred to that curiosity. There seems something limitless to it. Are there recessed equivocities in this drive of limitless curiosity? How does one connect this question with the issue of scientism? Do these equivocities have anything to do with the possibilities of misunderstanding the limitlessness of our desire to know? Are there temptations in curiosity itself to misform the potential infinitude of that desire to know? Is it possible for certain configurations of curiosity to produce counterfeit doubles of wonder? Has the scientistic impulse something to do with the temptation to this malformation? Has this something to do with how the infinity of our desire to know turns away from the true infinite—turns itself into the truth of the infinite?

Scientism bears on the place of science in the life of the whole from which there is no way to abstract science entirely. In the main, scientism understands science to be capable, in principle, if not in practice, of answering all the essential perplexities about the world and the human condition. I want to reflect on the temptation to contract the meaning of wonder in the scientistic interpretation of scientific curiosity. I will ask if this contraction of wonder paradoxically can be tempted with a limitless self-expansion out of which a kind of idolatrous knowing can come. I want to explore a connection with the determinateness or determinability of being, a connection present also in the idea of thinking as negativity. I want to explore a dearth of ontological astonishment in all of this.

We need to distinguish different modalities of wonder: wonder in the modalities of astonishment, perplexity, and curiosity. Curiosity tends to be oriented to what is determinate or determinable, perplexity to something more indeterminate, astonishment to what is overdeterminate, as exceeding univocal determination. The determinate and determinable curiosity of science, while capable of showing a face of unlimitedness, is not to be equated with the fullness of wonder. Throughout my reflection, the intimate relation of determination and self-determination will be of importance: there is a configuration of wonder overtly tilted to determination but which, more intimately, is ingredient in a project of self-determination that wants to bring itself to full completion. I am interested in asking if our curiosity, under scientistic influences, can come to communicate idolatrous outcomes. There is a religious issue here of how, in the name of high ideals, we secrete counterfeit doubles of God. The open infinitude of our seeking might be taken to reflect our *capax dei*, but there is a difference between a capacity for the divine, a capacity that finds in itself something divine, and a capacity that wills itself to be (the) divine. I am interested in asking if the scientistic contraction of curiosity creates a counterfeit infinity.

I offer some general observations about scientism. First and importantly, scientism is not science but an interpretation of science. The questions here are inevitably of a philosophical nature, with repercussions for the full economy of human life. In that full economy, it is unavoidable that we ask about the place of science in the life of the whole. There is no way to abstract science entirely from this sense of the whole, even though this sense may be more or less recessed in our self-consciousness.

Scientism is a philosophical interpretation of the whole, though it takes place within the whole. How is this life of the whole at stake in this interpretation? The answer to the question is that what we call science, at least in principle, has the resources to supply all answers to all the meaningful questions. It has not only the resources, but it has also the privilege and right to make this claim. There is something privileged about science on this interpretation. One of the considerations relevant here is a strong tendency to univocalize the meaning of the scientific impulse in terms of a master science that will offer this master key, or the hope of it, as opening all doors of remaining mystery, as overcoming all residual ignorances.

Of course, there are different scientisms, depending on the state of the current science, and depending on which particular science seems to be in the ascendancy in the epistemic stakes. One thinks of older scientisms in the eighteenth century with some of the *philosophes*; one thinks of how in the nineteenth century a variety of materialisms vied for this ascendancy.[1] One might associate determinisms of various sorts with the temptation to seek the one true cause, or set of causes, that will allow the scientific determinability of all being. One thinks of Freudianism: a certain understanding of eros as the one source of explanations, and if not explanation, illumination.[2] In the twentieth century, there have been various "master sciences." We now forget how Marxism was once considered so. One forgets how linguistics came on the scene as offering the power of the keys. The *potestas clavium* has passed variously to different sciences and more lately, perhaps, to genetics, for its reign as a brief god. Genetics offered a second coming to Darwinism.

How often do we hear it told that everything reveals adaptive evolutionary significance? Evolutionary psychology: evolution "wires" us so; neuropsychology morphing into neurophysiology will illuminate all. Cybernetic scientism: the mind is to be likened to a computer, and of course, it is like it, since the computer is the product of mind. I think there is a droll lesson from evolutionary aesthetics—it seems we are adapted to aesthetic perceptions laid down deeply in us from our time when we were getting by on the African savanna. It seems that the aesthetic scene most loved by humans is a variation of a scene on the savanna, with preference for some trees and some animals in the distance, a variation on a pastoral scene of some sort. The postmodern avant-garde is not amused to think that the earliest human beings have something in common with the "booboisie," H. L. Mencken's contemptuous phrase (dating from early in the twentieth century) for ordinary middle-class Americans. Despite the tastes of the advanced aesthetes, the aesthetic psychology that evolutionary unfolding seems to trump for is a deplorable love of kitsch. One thinks too of the transhumanism of a kind of cybernetic Nietzscheanism as having scientistic seeds.[3] I recall an advocate

---

1. One thinks of Darwinism; also of Marxism as a dialectical scientism; even of philosophic idealism as a kind of (speculative) scientism, especially in the hands of a Hegel. In the latter, as we shall see, here are complex qualifications, as his sense of *Wissenschaft* distinguishes philosophy from one of the particular sciences, which to Hegel are finite sciences. Still determination serves self-determination, a project marking most scientisms.

2. See the salutary and thought-provoking Frederick Crews, *Freud: The Making of an Illusion* (London: Profile Books, 2017).

3. Do not forget that many early Bolsheviks were as much enamored of the *Übermensch*,

of transplanting minds into durable matter. The soft and vulnerable flesh has no future. Transplanted into steel, we could be shot out into space as, say, chairs.[4]

How we understand the culture of knowing is in question. Culture: the deepest and widest sense in which the cultivation of the desire to know is nurtured; of course, culture and *cultus* are related members in the same family. *Scientia*: there is a more inclusive sense of knowing which in some ways is coincident with human being as a creature capable of coming to mindfulness of itself and being. This can include both self-knowing and knowing what is other. Obviously, much then hangs on what it means to know. There is also the relation between this more inclusive sense of knowing and the plurality of specific and determinate forms of knowing, among which are the knowings of the particular sciences.

With reference to this more inclusive sense, diverse forms of knowing are seeded in an original wonder. Indeed there is something about this wonder that is prior to the desire to know, insofar as such a desire is already a specification of an original porosity of being in us, an original porosity that is open to being. The desire to know takes shape in this original porosity, and the shapes it takes can be plural. Without the more original porosity to being in our porosity of being there is no desire to know, and no more specific determination of that desire. Curiosity about being and the determinate beings and processes to which we are opened is subsequent to, secondary to, this more original porosity. Scientific curiosity, such as we have come to know it in a long history of its diverse unfoldings, is derivative from this original porosity. But the diverse unfoldings can forget the maternal porosity out of which they are born, and take on an energy of determination that rides over the original givenness of this porosity.

Curiosity is born from original wonder but it is tempted to think of itself as self-born, self-activating. Its drive for determination is tempted

---

as were the National Socialists who were attracted to Nietzsche. See the science fiction, better scientistic fiction of Yuval Noah Herari, *Homo Deus: A Brief History of Tomorrow* (London: Harvill Secker, 2015), the final chapter of which ends with the prophecy of the best coming religion: "The Data Religion," the coming all-conquering religion of the future, given that intelligence is now said to be no longer dependent on consciousness, and presuming that we have the right algorithms and "data" enough to feed into our cybernetic machines.

4. I prefer flesh, albeit vulnerable and frail.

to think of itself as self-determining. It is hence also tempted to forget the original heteronomy out of which it is birthed. Self-determination and the determinability of being then tend to go hand in hand. The desire to know is driven by the desire to make given being more and more determinate; and this is tied up with our own desire to be the ones who determine the intelligibility of being, perhaps sometimes for its own sake but mostly for purposes of serving our own self-determination. The projection of curiosity to determine being as univocally as possible becomes the project of our self-determination as more and more absolutely autonomous. Our self-determination defines itself as more and more for itself, the more it can stamp its impress on given being as determined by it.

Parenthetically: Heidegger came in for a good deal of criticism when he said (in *What is Called Thinking?*) that "science does not think [*Die Wissenschaft denkt niet*]." In an interview explaining his view, Heidegger stressed the lack of self-reflection involved in science.[5] Surely he is not wrong about that, and in agreement with Husserl: science does not make itself its own object of reflection. But surely also there is more to the issue. The lack of thinking is not remedied by the supplement of self-reflection. The mystery of being in its given otherness is also at issue. Heidegger was trying perhaps to remedy the deficiency when he rightly advocates a dialogue of thinking and poetry. Even then was he perhaps *too dyadic* in his thinking? When Heidegger speaks of truth as *alētheia* and *orthotes* he is making an important point, an indispensable point in some ways. He is opening up the meaning of the nonpropositional as more original, and as at the origin of the propositional. I approach this issue somewhat differently in terms of the porosity of being. We need to avoid univocal unity as absolute, but also dyadic contrast as ultimate, as well indeed as the dialectical deconstruction of univocal unity and dyadic equivocity. The original porosity is better named and articulated in terms of a metaxology of being.

By comparison with the univocal, dyadic, and dialectical approaches, we need to think of the distinctions of system and being systematic, and of their connections with the trans-systematic. There is a metaxology of art, religion, and philosophy, beyond dyadic thinking. The same applies

---

5. YouTube. "Wissenschaft denkt nicht," accessed May 16, 2019; available at youtube.com/watch?v=HwuSmN5ptGA.

to the significance of science. Husserl said that he aimed to destroy the kind of thinking that he later, too late, sees Heidegger as doing. He wanted to make that impossible. Against naturalistic scientism Husserl wants to open up a transcendental philosophy whose path in and through "self-reflection" opens up also to being. Is it too transcendental? Is it possible to end up in a kind of transcendental scientism? I would pose the question in relation to the first crystallization of the impulse to transcendental absoluteness, namely the passage of philosophy from Kant to Hegel. Hegel and his system: is there not a danger of a kind of speculative scientism? The anti-idealists like Schopenhauer and Nietzsche do not offer consolation, in the end: Schopenhauerian monism of will; Nietzschean monism of will to power. It is the univocalization that is the cousin of the scientism.

The senses of being are at stake. In various forms of scientism the underlying presupposition is that being is determinate, and in a manner that invites science to make it as univocally precise as possible. Again the ideal of science as being as univocal as possible, bearing on the meanings of truth and intelligibility, is not separable from the project of self-determination. We would make being determinate in a scientistic spirit in order to further the project of our self-determination, via the determination of being as other to us. Cybernetic transhumanism strikes me as one of the latest forms of this.

I believe we have to take note of three modalities of wonder, keeping in mind that wonder is not a univocal concept. It is not first a concept at all, but a happening, and as a happening it is plurivocal. The three modalities are internally related to each other, but they reveal a different stress in the unfolding of our porosity to being. If we do not properly attend to these different stresses, we can mistakenly think that all wonder is subsumable into the curiosity that makes of all being an object of determinate cognition. This subsumption might consume curiosity, but it is the death of wonder. This is the temptation of the scientistic impulse, a temptation which in being enacted is justified in terms of a particular teleology of the desire to know. To the contrary, wonder is not to be solely reconfigured as voracious curiosity that spends itself in ceaseless accumulation of determinate cognition(s).

BETWEEN INDETERMINACY AND OVERDETERMINACY

To articulate the matter I find it helpful to invoke the notions of the indeterminate, the determinate, the self-determining, and the overdeterminate. They are relevant to understanding the dearth of ontological astonishment and the contraction of curiosity in scientism. They have a bearing on how we orient ourselves in thinking to being as given. I will say something about these notions, and then I will turn to different modalities of wonder, before returning again to the contraction of curiosity in scientism.

Looking back to ancient metaphysics the indeterminate tended to be seen in the light of the absence of intelligibility. By contrast, determinacy or determinability, so to say, keeps at bay the formlessness of the indeterminate (*to apeiron*). The epistemic process by which being is made intelligible involves the movement of thought from the indeterminate to determinacy, the former being left behind in the process. We begin with an indeterminate wondering, pass through a more definite questioning or inquiry, and end with a more or less determinate answer to a well-defined question. In truth, the unfolding here is more complex than a teleological process from indeterminacy to determination. We need to invoke the self-determining and more importantly the overdeterminate, in a sense to be addressed. The point is not to negate the indeterminate but to offer the more affirmative sense suggested by it: no longer as a formlessness to be overcome but as a "too muchness" in being that calls forth our ontological astonishment.

In everyday realism we think that things and processes have a more or less fixed and univocal character, and that this constitutes their determinacy. Nevertheless, determinacy cannot be understood purely in itself; it refers us to the outcome of the process of determination, a process not itself just another determinate thing. We tend to separate the determinate outcome from the determining process, and so take what is there as composed of a collection of determinate things. Determinacy is bound up with the fact that things and processes do manifest themselves with an immanent articulation and relative stability. Whether that immanent articulation can be expressed entirely in univocal terms is an important question. If we put the stress only on univocity, we can cover over the process by which the determinate comes to be determinate. Equivocal, dialectical, and metaxological considerations enter into a fuller account of determinacy.

When indeterminacy is invoked it is often by contrast with determinacy. This might seem to be essentially a privative notion, referring us to the absence of determinate characteristics, and thus hard to distinguish from what is void. I suggest a more *affirmative* understanding, one referring us to the matrix out of which determinate beings become determinate. As a kind of predeterminate matrix, this would reveal determining power in enabling the determinate things that come to be. This more affirmative sense makes us think of the idea of *overdeterminacy*. Void indeterminacy refers us to an indefiniteness which is only the absence of determination, rather than the more fertile matrix out of which determinacy can come to be. These two senses of the indeterminate are often mixed up. If overdeterminacy is presupposed by indeterminacy, our general tendency to oscillate between the indeterminate and the determinate will be seen not to go far enough. If determinacy is often correlated with univocity, and indeterminacy with equivocity, we need further dialectical and metaxological resources to do full justice to what is at play.

An additional consideration concerns the notion of *self-determinacy*. This refers us to a process of determination in which *the unfolding recurs to itself* and hence enters into self-relation in the very unfolding itself. This is particularly evident in the case of the human being as self-determining. The notion cannot be fully understood without reference to the ideas of the indeterminate and the determinate. Frequently self-determination is seen as the determination of the indeterminate in which a process of selving comes to achieve a *relationship to itself*. Again the human being is the most striking example of this, and particularly in modernity the idea of self-determination has received central attention. But both self-determinacy and determinacy refer back to something that cannot be described in the terms of self-determination or determination. This something other is not just the indeterminate understood in the privative sense, but the more affirmative sense which is the overdeterminate. Self-determinacy comes to be out of sources that are not just self-determining. Our powers of self-determining are endowed powers. There is a receiving of self before there is an acting of self. This makes the process of selving porous to sources of otherness that exceed selving.

This matter can be illuminated in a number of ways but I want to refer to the speculative logic of Hegel where the triad—the indeterminate, the determinate, and the self-determining (sometimes via reciprocal determination)—governs process as ultimately mediating itself in a self-becoming in which the other to the selving is the (self-)othering of the selving itself. The overdeterminacy does not enter systematically into the articulation of this understanding. I want to suggest that the overdeterminacy, as the affirmative sense of the indeterminate and not as the negative sense of the indefinite, refers us to the enabling matrix that makes possible determinacy and self-determination. There is something prior to the determinate but not a mere indefiniteness. It has an excess more than all determinations, as well as more than what we can subject to self-determination. There is a "too-muchness" that has a primordial givenness that enables determinacy, that companions our self-determination and yet also exceeds or outlives these. It is not to be equated with overdetermination understood as necessitation by an excess of determining causes. It allows the possibility of the open space of the indeterminate, and hence is not hyperbolic determinism, but hyperbolic to determinism in enabling the endowment of freedom. If Hegel's dialectic tends to be defined by the triad of the indeterminate, the determinate, and the self-determining, metaxology exceeds this triad in the direction of remaining true to the inexhaustible overdeterminacy. This inexhaustible overdeterminacy is multiply incarnated, for instance, in great artworks, persons, or communities.

ONTOLOGICAL ASTONISHMENT AND HEGELIAN NEGATIVITY

Let me now say something about Hegel's notion of thinking as self-relating negativity, because by this means we can see the connection between determination *qua* process and self-determination, as governing the whole purpose of the move from the indeterminate to the determinate. If to be intelligible is to be determinate—indeed to be, properly speaking, is to be determinate—the status of determinacy and determination opens itself for question. How comes the determinate to be determinate? How does it come about that being as determinate is determinable by thought and hence rendered intelligible? The issue of a *becoming* determinate is at stake, not just some entirely static sense of being. I see Hegel's connection of thinking with determinate negation, or more generally with subjectivity as self-relating negativity, as answering such questions. What is simply given to be is not intelligible as such; it is a mere immediacy until rendered intelligible, either through its own becoming intelligible, or through being made intelligible by thinking. Thinking as negativity moves us from the simple givenness of the "to be" to the more determinately intelligible; but the former (the "to be") is no more than an indeterminacy, and hence deficient in true intelligibility, until this further development of determination has been made by thinking as negativity. A further complication in Hegel's view is that thinking as process of negation is not only a determining; it is in process toward knowing itself as a process of self-determining. Hence his more complex description: self-relating negativity. The operation of negation is not only a determination of what is other to the thinking, it is the coming to itself of the thinking process. In that sense, the return of thinking to itself, in the process of determining what is other, is not just making determinate, it is *self-determining*. The determining power of thinking in negativity is hence inseparable from Hegel's understanding of the meaning of freedom. But there is an overall logic that governs the movement of thinking as negativity: thinking moves from indeterminacy to determination to self-determination.

In all of this there is a dearth of ontological astonishment, I claim. For instance, given being as a mere indeterminate immediacy can barely be said to be, and even less said to be intelligible until rendered so by determining thinking which mediates by negativity. Hence being becomes the most indigent of the categories that is all but nothing, until thought understands that it has already passed over into becoming. I do not want to rehearse the famous opening of Hegel's *Logic*, but want to suggest, among other things, that Hegelian negativity, via a logic of self-determining thought, is born of and leads to a dearth of ontological astonishment. Instead of a sense of being as the marvel of the "too much," we find rather an indigence of "all but nothing." To further illuminate the issue, we need to distinguish between different modalities of wonder: first a more primal ontological astonishment that seeds metaphysical mindfulness; second a restless perplexity in which thinking seeks to transcends initial indeterminacy toward more and more determinate outcomes; third, more determinate curiosity in which the initiating openness of wonder is dispelled in a determinate solution to a determinate problem.

Determining thought answers to a powerful curiosity that renders intelligible the given, rather than to a primal astonishment before the marvel of the "to be" as given—given with a fullness impossible to describe in the language of negativity, though indeed in a certain sense it is no thing. Heidegger, for instance, has a truer sense of this other nothing. My focus is less defending Heidegger as to suggest the need to grant something more than a *logos* of becoming and self-becoming—there is an event of "coming to be" that asks of us a different *logos*. It asks of us a different sense of being, a different sense of nothing—not the nothing defining a determinate process of becoming, or a determining nothing defining a self-becoming. Rather, a nothing in relation to which a coming to be arises—a coming to be that is more primal than becoming. In a way, we can say nothing univocally direct about this nothing; rather we need to attend to how becoming and self-becoming presuppose this other sense of coming to be. A sense of this is communicated in the happening of a primal astonishment before the happening of the "to be" as overdeterminate. In light of it every process of determination and self-determination is secretly accompanied by what it cannot entirely accommodate on its own terms. This granting of the overdeterminacy of the "to be" has significance in relation to the dearth of ontological astonishment in thinking as determinate negation, or self-relating negativity. It has a very important implication for the practice(s) of metaphysical thinking that try to stay true to metaphysical wonder in the mode of primal astonishment.

BEING OVERDETERMINATE: WONDER AS ASTONISHMENT

I now want to both deepen and widen our investigation by saying something about the three modalities of wonder.[6] We have to keep in mind that these three are internally related to each other as they reveal a different stress in the unfolding formation of our porosity to being. They are not three epistemic layers stacked one on top of the other. Taking form in the porosity, giving form to the porosity, there is a fluidity of passage

---

6. In this and following two sections, I am drawing from, and adapting, a longer discussion in my *The Intimate Strangeness of Being*, chap. 10.

of one into the other, indeed of permeability and mingling of one and the other. As Joyce says of the waters of Anna Livia Plurabelle, there is a "hitherandthithering" flow to them. But there are different stresses in the fluctuation, and if we do not properly attend to them, we can mistakenly think all wonder is subsumable into the curiosity that makes of all being an object of determinate cognition. This subsumption might consume curiosity, but it is the death of wonder. Wonder is not to be solely reconfigured as voracious curiosity that spends itself in ceaseless accumulation of determinate cognition, even unto the extreme of the counterfeit infinity of scientism. Equally, there is something other to thinking as self-relating negativity. There is something about wonder that exceeds self-relation. We do not possess a capacity for wonder; rather we are capacitated by wonder. This capacitation is not determined through ourselves alone. We alone cannot just will to bring it to be, or will to bring it to life again, if its power dies down. We do not just exercise self-determination over it. There is a given porosity of being that endows us with the promise of mindfulness. The self-determination of our powers of minding are derivative of this endowment.

Turning to the first modality of wonder, it is impossible to describe this astonishment in the language of negativity. There is a wonder preceding determinate and self-determining cognition. Wonder before the being there of being and beings is precipitated in this astonishment. This has not to do with a process of becoming this or that but with porosity to the "that it is at all" of being. That being is, that beings have come to be at all—this is prior to their becoming this or that, prior to their self-becoming. In a certain sense, all human mindfulness is seeded in this astonishment.

We have to be cautious here, as "wonder" is often seen in a way that is too subjectivized. It is the feeling of "gosh" or "wow" that is said to be experienced before what surprises us. One of the reasons I use "astonishment" is because it captures better the ontological bite of otherness. There is *the stress of the emphatic beyond expectation*. We say "The wonder of it is ..." and we mean to take note of a happening beyond expectation, one in which the surprising has been communicated with this stress of the emphatic. There is something of the blow of unpremeditated otherness in being struck by astonishment. The otherness seems to stun us, bewilder us, even stupefy us. We seem deprived of self-possession when we are *stricken* with a kind of amazement. We seem to be overcome with a kind of ontological stupor.

All of this seems to be rife with a kind of negation—not our negation but our being negated. It is not thinking as negation. Something of the affirmative "too-muchness," the overdeterminacy of being has been communicated in the astonishment. This is not free from a dimension of ontological frailty in that the surprising event might not have come to be, it might not have been at all. And yet it has eventuated, despite the possibility that it might not have been at all. We awake on a boundary between being at all and possibly not being. Our porosity to the overdeterminacy of the happening is linked with the intimation that the "too-muchness" is also a kind of "no-thing." The first appropriate way to think of this is not in terms of negativity. This might come later. First, in the opening of porosity, something strikes into us, while at the same time taking us beyond ourselves. Out of this, but derivatively, the self-transcending of thinking is possibilized. We see the inappropriateness of speaking of astonishment as just a subjective feeling. We are moved into the space of a *metaxu* where we are enabled to go toward the things, because in the porous between there is no fixation of the difference of minding and things. And so it is not quite that we go from our minds to the things, but more so that the things come to mind. The things come to mind. This is what "beholding from" also entails.[7]

Instead of thinking as negativity, already even before we more reflectively come to ourselves, there is the more primal opening in astonishment. There is a prior porosity in which there is no fixed boundary between there and here, between outside and inside; there is passage from

---

7. My use of the phrase "beholding from" is derived from William Wordsworth's "Lines Written above Tintern Abbey," i.e., "Therefore am I still / A lover of the meadows and the woods, / And mountains; and of all that we behold, / From this green earth; of all the mighty world / Of eye and ear." William Wordsworth, *William Wordsworth*, ed. Stephen Gill (Oxford: Oxford University Press, 1984), 134.102–6. The phrase occurs after Wordsworth speaks of the spirit "that rolls through all things" and before the lines that mention "of all the mighty world / Of eye, and ear,—both what they half create, / And what perceive." Was Wordsworth here caught in the tension of a kind of idealism, not fully true to the "from"? The problem is evident in Coleridge's lines in "Dejection: an Ode": "O Lady! we receive but what we give, / And in our life alone does Nature live: / Ours is her wedding garment, ours her shroud!" *Samuel Taylor Coleridge, The Major Works*, ed. H. J. Jackson (Oxford: Oxford University Press, 2000), 114. If we receive only what we give, there is no "beholding from." If there is "beholding from," we receive before we give.

what is, passage into an awakening of minding which is opened to what communicates itself to us, before our own efforts at self-determining cognition. We do not open ourselves; being opened, we are as an opening. Astonishment awakens the porosity of mindfulness to being, in the communication of being to mindfulness, before mind comes to itself in more determinate form(s). It is for this reason also that I would it correlate it with a more original "coming to be" prior to the formation of different processes of determinate becoming and the arrival of relatively settled beings and processes.

Because all determinate thinking already presupposes it as having happened, we find it difficult to think this more original porosity of astonishment. It is not yet determinate knowing, yet all determinate knowing proceeds from it. Yet it can be communicated. I behold the majestic tree and exclaim: "This is astonishing!" I am not projecting my feeling; rather, the tree is coming to wakefulness in me, while I am being awakened by the tree, and I am awakening to myself, in a more primal porosity. The striking otherness of this blossoming thereness has found its way into the intimacy of my receiving attendance. This astonishment is a porosity prior to intentionality; it is not a vector of intentionality going from subject to object; it refers us back to a patience of being more primal than any cognitive endeavor to be.

Porosity might seem like negativity in that it cannot be reduced to this or that determination, and allows dynamism and passage. At issue is not thinking as negation but rather a mindful *passio essendi* prior to and presupposed by every *conatus essendi* of the mind desiring to understand this or that. It is not first that we desire to understand. Rather we are awoken or become awake in a not yet determinate minding that is not full with itself but filled with an openness to what is beyond itself. Is it permissible to say one is filled with openness, given that such a porosity looks like nothing determinate and hence seems almost nothing, even entirely empty? Being filled with openness and yet being empty: this is what makes possible all our determinate relations to determinate beings and processes, whether these relations be knowing ones or unknowing. Thinking understood primarily as negativity does not have enough of this porous patience, even though its endeavor to know ultimately derives from it.

One might object that the desire to know is a drive to determination, a drive that when it comes to know itself becomes also more self-determining. It is a well-rehearsed theme that philosophy begins in wonder and Aristotle is often cited: "All men desire to know" (*Metaphysics* 982b11). Aristotle sees the connection of marveling and astonishment when he reminds us of the affiliation of myth and metaphysics, and also the delight in the senses. Nevertheless, the desire to know is understood essentially as a *drive to determinate intelligibility*, which on being attained dissolves the initial wonder setting the mind in motion. The end of Aristotle's wonder is a determinate *logos* of a determinate somewhat, a *tode ti*. This end is the dissolution of wonder, not its deepening. I find it significant that Aristotle calls on *geometry* to illustrate the teleological thrust of the desire to know (*Metaphysics* 983a13). Geometry can be taken as exemplary of determinate cognition: when the problem is solved, the wonder is extinguished and surpassed.

Plato is more suggestive in *Theaetetus* (155d3–4) when *thaumazein* is said to be the *pathos* of the philosopher. *Pathos*: there is a patience, a primal receptivity. This is at the other extreme to the self-activating knowing we expect from Kant and his successors, both idealist and constructivist. There is a pathos more primal than activity, a patience before any self-activity. There is no going beyond ourselves without the more primal patience and receiving. Patience is often denigrated as a servile passivity supposedly beneath our high dignity as self-activating powers. And yet no one can self-activate into wonder. It comes or it does not come. We are *struck* into wonder. "Being struck" is beyond our self-determination. We cannot "project" ourselves into "being struck." It comes to us from beyond ourselves.

While I will return to curiosity, let me offer a brief comparison between it and primal astonishment. I would correlate curiosity with a determinate cognition of a determinate somewhat (*tode ti*) or "object." By contrast, in astonishment an "object" as other does not simply seize us and make us "merely" passive. What is received cannot be thus objectified. What seizes us is the offer of being beyond all objectification, and the call of truthfulness to being. This is not first either subjective or objective, but trans-subjective and trans-objective. "Trans": we witness a *crossing between* "subject" and "object" and an intermedium of their interplay which is more primordial than any determinable intermediation between the two. The happening of this "being-between" reveals a porosity beyond subjectification and objectification and we are beholden to what eventuates in this between, making us answerable to its truth in our own being truthful. In the intimate strangeness of the porosity an excess of being flows, and overflows toward one.

We could say there is something *childlike* about this, but this is not to say it is *childish*. Childlike we find ourselves already in the porosity of being: astonishment is not produced, it *opens us* in the first instance, and there is joy in the light. The child *lives* this primal and elemental opening; hence wonder is often noted as more characteristic of earlier stages of life, often accompanied by an asking of the "big questions." Subsequent developments of curiosity and sophisticated scientific knowing are seeded in the primal porosity but what its grant enables we too quickly take for granted. The maternal porosity can be long forgotten when the project of science comes more fully on the scene. When the child points to the night sky and murmurs—"Look, the moon!"—the astonishing has won its way into its heart. Later, the astonished child is recessed, even driven underground, in the curious project of (say) space exploration which lifts off the earth.[8]

The more primal porosity is at the origin of all modalities of mind, but as intimate with the giving of the first opening, it can be passed over, covered over. Because it enables the passage of mindfulness it can be passed over, for we come to ourselves more determinately in this passing. It is first a happening and only subsequently is what happens gathered to itself in an express self-relation. In the latter, we risk the contraction of what the first opening communicates. We can contract the opening of the porosity to just what *we* will grant as given. The point is relevant to wonder in the modalities of perplexity and curiosity, and in modes of minding that are determinate and self-determining. The porosity is prior to determinate and self-determining cognition, and is neither of self or other but happens as the between space in which, and out of which, come to be a variety of determinate and self-determining mindings of being. The latter are derived, not original. What is more original is the between of porosity.

---

8. My thanks to Catherine Pickstock who responded to some of the remarks in this chapter in a presentation given in the series "Grammars of Wonder," organized by Philip McCosker at the von Hügel Institute, St. Edmund's College, University of Cambridge, February 23, 2018. I particularly note her acute remarks on Sylvia Plath's "The Moon and the Yew Tree."

BEING INDETERMINATE: WONDER AS PERPLEXITY

I think of perplexity as a second modality of wondering whereby we pass from the overdeterminacy to a mingling of the indeterminacy and the determinate. If one were to refer to thinking as negativity, it would be more appropriate to consider it in connection with perplexity. When we are perplexed we are often beset by doubt and uncertainty. Something puzzles us and we cannot quite solve the puzzle. We see the word "plexus" in perplexity, and what this suggests is a plaiting, a twining, an entanglement. The word "com-plex" points to something intricate and difficult to unravel: a knot we struggle perhaps to untangle. We find ourselves plagued by perplexity, tormented with some vexing matter. We are not sure what to think, and there is no serenity of mind. More often there is the threat of something bewildering, troubling, perturbing.

How does one think of perplexity as arising out of first astonishment? In astonishment we come to be granted as coming to mindfulness both of the overdeterminacy of other-being and a kind of indeterminacy opening in the porosity of our own being. We are granted as being for ourselves now in more express contrast to the overdeterminacy in which we more originally participate. We risk being overwhelmed by that overdeterminacy and want to reduce it to a more determinate measure, allowing us also to take its measure, to whatever extent is possible. Perhaps here some more express sense of thinking as negation can come into the open. The "too-muchness" of given being can seem to *oppress* us.[9] The intimation intrudes that we cannot be its full measure; yet we want to know it in full measure. A troubled disjunction arises: we do not know, we would know, we know we do not know. We endure the stress of a baffling difference between what we know is too much for us and our intimately known desire to know just that "too-muchness." In the baffling difference we are torn between our desire to know and our intimate knowing that the perplexing is too much for us. We are tempted to diminish the

---

9. Edmund Burke sees a connection of astonishment with horror: "astonishment is that state of the soul, in which all its motions are suspended, with some degree of horror." *A Philosophical Enquiry into the Origin of Our Ideas of the Sublime and the Beautiful*, ed. Adam Phillips (Oxford: Oxford University Press, 1990), part II, section 1. He is not wrong but he is not entirely right either. In terms of the analysis here, the sense of horror becomes more overt *on the turn* of wonder from first astonishment to perplexity.

stress in seeking a knowing which reduces the "too-muchness" to proportions that allow us to appropriate its difference. The desire to know can be developed as our way of subjecting the given "too-muchness" to our measure, that is, to the *proportionate* measure of ourselves as knowers. That said, wonder as perplexity is recurrently haunted by faces of otherness that are just so as *disproportionate* to the determinate measure of our determinative cognition.

Perplexity might be correlated with the *equivocity of being*. We are enthralled by the play of light and darkness, the chiaroscuro of things and ourselves. Enthralled as both enchanted by and in thrall to the dark light of unformed things and things forming, of ourselves formless and seeking form, of all things enigmatic and intimating, of ourselves as the most baffling of beings. This is not the reverse of astonishment but our awakening to the sometimes perturbing ambiguity of the overdeterminacy. Perplexity affects both the sides of self-being and other-being. Other-beings and selvings come from formlessness beyond form, are themselves as forming and coming to form, and finally point beyond themselves and all finite form. The equivocity can invade us with foreboding in the face of the mystery of life. Filled with dismay, we can be driven to distraction, can even be driven mad. At the same time, this perplexity can awaken an urgent *seeking* for what is true in all significant art, in all intellectually honest philosophy, in all spiritually serious religion. Mostly, however, the seeking has no fancy names, as ordinary persons in accustomed community, mostly out of the limelight, seek to tread the way of truth.

There is a saturated equivocity to perplexity: the *doubleness* of being *both* the dismaying destitution of not-knowing *and* the ignorance of a voracious desire to know. In perplexity we can wake up to ourselves before and beyond the determinate desire to know that we most often find in curiosity. Perplexity has something more primitive than what we normally call the desire to know, as well as something potentially touching transcendence as other. This more primitive perplexity is gestated in the intimate selving that comes to be out of the original ontological porosity. It is trans-objective and trans-subjective, and hence more than selving alone with itself. As being awakening out of the porosity, it is already an equivocal way of "being with" what is other than selving.

One could say in respect of the equivocal play of light and darkness, we are in a condition reminiscent of Plato's Cave. In perplexity, however, we are not in the Cave as prisoners who do not know they are prisoners. These latter do not know perplexity as an awakening. The perplexed have an intimation of being held in check by something too much for their own power. Being perplexed we can be nonplussed by the saturated equivocity of being. In moments of more porous mindfulness lucidity can break into perplexity, and we know that there is light. The light might be twinned with darkness, but that does not make it any less the light. *We ourselves* are double: perplexed between the burden of the mystery and the godsend of light that gives ontological uplift.

Perplexity can be haunted by *horror*: ontological horror before the being-there of being in its excess to our rational measure. It is not often enough remarked that in the Cave we can turn *downward* as well as upward. There can be a debilitating perplexity where we have the feeling of *being blocked from ascending into the light*. We seek to find the light, but instead we find ourselves darkened. We find ourselves in the dark in the very seeking for light itself. We lack the night vision of the wise. We are not the measure of the light; we are also not the measure of the darkness. We find we cannot go up on our own. In perplexity we find ourselves falling, though we do not want to fall.

I find it interesting that in the same dialogue, the *Theaetetus*, where Plato singles out *thaumazein*, the aporetic is also stressed again and again. The experience of *aporia* or impasse can show the working of extreme perplexity in thought. *Aporia*: a lack of *poros* and we cannot find a way across a gap. The aporia does not preclude further and new thinking, but it can also be addressed by myth or likely stories. Univocal theories are not enough. I am also put in mind of Kant: there are metaphysical questions we cannot avoid raising but cannot also answer or put to rest in a univocal science. There is the zigzag method for perplexity (Aristotle and Kant?): "on the one hand, this," "on the other hand, that." Perplexity calls to mind a fever where we restlessly rock this way, rock that way, unable to find peace. Thinkers like Kierkegaard, Nietzsche, and Dostoevsky had experience of this fever, sometimes suffering the unavoidability of thinking as a kind of sickness. They feel cursed by reflection as an unease, as a disease.

What here of thinking as self-relating negativity? Such thinking is inclined to claim that through its own self-determination it can counteract the falling into equivocity by means of its progressive determination of intelligibility. The Hegelian way of doubt (*der Weg des Zweifels*—notice the reference to the double) will overcome radical equivocity through its own self-accomplishing skepticism.[10] In accomplishing itself, skepticism overcomes skepticism, gives up its vagrancy (Kant described the skeptic as a nomad), and comes home to itself, in and as absolute knowing. Here knowing no longer feels the need to go beyond itself; it is finally at home with itself, having absolved itself from all alienating otherness, for all otherness proves finally to be its own otherness. It even surpasses the *desire* for wisdom, as in previous philosophy, and become possession of actual science, *Wissenschaft*. Previous philosophy was always *between* ignorance and wisdom; now there is no such between, because everything is between knowing and itself, in the circle of its own self-determination. In Hegel, after the old metaphysics, and the new critique, we are offered the new speculative philosophy which in post-transcendental form offers the totality of categories, each allegedly justified beyond critique, because having been radically critiqued by dialectic.

This dialectical way is carried on the labor of the negative to a mediation of the equivocity, through the many determinate intelligibilities, all the way to fully self-determining knowing. While this triadic movement from indeterminate, through determination, to self-determination has a certain qualified truth, it is not fully true to the dimensions of the perplexity suggested above. Here too there is something that exceeds determination, something also not to be described in the language of self-determining thought. If the latter takes itself to be the absolute measure of what is at issue, it suffers from the same bewitchment of the equivocity which it ostensibly claims to rationally mediate. It is within the Cave but has redefined its immanence as the whole, and hence is in an even worse position than those prisoners who know and grant with raw pain that they are still perplexed prisoners. The perplexity of the Cave has been dialectically domesticated: the Cave now is no Cave, because all that is

10. Hegel speaks of the journey of his *Phenomenology* as *der Weg des Zweifels*, the way of doubt, and we should note the reference to two, the double (*zwei*), something we also note when he describes the journey as a *Weg der Verzweiflung*, a pathway of despair. *Phenomenology of Spirit*, trans. A. V. Miller (Oxford: Clarendon Press, 1977), §78. There he also speaks of the *Phenomenology of Spirit* as a "self-accomplishing skepticism [*sich vollbringende Skeptizismus*]." See *Phänomenologie des Geistes* (Hamburg: Felix Meiner, 1952), 67; *Phenomenology of Spirit*, §49.

there is (self-)determined as immanence at home with itself and beyond which there is nothing greater to be thought. Without perplexity we settle into a false home at whose hearth flickers the fire of self-determining immanence itself as its own counterfeit god.

BEING DETERMINATE: WONDER AS CURIOSITY

I turn now to curiosity as a third modality of wondering, itself marked by its own doubleness, even despite its impatience with equivocity: the doubleness of being absolutely indispensable to the essential determination of being and cognition, and yet of always being tempted to run roughshod over the overdeterminacy of astonishment. The perplexity that can live on in thinking as negation can be further dulled, even unto the death of wonder. If to be is to be determinate, here to be is nothing if it is not determinate. Being is nothing but determinacy and to be exhausted in the totality of all determinations. The "that it is at all" of given being is taken for granted rather than as granted. The danger here is that the necessity of determinacy becomes a turn away from the overdeterminacy, and hence into a kind of hostility to ontological astonishment. Curiosity about the determinacies of being risks becoming a configuration of wonder which leads to the annihilation of the wonder of being itself.

It is necessary to assert the *constitutive* role of curiosity in getting as univocal a grip as possible on the intelligibility of being, in addition to as precise an articulation as possible of that intelligibility. We cannot but be curious, given that we are a desire to know the world around us and ourselves. When we are curious, our desire to know attends carefully to the details of things. Einstein admonishes us: "Never lose a holy curiosity." "Holy": it is as if the sacred companions the curiosity. In asking about curiosity we are also asking about the *worthiness* of knowledge, or at least certain kinds of claims to knowledge. In an adapted way, we are not far from Nietzsche's question about the value of truth. There may be claims to the true, forms bound to certain determinations of univocal truth, that carry us away from the sprit of truth, even as they are enabled at all by being carriers of the same spirit of truth.

We do think, of course, that sometimes curiosity can be excessive, that it can be addressed to unworthy things, that it can intrude too minutely into things. We speak of a healthy curiosity but there also seems an inquisitiveness that is too intrusive and that is taken up with what does not properly concern us. Curiosity, in a good sense, finds things interesting and surprising; its desire to know is open to the novel and strange.[11] It fastens on things in their interesting determinacy. It is open to what is unfamiliar and odd. The novel, the peculiar, the queer often draw the attention of the curious mind. We sometimes judge an argument to be curious: departing from expected ways, it is marked by ingeniousness or too much subtlety. There are those who are collectors of curiosities: in out of the way places, they are on the lookout for things or people out of the ordinary. We are familiar also with inquisitions, by contrast, where novelty is suspect. The inquisitor is particular about details because there are details which show forth the unapproved. We might approve of the openness of the desire to know, but we are more equivocal about something we think one has no right to know. There is such a thing as *prying curiosity*. We deem it to intrude on what properly does not concern it. Something is "off-limits" to the desire to know.

This double-edged character means that, *qua* wonder, curiosity is not a pure porosity to what is true. What we are in the intimate recesses of our being infiltrates our manners of being curious. There *can* be something closer to the purer porosity, the reception of astonishment, the awakening of perplexity. But it can also be the case that in the search for light something darker surges forth. From secret intimate sources, the desire to know can be marked by a *conatus essendi* that wills to overtake, subordinate, if not extirpate the porosity and patience that are intimate

---

11. I find it curious that the word "curiosity" became much more common in English usage, as well as in publications, and in a positive sense, sometime in the later sixteenth century. See Philip Ball, *Curiosity: How Science Became Interested in Everything* (Chicago: University of Chicago Press, 2013), 3–22. This was a time on the threshold of modernity, its turn to self, and the growing objectification of being. That said, and balancing, I think of Charles Dickens's *The Old Curiosity Shop*: the mystery of the human in the junk heap of flotsam and jetsam, bit and baubles, trash and treasures, treasure hidden in the trash heap. Ball details some premodern attitudes to curiosity that are more equivocal, if not deeply suspicious. St. Augustine, *vitium curiositas*; St. Bernard, *primum vitium est curiositas*. By contrast with *vana curiositas* only, Aquinas has an interesting discussion of *studiositas* and the issue of directing curiosity and knowing (*Summa Theologiae* II-II, qq. 166–67). See Gladden J. Pippin, "Directing Philosophy: Aquinas, Studiousness, and Modern Curiosity," *Review of Metaphysics* 68, no. 2 (December 2014): 313–46. To the degree that my analysis of the modalities of wonder is ontological/metaphysical, the equivocity of curiosity is not premodern, modern, or postmodern. There is about it a saturated equivocity that is ontologically constitutive, and hence to be found in, but not exahsuted by, premodern, modern, and postmodern forms.

to our being. The doubleness is not to be forgotten. There are formations of curiosity in which the will to make being as univocally determinate as possible takes on an all-pervasive momentum that presents it as an irresistible power of its own. Its sources in the more original porosity are forgotten, as well as its salutary interplay with the other modalities of wonder in astonishment and perplexity.

If perplexity is a first-born child of primal astonishment, curiosity is a second-born. If astonishment is overdetermined, if perplexity mixes the overdeterminate and indeterminate, curiosity dominantly stresses the determinate. Often we think of wonder in this third modality as wrestling with "problems." This does make sense—the "It is!" of first astonishment turns into the "What is?" (indeed "What the hell is it?") of perplexity, turning now into the sober "What is it?" of curiosity.[12] When we pose the question in this third form, we are asking primarily about the *determinate* being there of beings, or the determinate forms or structures or processes. We have moved from ontological astonishment before being as given at all toward ontic regard concerning beings, their particular properties, their intricate patterns of developments, determinate formations, and so on. This movement into wonder as curiosity is essential to the genuine becoming of our mindfulness of what is. This follows from the fact that the overdeterminate is indeed saturated with determinations. It is not an indefiniteness empty of determinacy. The more determinate question "What is it?" turns us toward the rich, given intricacy of this, that, and the other. There can even be something of ontological and epistemic reverence in this turn to things. After all, it too participates derivatively in our original porosity to the astonishing givenness of being. Curiosity can release our sense of marvel at these given intricacies of things.

I am interested, however, in a certain understanding of curiosity which turns the teleology of wonder into a movement from the indeterminate to the determinate, and thence from determination to determination, all the way to the totality of determinations which are held to exhaust the whole. I connect Hegelian negativity with such a teleological movement from indeterminacy, through determination to self-determining

---

12. If one tried to distill the three modalities and image them, it might look like this: Astonishment = !!; perplexity = !?; curiosity = ??.

knowing. While this understanding is not quite to be identified with the view that being is simply determinate, nevertheless he reveals something essential, and I think questionable, about such a teleology: what seems mysterious in the initial indeterminacy is brought into the light of full intelligibility at the end of the unfolding, intelligibility determinable by knowing as self-determining. This is evident at the highest level of absolute spirit: art comes to an end when the enigma of the origin no longer retains anything secret; likewise, in the end religion safeguards no divine mystery that ultimately is too much for the power of philosophical knowing.[13] Hegel's self-determination thus shares this crucial orientation with this understanding of the teleology of curiosity. This kind of curiosity negates the indeterminate, for this as such cannot be grasped, for only the determinate is thus graspable. Behind this grasping can operate a metaphysical *ressentiment* against anything in the ontological situation that exceeds its measure, a secret hatred of the overdeterminate. Equally all perplexity troubled by the "too-muchness" tends to be deemed an oppressive equivocity and as such no longer to be abided. There is no abiding with the mystery of given being. There is to be nothing abiding about the mystery of given being. If we look at the teleology of knowing in this way, we risk the eventual evacuation of spiritual seriousness not only in art and religion but also in philosophy. We come to suffer not simply from a dearth but from the death of ontological astonishment. For there is no room now for the *thaumazein* that recurs to the overdeterminacy in the never dispelled porosity of being. In claiming to fulfill its opening in fully self-determining knowing, it is no longer opened as a received porosity that sources the desire to know. Great artworks, like religious reverence or awe, may offer us striking occasions of

---

13. On this in connection with art in relation to the teleological movement from symbolic, through classical, to romantic art, see my *Art, Origins, Otherness*, chap. 3. In connection with religion, see *Hegel's God – A Counterfeit Double?*, and especially chap. 6 in relation to the idea of creation, which is for Hegel is a "representation" that does not get to the true Hegelian concept which is "creation" as God's own self-creation, God's self-determination. Creation is not the hyperbole of radical origination (see *God and the Between*, chap. 12), nor is the world as created the eventuation of finite being as given to be as other to the divine. The stress is not on such radical "coming to be" but first on becoming, then on self-becoming, indeed the self-becoming of God, and this following the teleological movement from indeterminacy, determination to self-determination. Just as there is no sense of hyperbolic giving to be, there is no sense of the baffling nothing out of which finite being is said to be given to be; there is determinate negation as the negativity immanent in the self-circling whole.

originating wonder that never dispel this ontological porosity but purge it of idolatrous lies. If original wonder is entirely impelled out of its initial hiddenness by determinative curiosity, the porosity is no longer kept open in philosophical mindfulness, and our ontological appreciation of the overdeterminacy of being withers. The wiser patience that waits on the renewal of first astonishment is betrayed.

THE IDOLATRY OF CONTRACTED CURIOSITY AND ITS LIMITLESS SELF-EXPANSION

Is there a connection between self-determining thinking *qua* self-relating negativity and the dearth of ontological astonishment of scientism? I believe there is, and it has much to do with overlooking the otherness of given being in its overdeterminacy. I want to return to the equivocity of curiosity in its impulse to overcome equivocity. The contraction of wonder that curiosity can become also, paradoxically, infinitely self-expanding. Curiosity *qua* wonder is a form of the original porosity, but *qua* contraction to this, that, and the other determinacy, it is a limitation of the porosity. And yet this limitation, again due its being sourced in the original porosity, can become limitless.

Curiosity is a contraction of wonder, but *qua* wonder, it can be limitlessly interested in everything. This seems something to be scientifically lauded, but suppose we ask now not about the "what" concerning which we are curious but the "how" or the way of being curious about something, about everything. What looks like the same curiosity can be informed by a kind of secret love of the object or subject of curiosity, but it might also be informed by a kind of hatred of its resistant mystery or marvel. It might hate the latter because it does not yield univocally to the curiosity, and will never do so. "Questioning is the piety of thinking" (*Das Fragen ist die Frömmigkeit des Denkens*), as Heidegger deeply remarked. What he did not remark is that the same question can be posed in the modality of love of the true, or in the modality of aggression, even hatred. There are ways of questioning that lack reverence for the thing questioned. They are impious. They are an assault on the thing.

Perhaps we all have some experience of being so assaulted by a questioner like this. I can recall a person who would spit out questions at me at first meeting, and of course one retracted into oneself because of being so attacked by questioning. Look at the way lawyers ask questions: sometimes insinuatingly, sometimes seductively, and sometimes too with barely restrained violence. There are journalists like this too. It is as if what might be an act of wooing, perhaps in advance of love, has no finesse for the reserve of the intimate and instead strikes impatiently and directly, as if that were the way to truth. This approach does not leave the space of the between open. It does not allow anything to be itself and to reveal itself in its own more intimate ontological terms. There is no wooing, no seduction, but more the rape of an erotic assault; for, after all, wooing and foreplay are full of equivocity, while the direct movement to union may well be an impatient univocity without reverence for the reserve of the intimate.

I have suggested a wedding of determination and self-determination, insofar as the determination serves the self-determination as the secret end of the "project" of knowing as a whole. Whether this wedding is made in heaven is the question of scientism. Scientism, as it were, draws on the gift of heaven in the infinite openness and restlessness of the desire to know. The wedding of theory and practice: this wedding is the binding of the theoretical desire to know with the practical desire for knowhow. My question is: If this restlessness of curiosity is turned away from the wonder of being, is it not inclined to generate a kind of *counterfeit infinity*? In what form? Answer: In the form of an infinite restlessness that is not in search of the true object of its desire but of the infinitely repeated excitation of restlessness without end.

If this happens, we are in the business of producing the counterfeit double of our infinite desire. Call it: infinite desire to desire without the infinite. For without the infinite the desire mutates either into a venture into limitless exteriority or into self-circling self-excitation (perhaps these two are the same, at a deeper level). It is not infinite restlessness as a kind of intentional infinitude which still is open to the answer(ing) of the truly and actually infinite. The latter would precipitate wonder in the modes of astonishment and perplexity, but wonder as univocally determining curiosity alone cannot stay for this revelation of the true infinite. Restlessness without end does reflect the intimate infinitude marking our desire to know but here its intention is not to be true to the real but (in the second option above) to realize itself as self-exciting without inherent limit. It is more like Hegel's self-sublating infinite rather than the human being's infinitude between its own self-transcendence and transcendence as other.

The wedding comes today perhaps dominantly in the marriage of science and technology. This is, in principle, a catholic marriage, catholic as having a bearing on the universal, as there is a globalized and institutionalized character to this now. But, in light of the self-expansion of contracted curiosity, one has to ask if this is a project of a universal that gives expression to our will to be the sovereign of the whole. Sovereign of the whole: proximately by drawing on the desire for the universal of the drive to scientific knowing; less proximately and indirectly, because energized by the drive for technological sovereignty in the form of the superiority of our project of unhindered self-determination (again both in a practical and theoretical respect). Is the universal of this globalized universal a counterfeit catholicism? One has to ask too, calling on Pascal: Does not this universal reveal itself in the dominance of the *esprit de géométrie*, not the *esprit de finesse*? It is not the intimate universal where ontological intimacy does not eschew geometry but ties it back to the gift of originating astonishment.

This wedding draws from the original porosity and wonder as astonishment but it determines the porosity in terms of human power, which means the mutation of the porosity, perhaps even denial of it. This leads to the contraction of the opening of curiosity in the very claim to fulfill it further and more fully. Hence the counterfeit infinity.

Is something of this is reflected in economics as under the sign of will to power, not under the *oikos* of the home on earth we are to build for ourselves? Will the counterfeit curiosity destroy all domiciles? For after all, in the *domus*, the domicile of the *oikos*, must not intimate life be allowed to be, allowed to be in receptivity to its deepest originating ontological sources?

The matter touches on death and life, especially in their ultimate extremities: war and health, the one dealing with our killing machines that emerge as the expression of our endeavor to be, the other dealing with the suffering that is unavoidable at the extremity of that endeavor to be. One hates our porosity and *passio essendi*; the other tries to keep at bay the *passio essendi* that comes back again and again, in suffering, and in sickness, and in death, as the ultimate return of the patience of being, now in the shape of not-being, and at the threshold of the mystery that is our entry into posthumous porosity. Look at how for a century at least so much of the scientific enterprise has been conducted under the patronage of either the military-industrial complex or the pharmaceutical industry. These are mass formations of the marriage of theoretical and practical curiosity. Astonishment and perplexity get in the way of scientistic determinability and superimposing self-determination.

I wonder also if this contraction of curiosity in its limitless self-expansion is connected with our determination of the whole of being in the light of serviceable disposability. A totalizing of the useful produces the reign of serviceable disposability: things are made to serve our instrumental desire, and hence be serviceable, but when used, they are used up, and are hence disposable. This point has some implications for wonder in the modalities of astonishment and perplexity. There is something about them that is deeply and intimately beyond serviceable disposability. One aspect of their indispensable service is precisely the way they open up for us the dimension of the given *qua* given, prior to use, and beyond use. There is a transcendence to use of what strikes us into astonishment and perplexity. What is there is not there to be used up. Art can sometimes refresh original astonishment and perplexity.

What of our being religious? Our being religious is pluriform, but if we consider the idea of the superior other, granted in light of divine transcendence, the space between divinity and us will not be best served by limitless curiosity, oriented to determination or self-determination. If wonder, especially in the modalities of astonishment and perplexity prepare and keep purged our intimate porosity to the divine as the superior other, then all our efforts at completing the project of seamless self-determination, via our determination of being as other, are not only prone to failure, but are already themselves expressions of a hubris on our part. The project to succeed thus is already a failure. It is true that if one were familiar with the longer religious tradition, this project itself would have difficulty avoiding the name of pride, the primal sin. Our turn to ourselves as agents of complete self-determination—and surely this is part of the agenda of modernity—cannot but look with suspicion on any claims of superior otherness. As a consequence, our relation to God as such a transcendent other must be itself relativized, called into question, perhaps even liquidated, if its resistance to our autonomy is ineradicable. In so many words, this is curiously reminiscent of the project of the serpent in Eden and its seductive promise: you too will become as gods. There is a certain modernity that is in the business of trying to prove the serpent right.

If there is a secret form of tyrannical will to power behind the scientistic desire to reconfigure all of being according to its dictates of a certain globalizing univocity, the serpent of counterfeit wisdom is its secret seducer to the false whole of reconstructed creation. Such a reconstruction has the tendency to fall into de-creation rather than creation. For it is always parasitical on the gift of creation which it can never acknowledge as such, since its project of the perfect future is just fueled by the energy of this refusal of the given as such. Its "creation" is de-creation: another voiding of being. To convert from refusal to acknowledgment would be to allow the offer of the more original porosity to give itself again, with all the painful surprise of marvel, long since eschewed as the brand of one's humiliation by the superior other. Humility before the gift of being would have to come again in place of the guarded protection against the gift of goodness that is perversely experienced as one's own humiliation. The original wonder gifts us with the gift of being able to receive gifts. If it is contracted or mutilated in scientific curiosity, then we cannot accept any gift, we cannot accept anything as given, for it is not given on our terms, and hence it is a burden to be dismissed, incompatible with our status as self-sublating gods.

Is it surprising that instead of the perfected earth we have the despoliation of nature and the oncoming night of ecological catastrophe? We are making gardens of the earth into fetid dumps. And it is our violent intrusion into everything, with no reverence that lets things be as they are, that loves things even as they are, that blights the goodness of creation. The blight is like the bleaching of the coral reefs. Almost suddenly, the blank counterfeit is revealed, and the habitat of life is made a dead zone for creatures who would otherwise enjoy the bounty of the maternal sea.

Both the will to reconfigure the whole, and the ontological loss that threatens more and more to come as the destiny we impose on immanence, are long-term consequences of the infinite self-expansion of the contraction of curiosity: its mutation not only of the original wonder but in that mutation loss of original love of the given mystery of being. In scientistic curiosity we see then an exploitation of the porosity but in a contraction of its purer openness. In the exploitation of the purer porosity there is the loss of porosity, and its being overtaken by an irreverent will to power, especially in the useful form of serviceable disposability. A counterfeit infinity of the desire to know: does it really desire to know, or does it want to be number one, be the alpha being, in order to be the omega being? We can never be alpha beings because we are always seconds: we come after, because the alpha gives us to be, gives us to be as porosity to being other than ourselves. The true alpha being gives being to be, and not in the domineering form of imposing sovereignty—rather, in the gift of agapeic letting be: from surplus, not from a lack that has to counterfeit infinity to feel immanently in itself its own absoluteness. The true alpha is already fully itself: super-plus, overdeterminate, the generous infinity. Fully itself: even when it agapeically makes way by giving a way, and lets be kenotically, as if it were nothing in the way. All counterfeits come down to wanting to be it, but not in the reverent modality of wanting to be like God but in the irreverent usurpation of wanting to be god. The essence of scientism is thus at core religious. Its "project" is the construction as the graven image of our time: self-determined, self-enclosed immanence as the changeling of true infinitude. As secreting a counterfeit infinity its essence is idolatry.

4 ∽ Are We All Scholastics Now?
On Analytic, Dialectical, and Transdialectical Thinking

SCHOOLING PHILOSOPHY

What is Scholastic philosophy? The experts may say one thing but in the lay mind the image will be conjured up of church-dominated clerics juggling with abstractions remote from concrete life. The Scholastics were hairsplitting mandarins of the Catholic church, supine to Aristotle or Aquinas or some other authority. The modern inheritors of the Enlightenment will bridle at this. To them it is a smart to the dignity of autonomous reason to be subject, or to subject itself, to such traditional authority. The word "school" is important. One is referred to a group activity. There are no solitary Scholastics, though there are singular Scholastics. A school enables study in common, in community. Unkind observers might think of the masculine character of the gang—celibate clerics of high intellectual caliber, given to forensic debate with other alpha male logic-choppers. The goal of truth may be in mind but out of mind is perhaps the secret aim of establishing a pecking order of alpha intellects, a hierarchy. Celibate erotics become rational(ized) eristics. The *disputatio* ritualizes the contest of thought—the *agon* of analysis.

I report, I do not endorse. The historical experts will say this picture is to paint a fantasy and perhaps there is much in it of a resume of prejudices, but in many minds some such a picture has often lingered after the demise of Scholasticism.[1] Among important points not to be forgotten

---

1. The Webster dictionary associates "scholastic" with the "pedantic" and the "dogmatic." John Locke, *An Essay Concerning Human Understanding*, ed. Roger Woolhouse (Harmondsworth: Penguin, 1997), book III, chap. X ("Of the Abuse of Words"), speaks of "the several

are the following. The practice of thought by the Scholastics was integrated into a way of life more encompassing than just analytic thought. Pierre Hadot has reminded us that philosophy itself was bound up with a way of life in ancient times, but *mutatis mutandis* the point stands here too.[2] The permeability of thought and the religious is not to be neglected in understanding this way of life. In addition, the excellences of all of this are worthy of remembering. Josef Pieper, in his singularly engaging way, recalls us to the tremendously fertile and varied intellectual life that persisted for centuries under the banner of "Scholasticism."[3] There is the fact too that the form of communication of Scholastic dialectic embodied a kind of dramatic dialogue, a kind of intellectual theater of the *metaxu*, between reason and faith, freedom and authority, respect and contestation, one thinker and another, *scientia* and *sapientia*, the human and the divine, the divine and creation. There is a plurivocity about this intellectual theater of the *metaxu*, sometimes tilting more analogically, sometimes more univocally (I think of Abelard, for instance). The form of exposition of Aquinas: a question, with objections first stated, often with an impressive directness and a compactness that tries to get to the heart of the issue, then a response embodying the best the argument can bear, and finally, a reply to the objections, taking into account the sometimes dissident other. Artificial in one sense, yet also a tremendous distillation of the to and fro of dispute, the hither and tither of thought, the fertile *sic et non*, that arises from prephilosophical sources, and in the formal rubrics of an intellectual give and take seeks to offer a fully-rounded response to the perplexity at issue. There is a plurivocity in this theater where the drama of differences points beyond opposition to a truthful fullness.

---

sects of philosophy and religion [that] have introduced" words without meaning, so as to "cover some weakness of their hypothesis ... [they] seldom fail to coin new words, and such as, when they come to be examined, may justly be called insignificant terms." Who are the sects that do this? "The great mintmasters of this kind of terms, I mean the Schoolmen and Metaphysicians." In relation to words: "plain sense" as recession of the figures of analogy, coupled with forefronting of the univocal?

2. Pierre Hadot, *Philosophy as a Way of Life*, trans. Michael Chase (Oxford: Blackwell, 1995).

3. *Scholasticism: Personalities and Problems of Medieval Philosophy*, trans. Richard and Clara Winston (South Bend, Ind.: St. Augustine's Press, 2001). Etienne Gilson has a tender phrase for Scholasticism: "the honeymoon between theology and philosophy," a honeymoon which he sees as ending with the Condemnation of 1277. *History of Christian Philosophy in the Middle Ages* (New York: Sheed and Ward, 1955), 456.

Scholasticism, of course, is often identified with the Catholic church.[4] Yet, of course, there were Protestant Scholastics. We think of the Middle Ages but we find instances of Scholasticism in different forms through later history. One thinks of the rationalism of the eighteenth century with illustrious practitioners like Wolff and Baumgarten.[5] One thinks too of the renewal of Scholastic philosophy at the end of the nineteenth century, reflecting the exhortation of Pope Leo XIII, carried through under the influence of Cardinal Désiré Mercier. The Higher Institute for Philosophy at Louvain/Leuven, established through Mercier, was perhaps the major center for this revival. In the case of Mercier the debate with modern science was very important. Moreover, the study of medieval thought was not primarily or only historical but systematic. The intent was to develop a form of philosophy inspired by the great Scholastic thinkers, especially Aquinas, and with the aim of entering the lists of modern controversies. The point was not ghetto of thought but quite the opposite—the conviction that there was a truth to be thought and rethought—a truth, moreover, to be communicated outside the charmed circle of those more intimate with the original medieval sources. Over time this emphasis lessened and a more pluralistic Institute showed the influence of continental philosophy generally, with thinkers like Husserl and Heidegger and other phenomenologists being seriously studied. In due course the conviction diminished that some form of Thomism was a living philosophical option and was more or less replaced by high-class historical scholarship. One looks for a Thomist but often one finds an

---

4. This chapter was originally written in dedication to the memory of Fr. James McEvoy, last professor of scholastic philosophy at Queen's University, Belfast. A version was given as the keynote address to the autumn conference of the Irish Philosophical Society, at Queen's University on November 27, 2010. My title is to be seen in relation to the theme of the conference: "Convergences and Divergences: Philosophy in the Scholastic, Analytic, and Continental Traditions." In Belfast the Department of Scholastic Philosophy was originally established to serve primarily the philosophical needs of its Catholic students. Not long ago in Ireland Scholastic philosophy was the reigning establishment in the National University. When I was an undergraduate during the late 1960s and early 1970s, there was still a significant influence of Scholasticism. Prof. Brendan O'Mahony (a graduate of Leuven, as was his uncle, James E. O'Mahony, also professor of philosophy) practiced a form of teaching in University College Cork that mixed attention to a kind of moderated Scholasticism, with openness to both continental and analytic philosophy. Some of this teaching was influenced by the Louvain (Leuven) model.

5. Pierre Hadot also reminds us that Kant is concerned with wisdom in an ancient sense in *What Is Ancient Philosophy?*, trans. Michael Chase (Cambridge, Mass.: Belknap Press of Harvard University Press, 2002), 258–70.

expert. There seems to be more, so to say, "practicing Thomists" in the United States—those committed to some form of Thomism as a living option of supremely defensible philosophical wisdom.⁶

All this is by way of my own intimacy with some aspects of Scholasticism. That earlier neo-Scholasticism now seems dissolved, no doubt in reaction against the manual tradition of teaching Scholasticism. This seemed too much of a merely external way of doing philosophy: one had the answers before one even felt the force of the questions. Replaced by what? Has Scholasticism vanished or are we all, *mirabile dictu*, Scholastics now? I ask because when one looks at the two supposedly main "camps" of contemporary philosophy, the continental and the analytic, one sees something like this: on the one side, more and more of the hermeneutical Scholasticism of the text; on the other side, something like the Scholasticism of the technical or quasi-technical analysis. Let me remark on these two.

HERMENEUTIC AND TECHNICAL SCHOLASTICISM

To hermeneutic Scholasticism: Hermeneutics is a rich practice, or set of practices, but there are too many times when we find commentary on commentary on commentary. Sometimes one thinks that some texts have become canonical—for instance, Heidegger's *Being and Time*. I cannot count the number of theses I have read on *Sein zum Tode*. The refrain of Job's wife comes to resound: Curse God and die! And there is a minor industry in commentaries and handbooks and companions, mostly, I suppose, for graduate students. I am reminded of commentaries on the *Sentences of Peter of Lombard* that theologians tended to have to do in the Middle Ages. Heidegger is our philosophical Peter of Lombard. The commentary is, of course, a school exercise showing that the student can carefully read a text, as well as offer some intelligent observations. By the nature of commentary it is not always, or only rarely, a direct thinking about things. *Zu den Sachen selbst*, this was the original war cry of

---

6. There are also interesting crisscrossings. Louvain Scholasticism has had an influence in the United States and this faded influence of the dead generations still is spread. The Institute of Philosophy lives off shades of this former glory, even if this glory is past or passing. Not a few students come to Leuven or are sent because they have been told of its repute by teachers, some of whom still think of a time when Thomism was more in the ascendant.

phenomenology. Now "to the things themselves" has been hermeneutically overtaken by "to the texts themselves."

Of course, the thinkers to whom we keep returning were not just thinking about texts but about things. The great texts are not simply about other texts. They are about the great and elemental perplexities that no text will ever encompass entirely. Nor is any text self-authoring, self-authorizing. In some hermeneutical quarters one wonders if Aristotle's God, thinking thinking thinking, has been replaced by the Arch Sacred Scribbler: *texting texting texting*. What is worrying about this is that with it can come the muffling of a more direct address to the perplexities themselves, as well as a skirting of the systematics of philosophy. Hermeneutics offers a constellation of Scholastic skills, acquired through initiation into a school of reading. The novice must pass through various ritual points of passage—rites of initiation. All of this is often a matter of learning the specialized language of the insider where words become shorthand for things only the insider can understand.

This Scholastic nature was accentuated paradoxically by the hype of deconstruction. I mean hype as connected with *huper*—deconstruction as hyperbolic hermeneutics. To all appearances, deconstruction seems to be on the margins of Scholastic, academic philosophy. Nevertheless, when one tried to jostle one's way to the margins in the heyday of deconstruction, one was amazed to meet only crowds. The center was empty, the margins were crowded. You might say school was out. But outside, on the outside, the school reassembled. The margins made a new center. This was evident in the fact that while the rhetoric was the rhetoric of difference the practice was the practice of the same. Everyone spoke about difference but everyone spoke the same, said pretty much the same thing. I take this to be one of the temptations of a kind of Scholasticism, even indeed of exotic Scholasticism, as deconstruction often seemed to be. I can understand that a finesse for small differences can develops in all schools—small differences rather than difference with a big *D*. At a certain point intellectual finesse passes over into finicky conceptual parsing—or deconstructive overreading.

Of course, the heyday of deconstruction has now gone by. The bloom of revolutionary newness has worn off and old age brings weariness. I taught in America during the heyday of deconstruction, but recently on a visit I asked a colleague who was director of a Humanities Center about the presence of deconstruction in the literature departments. The answer I got was that the younger faculty now looked on the deconstructionists as the "old guys." Deconstruction was latterly the province of the "conservatives"! Time tells all. Settling into a school of sorts means also the inversion of novelty into something, alas, too *passé*. A new class of freshmen enters the school and the mantras of the older members become stale.

To technical Scholasticism: Sometimes in relation to such outcomes the analyst was inclined to say: "We told you so; we always knew that continental philosophy was 'wooly nonsense'—there you have it now." Perhaps the current return to Husserl (and Frege) is a reaction against this—even within continental philosophy itself. In the origins of analytic philosophy one can see a kind of revolt against such "wooliness." Issues and questions are to the forefront, not texts. We are offered redirection to problems. History and authority count for nothing in the assault of argumentative force. A problem-based orientation replaces a text-based commentary. Problems in principle are soluble if stated in the right form. Hence the need to state the problems properly. It may be that some problems are not genuine problems if our formulations produce pseudo-problems. Concern with the issues of language inevitably follows. In some forms of analysis, the equivocities of everyday usage, for instance, are seen as sources of possible confusion. We find this in the early history of analytic philosophy: we pursue an ideal logical language which would put univocal clarity in the place of the equivocities normally nested in sloppy everyday language. An analogous sloppiness is nested in traditional metaphysics. The problems of traditional philosophy are pseudo-problems. A cry of intellectual revolt arises against this mess of metaphysics. The revolt is braced by confidence in the successes of science and the precisions of mathematics. In philosophy too, where before confusion reigned, now purer techniques of analysis will create proper clarity.

I will come back to these issues but here I only note how as this movement takes shape it does take on more and more a Scholastic character. The practices of a kind of *forensic thinking* are not far from both Scholasticism and analytic thinking. I mean also to stress the needed *schooling* in analysis. Over time, and even though historical authority is eschewed, we find the *historical institutionalization* of certain practices of thought—and these are embodied in the social forms of education in the so-called best graduate departments. One notices that one has to learn the philosophical patois—the right way of talking—*the* ways of talking. It is true that these ways are now much more diversified than ever. Nevertheless, in the plural practices of analysis the goal often persists of putting precise univocity in the place of the initial wooly equivocity. Being initiated into the practice is a matter of passing successfully through the prestigious graduate school and getting the approved doctorate—becoming professionalized, that is to say, becoming *house-trained* in the ways of the school.

The continentals have regularly charged the analysts with being remote from the problems of life. The charge is not one they themselves always escape. Jonathan Swift failed to notice that besides mathematicians there are hermeneuticists on the flying island of Laputa. Is not this the charge—remoteness from life—that has recurrently being formulated *against Scholasticism*? Every school risks becoming a ghetto of insiders. There on the inside we understand each other but we do not care to communicate with the outsider. This is true between different schools, and it is also true between the school and the great unwashed surplus of nonphilosophical persons. This is a lamentable situation which can only bring philosophy into disrepute. I am not objecting to the technicalities of sometimes necessarily arcane discussions. But this surely has to be complemented by the voice of a wise sanity that restores thought to the flow of life as lived, or to the larger community within which the specialized school is situated. We schoolmen are privileged with a relative freedom from the more pressing practicalities of that larger life, but we are indebted to it, draw from it, and finally always return to it, as our deepest participation is in its enigmatic flow. One does not have to tell any genuine philosopher that this is true. Sometimes with us alas it is this that happens: the mountain groans under immense labors of professional heaving, be they hermeneutical or technical, and gives birth to the mouse of an inoffensive platitude.

Bound up with both forms of the new Scholasticism we find today a stress on the professionalization of philosophy. Young students are turned into academic scribes when they are barely out of swaddling commentary or first-order predicate logic. Publish and be professional—otherwise there will be no grants, no postdocs, no jobs, no promotions.

The graduate director baptizes young students as initiate scribblers under the sign of inputs and outputs. This is a very restricted notion of a school, to be sure—a factory for the production of publications read by a tiny number. Remarkable also is the stress on the article rather than the book. Articles are like science reports. A book shows an effort at more holistic thinking, shows the strengths, shows also the weaknesses in the stretch of mind involved in the lengthier form of writing. Who writes a real book today? Who reads? Books ask more "big picture" thinking, articles more piecemeal problem solving. There are programs where one can get a doctorate by publishing three or four articles in the "top" journals. Top: defined by self-selection, self-stipulation. Top: even to the self-congratulation of the insiders, and ultimately to self-satisfaction, intellectual smugness, and decay. We write for our "top" colleagues—our participation in larger life can go whistle.

To conclude this opening sortie: the exotic Scholasticism of the hermeneuticists and deconstructionists is matched by the technical Scholasticism of the analysts. In both there is an initiation into a practice of thought or writing—a school—a shared way of doing things. The danger is that we are buoyed up by the courage of crowds and the enigmatic resolve to address the elemental perplexities weakens. In allowing the school to do one's thinking there is a loss of the courage of philosophy. Professional success can quickly recess issues not textual, issues not problems. Yet there are more intractable perplexities that cannot come directly from texts or from technical thought.

ANALYTIC THINKING

In what now follows I turn to a somewhat more systematic consideration of three forms of thinking: analytic, dialectical, and transdialectical (as I will call it). To anticipate what is to come in the systematic terms I use: in analysis we find an oscillation between equivocity and univocity; in dialectic we find a self-mediation of these two and the constitution of a more embracing perspective, inclusive of the opposite sides of a question; in transdialectical thinking we find an intermediation of equivocity beyond univocity and dialectic, with metaxological finesse for nuances of otherness, not appreciated in univocity, and not properly minded in dialectic. Analytic thinking is driven by curiosity, dialectical by perplexity, transdialectical by the resurrection of originary astonishment which itself is more primordial than curiosity and perplexity, and hence more original than analysis and dialectic.

First to analytic thinking: here my interest is not in analytic philosophy and its many varieties but in analysis as a *constituent* part of philosophy itself. While analysis is not the whole of philosophy, nevertheless it is constituent of its plurivocal practice. Analysis in this sense is as old as philosophy itself but not identical with it, and is perhaps wider than the current practices of analytic philosophy. The situation is elemental: we are in perplexity before what exceeds our understanding, and this perplexing something is most often something complex. How deal with the com-plex? As noted earlier, the word "plexus" in "complexity" brings to mind a plaiting, a twining, an entanglement. That is to say, we encounter something intertwined, interwoven, or twisted together. We meet something intricate and difficult to unravel, something knotted that we must try to untangle. "Per-plex" contains the same sense of the plaited together. How to understand the complex that perplexes? By unknotting what is intertwined in itself. A knot is something to be untied and in the untying we hope to unbraid the different threads that make up its complexity.

One thinks of somewhat more formalized ways of unpleating the folds of a complex: for example, the diaeretic method in Plato's *Sophist*; the resolutive/compositive method in Aristotle's *Posterior Analytics*; of this method as taken over in terms of the composition and division of discursive thinking in Aquinas and other medievals; of the same method again as turned against Aristotelianism in Descartes's rules, the first two of which address the resolution of the complex into the more simple. Needless to say, one thinks also of diverse practices of linguistic analysis where we seem to be untying the knots of complex ambiguities. A consideration to be kept in mind: a knot is also something that ties things together—and perhaps the knot needs to be allowed to hold fast—a binding is not always something that puts one in a bind.

Analusis: the Greek word refers us to an unloosing, a releasing. *Analusis* also carries the connotation of a dissolution and a death. Analysis would then be a kind of *autopsy*. This suggests another metaphor: the butcher who cuts the carcass along the joints. Analysis follows the articulation of the organic being, and the jointure of the matter is laid out. Whatever we make of the image of the matter being dead—"we murder to dissect," in Wordsworth's famous plaint—what also comes to mind here is the image of the surgeon. The cutting activity of the surgeon is finally in the service of life. The point of surgery is to save life in the face of the sickness of life. Analysis might thus be like a therapy, a paring away of sickening distortions and a preparing for a new health, especially if there is something that takes hold in the organism that distorts the truer jointure of the thing. Analysis might seem to be the therapeutic surgery of thought and language. One sees this in modern analytic philosophy, probably more explicitly so at the beginnings of its unfolding when there was more anxiety to define the distinctive nature of what then presented itself as a new turn in philosophy.

I think of analytic thinking as addressing a perplexing matter which, as perplexing, is complex and lacking initially in the more fixed determination that allows us to get a clear hold on its constituents. Perplexity before the complex is hesitant about the equivocal "too-muchness" of the matter and by mustering a more *definite curiosity* about the constituents of the complex, there is a loosing of the knot. The unplaiting of the twists of the complex brings before the curious mind more univocal determinacy where before there seemed to be something bordering on indeterminacy or overdeterminacy. Analysis can be driven to transform an indeterminate perplexity into a more determinate curiosity of mind which takes hold of the matter in view, precisely by articulating the determinacies that compose the complex and that otherwise seem to melt into one another in an undifferentiated miasma.

One sees the gain in perspicacity that analytic thinking can bring as it replaces confusion with clarity, equivocity with univocity. But this cannot be the end of the matter. The issue is not just a matter of how, after analysis, we find our way to synthesis—though this is very important, if we are to avoid the infamous "murder to dissect." An initially undifferentiated puzzle is replaced by a more articulate differentiated sense of the puzzle, and the differentiation aids in the resolution or dissolution of the puzzle. But are all our perplexities only puzzles subject to univocal determination? If our perplexities are only a matter of mere puzzles, we already begin to suspect the visionary poverty of some practices of analysis. The question is whether there are perplexities that are not determinate or determinable puzzles. If there are, how are we to address them?

There is no question of rejecting analysis, but at certain crucial points we do more than analyze. We can begin to analyze the nature of analysis itself, and then we are pointed to something more than analytic thinking. We do this to make sense of the necessity of analysis itself and find that there is something at work more than any analytic technique. There is an ethos within which analysis is done, and which, at least in part, makes intelligible why the analysis is to be done, and why it is done this way. This ethos is not itself an instance of analysis. It is the originating occasion and milieu which gives rise to the perplexities, to the responses deemed appropriate to these perplexities, in this instance the transformation of perplexity into a curiosity that takes apart the complex. The originating ethos also shapes the purposes for whose sake the analysis itself is undertaken. In short, analysis takes place in the middle—in the midst of an ethos wherein problems are precipitated in a perplexity not initially analytic, an ethos which is always more than a set of problems. The ethos indeed may give rise to perplexity about the sources of intelligibility in a non-analytic sense, as indeed to perplexity about the end(s) of the process as a whole to which the analysis contributes. For in the end, purposeless analysis does not make much sense. We analyze "in order to …" The point of an analysis might be reasonable but its reason need not be analytic.

This means that our choice is not between analytic technique and surrender to unreason. There are forms of analytic reason but there are reasons for analysis for which analysis itself does not supply the reason. Once again we must think about the pre-analytic ethos of thought itself. This indeed is the everyday world, what the continentals call the *Lebenswelt*. The everyday world now, of course, also includes the developments of the sciences and technology. In our time science and technology have exercised huge influences on our reconfiguration of this ethos of everyday life. We have to presuppose a variety of pre-analytic identifications for any analysis to take place in that ethos. It is not coincidental that where some forms of analytic philosophy open an interest in the everyday, continental thought raises the question of the *Lebenswelt*. In either case, a non-analytic form of discrimination and discernment must already be at work. What do we do with that? Do we rationally reconstruct it because it is full of ambiguity? Or let it be in its own terms? The contrast of these two questions says something about the earlier and later Wittgenstein. In the earlier, we find the search for an ideal univocal language; in the later, we find a return to the equivocity of the everyday, the multiplicity of language games which are quite right in their own terms, and not in need of logical reconstruction according to the ideal of a univocal language.

If there is such a thing as pre-analytic intelligence, it is notable in our contemporary reconfiguration of the ethos of being how science and technology influence *the how* of our response to this already given ethos. Not surprisingly, contemporary analytic philosophy has often prided itself on its alleged precision, with its unprecedented emphasis on technical mastery. In the name of so-called conceptual rigor and clarity, it embodies the eschewal of all confusion and abhorrence of wooliness. It is an heir of the rhetoric of rational Enlightenment that seems to believe that traditional philosophical problems can either be solved or resolved or dissolved (as we know, sometimes by resort to quasi-mathematical technique).[7]

The dominance of analytic philosophy in the Anglo-American world as an academic school has sometimes meant that its diverse presuppositions are not always subject to scrutiny. There can be an unspoken assumption that this is how we do things, for a dominant philosophical school has a tendency to colonize other practices of philosophy. One sees this in the way, for instance, that the history of philosophy is reformulated in the light of contemporary analytic practice. The study of the ancients, say, the reading of Plato can be exhilarating in its own way but when reformulated in the favored vocabulary of the dominant group the results are not always inspiring. If the other is made to talk one's group language, the other is at a disadvantage and hence the more easily tamed or corralled. The challenge to us of other practices of philosophy is tamped down. Some problems are bypassed rather than addressed when they do not fit our terms. This can happen also in continental philosophy when certain traditional perplexities, such as those connected with God, are baptized as "ontotheology," and henceforth what amounts to a philosophically sanctioned silence about them is allowed to reign.

Again at issue is initiation into a practice of philosophy—a certain professionalization of thought—and this means playing by the rules

---

7. On the self-images of the philosopher as a technician and as a scientist, see William Desmond, *Philosophy and Its Others: Ways of Being and Mind* (Albany: State University of New York Press, 1990), chap. 1.

of the game to which we are enculturated by passage through graduate school and beyond. It must be said that not to ask about the practice and its presuppositions does finally amount to a philosophical weakness, indeed failure. The call may be to do analytic philosophy, not to reflect on what it is to do analytic philosophy; but this last matter is not a mere "meta problem." Philosophy is in the business of the most truthful self-knowledge possible. Otherwise we end with a Scholasticism of the dominant professional practice. Rorty's ironical sophism reflects this unwittingly: truth is what your colleagues let you get away with.[8]

There is the need for a reasonable account of analytic reason that is not itself analytic—there are other senses of reason. What offers determinate reason is not exhausted by determinate reason—there is something more. This is one reason why in relation to the everyday world or the *Lebenswelt*, thinkers have been driven to inquire as to the origins of analysis itself. One might want to offer a genealogy of analysis. Sometimes we are offered a quasi-Nietzschean genealogy: the origins of analysis are in terms of will to power, for instance. There can be something to this, obviously. In analytic thinking we are getting a handle on things, getting a hold—all with the intent of not being at a loss before the perplexity. We take apart what overcomes us. Why? To overcome what might otherwise overcome us, in its excessive "too-muchness." But if analysis has an origin in will to power, in what does Nietzschean genealogy have its origin? Will to power? Then the same question applies to it. Lesson? There must be another commitment to truthfulness not exhausted by will to power. Otherwise all genealogies of analysis are finally no different than the analysis itself, now accused of secret will to power, and then there is no basis for accusation.

I would argue that this must be one-sided. The reasonableness of analysis is emergent out of a non-analytic sense of reasonableness, but

---

8. Rorty might criticize analytic philosophy for retaining scientistic or positivistic residues, yet in the end he defers to the scientific orientation as an oracle of truth before which we must bow. His conversion to hermeneutical edification did not entirely root out the old Adam of modern Enlightenment. Rorty's celebrity was that of the apostate to the dominant guild. He was a renegade theologian whose apostasy brought unapproving quietness among the orthodox and a lot of tut-tutting, but roused jubilation among the unbelievers. Behold the great thing: look he has become like one of us, knowing Hegel and Heidegger. A prominent insider of the ruling sect has come to the outside, has come over to us. Let us kill the fatted calf and sing a *Te Deum* to hermeneutical edification.

this is not to be seen simply as the mask of a secret will to power. It is a non-analytic opening to what is. Perplexity and curiosity always show this opening, or take form in it. However finite we are, there is this prior openness, or else we could not know or say that we are finite. Will to power itself presupposes this porosity. There is a fundamental porosity of mind which later comes to determination in analytical form but which is prior to and exceeding analysis. The porosity is more intimate with the overdeterminacy of the ethos of being. I think professionalized analysis runs the risk of closing down that porosity. It often weighs it (down) with self-imposed conceptual chains. One thinks again of the later Wittgenstein as trying to escape these chains in his return to the ordinary—the pre-analytic context of analysis. Analysis serves as a non-analytic catharsis or release—an exorcism of concepts that bewitch us—and in the form of a precision of thought that is not simply a matter of technique. I would call this the renewal of a certain finesse. This is closer to something like the turn to the ordinary *logoi* that we find in Socratic dialogue. We turn to the words, to what people say ordinarily, seeking to *find the logos* in these *logoi*. But this dialectic is more than *diaeresis*. I will remark on this again later.

What do we do with the equivocities of the ordinary? I would say that Socratic dialogue is double: there is a turn to the ordinary *logoi*, which both respects and criticizes these *logoi*. By contrast, the Wittgensteinian practice seems more aimed at the bewitchments of the philosophers, and being freed from them. There is perhaps an element of a too one-sided reactiveness against such philosophical bewitchments—rather than the fuller finesse that knows there is no sanctification of the ordinary either. For common sense often is too infected with common nonsense. There are many and different "ordinaries": there is an Irish, there is a British, and they are not the same. There is a Russian "ordinary," for instance, which opens to a world like Dostoevsky's where astonishment and perplexity touch the ultimate exposures of human existence. There is an Oxbridge "ordinary" where dons converse in a world not replete with metaphysical perplexity or ontological astonishment, a world not overtly exposed to the extremities. In the return to the ordinary there is more than the ordinary and more than analysis also.

Likewise, the question of the end or ends of analysis is unavoidable. Here we are concerned with the purposes which analysis serves. One must say that mindfulness of the ethos of analysis must be turned into an *ethics of analysis*. Traditionally this was often put in terms of the problem of synthesis. We dissolve a complex whole or constellation into the parts, and the parts into parts—a kind of deconstruction of the whole. Not only do we call on some non-analytical recognition of the whole that is analyzed, but this recognition is non-analytic, although intelligent. How to recognize that we have completed an analysis? Or that we have reached the end? What do we see when the analysis is satisfactory? That this happens is undeniable but it is not itself an analysis. (This is related to what is called by some the "paradox of analysis.") We say: "Ah yes, I see the point, I *see* the point better now..." I think of Wittgenstein's metaphor: "Once I have exhausted the justifications, I have reached bedrock, and my spade is turned."[9] But what is analytic about such a metaphor? There are so many metaphors in Wittgenstein and we appreciate them but we appreciate them not because they are analyses but because they embody the pithy formulation of a surprising and striking insight. Utterances as enigmatic as Heidegger's stud Wittgenstein's writings. In the *Tractatus* one recalls the famous image of the ladder we must throw away, once having used it. When we are told there are things that cannot be *said* but that can be *shown* or that show themselves—surely we are at the limits of analysis? *Philosophical Investigations* offers another famous image (§309): "What is your aim in philosophy? – To show the fly the way out of the fly-bottle." What has the buzzing of a trapped fly got to do with conceptual analysis? It is a riddling image, more memorable than any concept. Its significance is not grasped by analytic thinking, and yet it is grasped, and grasped as signifying something of the point of analytic thinking. "The results of philosophy are the discovery of some piece of plain nonsense and the bumps that the understanding has got by running up against the limits of language" (§119). What bumps? Again we have memorable images, not univocal analyses. Scholarly careers have depended on these bumps and buzzings, and on the deciphering of their riddle.

I noted above how analytic philosophers sometimes direct the charge of "wooliness" at the thought of continental thinkers. I say "Your concepts

---

9. Ludwig Wittgenstein, *Philosophical Investigations*, trans. G. E. M. Anscombe (Oxford: Blackwell, 1953), §217.

are wooly"; but sometimes this really means "I don't understand you"; and this in turn means "You are not understandable"; which again in turn means "What you say is not intelligent, perhaps not even intelligible"; and why is this so? "Because I don't understand it"; "Why don't I understand it?"; "Because your concepts are wooly"—and *voilà*, the circle closes. But does not this mean: when I say you are confused, this conceals my confusion and does so with technical conceit? I see the tiny spot in your eye, I do not see the gross beam in my own. I only briefly note this paradox—the concept of "wooliness" is itself a wooly concept. There is no way to give an entirely univocal analysis of "wooliness." The standard against which wooliness is judged, and condemned, is itself wooly. One could not make use of it without presupposing some non-analytic sense of reasonable discernment. Mindful discernment can see some non-analytic reason in the very notion of the "wooly" itself—without being able to, or indeed needing to give a fully univocal account of what it sees.

The issue of ends is connected with the search for a balance of analysis and synthesis in earlier forms of analysis. We see this, for instance, in the ancient *sunagōgē*, or in Descartes's rule concerning enumerations so complete as to leave out nothing. Without some non-analytic sense of a whole it is hard to make sense of analysis as a whole. This something more at play, suggesting a sense of synthetic reason, will bring us to dialectical thinking: *an immanent holding together of the terms of analysis*, even when these terms seem to lead to breakdown, indeed to a falling apart of an integral account of things. To know that an analysis fails or succeeds presupposes the immanent working of a sense of togetherness of elements beyond analysis. This leads us back to the plaiting or twining together of elements in a complex, and with which perplexity always is faced, even when it cannot make sense of them. Dialectical thinking mediates some intelligible sense of the complex of this "holding together."

I would say that *trans-analytic thinking* is occasioned by the nature of analytic thinking itself. If analysis is an *unfolding* of what otherwise is plaited together, does not this unfolding point to a *dynamism* of thinking? Analytic unfolding suggests a pointing beyond itself of dynamic thinking. What is this dynamism and this beyond? However we answer this question, it is a pointing beyond what is emergent through an immanent analysis of analysis itself. There is a self-transcending motion of thinking that is impossible to fix finally in terms of a collection of analytic elements. We are forced to ask if there is not a pre-analytic and post-analytic sense of "the whole" inarticulately at work in analysis itself. Or if not of "the whole," certainly of the between, as I would prefer to put it. If so, how to think this "whole," how to move through this "between"? How does determinate thinking itself transcend from determination to determination? The transcending is not just another fixed determination. If we say all thinking is a fixation of determinations, we cannot think this transcending, and hence cannot made sense of the energy of thinking itself. This transcending would be a matter of determining, not determination. Dialectic has much to do with this motion, seen either as a motion of thought or a motion of being; a becoming of intelligence or a becoming of intelligibility; or a becoming *between* thought and being, *between* intelligence and intelligibility.

DIALECTICAL THINKING

One can see a continuity between analytic and dialectical thinking. Where the former tries to fix determinate thoughts, the latter sees a surpassing of thinking that is more than every fixation. Analytic thinking often lives off the fact that some determinacies are not compatible with other determinacies, and is impelled to think through and beyond contradictions. Dialectic takes over the energy of that "thinking through," moving thought into a space where the contradictory determinations can be thought together, in a many-sided framework where otherwise incompatible fixations can coexist, or be adapted to coexist. Analytic thought fixes univocal determinations; dialectical thinking understands how these determinations become unfixed, give way to other, not unrelated thoughts, though there is more than an equivocal flow of thought, for the flow is not formless flux but rather puts us in mind of claims like that of Heraclitus about the *logos* that runs through all things.[10] Dialec-

---

10. Heraclitus: "although all things come to pass in accordance with this *Logos*, men seem to be quite without any experience of it" (fr. 1). "We should let ourselves be guided by what is common to all. Yet, although the *Logos* is common to all, most men live as if each of them had a private intelligence of his own" (fr. 2). "The thunderbolt pilots all things" (fr. 64). "Although intimately connected with the *Logos*, men keep setting themselves against it" (fr. 72). I refer to the Diels-Kranz numbering of the fragments in *Die Fragmente der Vorsokratiker*, 6th ed., ed. Walther Kranz (Berlin: Weidmann, 1952). See chapter 9, below, for a fuller discussion of Heraclitus.

tical thinking can sometimes become arrested with the equivocal, even while claiming to be beyond the equivocal. But at its most truthful, it brings the equivocity of univocal analysis to a self-knowledge wherein the inseparability of univocity and equivocity points beyond them both, to an intelligent and intelligible mediation of univocity and equivocity. In this respect, it is attentive to the sense of the whole often out of focus with analysis as such. Not surprisingly, in this light, dialectical thinking is concerned to address the beginning and the end and by means of a mediating thought that seeks to bind up the whole.

Different forms of dialectical thinking encompass the entirety of the philosophical tradition, and hence my discussion here can only reflect what I take to be *some* essential considerations.[11] It is important to note the plurality of forms of dialectic. Perhaps relevantly, these forms occur within certain extremes. On one extreme, dialectic has been identified with a kind of specious reasoning; on the other extreme, it is said to be the method for overcoming all specious reasoning. Here are some forms. It tends to be identified with logic, as in the Middle Ages. Kant sees it as policing the boundary of warranted knowing and guarding against transcendental illusion. Hegel sees dialectic as passing beyond the antinomies of Kant to a higher speculative unity of opposed determinations of understanding. Marx claimed to demystify dialectic in relation to historical praxis. Dialectic is often viewed with suspicion by analytic philosophers who worry about specious reasoning and what they see as the pseudo-thinking of speculative idealism. We find an analogous suspicion in many of Hegel's continental successors. They revolt against what is said to be idealism's totalizing claim. Their revolt against Hegel tends to decry the entire tradition of metaphysics in similar terms. It is a fair question to ask if this does justice to the practices of dialectic connected to Socratic *maieutic*, or indeed to the description of the highest philosophical thinking in Plato's *Republic*.

This last puts us in mind of the previously mentioned diaeretic method that we find in Plato's *Sophist*. It raises again the intimate connection between the putative precisions of philosophical thinking and the putative equivocities of ordinary thinking. I illustrate with the case of Zeno, considered by Aristotle as the inventor of dialectic, a claim which

---

11. On the points made here more fully and on many other points, see *Being and the Between*, chap. 4.

Hegel endorses. As a disciple of Parmenides, Zeno came to the defense of the thesis of the One, and against the equivocities of the many (the double-headed many of common sense). He does not directly refute the equivocal many but inverts their views on their own terms. Deriving contradictory consequences from their views, showing the inherent self-contradictory nature of ordinary claims, a space is opened for the thesis of the One. Thus conclusions scandalous to common-sense equivocity are drawn from considerations of motion, as with the arrow or Achilles and the tortoise. From motion follows the impossibility of motion. What lies behind this practice of thought is the attitude that the seeming univocity of common sense is really infested with equivocity. Dialectic brings out that infestation, and in the process seems to discredit these univocities of common sense. Not surprisingly, this practice of dialectic creates suspicions of sophistry. There may be *philosophical* equivocities at work in this Zenoian practice of dialectic also.[12]

Perhaps we can say the following in more general terms. Dialectic has to do with an *immanent* development of thought and indeed a confidence that there is an inherent intelligibility unfolding in being, or in a process of becoming. Trust in an orientation to truth immanent in thought is correlated with confidence in intelligibility inherent in being or becoming, and the inseparability of thought and being. Interestingly, Zeno assumes the position of *the other*, and in an interplay with that other he brings thought around to something opposite to the articulated view of the other, in which what is secretly immanent is more expressly and intelligibly articulated. There is no need to impose any external standard on the other. If this is *analusis*, it is marked by an immanent dynamic and not by extrinsic imposition on a matter to be taken apart. There is an interplay of same and other, identity and difference. An intricate intelligibility comes to complex articulation in an immanent unfolding. Beyond the sameness of univocity and the difference of equivocity, beyond their oscillation, an intelligibility emerges that takes analysis beyond the motion of separation and returns thought to the complexity of many-sided intelligibility. Dialectical thinking is here obviously not

---

12. Kant on Zeno, *Critique of Pure Reason*, A502/B530: "Zeno of Elea, a subtle dialectician was severely reprimanded by Plato as a mischievous sophist who, to show his skill, would set out to prove a proposition through convincing argument and then immediately overthrow them by other arguments equally strong."

the opposite of analytic thinking, but rather a riding of the wave of dynamic thought that is actually at work in analysis, though often analytical thought thinks of itself as fixing a process in terms of cut-and-dried determinations. There is more than cut-and-dried fixity, more than dissolving flux. There is a thinking and an intelligibility that is dynamic. What I am here saying is not Parmenidean but closer perhaps to what Heraclitus insinuates concerning the *logos* in all things.[13] A more ultimate sameness of univocity seems to be Zeno's goal as a Parmenidean. Here I stress the dynamic of the activity of thought, even though that dynamic is often hitched to a goal that seems to want to transcend dynamism.

This is not to deny a certain proximity of equivocity and dialectical thinking. One notes certain uses of dialectic for essentially *negative purposes* such as were evident, for instance, in antiquity with the sophists. The sophists were often virtuosi of a dialectical *technē* that could be put to the services of *any* point of view, making the weaker appear stronger, the stronger weaker. The dialectic could be turned into an instrumentalized strategy of thought that could be directed to contradictory ends, like truth and deceit, or justice and the unjustified exoneration of the wrongdoer. We come across again a certain doubleness with the practice of dialectic: specious reasoning and the very heart of reason itself.

This *double possibility* for dialectic is significant. In some deployments dialectical thinking can camouflage a will to power to dominate the other or the opponent. This is a charge sometimes laid against *all* dialectic by contemporary continental philosophy, but to put it thus is to put the charge too coarsely. Throughout the longer tradition the temptation to put dialectic to a more equivocal employment was understood. I am thinking of how both Plato and Aristotle took pains to dissociate a truer dialectic from dialectic in the services of a more instrumentalizing, or even tyrannical orientation. A strife of thought is at stake with dialectic, and the strife can turn to conquering the other rather than pursuing truth in common. When Plato draws our notice to the eristic uses of reason he was warning against this abuse of dialectic, an abuse most in

---

13. Heraclitus (fr. 10): "The bones connected by joints are at once a unitary whole and not a unitary whole. To be in agreement is to differ; the concordant is the discordant. From out of all the many particulars comes oneness, and out of oneness comes all the many particulars." See above on analysis, jointure, and the butcher.

evidence in the absence of a ballasting ethical wisdom. The desire to triumph over the other in eristic argumentation instrumentalizes our mind as a means to domination. True dialectic must be free from this instrumentalization. Nietzsche was by no means fair in charging dialectic as masked will to power.

This is an old issue. Aristotle attacks the sophists in *De sophisticis elenchis* in order to free the use of dialectic from the abuse. Generally, he thinks of dialectic as dealing with the scrutiny of premises that are generally accepted, or of premises that are probable, or generally accepted as persuasive. Dialectic also has a function in intellectual training. It is not a method of demonstrative knowledge which offers valid deductions from true and self-evident premises. It has value for arguing with others in terms of their presuppositions and premises. It helps us, Aristotle importantly says, in our approach to the first principles of demonstrative science, principles that are not themselves demonstrated or demonstrable. The ultimate principles of sciences cannot be approached within the terms of the determinate science itself, as these principles are prior to and presupposed by the determinate science. These principles are to be approached through the discussion of the generally held opinions—to do this is a proper function of dialectic. Thus in *Topics* 101b3–4, dialectic offers "a process of criticism wherein lies the way [path] to the principles of all inquiries."

I take this to be, among other things, an indication of the limits of analytic thinking. It can be taken to acknowledge, so to say, the other to determinate intelligibility that is not, however, simply unintelligible, because without these principles demonstration could never be demonstrative. Determinate demonstration is made possible by ultimate principles that are not themselves univocally demonstrable. While there are many implications to this, I will just note that a thinker like Hegel rightly saw something of the importance hinted at here. One might put it thus: there is a *determination process* more ultimate than *determinate products*. Further, analytic thinking cannot do justice to this determining process as such, because it is defined as one of its products. There is a dynamism of self-transcending to thinking and this is more than a series of fixed determinations, more even than any set of formal rules that are said to govern their connections. In Hegel's case, the systematic determinations of formal logic will not do justice to the process of determining as other to fixed determination. This is a major reason why he thinks that a "dialectical logic" is needed.

Hegel claimed that Kant's discovery of the antinomic character of reason was here ripe with a significance Kant himself did not pluck. Kant says that ancient dialectic was always the logic of illusion (*Logik des Scheins*, in *Critique of Pure Reason* A61/B85–86), though this misrepresents the variety of ancient views. He is concerned with the critique of what he calls dialectical illusion. Transcendental dialectic deals with the illusions that inevitably arise when we try to surpass the limits of experience, purely by understanding. There seems to be something unavoidable about such transcendental illusions, and it is not clear that we can dispel them definitively. The antinomic character of reason suggests that reason inevitably comes to an ultimate impasse. For Hegel these *aporiai*, as we might also call them, are not unsurpassable. At this limit, thinking opens into the space beyond determinate thought, and in answer to Aristotle's dialectic as a path to the principles of all inquiries, discovers itself as *self-determining*.

We might say that dialectical thinking need not oscillate between univocal determinacy and equivocal indeterminacy, as we suspect Kant did. There is a more primal dynamism of thinking at work, even in this oscillation. This dynamic of dialectic is made possible, for Hegel, by another side of Kant that also takes us to the edge of determinate univocal intelligibility, though here from the side of the self, and not, as in Aristotle, from the side of being. This is Kant's sense of the transcendental: *self as a process of synthesizing* prior to all determinate analyses and syntheses. We are asked to consider the very dynamism of thinking as a determining activity within minding itself. Kant's "deduction" of the transcendental unity of apperception is not to be thought of as just a formal logical deduction. It is marked by a regressive movement toward what exceeds determinate form. In Kantian terms, we are seeking the source of the formal intelligibility of the categories and their unification with the manifold of sense constituting our ordered experience of the world. The more original source of the formal and the determinate is not a form or a determination. It is thinking as self-determining.

Hegel held himself to have transcended the *aporiai* of Kant's transcendental philosophy in his speculative thinking; nevertheless, the latter is made possible by the former. Hegel does not offer us a triadic formalization of thesis, antithesis, and synthesis (this is more Fichtean than Hegelian, as scholars recognize). There is a passing of opposites into opposites where contradiction is not so much denied but made to assume an *enhanced role* as a way to truth. Comparing Zeno, Kant, and Hegel, we might say: Zeno exploits the truth-claim of the other to show its untruth, and so mediately leads us back from the many to the One. Kant brings us to a point of rational undecidability: both sides of an antinomy might be true, might be false and so the ultimate truth must be left undetermined. Hegel sees that both sides might be true, even in their being false; indeed the falsity of each might contribute to the truth of the other. Rather the truth is shown in a reciprocal implication of the true and the false. The process of this mutual implication only reaches *the* truth in the true as whole. Then the one-sidedness of different antitheses has been transcended in the absolutely self-mediating totality. Dialectic articulates the internal instability of partial truths, false in their truth because partial, yet true in their falsity because the part dynamically points beyond its own internal instability to a more complete determination of truth. All of being will be said to be dialectical by Hegel: nature, history, God. When Hegel claims to articulate the logical necessity in all this, his speculative dialectic purports to offer the *logos* of the whole.

TRANSDIALECTICAL THINKING

I distinguish this dialectical *logos* of the whole from a plurivocal *logos* of the *metaxu*. The latter is a metaxological wording of the between, a *logos* of the *metaxu* that calls forth a philosophizing that might be called transdialectical. Its desideratum is to do justice not only to the inexhaustible otherness of the between, but to the communications of transcendence as other that exceed immanence closed in on itself. I would speak of transdialectical rather than postdialectical thinking. I briefly suggested in chapter 1 how "post" is more of a temporal qualifier, while there is something more systematic at stake in "trans." A remark on both the historical point and the systematic is needed. The justification for using the term "post" concerns how post-Hegelian philosophy, philosophy after Hegel's heyday, is marked by revolt against the Hegelian practice of dialectic, or by efforts to adapt or modify it for non-Hegelian purposes. We find this in both continental philosophy as well as analytic, with these now understood with reference to the two contemporary "schools."

To the continental post: I repeat how Merleau-Ponty notes the debt to Hegel incurred by almost all the strands of contemporary philosophy, among which he mentions Marxism, phenomenology, and existentialism.[14] Often, in fact, an aspect or significant side of Hegel is taken over to scold or "overcome" the same Hegel. One of the *disjecta membra* of what Hegel himself claims to be a healthy organic body is used for anti-Hegelian, or post-Hegelian purposes.

To the analytic post: The historical narrative that defines the initial sense of identity of analytic philosophy has its origins with G. E. Moore and Bertrand Russell and their turn against the idealism of thinkers like T. H. Green, Bernard Bosanquet, J. M. E. McTaggart, and F. H. Bradley, all of whom were dominant figures at the end of the nineteenth century and the beginning of the twentieth. Russell reacted to Bradley proximately and was himself once a kind of idealist, but Hegel (and Hegelianism generally) becomes the bogeyman whose name is henceforth uttered only to sneers.[15] I would have to add a note on the *post-analytic*: the still not entirely unexorcised ghost of Hegel seems to rise again; but more on that below when I ask about deschooling dialectic.

Transdialectical thinking better expresses the systematic rather than just the historical point, given that "trans" indicates a beyond or a going beyond, and it is questionable if Hegelian dialectic is faithful to both the going beyond of thinking as well as the beyond of thinking. This is not

---

14. Merleau-Ponty, *Signs*, 63. Hegel was hugely influential in France from the 1930s onward through Alexander Kojève's lectures on the *Phenomenology of Spirit*, influencing, among others, Maurice Merleau-Ponty, Jacques Lacan, George Bataille, and Raymond Aron. Forty years later the anti-Hegelian reaction turns to Nietzsche, and we might think of Michel Foucault's opening lecture at the Collège de France in 1970 (speaking of his debt to Jean Hyppolite): "our age, whether through logic or epistemology, whether through Marx or through Nietzsche, is attempting to flee Hegel." *The Archaeology of Knowledge*, trans. A. M. Sheridan Smith (New York: Harper and Row, 1976), 235. Gilles Deleuze in *Nietzsche and Philosophy*, trans. Hugh Tomlinson (New York: Columbia University Press, 1983), is unequivocal in profiling Nietzsche as the absolute opponent of dialectic; for Deleuze there is to be no compromise between Hegel and Nietzsche.

15. See Peter Hylton, *Russell, Idealism, and the Origins of Analytical Philosophy* (Oxford: Clarendon Press, 1990). It should be acknowledged that there is great diversity within analytic philosophy in relation to metaphysics, whether antipathetic or sympathetic. See Aaron Preston (ed.), *Analytic Philosophy: An Interpretive History* (New York: Routledge, 2017); the stress of the contributors in this volume is on the role of interpretation in analytic philosophy treated as a tradition.

to deny that there *is* a going beyond of thinking in Hegel. Nevertheless, because this is an immanent transcending, in the end there is no "beyond" in a sense other to, or more than, the immanent transcending of thinking. There is no overdeterminate sense of otherness and transcendence that finally does not submit without remainder to the appropriating power of immanent dialectical thought. Transdialectical thought is not antithetical to dialectic but looks at the movement of (inter)mediation differently. There is a "trans" of thinking in the middle, a passage in the between, but in intermediation with what is other to thought thinking itself. The "trans" opens a plurivocal intermediation with the other to thought thinking itself. It also allows metaxological thought to look again with hermeneutical generosity on earlier practices of philosophical dialectic, where mindful porosity to the "more" of transcendence as other is less sealed off than in the immanent categories of a modern rationalistic system.

I asked before if Hegel's own practice of thinking manifests an *equivocal dialectic*: what he took as a speculative unity of the opposites (say of immanence and transcendence, or the human and the divine) equivocates on their unity which itself then soon splits in terms of the rival demands of the right and the left Hegelians. There is an internal instability already there in Hegel's speculative unity distributed between sameness and otherness—an equivocation on otherness, a prioritizing of sameness. Some instability is hard to avoid if the issue is the *movement between* identity and difference, and such movement can be balanced or it can be unballasted. It is no easy matter to attain the proper poise between them.

One way to approach the point is in terms of the contrast of two practices of dialectic: dialogical dialectic *à la* Socrates and Plato, systematic dialectic *à la* Hegel. The dialectic of Hegel is always a self-determining dialectic. One sees different possibilities in the Socratic-Platonic practice of dialectic. Hegel's dialectic is not truly dialogical in the Platonic sense, where there is not only an ever renewed openness of dialogue, but there is also an erotic openness to the beyond, to the transcendence of the Good as other to our own self-transcending. An immanent dialectic, it is not entirely immanent but rather is porous to what exceeds immanent determination. Metaxology as transdialectical thinking is more Platonic than Hegelian with respect to keeping open the porosity of philosophical eros to transcendence as other. Interestingly, many anti-Hegelian post-Hegelians are often deeply in agreement with Hegel on this score. That is to say, they are anti-Platonic, in claiming to be entirely immanent in their view or in their practice of philosophy. They may deconstruct the Hegelian totality but they share with Hegel the finally non-negotiable commitment to immanence as such. I take Deleuze to give expression to this, even though he is sharply critical of Hegel from a Nietzschean point of view. As a philosopher of immanence, he is in complete agreement with Hegel. We might think of Spinoza as the founding father of modern immanence, but for Deleuze to cite him again, Spinoza is the "Christ of the philosophers," and so more a redeemer rather than a founding father. In any event, it is not unexpected if a family relation on immanence should turn up between Hegel, Nietzsche, and Deleuze himself.

This equivocity of speculative-dialectical thinking can be looked on in terms of the contrast of the open and the closed. Dialectical thinking points to dynamism, and this dynamism seems to be open to the future. By contrast, the speculative side of Hegel seems to lead to absolute unity or the closure of system. It is this latter which is most criticized, and in its place we are sometimes offered a form of dialectic, without the system. One can find something like this in Marx's use of dialectic, though he was in search of the necessary intelligibility of economic system(s). We also find it in some recent interpretations influenced by Derrida and deconstruction.[16] We can also find an *equivocal anti-dialectic* which, as equivocal, has some relations to negative dialectic, and again without the system.[17] On one side of this line we might cite either Kierkegaard or Nietzsche, on the other side, someone like Adorno.

One can see the point but I think the issue of the equivocity must be addressed at the systematic level. It is not enough just to uncouple dialectic and system and not consider that something about the form of self-mediating dialectic brings us to the system. Without more deeply reformulating the sense of dialectic we are going to be pushed again in that direction, back into Hegel's arms. The meaning of dialectic and

---

16. I am thinking of Catherine Malabou, *The Future of Hegel: Plasticity, Temporality and Dialectic*, trans. L. During (London: Routledge, 2005); and Karin de Boer, *On Hegel: The Sway of the Negative* (New York: Palgrave Macmillan, 2010).

17. I treat of these themes, among others, in *The Intimate Strangeness of Being: Metaphysics after Dialectic*.

its practice has to be revisioned in terms other than the Hegelian way where the rhythm of relation between self and other, identity and difference, always dominantly closes on a more inclusive sameness or unity. This does not mean giving up on the systematic side of philosophical thought, though it does mean a distance from claims to possess the system as an entirely autonomous self-circulation of encyclopedic thought. This means returning to revise the "dia" of dialectic in the direction of an open "dia" of a more dialogical dialectic. A reason I prefer the locution of the *metaxu-logos*—wording the between—is that it entails no denial that we may also require analytic univocity, finesse for the equivocal, and a dialectic of strife and striving. But there is more at play in the porous between than in all these possibilities. Indeed they are enabled to be what they are by virtue of their secretly drawing forth some of the rich promise of the between. To repeat: wording the between is plurivocal.[18]

One might suggest that one of the things we have been dealing with, whether we reside on the analytic side or the continental, is the aftermath of the self-inflation of idealistic thought. This led to a rational bubble which in time burst, leading to a painful deflation, and a long recession of reason, even to a depression, or certainly a diminution of our confidence in reason. In the wake of Hegel's post-Kantian rationalism (rationalism itself a kind of Scholasticism), we are still suffering from the depression of reason. Something of this depression can be seen in the Scholastic apotheosis of the everyday platitude parading as a superior clarity. The self-determining subject of idealistic reason has become the sometimes abject and self-lacerating nonself of postmodernism, with brief flares of ecstasy flashing out of its fervent Dionysian dismembering. We need a new confidence of reason somewhere between the over-self-confidence of modern rationalism and idealism, the studied overcaution of analytic ordinariness, and the abjection of postmodern antirationalism.

Transdialectical thinking takes issue with the modern ideal of autonomous thought, so far as this leads to a self-determination wherein openness to the other of thought is either rejected, or subordinated, or appropriated, or reconfigured, or passed over, or even exploited with-

---

18. See my essay "Wording the Between," in *The William Desmond Reader*.

Are We All Scholastics Now? 153

out crediting it.[19] I will briefly make the point in terms of the equivocal relation of philosophical thought to its significant others, especially art and religion. Among the things required by transdialectical thinking is a metaxological rethinking of what Hegel denominates under "absolute spirit," within which fall art, religion, and philosophy. There is something in all three which is transdialectical, and their dialogical relation is not just a matter of a speculative *Aufhebung*. It is in the *movement between* them that the most challenging and deep perplexities emerge. The otherness of art, the transcendence of religion, both reemerge in this between.

Instead of self-images of the philosopher as scholar, technician, or scientist, the figures of the poet and priest become important.[20] I think of Heidegger and the dialogue of poet and thinker. The poet here is not a post-Kantian specialist of aesthetic experience. He is a sacral figure, sacerdotal in the way of Hölderlin. The poet has to do with the holy. This is the old quarrel of poetry and philosophy perhaps, but it is not the same quarrel as in Plato's finding for the philosopher and Nietzsche's inversion in favor of the poet. It is a family quarrel, even a lovers' quarrel. The between space is irreducible, and in this dialogue both are in the middle. Philosophy is challenged to reformulate its own identity in that between.

Then there is the abandoned condition of religion, often doubly abandoned by the intellectuals. This is not entirely the fault of the religious. Deeply ingrained in the modern and to a degree the postmodern is at worst a hostile, at best an equivocal attitude to religious transcendence. In light of the postmodern stress on otherness as such, religious transcendence at least must be considered in its importance. Transcendence is not the problem that Hegelian dialectic made it out to be. This is more a problem with that version of dialectic than the other way round. The transdialectical will dovetail certainly with the turn to religion in the continental tradition. I would speak of a new poverty of philosophy.[21]

---

19. Recall again how beyond the acme of thought thinking itself in Hegel, thought thinking the other of thought thinking itself emerged variously with Marx, Kierkegaard, Schopenhauer, Nietzsche, Heidegger, and other thinkers of the twentieth century. Worth noting again is something of a revival of the study of Schelling among postmodern thinkers. The other to thought thinking itself is at stake, the "indivisible remainder" exceeding the system of idealism. A tie to Spinoza still binds Hegel and Schelling, for each is in love with an immanent God, even though each thinks also in the space of a Christian economy of spirit.
20. On these self-images see *Philosophy and Its Others*, chap. 1.
21. On this see my *Is There a Sabbath for Thought?*, chap. 3.

The field of metaphysics, too long lying fallow, can be cultivated for new shoots of promise. The agapeic spirit of true astonishment can grow out of postmodern perplexity.

DESCHOOLING DIALECTIC: WITTGENSTEIN OR HEGEL AGAIN?

What about our relation to the *equivocities of the everyday* in transdialectical thinking? Will it be a further twist on Hegel or will it be what I will call a *deschooling* of dialectic? I would argue for the latter in the sense of a release of thinking from merely Scholastic containment and its return to the *metaxu* of being. Such a metaxological philosophizing, while at home in the systematics of thought, opens to what exceeds system, namely, the ethos of life that sustains the search for systematic connections in the first instance. It seems to me that contemporary philosophy gives some signs of both these possibilities.

Thus while the place of Hegel in the narrative identity of analytic philosophy is negative, there has been talk of a post-analytic philosophy, indeed postphilosophical philosophy wherein Hegel plays a diffidently returning role. Two figures prominent in this regard are Robert Brandom and John MacDowell.[22] The former draws intelligently from Hegel's *Phenomenology*, pointing toward something not unlike a version of objective idealism (not absolute idealism); the latter develops a position closer to idealism in *Mind and World*. MacDowell offers an account of American philosophy in a trajectory between Quine through Sellars to Rorty and Davidson and then at the end of the process we seem to have to come again into territory that looks a lot like the neglected land of Hegel. Hegel seems irrepressible.

Thus also Richard Rorty once claimed that the question for the future of analytic philosophy was: "Who now is going to teach Hegel?" In some ways this was a taunt to the analysts—a dare to invite the bogeyman into the parlor. It was also in his eyes a step beyond analytic thinking, toward what he termed edifying philosophy, philosophizing with a kind of hermeneutical (and ironical) character. He spoke of philosophy's place

---

22. Robert Brandom, *Reasoning, Representing, and Discursive Commitment* (Cambridge, Mass.: Harvard University Press, 1994); John MacDowell, *Mind and World* (Cambridge, Mass.: Harvard University Press, 1994).

in the conversation of mankind. The phrase was taken over from, while adapting, Michael Oakeshott's reflection on "poetry's place in the conversation of mankind." One of the self-images invoked by Rorty then was the "strong poet" (the other was the "utopian revolutionary"). Obviously the Hegel of the system was not embraced by Rorty. Nor was it quite the Hegel of dialectic, understood as a systematic practice of thought which has promise to address some of the *aporiai*—if not limits—of analysis, particularly regarding origins and ends, ethos, presuppositions and purposes. It was a historicist, hermeneutical, even ironist Hegel. Be that as it may, I once invited Rorty to a conference of which I was the organizer on the theme "Hegel and His Critics." His answer was a polite demurral, and the confession: "I know nothing about Hegel."[23] Whether this was a form of *docta ignorantia* I cannot say, but Rorty's version of postdialectical philosophy would not be (as he put it) philosophy with a big P but philosophy with a little p. Big P philosophy is that of someone like Plato, and I would say, Hegel. Is the little p a legacy of ordinary language philosophy? One might be inclined to say that Rorty can have his little p. One would rather keep the big P, even if it means still having to wrestle with Hegel's system.

I propose that we take Wittgenstein as an example of deschooling dialectic. Why? Our metaxological task is not to "improve" the ordinary by means of abstract univocities. Equivocal though it be, there is rough work already going on in the ordinary, fulfilling in itself without need of a higher or purer logical reconstruction. In the eyes of some on the continental side, Wittgenstein often is taken to be very present in analytic philosophy but the story seems somewhat more blurred. I recall Stanley Cavell once saying in conversation (in almost an echo of Rorty's question): "Who is there now to teach Wittgenstein?" He was referring to a perception of the current state of analytic philosophy wherein the groundswell of a new quasi-scientism might be detected. The unsystematic character of the later Wittgenstein's observations, as well as worries

---

23. The results of the conference saw the light in William Desmond (ed.), *Hegel and His Critics: Philosophy in the Aftermath of Hegel* (Albany: State University of New York Press, 1989). John Dewey was a great hero for Rorty whose pragmatism he would resurrect as neo-pragmatism. Dewey was a Hegelian before becoming a pragmatist, and always admired Hegel's *Phenomenology of Spirit*. Dewey's pragmatism was a naturalized Hegelianism without the Hegelian absolute.

about the implications of various forms of scientism, find not enough echo in such an ethos of analytic philosophy. Cavell bemoaned that.

There is a kind of haunting again by the figure of Hegel. I like the following story about the older Wittgenstein, walking in the Phoenix Park in autumn 1948, in conversation with his Irish friend Drury, whom he had dissuaded from becoming a professor of philosophy, from entering "the profession," as we now say. Drury asked him: "What about Hegel?" Wittgenstein:

> No, I don't think I would get on with Hegel. Hegel seems to me to be always wanting to say that things that look different are really the same. Whereas my interest is in showing that things which look the same are really different. I was thinking of using as a motto for my book a quotation from *King Lear*: "I'll teach you differences." [Then laughing:] The remark "You'd be surprised" wouldn't be a bad motto either.[24]

The story reflects what might be called the pluralism of the later Wittgenstein, developed in reaction to the will to univocity of scientism and positivism, and shaping the younger Wittgenstein. One understands the emphasis. Everyday responses can have about them something quite right, requiring no reconstruction in a more logically coherent univocity. Ordinary ways often have an ear for nuances that do not need the artificial hearing aids of a scientistic or philosophical theory. Such theories can garble what calls to us, clog our ears, and muffle the music of everyday life. "Return to the ordinary" might mean the dismantling of the abstractions of an ideal univocity, constructed out of the ordinary but in a fugue state about their own origin there.

"I'll teach you differences." One might see this teaching of differences as a school for the deschooling of dialectic, and hence as an education in transdialectical thinking. Beyond the closure of the Hegelian system, you would be surprised at what happens in the midst of things, in the between of being and its intimate strangeness. *To on legetai pollachōs*: why

---

24. In M. O'Connor Drury, *The Danger of Words and Writings on Wittgenstein*, ed. D. Berman, M. Fitzgerald, and J. Hayes (Bristol: Thoemmes, 1996), 157. Transdialectical thinking cannot absolutize either sameness or difference, for it is the *interplay* between sameness and difference that concerns it. In the introduction to *Philosophy and Its Others* I described my view as somewhere between Hegelian holism and Wittgensteinian pluralism. We may not have the self-certainty of a univocal or dialectical absolutism, but this does not mean we must settle for something like Richard Rorty's chirpy relativism, not to say, cheerful nihilism.

not see Wittgenstein's emphasis on the plurality of forms of life or language games as a surprising variant on Aristotle's dictum that being is said in many senses? I would add that Wittgensteinian pluralism recalls an earlier practice of dialectic already mentioned, namely, the Socratic-Platonic approach, an approach with promise of an openness to otherness suggestive of transdialectical thinking. Of course, an established view of the Socratic-Platonic approach sees it as unrelentingly hostile to the ordinary—we must transcend the everyday opinions and their equivocity, and have a more univocal *epistēmē* that conquers confusion. It is true that there is a transcending movement in the Socratic-Platonic practice of dialectic, but this occurs in the ethos of the ordinary, where the thought of the extraordinary emerges. The guiding examples of Socrates all spring from the world of common sense, and our philosophical conversations never quite renege on a trust that there is something at work more ultimate than common confusion, and to which the philosopher must give mindful ear. A new mindfulness, born of attention to what the *logoi* reveal, is needed, a mindfulness flowering in attention to the suggestive equivocities of ordinary univocities.

The Platonic dialogue enacts a plurivocal practice of philosophizing in which there is both the schooling of dialectic and the deschooling. Hence we find analytic, dialectical, and transdialectical thinking, and all with essential reference to the *metaxu* of life as the ethos wherein all thought comes to articulation. Plato was a metaxological thinker and as such also a philosopher of the equivocal. Philosophical thinking must move around in the equivocal, and get its bearings from the differences manifest in *doxa*. We can see Socrates's turn to the *logoi* as a sign of his conviction that what people say is the sediment of ambiguous truth, and is not necessarily a defect. The dialogical emergence of philosophical truthfulness from attention to *doxa* witnesses to a vigilance to the equivocity of the ordinary. We must learn from the wisdom of the ordinary, even while on guard against its possible corruptions. The goal is not pure univocity but a more metaxological dwelling in the equivocal. Dialogue dramatically enacts the truth of the equivocal—without reduction and falsely fixed univocities. We must pass into and through these ambiguities to gain direction to the more ultimate truth of the ideas and the Good. Our approach to the One cannot neglect attention to the many.

One thinks also of the implication of Parmenides's stunning question to the younger Socrates (*Parmenides* 130c7–d2): Are there ideas of things like hair, mud, and dung? The question is posed in the company of Zeno whose dialectic we have earlier met. To me Parmenides's reply delicately rebukes the callow philosopher who averts his gaze from revolting realities such as these. The transcending energy of thinking is not outside of some relation to such things, though it is not exhausted by that relation. We normally see Socrates putting the question but here we see him as put into question. And suppose even one were to glimpse the Sun, still nothing would be cut and dried, nothing univocal. The excess of the light first makes us blind, and we must pass through the night of the soul that the excess of light occasions. The philosopher must also learn *night vision* and adaptation to the darkness, when justice for the Cave requires him to return to the Cave. Transdialectical thinking requires night vision of us.

SCHOOL DAYS OVER: BACK TO *SKOLĒ*

Philosophical finesse for the equivocity of the ordinary and its connection to Socratic-Platonic dialectic brings us back to the *metaxu*. We are down in the Cave of life and because our theme is also Scholasticism I think of the song, "School Days Over," sung with true feeling by inimitable Luke Kelly:

> School days over, come on then John,
> Time you was putting your pit boots on
> On with your sark and moleskin trousers,
> Time you was on your way
> Time you was learning the pitman's job,
> And earning a pitman's pay.

The song sings of it being "time to go, time one was working down below." Making a living calls on us. Can we be philosophical pitmen and still carry schooling with us—even when dialectic is deschooled? I asked at the outset: "Are we all Scholastics now?" and also connected the question with making a living as a professional. But is there another sense in which we would love to say that we are all to be Scholastics now? I am thinking of a meaning hidden in the word *skolastikōs*, namely, *skolē*—leisure, as it is sometimes translated—freedom from the pressing worries of practical life, freedom not as an ivory tower luxury but as release into the space of a mindfulness that itself is released to the things as they offer themselves to us. This is, one might say, a *skolē* beyond the professional schools of analytic and continental Scholasticism.

Against Kantian critique, Hegel liked to repeat the story of the Scholasticus who refused to get into the water before he had learned to swim. His point, and he had a point: one must do it, do philosophy. One cannot learn it before doing it. Just do it! Yes, one must do it, but I would say, there is more than doing. There is listening and hearing. *Skolē* allows one to listen, in the flow of speech, in the middle give and take of words, before one speaks oneself. Listening to the word: there is a porosity of being and a porosity to being, before there is the endeavor to be (*conatus essendi*) of determining or self-determining thinking. There is a passion of thought, a *passio essendi* wherein we are endowed to be, whence we can become what we are to be. Our speaking, as responding, is an *endowed wording* of being. But this means a receiving more primordial than any doing or constructing on our part. This is true to the original astonishment that seeds the more analytically determinate and even dialectically self-determining thought that later may come to be. *Skolē* has much to do with this more original receiving.

Being at *skolē* releases us into the astonishment that, as we recall again, Plato suggested was the *pathos* of the philosopher (*Theaetetus* 155d3–4). This pathos is transdialectical but it is not the enemy of either analysis or dialectic. It witnesses a porosity of mind in the between, seeding the *passio essendi* of our being, out of which can flower a passion of philosophizing that is more than analysis and dialectic. This passion of philosophizing may crystallize into analytic clarity, it may take form in the dialectical self-transcending of dynamic thought. But more than these, and enabling them, it reveals a patience of mindfulness to the intimate strangeness of being. Philosophy must be *skolē* in that sense, Scholastic in the crucial respect of offering a *paideia*, an education in listening to the *logos*. The true schooling of philosophers would be our efforts together to listen to the *logos* and mindfully engage with it, in its wording of the between.

5 ∞ Between System and Poetics
On the Practices of Philosophy

VOCATION

There are many practices of philosophy. The plurality is remarkable. I repeat and explore further an important point: postmodern thinkers often take plurivocity as a mortal strike against metaphysics, but I take it rather as its lifeblood. There is no univocal essence of the plurivocal practices of philosophy. There is no Platonic form of philosophy reserved in heaven. Moses, stumbling down from Mount Sinai, did not forget an eleventh commandment that would charge us on pain of sin against reason to philosophize thus and thus only. Further, the practice of philosophy is not the same as the job of a professor. I get paid to be a professor, but no one pays me to be a philosopher.

No one ever asked me to be or become a philosopher. From where then does a call to philosophy come? Is it a calling? I think it is. I know we are more likely than not these days to squirm with such language of calling. We uneasily suspect something of the religious behind it. And maybe our suspicions are not entirely wrong.

What does it mean to be? What does it mean to be good? To know? To be truthful? To create? To speak? To communicate? To be a thing? To be intelligible? To be a human being? What does it mean to be God? There is no specialty of being, of life, of mindfulness that would exhaust such questions. Professionals get paid for their expertise, and hence scholars, technicians, scientists can be rewarded for what they produce or contribute. The scholar, technician, scientist, poet, priest, revolutionary, hero, sage were the significant others, diversely defining the self-image of the philosopher that I portrayed in the first chapter of *Philosophy and Its Others*.[1] The practices of philosophy are not solely self-

1. *Philosophy and Its Others*, chap. 1.

defined but come to shape in the interplay between it and its significant others. The poet may get his grant, the technician his patent, the scientist his Nobel Prize, the scholar his honorary degree, the priest his dues, the revolutionary his Mercedes when he comes down from the hills, the hero may now ascend to the exalted status of the celebrity intellectual, and where oh where is the sage, except perhaps in California or some points eastward of it. What are the rewards of philosophy? All said, it is a practice of mindfulness for free.

Professionalization is excellent, but it can be the death of philosophy as the practice of a certain kind of mindfulness. There is no specialty of the whole of life, no specialization of porosity, no technique of ultimacy. Finesse is needed for a way of life. Philosophy is a way of life, in which thoughtfulness about first and last things shapes one's relation to the between of being at all. There is a theoretical side to it, but this is less the modern sense of theory as an instrumental hypothesis as the earlier sense of theory as delight in seeing what is. There is a practical side to it, as it is the enigmatic charge of what it means to be good that perplexes the thinker. What does it mean to be? What does it mean to be good? These questions have a bearing on how one is to be, and how mindfulness enters into our own being between ignorance and wise humanness. The practice of philosophy is as much in the living of the thought, as in the life of thought. The life of the mind is inseparable from a mindful life.

BETWEENS

My concern here will be to explore the plurivocal space between system and poetics. Between system and poetics: here the word "between" can have different meanings. It could signify something like "versus." Consult, for instance, the old quarrel between philosophy and poetry. I will come back to this, since this quarrel is by no means univocal, and its meaning for philosophy is still in question, philosophically. In any case, one implication here seems to be this "between" as "versus" faces us with a choice: one or the other, but not both together; either system or poetics but not both.

Other meanings of "between" are less overt. Thus, it might mean less a tension or agon between these two, as more an opening to something *beyond* system. One might say: into that space between system and something beyond, the poetic inserts itself. Thus, there are philosophical occasions when system no longer seems relevant and appropriate and something beyond systematic encapsulation calls forth a different response at the limit. Instance: think of how in Plato, when discursive reason reaches a certain limit, there is a resort to more poetic, and crucially, more mythic ways of speaking. This space of the beyond of system requires a different voice, and this is not necessarily an abjuration of philosophical reason but a response called forth from philosophical reason at the limit, or at the utmost reach of its explicitly discursive powers. This too is an important sense of "between" to which I will return.

Another meaning of "between" points in the following direction, and here we are perhaps on more familiar ground. I mean there is a space between system and poetics, but that space refers us to *origins* rather than to what is aimed at "beyond" system. I am thinking here of the view that the more original sources of articulation are poetic rather than conceptual, imaginative rather than intellectual, and hence there is a *beyond in the root of articulation*, in relation to which the poetic is initially more intimate. Poetry first, philosophy later. So the view of Vico, to mention an important instance.

Again different postures to this are possible. One is the response of the philosopher who looks at this original space as the source of *equivocation*: something to be overcome by an articulation that is more intellectually univocal. That is to say, poetics is enmeshed in the equivocity of origins, philosophy transcends this equivocity and replaces it with univocal *ratio*. Not myth beyond philosophy, but myth prior to philosophy, but myth now that inevitably must be demythologized, that is, displaced, surpassed, and replaced. The space between system and poetics is one between the equivocal and the univocal, but for philosophers the former poses a problem, the latter alone the promise of its solution. Interestingly, in Socratic practice you find something of this in the *elenchus*: investigate, search, interrogate, put to the test the insinuations of the equivocal and replace it with the intelligible constancies of univocal definitions.

Then again we must consider this further different view. Suppose the space of the origins to which poetics is intimate is less an indigence of intelligibility than a *reserve of importance* to which every intelligibility is indebted, but which no univocal or dialectical intelligibility can exhaust. Then the equivocal is deeply fertile, and without it there would be no living intelligibility. It is a matrix, but a matrix that is never exhausted by its more univocal offspring. If religion and poetry are the first born of this matrix, philosophy is second born. To continue to be (re)born and to thrive, philosophy must find its way to honor its mother and keep alive its familial bond with religion and poetry.

Two responses would seem to be precluded by this rebirth. First, that *dualism* of poetry and philosophy, in which opposition defines the exclusion of the putatively more primitive partner, that is, the poetic or the religious. Second, that *dialectical sublation* that grants provisional rights to the poetic, or the religious, only to go on to claim that everything essential will be preserved in the conceptual overtaking of the image or the religious story. When philosophy thus overtakes the poetic, or the religious, there will be no more need of image or story—perhaps not for the conceptually unsophisticated, but certainly for the philosopher. This second response is obviously closer to Hegel's *Aufhebung* than to either a Platonic exclusion or Platonic transcendence.

METAXOLOGY

I think a *metaxological* response can make sense of all these responses, but it need not, cannot endorse them simply. It can accept some more readily than others, and with appropriate qualification. As the between here is plurally possibilized, so also there may be needed a plurivocal dwelling with the between, issuing into mindful expression that asks for a more plurivocal practice of philosophizing. The stress in this practice would be sympathetic to acknowledging that the poetic, or the religious, does show a certain intimacy with the original sources of articulation, intimacy in both a nonreductive and nonsublatable sense. There would be a philosophical willingness also for the transcending character of the between in which the utmost reach of *system finds itself "overtaken"* or exceeded by nonsystematic considerations that nevertheless ask for some articulate and thoughtful response. With this too the reserves of the poetic, or the religious, again must come into play.

That said, I think we have to attend to yet another sense of the "between" in which we always are: not so much at the limit of origin or verging on the "beyond" of given immanence, but *constitutively* in that given immanence, relative to our daily being just so in the midst of things. We find ourselves *in medias res*, and often so seemingly without our faces turned to any extremity of origin or beyond. I say "seemingly," because the everyday is the milieu of "seems" where what seems so is not always so. In a word: this everyday between is a *milieu of the equivocal*.

How do we address this equivocity? Obviously, in many ways. I will later say something about the mind of finesse. The question comes: Does the everyday itself harbor reserves of importance? Would not being in the midst of things, in the givenness of the ordinary and its reserves, ask for both a systematic and poetic response—and this in philosophy itself? The answer must be yes, if all knowing at some point must turn to what shows itself, must turn to the phantasm, as Aristotle and Aquinas aver? Perhaps too what we mean by "phantasm" now must have a sense more surplus and saturated than it always seems to have with these two thinkers: excess there in the midst of things in their givenness and intimate reserves? Equivocal excess, since the showing too is inseparable from seeming? I have come to call this a saturated equivocity.

And are not *we too* a middle in that midst? Are we not ourselves a "between," insofar as we are as intermediating with the surplus of that reserved givenness? More, do we not also have to mediate (with) *our own* reserved givenness, the surplus of our own originality and transcendence, at once both intimate to us and strange? Are we too not a concretion of saturated equivocity and a fertile sign of its signifying? Can we be the absolute measure of seeming, because we ourselves are a seeming show? Can we be the full measure of equivocity, if we too are constitutively equivocal? A perplexing question for systematics, a provocation for poetics.

It is also a perplexity for our being religious. Let the human being be the measure of all finite things other to itself, is the human being the measure of itself, of its own fertile equivocity? Is there an other originality and transcendence, in the dimension of the hyperbolic, more than the human measure, or more than any human measure? In the deepest intimacy of being religious, there is an elemental porosity to the hyperbolic. There is no finite measure, no human measure of this porosity, ultimately.

SYSTEM

I will come back to this, but let me backtrack a little and say something about *system*. "System" indicates an organized whole composed of many parts; and there can be many such organized wholes, material or bodily, musical, intellectual, social and political, and so on. *Sustēma*, deriving from *sunistanai*, refers us to a togetherness (*sun*) that is brought to stand (*histanai*). That *sustēma* brings a togetherness to stand, suggests less a block unity than a "being with," a between of relation. The question is the character of this between of relation, the how of the togetherness, the openness of it; or how closed it is, or must be on itself. Thinking in terms of this between, what is to preclude the thought of an open system?

In modern philosophy one associates the systematic impulse with Kant's desideratum of categorical completion, and with the impetus of his successors to develop or deduce such a categorical completion from one principle, culminating in a totality of thought determinations that constitute an absolute whole. The term "system" now evokes distaste, if not abuse. I think of Nietzsche to the effect: the will to system evidences a lack of integrity. One can sympathize: I think of those systematizers who (mis)behave like the ugly sisters of Cinderella; the glass slipper will fit the foot, must fit the foot, never mind the blood on the carpet! I often imagine how things were among academic philosophers in Germany, in the wake of Kant's transcendental turn, and then Hegel's idealism—for a while, all bewitched, besotted with system. Such were the times when Hegel "came on the scene." Let us not be too snide. It is easy to mock those Hegelians, as they are all mostly dead. Idealistic reason is not alone in being susceptible to bewitchment. Think of, in our day, the Scholastic Heideggerian, indeed the Scholastic deconstructionist, and the most grotesque of all, the Scholastic Nietzschean.

To be fair to the earlier systematizers, there is something disingenuous in Nietzsche's denunciation of the will to system. The dazzling surface of his own rhetoric often dissimulates the systematic recurrences of certain basic themes in his way of thinking, recurrences that honesty would prefer were sometimes set forth by Nietzsche more forthrightly. Many of these recurrences have a family relation to idealism, and the blood of Schopenhauer always circulated in Nietzsche, even granted it nourished another body and helped grow a different flesh. Schopenhauer is often the "system" recessed in the unsystematic Nietzsche. In that respect, to know the more systematic Schopenhauer is to be able to detect more clearly an ensemble of certain basic ideas with which Nietzsche plays. Plays, as he plays with us a game of poetic peek-a-boo: now we see it, now we don't. Some readers are not always blessed with memory long enough to recall what they then saw, and now don't, hence to see that one and the other don't always easily go with each other. And Nietzsche's rhetoric sometimes keeps such things from us, as it always ushers us on, relentlessly keeps us on the move.

System, for many today, is identified with a certain closed arrangement of concepts or ideas, themselves tending to highlight the sameness of things and lowlight the differences. We live reactively in the wake of system, in which previously recessed differences are brought forth to parade, sometimes in very showy or gaudy garments. Of course, we identify system most strongly with Hegel and idealism. But one can argue that the desire for system takes on a particular character in modernity, not entirely unrelated to the upsurge of a more radical univocalizing trend in *all spheres of human life*, but especially in science, and strongly reflected in philosophy itself.

I refer, for instance, to the powerful univocalizing mathematical tools developed in modernity to transform the notion of science, in terms of method and of strict standards of coherence and exactness. In previous times, there seems nothing quite like the limits to which this now is driven. One can see this as a response to the seeming of the equivocal. One thinks of mathematics in terms of exact univocity and a rigorous internal coherence of connections. One thinks of a system of relational implications, implicit in the beginning but needing proper methodical development to be laid out in its fullest and most explicit rational intelligibility. The implications extend beyond pure mathematics itself. For some such ideal of system is also pervasive in the reconfiguration of everyday life in the last centuries. Coming from some enigmatic source not at all mathematically univocal, one hears the relentless urging: make it systematic! Make science systematic, make medicine, make transport, make economics, make education, make politics systematic, making child-rearing systematic; the list could be continued. The culmination comes in talk of THE SYSTEM. This is the word used simply for that *pervasive configuration of everyday life* under the dominion of variants of scientific-technical rationality, variants themselves particular offspring of Enlightenment reason in its univocalizing mission.

ANTISYSTEM

Not surprisingly, there arose the *rebels* against THE SYSTEM. And then too the rebellions they led were themselves made possible by the system, and the conveniences of life that it produced, not least the material reserves it offered. Not unexpectedly also, the rebels, grown a little older, I will not say wiser, often become mainstays of the system. One sees this expressed in the swing between Enlightenment and Romanticism, variations of which swing are still with us to this day. See the loopy flowers of hippy counterculture versus the straights and squares of the system (1960s) as a variant of Pascal's contrast of finesse and geometry. Today we have made our peace with a more or less (self-)satisfied collusion of the two: cybernetic systems of information-processing effectively produce comfortable cocoons for consuming subjectivities. The two go hand-in-glove: technology and our comforts; the computer and pornography; hard reason and the mushy mess of eros. The collusive "dialectic" of Enlightenment and Romanticism, of modernity and postmodernity, of (calculative) cybernetics and (recreational) sex expresses something of the late modern reconfiguration (if not the corruption) of the fertile space between system and poetics.

To consider something of the philosophical expression of this, think of the turn to self in Descartes, the *cogito* as the one principle. One thinks of this more radically in Kant's transcendental unity of apperception. Then "come on the scene" his more extreme sons among the idealists. And we hear the loud complaint of these first rebel sons at father Kant's failure to deduce all the categories from one principle. These rebels were dutiful sons as well, and there is an almost lethal earnestness in their working out of the ideal of system in terms of systematic coherence and completeness with reference to an absolute unity. Consult Fichte, consult Hegel, but not them alone. We find a post-transcendental offspring of the homogenous unity of original Eleaticism, now become a self-differentiating One which develops itself and contains all the essential differences in itself. We find a post-Kantian Spinozism in this sense: not Spinozism as geometrical univocity; more a transgeometrical univocity, defined by the self-development of the absolute subject, not substance (Hegel: substance become subject). All of this is oriented toward totality, or an absolute holistic unity to which all differences are immanent, or self-differences.

There are admirers of Kant who breathe a sigh of relief with the cautions of a Kant versus the extravagances of a Hegel, but it was the canny Kant who raised the stakes about completeness and unity with respect to system. For that matter, there are claims Kant makes on behalf of his own work which are pretty close, in their hyperbole of self-congratulation, to claims such as Hegel made to turn philosophy from love of wisdom into accomplished *Wissenschaft*. And in all of this there is the issue of radical immanence, and the opening of the between to ultimate transcendence.

It is important to remind ourselves that these post-Kantian idealisms are philosophies of *radical immanence*—a radical immanence under the *sign of unity* and totality. Kant is not quite so radical a philosopher of immanence, though he made possible and influenced the genesis of such a philosophy. His "postulatory moral deism," itself a kind of philosophy of finitude, inspired and ceded to a kind of "sublationary infinitism" in which the absolute, self-determining subject of idealism comes ultimately to include all otherness within itself.[2] The immanent whole knows only *its own otherness*. From first to last there is the absolute one and this is the immanent whole beyond which there is no other.

There are later philosophies of radical immanence under the *sign of difference*. These are philosophies of postulatory finitism, philosophies no less hostile to radical transcendence (consider here God's irreducible otherness) than, say, Hegel's "sublationary infinitism." I think of Nietzsche and Deleuze. The postmodern Spinozism of Deleuze is evident: I recall one more time his sanctifying elevation of Spinoza as the "Christ of the philosophers." Something analogous holds for Nietzsche, the anti-Christ of the postphilosophers. While the idealist philosophies of totality and the anti-idealist philosophies of difference are ostensibly opposed, in fact, they are deeply at one in this stress on radical imma-

---

2. See *God and the Between*, 93–100. I know Kant's God has "theistic" and not simply "deistic" characteristics, but this God in the end seems so to back off completely from any concurrence with human freedom that for practical purposes it seems more "deistic" than "theistic." Kant, one suspects, dreaded the ontological intimacy of the "theistic" God, and was relieved to be able to keep that God at a distance by the interposition of the moral law. The ontological intimacy of which I speak would require a metanoetic transformation of the metaphysical meaning of "immanence."

nence; and even though the latter stress the poetics rather than the systematics, as do the former. I myself do not think that the intermediating space between immanence and transcendence is to be described in dualistic, dialectical, or deconstructive ways. I would rather a metaxology of immanence in which the hyperboles of being bring us to ontological thresholds exceeding fully immanent determination. The ontological intimacy of given being is an immanent hyperbole of what itself cannot be contained in any completely immanent frame.[3]

As a philosophy of immanence postulatory finitism complements, even while deconstructing, sublationary infinitism. The metaxological way of being between system and poetics is other than both, because the between cannot be closed into radical immanence, either under the sign of unity as with speculative dialectic, or the sign of difference as with equivocal (anti)dialectic. The conjunction of Spinozistic holism and (post-)Kantian transcendental autonomy generates a new configuration of immanence closed off from radical transcendence. The metaxological practice of philosophy, systematically without being the system, dissents from this. On this point, it is as much anti-Nietzschean as anti-Hegelian.[4]

It is fair to say that much of the negative reaction to system is conditioned by a long and complex development in modern philosophy. The hyperinflation of the systematic claims of reason generates a variety of seditious deflations of all claims made by reason. Many of these negative reactions are defined by exploiting one part of the ensemble of ideas developed previously in a systematic context and using them as weapons against the claims of completeness made on behalf of the system. Call it deconstructed, or discomposed Hegelianism, if you will. Or for that matter, rebellious Kantianism: the good will of rationality has recessive genes that are later born in some black sheep of the idealist family, most evidently in that bad boy Nietzsche and his unruly will to power.

And—interestingly for our theme—it is in bad boy Nietzsche that the urge for poetics *against* system is most powerfully expressed in post-idealistic thinking. At one level, this is a *return* to the ancient quar-

---

3. On the hyperboles of being, see *God and the Between*. In the next chapter I treat of these hyperboles and Marion's saturated phenomena.
4. See, *inter alia*, my *Hegel's God: A Counterfeit Double?*; on postulatory finitism, sublationary infinitism, and related issues, see my *Is There a Sabbath for Thought?*, esp. chap. 1.

rel of poetry and philosophy; at another level, it is a *turn away* from system, in that it seeks to resolve the quarrel with a different stress on the poet than the one held in the rationalist and idealist lines of inheritance. Not poetry to the exclusion of philosophy, but a redefinition of the range and ambitions of philosophy in terms of a far more sympathetic and symbiotic relation to the poetic.

BEING SYSTEMATIC

I have much sympathy with this last proposal as a desideratum. I have less sympathy with the way the desideratum is pursued. Why? Because it is too unselfconsciously *heir* to many of the views it claims to be deconstructing. It is too totalizing, in its own way, of the longer tradition of philosophy, where I am impressed by a more plurivocal practice of philosophy. It is too asleep to the other senses of "between" that I more "systematically" outlined above, and especially to those senses bearing on the excess of origin and the "beyond." It is too negligent of the issues of origin and transcendence in the favor it gives to a certain radical immanence or postulatory finitism.

We need to think through the hyperboles of being in the between. Hyperboles of being: happenings in immanence which yet exceed the terms of immanence. We need to pay attention to the different senses of "between," and to do so more "systematically," in order to get clearer for ourselves that there is an issue here that is not a local one for late modernity, but a deeper one that is elemental and constitutive of our ontological endowment; and this particularly with respect to the between defining our relation to the origin, and our relation to the "beyond," and how both these enter our passing sojourn in the middle of a given life.

For one can reflect systematically without necessarily claiming possession of the system in the closed and totalizing sense. Let such a being systematic be called "systematics," by contrast with "the system." The practice of philosophy necessarily requires some sense of systematics, again by contrast with the system, if one's ultimate sense of being and mindfulness is metaxological. Such metaxological systematics is not fixed by the univocal sense of being and by unmediated unity; not totalized by self-mediating dialectic and its inclusions of difference within one comprehensive unity; and not just cast abroad on unrelated diversity by equivocal heterogeneity or deconstructive difference that holds itself in suspension over the promise of a certain togetherness of and in the between. There is a complex and rich togetherness in the nature of things, a community of being, reaching all the way to ethical and religious community; a community impossible without irreducible otherness, but also defined by constant identities, themselves not beyond the processes of passage that constitute our ambiguous emplacement in creation as the universal impermanence. We need systematics in the sense of a disciplined understanding of connections; connections stabilized but not frozen by samenesses; connections defined and developed by dynamic differences; connections not enclosed in one immanent whole; and all in all, connections enabling complex interplays between samenesses and differences, interplays exceeding the closure of every whole on itself.

I would also say: Without poetics, no systematics. And: Without a more original porosity of being, and our given *passio essendi*, no poetics either, and hence also no systematics. This means that there is a more original sense of being religious prior to being artistic and being philosophical. Poetics and systematics are ultimately less original than the porosity of being that opens us up as a being between, or as being a between. We human beings are a medium of passage, a middle capable of becoming mindful of what has passed, what is passing, and what is coming to pass. It is being religious that lives this porosity in the form of the finesse of prophetic mindfulness. Ultimately this is gifted and perhaps is one of the ultimate gifts. I will come back to this.

To the present point: without the poetics of coming to be, for us there is no systematics of being at all. Poetics deals with a bringing or coming to be; systematics finds interconnections in what has come to be. Poetics deals with creative overdetermination; systematics with created determinations and self-determinations. Poetics reveals the more original coming to be, or showing; systematics articulates forms of interconnection that issue from the more original forming. Poetics concerns the forming power(s), prior to and in excess of determinate form, for it is intimate with the overdetermination of the original source(s). Thus, in truth, systematics makes no intelligible sense without presupposing the poetics, poetics often forgotten when more formed intelligibilities have arrived and when what they bring has come to occupy us.

Modernity after Descartes has often been infatuated with the systematics to the neglect of the poetics. This neglect verges too often on a betrayal of finesse; though, in fact, the best moves of systematics are themselves in debt to what overtly they seem to slight. Differently put: first and last, finesse is more original than geometry. You have to discern differences, see differences as differences, and thus discriminate them as identities, before you can analyze their forms of interconnection. Finesse is even more the first requisite, if the form we seek to comprehend is not static but a dynamic forming. Even in the (static) form that has come to a stand there is hidden the memory of a dynamism of coming to be formed. Recall remarks above about *sustēma* as deriving from *sunistanai*: *sustēma* brings a togetherness (*sun*) to stand (*histanai*). Finesse does not so much fix the form as move intelligently with the dynamically forming—in coming to be itself activated mindfulness. Poetics is alive to this energy of coming to be. Poetics itself, in its finessed mindfulness, is alive with this energy.

There have been practices of philosophy that are systematic, without being obsessed with the system, and in search of interconnection out of resources seeded in the poetic. Such thinking seeks out connection; knows that to think of one thing means to think of another, and vice versa; knows that there are articulations already at work to which we must be faithful; knows that we construct connections in a field of being that is open to further determinations; knows also that the universal impermanence will dissolve in time these finite constructions.[5]

We think from the midst, and work our way out, so to say, from where we find ourselves there. And we do not say: there *must* be a unity whose circumference must be laid around the totality of things, and which we can *project* from our place in the midst. Porosity is more primal than projection. A thinking in the midst, while systematic, can be much more open to the ruptures that define difference and sameness there; can be much more diffident about extrapolation to a putative whole of wholes from its middle condition; can be porous to the hyperboles of being, happenings of finitude that exceed finite determination.

Hegel was not unaware of some sense of the middle condition, but his approach to and understanding of it is not fully metaxological. He-

---

5. See, for example, Plato's *Philebus*, where an ensemble of supple systematic resources—one and many, like and unlike, same and other, and the fourfold of limit and unlimited, mixture and the cause—are deployed to fruitful effect.

gel has a dialectical feel for the dynamics of forming, prior to and beyond the fixations of form. But with him the system overreaches the poetics and the systematics. The overdetermination of poetics becomes an indeterminacy lacking intelligibility until it is given determinacy and form by the systematics; while systematics itself is overtaken by the absoluteness of the system as the apotheosis of self-determination. Absolute self-determination comes to itself absolutely through its own otherness. This is the one form of (self-)mediation in all interconnections, within which fall all determinations, through which is overcome all indetermination, and because of which the overdeterminate is neither recognized nor minded. System overtakes poetics, and closes down the porosity of systematics to what is beyond system.

Hegel highlights important considerations in our being in the midst, most particularly connected with the power of (inter)subjectivity to be in relation to itself, while being in relation to what is other. The recurrence of this structure of relation, he "projects" onto the whole; or perhaps projects a whole, in claiming this to be the dynamic of structuring of the whole. This claim about the whole is built upon a certain understanding of otherness, and sameness, which puts into recess forms of otherness that cannot be contained in the dialectic as he understood it, that is, as too under the influence of the modern turn to the one and the self. Hegel is, in that regard, another ugly sister of Cinderella in his practice of philosophy. I cannot detail here the small horrors of what little toe is here and there cut off, nor stay to mop the blood on the ground. I will only say that the amputations and squeeze affect how he thinks the between, relevantly to our current theme, in the interplay between art and philosophy, and between religion and philosophy.

FINESSE

Being systematic in one's philosophizing is not the same as having THE SYSTEM. Yet there are ways of being systematic that are truer to what is at play in the milieu of being, and that develop modes of mindfulness that are more finessed for the fuller subtleties of what is there at play. When I mention finesse I inevitably bring Pascal to mind with his marvelous distinction between *l'esprit de finesse* and *l'esprit de géométrie*.

I am no enemy of geometry, but its great helpfulness with univocal exactness is not always the most helpful. This is particularly true when we are dealing with the equivocities of the human condition. Pascal is an admirable contributor to the tremendous advances in the modern scientific univocalizing wrought by empirical and mathematical science. But he was not so bewitched by it as to deem it the one and only way to truth. Spinoza does not lack for in finesse, but in his ethics *more geometrico* I can find no appropriate name for its generous acknowledgment. Quite the opposite, geometry seems to be usurping the role of finesse.

I find astonishing his statement to the effect that the human race would have lain for ever in darkness were it not for the development of mathematics. "Truth would be eternally hidden [*in aeternam lateret*] from the human race had not mathematics, which does not deal with ends but with the nature and properties of figures, shown to humankind another norm of truth" (*Ethics*, Part I, appendix). If I read this right, a (quasi)soteriological power is being claimed for mathematics. Prior to the geometrical sages of modernity, humanity seems to have been lost in the Caves of night. After the new mathematics, rational salvation offers humankind the possibility of release into light, into blessedness. What release, what blessedness? If mathematics saves us from purposes and ends (*fines*), its knowing would be a purposeless knowing in a purposeless universe. If this is an advance beyond darkness, it is also an advance into a different darkness, darker in its intelligibility than the unintelligible darkness we have now supposedly left behind. This to me seems more like a geometrical counterfeit of saving knowing.

Finesse is more a readiness for saving knowing, bearing on what is prior to and beyond geometry. I would say that finesse bears on a mindfulness attuned to the signs of the equivocal, where the point is not the conversion of these signs into a univocal or dialectical-speculative system. It is here that the powers of the poetic come to the fore. To the extent that philosophy itself requires finesse, it must go to school with the poets. If it wants to approach saving knowing, it may need finesse further again. I mean finesse that is the sister of religious porosity.

Finesse is by its nature an excellence of mindfulness that is singularly embodied. It cannot be rendered without remainder in terms of neutral and general characteristics. It cannot be geometricized. We come first to know of it, know it, by witnessing its exemplary incarnation in living human beings of evident finesse. There is no geometrical "theory" that could render it in an absolutely precise univocal definition. It refers us to the concrete suppleness of living intelligence that is open, attentive, mindful, attuned to the occasion in all its elusiveness and subtlety. We take our first steps in finesse by a kind of creative mimesis, by trying to liken ourselves to those who exemplify it, or show something of it. This creative likening renews the promise of finesse, but it also is itself new, because it is openness to the subtlety of the occasion in its unrepeatable singularity.

Singularity here does not mean a kind of autism of being, nor does it mean that we must forsake any communication of its significance to others. Such singularity is rich with a promise which, though perhaps initially not fully communicated, is yet available for, or making itself available for, communicability. What is communicable cannot be confined to what can be articulated in neutral generalities, or in homogeneous universals. We are here called to attendance on the intimate universal. Finesse is in attendance on what is elusive in the intimacy of being, an intimacy that is at the heart of living communicability.

The poetics of a metaxological philosophy must seek to be true to this intimacy. Its very efforts at systematics must show themselves to be open to this promise. That is, the systematics must be born of an intimacy of being that the more determinate systematic articulations of thought never completely exhaust. It must be open beyond itself to what transcends itself, precisely just so as systematics. Earlier I drew attention to a sense of "between" as at the origin, and as at a boundary pointing to the "beyond" of the immanent middle. This "beyond" (as well as this "before") cannot be uprooted from the intimacy of being, and hence requires more than "theory."

The *occasional* nature of the happening of being turns us to the poets, turns us into poets. *Being as occasion* also brings us into neighboring with being religious. And this, in our attendance on the amazingness of the everyday, the mystery of our being in the midst. A genuine occasion has something of the momentous about it. Systematics may not always avoid the seductions of the neutral universal, but it can at least be ready to confess its sins and grant that there is *more* than *that* neutral universal. The practice of philosophy can be a reminder of this "more." Finesse may require a love before and beyond purposeless "theory."

POETICS

Given this singularity, perhaps I can say, must say, something about my own itinerary in finesse, or lack of it, and some occasions of its evocation. I recall as a young person my attractions to the ordered thought of mathematics. This was balanced by being disturbed, imbalanced, by the darker perplexities induced by, for instance, the study of *Hamlet*. On the one hand, the consolations of coherence and systematic univocity; on the other, the slippery ambiguities of the human being awakening to itself as a question to itself, a question that nothing definite can determinately answer, univocally. What to geometry is this quintessence of dust? Nothing. To itself this creature, the human being, though it fears it is nothing, is something—something in question to itself. This creature of dust is a creature of finesse, hence more than a quintessence of dust.

Then there were, there are the extreme claims made in being religious. I mean not first doctrines whose claim to be revealed mysteries cast all pretensions to univocity into disarray, but also the extreme claims made on the practice of a life, if this first claim has any truth: to be as truthful, in accord with a certain trust in God. This reflected something of the ethos of Irish culture at the time. Religion, Roman Catholicism, provided the hegemonic overarching, overreaching horizon within which questions of the meaning and practice of life were to be answered. A between opens up for a philosopher who is perplexed by these claims. Thinking is here double-edged: it can be critical in a destructive way; it need not be so destructive, may be moved by its own proper reverence. There is a practice of philosophy that ultimately is seeded in reverence as religious, but grown into thoughtfulness about religion by the press of ambiguous life itself. If there was a single tradition of philosophy in Ireland while I was growing up, it was a form of Scholasticism, newer forms influenced by teachers trained at Leuven: ancient and medieval philosophy, combined with phenomenology and existentialism—a not unfertile mix. But to go to school with some questions means there are no schools that will do. One may find oneself outside the guilds, be they analytic or continental.

The poets: there was always a very long line of respect for these in Ireland. When I first studied at University College Cork a few of my friends were budding poets. I do not think I entirely lack poetic powers but I went my own way, though that philosophical way does call upon early affinities with the poetic. I think I came to poetry from religion and came to philosophy perhaps directly from poetry, but certainly religion stood over this transition as the elder sister. One could make a cultural claim in Ireland if one were a poet, but of course in Ireland, as Patrick Kavanagh said, the standing army of poets never falls below three thousand. I did not join the army, nor was I recruited or dragooned. I went my way. I do not think I have been unfaithful to a certain muse whom I have not ceased to woo, or scatter tokens of affection throughout my writing. It is not quite, in Eliot's words, a matter of making "raids on the inarticulate," for there is articulating and thinking that is not thievery. And with all due respect, among the poets I did not always find enough of the kind of thought I instinctively sought, often not quite knowing what it was.

In the practices of my own philosophizing, one can find some extremes of abstract dialectic, leaving some readers exasperated or gasping for more familiar concreteness—and then, by contrast, the eruption of another (poetic) language, seemingly entirely other, imagistically concrete, too concrete for some abstract thinkers. Some of my readers are discomfited by this doubleness. Others, I am happy to report, approve of it in some way. Perhaps the mixture of being discomfited and being moved has something right about it. We can be lulled into a false sense of philosophy with respect to abstract dialectic; as if that, and only that, were philosophy; and not the emergence of thinking from an ambiguous ethos; not also the reinsertion of thought in the flow of life itself. For me, the thinking must address the *movement between*: up from the ambiguous matrix, above the flat wastes of thoughtless life; down again from the dry, oxygenless ether into the red blood of life, feet contacting once more the rougher ground. True, in the movement up, we may suffer from altitude sickness, we cannot breathe, and our minds become dizzy; in the movement down, the glut of life may be too much for us to digest, and we settle on a vanishing diet of anorexic abstractions.

The movement between: a process of transcending in being mindful, that emerges from roots often lost to thought in darkness before articulation; that points above univocal articulations; that puts pressure on the reassuring forms of domesticated life; that also paradoxically returns us to these daily forms but now with some shift in seeing, or some hidden access of light allowing one to see things differently, or see not quite straight anymore. For this turn back down may require of one a kind of *night vision*, and initially all one can make out are dull shapes shifting in a gloaming. There is nothing simple about this at all. Even with one's feet back on the rough ground, one may stumble on the trivial thing. Falling over the everyday: "falling over" is a being off balance; it is also one of our ways of describing love. Not only, only connect; but also making one's peace with the many farewells of life. And there may be portents that there is an under-ground to the firm earth, as before there appeared a sky above one. Being willing to enter the under-ground might have much to do with communicating with the more intimate sources of thinking and speaking and creating. Going into those sources is to risk a kind of dying, for this under-ground is as much tomb as womb, and it is the death of false selving that is terrifying for those singers who must spend a season in Hades.

The poetics of my own practice of philosophy: this is not a matter of giving to thought a kind of "feel"; not simply a kind of evocation, though it can be both; not just a rhetorical embellishment that otherwise puts drapery over the sturdy drab furniture of thinking. It has more to do with *enactment*: the very concreteness of thinking itself as performed in fitting words. The words are not just a matter of "talk about" something, but are uttered or written somehow to bring to pass a happening, to enact it mindfully. Performance is a (per)forming, a coming-to-be of significant form, through (*per*) a passing from silence to speaking. The saying is as important as the said; and sometimes the saying says more than the said. The faithful thought finds fruits in its fitting word.

The mindful enactment, the performance of thinking, has something to do with a wedding of form and content. The form is the forming of the content, a bringing to form, not the superimposition of a form on a matter or content already fixed. Thinking, in this regard, is like a *poiesis*: a coming or bringing to be; an emergence as if from a kind of nothing; but then also a becoming in terms of a forming. There is something prior to form: intimate, originally idiotic sources of thinking. The form that *has* become is not the end of the matter insofar as it points back to these, its own hidden original sources. Yet formed thought also points beyond itself, either in terms of its own dissolution, or self-surpassing, or in terms of an other exigence emergent with it at the extremity of its own self-becoming. Then something other than the self-becoming of thinking is communicated: the other beyond the self-determination of thought. This other calls further the self in self-becoming beyond self. It also calls for thinking what is other to thought thinking itself.

So images, metaphors, and such like are not mere rhetorical adornments in my practice of philosophy. There is a rhetoric, yes, but this can aim at a fidelity to coming to be and the forming of the content: the thinking itself in its own singular forming. I would say that there is always the taste of singularity to fresh thought, even if it repeats thoughts that are the same as those that have already been thought by others, or that can be thought again. The freshness comes from a dipping of mindfulness into the original sources of articulation. This is impossible without imagination, whether poetic or philosophical or religious.

This for me is not an optional thing. It is a fidelity to what is communicating itself or being communicated. The fact that some professional philosophers might not recognize themselves in this does not settle the question between us. We all tend to be initiated into a practice of philosophy, but no practice is entirely immune from question. A thinking that seeks immunity for itself, while accusing or judging everything other, immediately makes itself suspect. By claiming to be above suspicion, it straightaway arouses suspicion. Some pretensions to the system can claim a kind of immunity from incompleteness. Who or what grants the immunity? Can philosophy grant immunity to itself, and still remain a creditable witness to thought? Essential to *any* practice of philosophy is its willingness to call itself into question. Professional, professorial philosophers ought to remember this and not feel self-satisfied that they are safe insiders of a professional guild. A different nakedness and exposure to the outside is needed in philosophy: this is also a "being between."

SINGING THOUGHT

This recalls the theme of different betweens earlier laid out. There is clearly a "between" that yields to more systematic treatment: an interconnected web of thoughts, or happenings, each related to others; and a systematic thinking can follow along the lines of articulation defined by the web of such interrelations and interconnections. Hegel exploits this, and makes a certain claim to complete the explications of the web of interrelations of thought and being. But this sense of between is one which is primarily *immanent*. My question is whether this immanent between gives witness to another sense of between that is at the boundary of immanence, or itself between immanence and transcendence. I do not want to put the point too dualistically, for I think that signs of this other between emerge in immanence itself. These signs are signally given in the hyperboles of being: happenings in immanent finitude that yet cannot be determined completely on the terms of immanent finitude. They point beyond, and again in no dualistic manner, but rather in terms of the excesses given to showing in the immanent between itself. The immanent between is porous to something other to it.

How then to be in this *other* between? And how to address it? This is not an easy question. I am not sure one can give a direct answer. I am not sure what an "answer" might mean. I have offered a response in *God and the Between*, though responding is present in other works too. Addressing this other between, or letting oneself be addressed by what is communicated in and across it, is, I think, inseparable from the religious. But there is a poetic side to this address and openness, that asks for the allowance of attention to the hyperboles of being in the immanent middle: hyperboles, however, *occasionally communicated*, and not simply in terms of neutral generalities.

The poetic and the religious are familially intimate, as I suggested. I would speak of what it means to be in the between beyond system; which is again both a pointing beyond, and yet a return to something very elemental. If the pointing beyond is recognizably *religious*, in a more usually accepted sense, the return to the elemental is *poetic*. I would say however, that the poetic is also pointed beyond in the elemental, just as the religious, in its transcendence, brings up back into intimacy with the elemental. Poetry is exposure; religion is nakedness; both are ultimate porosities. But how to remain *true to the occasion*? Can philosophical thought ever find the fitting words?[6]

I have written some more systematic works, and have brought a trilogy of systematic works to a sort of "completion" with *God and the Between*. One would be deceived to think of this as "system-building" in a

---

6. Worth recalling is how the letters of St. Paul's are in the main *occasional*, directed to a particular community, with particular characteristics and issues. They are intimate and universal: singular in address and yet they come to be addressed to both Jew and Gentile, the whole of humanity.

more traditional sense, where things are put in their place and then it is done. Not at all: I see systematic thinking is a *working through* of fundamental possibilities of minding and being, which having been done might *release one* to be again, to be mindful again, otherwise. I cannot entirely evade the desire of which I spoke in *Philosophy and Its Others*, namely, of thought singing its other. Not thought thinking itself, nor quite thought thinking its other, but mindfulness as thought singing its other. What would singing thought be? I speak metaphorically. I speak in a way that an admirer of Vico might understand when he says that song is the source of speech. But there are songs also beyond first speech, the songs of a second spring beyond the self-becoming of the middle of life. There are songs proper to a before, to a middle, to a beyond. Perhaps, *apropos* the latter, these are the songs of age, the songs of time. If, on one side, we are directed to the *poetically immanent*, on the other, we are solicited by the *religiously beyond*.

This dream of singing thought might be expressed, for instance, in mindfulness of the processes of selving, the selvings of a life, the communicabilities of living. Could one do that philosophically, and in terms of thought singing its others? This would be very difficult. One knows of *artists* who have told the stories of various selvings, and without loss of either the intimacy of occasions or of communicability beyond oneself. Examples: the beginning of James Joyce's *Portrait of the Artist as a Young Man* seems to enter immanently into being in the between as a baby, whose later selvings are said by some commentators to be modeled on Aristotle's *De Anima*. Charles Dickens's *David Copperfield*: early chapters are written from the viewpoint of the child, more or less; there are touches that sketch the occasion of being small, as in David Copperfield's being struck by Mr. Barkas swallowing the pie whole, like an elephant; or the child enduring the impenetrability of adults, in the heavy woman descending from the mail carriage, like a haystack; there is a later episode when David gets drunk on the first occasion, and Dickens marvelously enters into the skewed self-intoxication of a first getting sloshed.

Other artists could be mentioned, but one might say: great art tries to remain imaginatively true to the occasion of being. For instance, consider Joyce's *Ulysses* as an extended fidelity to the occasion of June 16, 1904—now artistically immortalized as Bloomsday. But how to *think*, in the middle, of the *surplus of the occasion*? For there is, in the between, a *surplus immediacy*. But when we think, do we not distance ourselves, mediate this surplus, and so seem to deal with something other to the surplus? We seem to have to choose either the surplus occasion or the thought. How then is a singing thought possible, faithful to both the surplus and the thought? This would ask a mindful fidelity to the surplus occasion, as much affirming the occasion as articulating its surplus. But can that be done by philosophical thought? Is it only the poetic image or the religious story that is both surplus and articulate, and each in its own way faithful to the occasion? If we desire fidelity to the surplus occasion, must we be confined to the intimate only, the intimate as the "merely" private? Or is there an intimacy of being not private? Is there an *intimate universal*? I think there is. Is it only in being religious that we enter into the intimate universal: an enabling middle between the human and the divine; a between that neither betrays our intimate singularity of being nor abdicates responsibility for a more unconditional communicability? Would one not need something like *agapeic mindfulness* to be true to it? Who has that mindfulness? Perhaps nobody except God: mindfulness as knowing love of the singular, communicated as care for the mortal creature.[7]

The artist has poetic license, we say, and the story. But what kind of license does philosophy have? What licenses philosophy? The language was still in use until very recently of speaking (in Belgium, where I taught) of earning the degree of a *licentiate* in philosophy. A college of professors confers that license, but is there a deeper *authorization* of philosophy? Is a storied philosophy possible and who or what would authorize it? I do not mean a philosophy of stories but a storied philosophy—enacting something of the occasion of being, not just reflecting on it. This is a point I put above about a certain poetic practice of philosophizing: participating in the occasion, not just talking about it, and yet both participating and speaking in a philosophical register.

This point might be said to be consistent with a metaxological prac-

---

7. On some of the themes mentioned above see: "Surplus Immediacy, Metaphysical Thinking, and the Defect(ion) of Hegel's Concept," in *The Intimate Strangeness of Being*, chap. 3; agapeic mindfulness, chaps. 4 and 6 of *Perplexity and Ultimacy: Metaphysical Thoughts from the Middle* (Albany: State University of New York Press, 1995); on the intimate universal, see *Is There a Sabbath for Thought?* as well as *The Intimate Universal: The Hidden Porosity Among Religion, Art, Philosophy and Politics* (New York: Columbia University Press, 2016).

tice of philosophy, if we connect the *metaxu* with a reformulation of the idea of philosophy as a "meta" discipline. Philosophy as a "meta" discipline is often thought of as a second-order discipline, reflective of and on a first-order activity, but I would stress the doubleness of the meaning of "meta." "Meta" can mean "in the midst," as well as "over and above, beyond." If "meta" as "in the midst" refers us to a first-order activity or performance, "meta" as "over and above" refers us to reflection on this first-order activity. A metaxological practice of philosophy could not endorse any sharp division of these two senses of "meta." This practice would seek to be at once first- and second-order: not one, not the other simply, but both, and the movement between the two, in which the intimacy of the one to the other is shown both as "in the midst" and "over and above." This would also have implications for the movement between immanence and transcendence.

I can envisage a story line that would bear on the poetic, religious, and philosophical significance of human selvings, or our being in communities. How to relate the story or stories, and to do so philosophically, and yet not to betray the poetic and the religious, and to relate it from within out, as well as to be true to what we have received? Inevitably we think of life being lived forward and understood backward. How then to think the promiscuity of the forward and the backward, doing justice to something of the systematics and the poetics? Would one perhaps have to invent a *new genre* of writing in the process? Not the philosophical novel, but storied philosophizing, where the stories are not mere illustrations of concepts. I do not know if it can be done, I do not know if I can do it. It might mean that one must simply turn into a poet, a religious poet perhaps. Even if so, could philosophy still be carried (over) in hidden reserves, offering accesses to what more often than not is closed to poets and perhaps religious thinkers. (Is Kierkegaard someone here to think of as showing a way?)

Whatever one might think of these suggestions, important for all of this will be to come anew into the *elemental porosity of being*. This coming anew is first dependent on a kind of *metanoia* of selving, and a renewed release into the space of communicability. Only later do the imaginative or reflective articulations come. I know, of course, that the turn about, the renewed release, and the new saying cannot be separated into detachable phases; though there are those who have been in the turn about and release and who do not have the resources to articulate what is occasioned there; just as there are the loquacious who talk too much and do not know what they are talking about, for they have not undergone the *metanoia*, and their loquaciousness counterfeits the passage of the true word.

RELIGIOUS POROSITY

Mention of this porosity of being makes me turn from the poets to *the priests*. I was myself attracted to the priesthood. The complications here for the philosopher, for the thinker between religion and philosophy, are multiple. There can be religious cultures that are inhospitable to philosophical thought. Perhaps earlier in the Ireland in which I grew up, there was a certain conservative bent that either looked askance at the asking of questions, or else gave its permission as long as the pursuit kept clearly to the sanctioned pathways. Rural people are often skeptical about fancy talk, while bourgeois city dwellers may have justified pretensions to education but often hesitate before taking directions too disturbing to more settled pieties. I once published some articles on Marx in the *Cork Examiner*, and my granny immediately pronounced I was finished. She was not entirely wrong. Among some, my own studies of Hegel, against whom I have struggled, led to my being deemed guilty by circuitous association: Hegel, Marx, Lenin, Stalin—and now we are being shot.

While the circumstances that occasioned these associations do not now quite press home on us, in every occasion genuine philosophy requires a different amplitude of mind. Arrogance *vis-à-vis* the others is not called for or justified. Nevertheless, it may well be that the pursuit of thought puts a person on an edge relative to others, and sometimes pits them against each other. That said, there is now a culture of severe criticism, if not undisguised hostility, toward the religious orientation of that earlier time. One understands this, in part, because of the sometimes heavy-handed use of hegemonic power by ecclesiastical institutions. Nevertheless, the hostility is not justified if we take the viewpoint of that ampler horizon of mind and consider the human being as *homo religiosus*, and without excessive fixation on the putative hangups of (Irish) Catholicism. Being religious is immensely plurivocal, and yet at the center of it all is the most elemental of all elemental relations: the human in relation to the divine, the divine in relation to the human—let the divine be interpreted how you will.

And then too there is the tunnel vision of retrospective score settling that often descends on "enlightened" discussions of religion. I tend to think that human generosity has a certain fundamental constancy, as do malice and small-mindedness. To think there was nothing of generosity in former times, smacks of the ultimate self-righteous arrogance on our part. In any case, my own experience of being religious in Ireland was on the whole something that deeply impressed me: impressed itself on me, and in a manner that I think was indelible. Images: neighborly generosity; some individuals marked by a sense of marvel and gratitude for life; the immense delight (not exclusive of a mockery, itself a kind of delight) in the stunning mystery of human beings, coming and passing in all shapes and sizes; guilty sympathy for those less fortunate than oneself in a time when the material resources to help them were far less than is now the case; unselfconscious enactment of the urge to pray, and so to place oneself in a space where the presence of the divine offers itself to us; rituals with their own majestic aesthetics, and indeed a magnificent sensuousness by comparison with which the stripped-down efficiencies of recent years strikes one as dull and devoid of any sacred flamboyance. For there was more unselfconscious excess in that direction. But then the human being is excess; and if the exceeding will not be given its out in the religious direction, it will find other, less wholesome, even vicious, sinister, malignant expressions. Vice too can be in the dimension of the hyperbole. (Had Hitler been accepted into art school, or succeeded as an artist, who knows what would have followed? A dark, dark instance of Cleopatra's nose.)

I fully understand and endorse those who decry pedophilic priests. The violation of the innocents is a desecration of the holy. I cannot understand those who decry such priests, and then go over to the party of Herod and endorse the legally licensed killing of the innocents. Pedophilia is perverted love, but killing the unborn innocents is still killing. I have wondered if the claimants of a certain form of secular enlightenment have need of an enemy over against whom to arrogate the superiority of the supersessor. Sometimes this results in repeatedly digging up the same bodies, well beyond any generational statute of limitations. When are the dead allowed to remain dead and buried, and not again to be exhumed, put on trial, and buried again by the dead? Exhumed to offer a needed target for appalled outrage in the present. I am reminded of the famous case of digging up the body of Pope Formosus to put him on trial many years after his death (I refer to the infamous Cadaver Synod, *Synodus Horrenda*, in 897). The dead papal corpse, propped on a throne, was delivered over to judgement and found guilty. The body was interred again in a graveyard for foreigners, only once again to be dug up and thrown into the Tiber, loaded with weights. There are analogous secular, antireligious versions of such Cadaver Synods.

To return to my main thread of thought: the urgency of ultimacy marking being religious is the familial, intimate other to a similar searching of ultimacy that can consume the poetic or philosophical quest. This by no means entails a decamping from the splendors of ordinary life and their unappreciated mystery, too often to us invisible. It is true that the search for system in modernity has put strain on this familial relation. We see this in more scientifically oriented systems: religion becomes utterly subjective and privatized—more often than not this is a bad subjectivity, resulting in a betrayal of the intimacy of being to which religion answers. We see something similar in more idealistic systems: the betrayal of the intimate universal of being religious is covered up by its substitution by an impersonal rational universal, deemed more ultimate than the God that is "merely personal." I have repeatedly posed the question as to whether this way of thinking is a systematic violation of the sense of mystery and transcendence, intimate to religion, and especially religions sourced in biblical inspirations. Reflection on this space between philosophy and religion, as well as between philosophy and art is crucial for a metaxological philosophy. I mention my ongoing quarrel with the Hegelian sublation of art and religion in this regard, but I will not go into it here.[8]

---

8. See *Hegel's God* and *Is There a Sabbath for Thought?* This matter is also a concern of *Art, Origins, Otherness: Between Art and Philosophy*. These last two books try to give some indication of what a metaxological dialogue between art, religion, and philosophy might look like. I am suggesting a kind of metaxological rethinking of Hegel's absolute spirit and the triad of art, philosophy, and religion—though perhaps we must make that a quaternity, because the ethical cannot be excluded, in that the good of the "to be" is at stake. With these others, philosophy is one of the essential ways of being true to the between, though not the only one. Metaxological philosophy does not crow on the conceptual apex, for in the porosity of the between there is no such apex, though there are songs of passage.

I think these betweens ask philosophy to be open to the religious, as perhaps a more intimate and ultimate between: in the sense of having intimacy with the primal between, the porosity of being between the human and the divine. I would claim that being religious is dedicated to keeping unclogged this porosity which is at the wellspring of life itself. Indeed without that porosity being kept unclogged, the deeper sources of philosophical thinking would themselves come to dry up. If so, should one be surprised if the end of one of the triad—art, religion, philosophy—goes hand-in-hand with the alleged end of one or more of the others? The so-called end of art, death of God, and end of philosophy: are these Siamese triplets whose lives rise and fall, die or are wasted by the sickness of the others?

The matter at issue does not bear exclusively on one or the other of these three. There is a sense in which the matter is more deeply religious than anything else: it bears on that primal porosity in which the seeds of reverence, of inspiration, and the grounding confidence in truth and thought either grow or perish. We live in an ethos of autonomous humanity in which we have reconfigured the space of porosity in terms of our own self-determining powers, sometimes blocking the space of communication between us and transcendence as other. The reverence at issue suggests the thought of something strange: not seeds growing in a fixed ground, but because the ground is a porosity, we must think of seeds growing in a kind of openness or a seeming nothing. We are asked to think an energy of passing, or passage in which we are first opened before we open ourselves. We are a *passio essendi* before we are a *conatus essendi*: first given to be, before we endeavor to be. The issue is one of gratitude for this being given to be, and reverence for its source.

What I am here calling the primal porosity is connected with that between (discussed before) relative to the origin, and relative to the "beyond." This between bears on the extremities of the between of finite immanence. Life in the midst is a between, but this middle is bound by extremes that are the threshold of the more ultimate between—between finite immanence and its more ultimate origin and transcendence. The primal porosity is always configured one way or another in the daily, more domestic middle. A great task for the practice of life itself in the daily middle is to keep this porosity unclogged. Being aesthetic, religious, and philosophical, practiced in the mindful spirit of truthfulness, are the indispensable helpers that keep us on the way. Nor must we forget being ethical: this is our willing care for the good in the ethos of being. A deeper understanding of this ethos brings us back to the *passio essendi* and to the porosity, and transforms being ethical in a more agapeic direction, that is, in the direction of the service of the other that has been recommended to us by the great religious traditions. Neither a culture of autonomous art, nor autonomous ethics, nor autonomous philosophy is best suited to dwelling thus in the between, or the ethos or the porosity.

Beyond the hegemonies of past sacred univocities in which worldly and spiritual will to power too often colluded equivocally with each other, we need a new, or renewed way of being religious. Without gratitude for what has being given, it is hard to see how we could find our way to the renewed reverence.

BEYOND THE SOLITUDES OF IMMANENCE

That reverence has come under attack in modernity, for reasons complex enough to require an exploration of its own, but among them is the extremely strong drive in modernity to univocalize all being.[9] In postmodernity there are assaults on that univocity, and celebrations of equivocity, assaults and celebrations that arouse in us our own equivocal assessment. By contrast with both the drive and the counterdrive, it needs to be reiterated that the longer tradition(s) of philosophy testify to something of the plurivocity of philosophy itself. This plurivocity betokens a rich sense of the space between system and poetics, and asks finesse for its fertile equivocity. On occasion that finesse might have to confront wrongheaded univocalizings, as well as celebrate, with postmodernity, the richness of the equivocal. But there are other occasions when it must allow the fitting univocity its proper place, as well as demurring about any apotheosis of equivocity that reneges on mindful intermediation and communicability. Flinging in our faces absurdities that repress intelligibility is no response to false clarities oppressing honest mindfulness.

Still, one might press the objection that in all these past practices of philosophies there is a central quest for an understanding as univocal and systematic as possible. Certainly philosophers often do show a strong

---

9. See *Is There a Sabbath for Thought?*, chap. 8.

predilection for univocity. Yet even if proper univocity is one of philosophy's desiderata, the practices of *philosophizing* extend beyond that. Thus there is the search itself—this cannot be univocalized, even if it searches for univocity. There is the origin of the search in a radical astonishment that may give rise to the search for univocal cognition but that itself cannot be univocalized completely. Even if we begin in the negative of astonishment, namely, doubt, doubt itself cannot be completely univocalized, even when its secret desire is for a certainty that gives absolutely univocal knowing. There is the eros of the search—eros for univocity cannot be itself univocalized. Thus, for instance, the passion for scientific and mathematical truth is not itself scientific or mathematical: it exceeds what it seeks; were this not so, there would be no seeking at all. The passion for objective knowing is not itself fully objectifiable.

There is also the fact that the practice of philosophy can never be absolutely solitary. There are solitudes, and philosophy drives one into many, but these are finally always qualified by communicative intermediations with others, whether overt or *incognito*.[10] This is evident in the dialogical practice of philosophy, if we go back to the beginning of dialectic (*dia-legein*) in conversation. The *dia* is always a double, even as it is also a porous medium (as when we say something is diaphanous: the *dia* names a middle, via which a light passes). There is always a pluralization at work.

The communicative practice of philosophizing is more than the said: in the communal saying, and in the being truthful of the speakers, something of the true comes to be communicated. This saying and this being truthful cannot be univocalized or systematized. You could not have a conversation at all, if all speaking were reduced or reducible to complete univocity. Even more evidently so, there would be no eros; nor could our conversation be marked by irony or laughter or mockery and such like. Nor could you have a conversation if all speech could be systematized. You might have a monologue of thought alone with itself. I do know that Aristotle and Hegel named their god as thought thinking itself, but this to me smacks of a return on the speculative heights of a certain acme of univocity. One might call it the "religious poetry" of speculative univoc-

---

10. See "The Solitudes of Philosophy," in *Loneliness*, ed. Lee Rouner (Notre Dame, Ind.: University of Notre Dame Press, 1998), 63–78.

ity, but even then, it is not enough. That it is religious poetry shows that there is more than univocity at the highest acme of speculative univocity.

Religious poetry has not been to the tastes of modern philosophers whose practices of philosophy have especially been influenced by a scientific and mathematical self-image. Sometimes one finds in the not distant past philosophy denounced as "secret theology." But is not *all* philosophy, in a way, a secret something or other, or in open or screened relation to its own significant others? Otherwise, the limit of such solitary self-containment of philosophy would be a kind of autism of being and mind. In truth, an interplay with significant others, expressed or reserved, always influences the self-understanding of the philosopher. And this even when philosophy lays claim to complete autonomy. To grant this interplay, of course, immediately undercuts the claim to complete autonomy: what autonomy is claimed is itself dependent on something received. In *Philosophy and Its Others* (as I mentioned at the outset) I speak of the plurivocal practices of philosophy in terms of the following significant others: the scholar, the technician, the scientist, the poet, the priest, the revolutionary, the hero, the sage. Being in relation to an other or others is always important, indeed constitutive. Depending on the significant other(s), the self-understanding and practice of the philosopher will differ. The scientist, technician, scholar, and perhaps revolutionary have been important in modernity, but all these influences are qualified by a belief in system as autonomous knowing.

What is wrong with that? The disingenuousness of the claim to autonomous knowing; and the occlusion of the between, that is here, of philosophy's own being in relation to an other or others, that shape the self-image and practice of the philosopher. This is so willy-nilly, let the overt rhetoric say the opposite as much as it please. We neglect the fact that the practices of philosophy are between philosophy itself and these others. We lose sight of the fact that it is perhaps philosophy's special vocation just to attend to that space "between," as it attends to both itself and its others. This is more than a simplistic emulation of the other held significant. It is being in relation in a double sense: *defined as self by being defined in relation to what is other*, inhabiting the space of thought in a metaxological manner. The modern ideal of self-determining or autonomous knowing has put this into recess, while, in fact, it is always parasitical on that which it has recessed. The autonomy of philosophy is not univocally self-produced. What freedom philosophy gains comes from the manner in which it inhabits the *metaxu*. There is always indebtedness to the other, and indeed the possibility of gratitude for what is given to it, and not simply produced through itself alone.

This stress on autonomous knowing, coupled with the turn to self, with the increased demands made on univocity in modernity, and with decreased patience for the sometimes intractable equivocities of being—all these feed into a formation of the systematic impulse that itself makes more and more demands on the desire for absolute unity and completeness, culminating in its conceptual hyperbole in Hegel's system. It is entirely just from that point of view that many of the discontented thinkers of modernity since Hegel would find some bone to pick with him. Latent in his ambitions and claims to achievement are many of these questionable assumptions. Admittedly, they are given their own form by Hegel, and as we might also grant, in his own way he did struggle against some of their deficiencies, even while being their victim, also in his own way.

Do the anti-idealist deconstructors of totality offer us enough? I think neither Hegelian system nor the detotalizing practices of such critics opens for thinking the porosity of the needed reverence that releases us beyond the solitudes of immanence. Hegel offers a "sublationary infinitism": the finite is sublated in the infinite, and the results are a self-circling immanence. The detotalizing practices of the critics of "sublationary infinitism" are often marked by postulatory finitism. And it is by virtue of opposition to such sublationary infinitism as untrue to finitude, or not true enough, that postulatory finitism borrows much of its contemporary persuasiveness. But postulatory finitism is also given over to self-circling immanence, though the self-circling is tortured rather than reconciled. In truth, both sublationary infinitism and postulatory finitism share the fact that they are philosophies of *unremitting immanence*.

If and when these two come to the boundary between immanence and transcendence, they swerve off that boundary, back to immanence; swerve differently certainly, whether in dialectical-speculative or in detotalizing form, but both offer us at most an immanent self-transcendence. Neither robustly addresses the ultimate between where, in intimate immanence, all solitudes are surprised by, or overtaken by, or shocked into an unexpected porosity to transcendence as irreducibly other. This is not a transcendence defined by immanence, but a transcendence that gives immanence itself to be, and endows the immanent between with the plurivocal promise of immanent self-transcending beings.

A philosophy of this ultimate between requires something other: a philosophy of finitude not postulatory; a philosophy of infinitude not sublationary; a philosophy in which we are not closed off from rethinking transcendence in a sense other than either of these positions can, or will contemplate. Perhaps some deconstructions of Hegelian system seem to look for something reminiscent of metaxological philosophy, but do they have the resources needed for thinking in the space *between* system and poetics? If their reaction to positions like Hegel's are bewitched by the notion that he has the monopoly on "system," the temptation will be strong to turn that between into a "versus," undervaluing the systematic, even while granting the poetic a new respect.

As I suggested at the outset, this "versus" is not the most fruitful for us, in addressing the different betweens that call for thought. A transdialectical practice of philosophy must enact something of metaxological mindfulness that, while not claiming to be the system, does justice to both the systematic and the poetic—and the religious. If I am not mistaken this means for philosophy a return to the plurivocal condition of the *metaxu*, to permeability to the others, and to the porosity of being in the between. This porosity looks like a return to zero and yet it is not an empty nothing. In and through it, we are offered, so to say, a fertile poverty that, in a new interface with creation, and in dialogue with the others, especially the poetic and religious, occasions the release of philosophizing from the solitudes of self-circling immanence.

6 ∞ Saturated Phenomena and the Hyperboles of Being

On Marion's Postmetaphysical Thought

OPENING METAPHYSICS: NOT QUITE A HAS-BEEN

I want to offer a study in contrast between Jean-Luc Marion's saturated phenomenon and the hyperboles of being.[1] There are significant overlaps between these, and some striking convergences, but at the outset there is a crucial divergence of a more general sort that is worth mentioning concerning the status of metaphysics. Marion's work is saturated with the rhetoric of postmetaphysical philosophy, represented paradigmatically in his version of phenomenology. What he means by "metaphysics" is very much in line with what Heidegger says about it. In opening remarks while introducing this work I tried to make clear my resistance to such talk about "postmetaphysical" philosophy, and I do not have to repeat what I have already said. Marion's claim is that phenomenology now replaces metaphysics as first philosophy.[2] By contrast, I stress the plurivocal practices of metaphysical thinking. To take just both the Aristotelian and Scholastic-rationalist definitions and practices of metaphysics: it may well be that they do not fully answer thought, perhaps even about

---

1. The reflections in this and the following chapter were developed in connection with a 2013 symposium sponsored by the Theology Institute at Villanova University on "Truth and Mystery," at which Marion also spoke. In the present chapter I deal primarily with my engagement with Marion, and in the following chapter I take up being true to mystery, but it is worth pointing out the intimate connection of these two chapters, which were originally composed as "Being True to Mystery: On Saturated Phenomena and the Hyperboles of Being."

2. See *In Excess: Studies of Saturated Phenomena*, trans. R. Horner and V. Berraud (New York: Fordham University Press, 2002), chap. 1, "On Phenomenology of Givenness and First Philosophy"; also *The Visible and the Revealed*, trans. C. M. Gschwandtner et al. (New York: Fordham University Press, 2008), chap. 3, "Metaphysics and Phenomenology: A Relief for Theology."

the unavoidable questions they themselves pose, but they do not exhaust the possible plurality of practices of metaphysical thinking, even within the so-called tradition of metaphysics itself. To reiterate why I take seriously Aristotle's canonical saying that being is said in many senses (*Metaphysics* 1003b5 and 1028a10): it still possesses the power to release us to this plurality of practices. The significance of this saying I develop in the direction of a metaxological metaphysics.

There is no overcoming of metaphysics as such for there is no univocal essence of metaphysics to be overcome. That there are *many practices* of metaphysics, Platonic, Aristotelian, Thomistic, rationalistic, transcendental, realistic, and so on, means that we too must live up to this plurality in thought. To determine this plurality as if it were some univocal essence is too reductive. Hence the worry that there is a secret univocalization at work in philosophical rhetoric about our being "postmetaphysical," even as that same rhetoric often is brought to bear on "deconstructing" the univocity of "metaphysics." That means too that one can continue to speak of metaphysics as first philosophy (*protē philosophia*), in its being mindful of the meaning of the "to be." The plurivocity of meanings to the "to be" can be reflected in the plurivocal practices of metaphysical thinking. Metaphysics need not be seen as a "has-been," and can be fruitfully pursued in a metaxological register. This allows us a different orientation to earlier practices of metaphysical thinking; allows us to address some of the key post-Kantian developments in philosophy; allows us also fruitfully to do metaphysics in a robustly contemporary way.

Despite differences in starting points, despite differences in how we understand the tradition of metaphysics, despite differences in how we see the heritage of metaphysics and the promise of its future, there are significant overlaps in where I and Marion sometimes end. I have developed the notion of the hyperboles of being most proximately in connection with finding a way to God (in *God and the Between*), developed in a manner that is consistent with a fuller explication of what is entailed by a metaxological metaphysics. These hyperboles of being dovetail with the fourfold sense of being involved in a metaxological metaphysics, and thus too offer their testimony to the plurivocal nature of being, and the guiding orientation that being is said in many senses. And yet I have been struck by how in the field of these ultimate considerations key notions of Marion, articulated from the direction of his own development of phenomenology, come to some convergence with the hyperboles of being. In this light, I will first offer a general contrast of saturated phenomena and the hyperboles of being. Then I will look more particularly at the four hyperboles of being in turn, indicating their natures, and where they come into contact with, or diverge from, Marion's saturated phenomena.

GENERAL CONTRAST OF SATURATED PHENOMENA AND THE HYPERBOLES OF BEING

First to the general contrast: the hyperboles are happenings within immanence that yet cannot be entirely determined in the terms of immanence. Finite immanence, I suggest, is best described as a *metaxu*, articulated by a creative pluralization of happenings, beings, and processes, held together and sustained in differentiations by proliferating networks of relation, and yet impossible to close into one single totality, because within the between of finite immanence the boundaries we encounter again and again prove porous. The between itself is porous to what is itself impossible to finitize fully. I would say our being religious is the most intimate and ultimate testimony to this constitutive porosity, always and everywhere on the verge of mystery beyond finitization, even when communicated in finitude. This is one reason why *figurative* communication is crucial on just this issue. I have spoken of metaphor, analogy, and symbol, as well as hyperbole.[3] Passages in the between, and not least its religious crossing, are witnessed in the watchwords of each of these figures: the "is" of metaphor, the "as" of analogy, the "with" of symbol, the "above" of hyperbole. The passages of these figures go in, go out, go down, go up. The passages are a "trans"—a going beyond, even in going in, or out, or down, or up. The very word hyperbole catches something of this passing, here this "throwing above," or "being thrown above": *hyper-ballein* in Greek. In the between we are thrown down, but also thrown above, being thrown above the between. Hence the suggestion that the hyperboles communicate more than the terms of immanence can circumscribe. And given the figurative dimension, if philosophy is to have any hope, it has to be porous to its most significant others—art and religion. If its practice is only in-

---

3. *God and the Between*, esp. chap. 6.

sistent on self-determining thinking, then this enabling porosity is inevitably disabled. The hyperboles reveal certain *threshold* happenings, and again not least in opening the intimation of mystery in relation to the divine. In living they witness to happenings of opening to ultimate transcendence as other to the immanent between. Philosophy apart, we live these hyperboles, live in and out of them. Rarely do we comprehend their significance, and often in our lives we betray their promise. Without genuine metaphysical mindfulness of the primal ethos of being, it is hard to do them justice in philosophical thought.

Marion's account of the saturated phenomena has an *intensive side* in terms of the inherent structure of the matter at issue and an *extensive side* in terms of the range of phenomena to which our attention is drawn. First on the intensive side, we see a complex exposition and development within phenomenology itself, in which Marion sees himself as inheriting and extending the essential insights of Husserl and Heidegger. If Husserl offers a first reduction to objecthood, Heidegger a second reduction to the being of beings, Marion proposes a third reduction to givenness. The terms inherited from Husserl do shape his account. Generally in Husserlian terms, the meaning of phenomena is understood in terms of a conditioning horizon, in terms of intention and intuition, and the fulfillment of the intention in the intuition of givenness.[4] However, in the case of the saturated phenomena, the conditioning horizon seems to give way and the phenomenon is said to be unconditioned. Moreover, there is an excess of intuition to intention: something exceeding intentionality, one might say, a "too-muchness," an overdeterminacy that yet is given. Among other things this seems to lead to a reversal of what we take to be the normal priority of the transcendental ego relative to which the phenomenon is defined—as for us. Now it is for us, in a kind of reversal of intentionality, to be for what shows itself: we are the *interloqué*, the ad-

---

4. I will draw especially from the important essay "The Saturated Phenomenon" in *The Visible and the Revealed*. Thus Marion says (24) that he wants to envision "a type of phenomenon that would reverse the condition of a horizon (by surpassing it, instead of being inscribed within it) and that would reverse the reduction (by leading the I back to itself, instead of being reduced to the I)?" Further this is "not a question here of envisaging a phenomenology without any I or horizon" but "of taking seriously the claim that since the formulation of the "principle of all principles," that "*possibility* stands higher than actuality," and of envisaging this possibility radically. Obviously at work here is furthering the Heideggerian reversal of the priority of actuality to possibility in Aristotle.

dressed.⁵ There is also something about the saturated phenomenon that exceeds all the concepts we might bring to bear on it. Marion points out that there are weak or banal phenomena, such as everyday perception, or mathematical form, where the intuition is relatively empty, hence phenomena where it is easier for intention and intuition to be adequate to each other. In the saturated phenomenon, by contrast, it is the inadequacy or inequality between intention and intuition that tilts in the direction of the excess—the excess that yet *qua* phenomenon is given.⁶

These observations bear on the intricate structure of the saturated phenomenon, but what of the extensive range of such phenomena? Here Marion cites a number of instances from the history of philosophy, including Descartes's idea of the infinite and Kant's idea of the sublime.⁷ This extensive range includes for him the painting as spectacle (idol), as well as a particular face I love (icon). Finally, the religious threshold is reached when he suggests that the theophany in connected with the saturated phenomenon. "The theophany," as he puts it, is "where the excess of intuition lead to the paradox that an invisible gaze visibly envisages me and loves me. And it is here that the question of the possibility of a phenomenology of religion would be posed." Further: "In any case, recognizing saturated phenomena comes down to thinking seriously 'that which none greater can be conceived [*aliquid quo majus cogitari nequit*]'—which means thinking it as a final possibility of phenomenology."⁸

---

5. Ibid., 44: "The I experiences itself as constituted by it.... The I loses its anteriority and finds itself, so to speak, deprived of its duties of constitution, and is thus itself constituted: it becomes a me rather than an I ... one meets here what I have thematized elsewhere under the name of the subject at its last appeal: the *interloqué*.... This reversal leaves it interlocuted (*interloqué*), essentially surprised by the more original event that detaches it from itself.... As a constituted witness, the subject remains the worker of truth, but is no longer its producer." On the *interloqué* see also "The Final Appeal of the Subject," in *Deconstructive Subjectivities*, ed. Simon Critchley and Peter Dews (Albany: State University of New York Press, 1996), chap. 5.

6. Ibid., 37: "Finitude is experienced (and proved) [*s'éprouve (et se prouve)*] less in the shortage of the given before our gaze than in that this gaze sometimes no longer measures the amplitude of givenness. Or rather, measuring itself against that givenness, the gaze experiences it, sometimes in the suffering of an essential passivity, as having no measure with itself. Finitude is experienced as much through excess as through lack—indeed, more through excess than through lack."

7. Ibid., 46n: "And I insist that here it is purely and simply a matter of the phenomenon taken in its fullest meaning."

8. Ibid., 47–48, where Marion offers a recapitulation and classification of phenomena. Pure historical events need a hermeneutics. Of revelation he says: "I here intend a strictly phenomenological concept: an appearance that is purely of itself and starting from itself, that

Before turning more fully to the hyperboles of being, I return briefly to how one's understanding of "metaphysics" has relevance for the matter under consideration (see my opening remarks above). Phenomenology as addressing saturated phenomena or being addressed by them is not "metaphysics," nor is it metaxological metaphysics as open to a wording of the between in which the hyperboles of being are communicated. I note that Marion defines the phenomenon in relation to Kant and Husserl. I would say my own (metaxological) thinking is more a response to Hegel, and this is relevant to how we understand the nature of phenomena. For one thing, *apropos* of the transcendental nature of the Kantian approach, there is a significant working through of some of its difficulties in classical German philosophy, with Fichte, Schelling, and Hegel not least. In relation to that "working through," I see a metaxological metaphysics as postdialectical, more precisely, transdialectical, and hence post-transcendental in a complicated sense in which an effort is made to take the measure of Hegel. Worth recalling with Hegel is his critique of the emptiness of the thing in itself as we find it in Kant. There is here a dialectical critique of the idea of phenomena as such. It is impossible to rest with a dualism of phenomenon and noumenon—the essence appears. If the essence did not appear we could say nothing of it, and not even say we know nothing of it. One might say that Hegel is trying to turn the screw on an equivocity said to mark the Kantian dualism in which the phenomenon is never an empty appearing, because the essence, so to say, fills itself, fulfills itself in coming to articulated appearance.

Of course, there is no excess finally to what appears, in Hegel's claim to have fully unfolded the essential possibilities of the manifestation of the absolute. The immanent consummation of the essential, without excess or mysterious remainder or transcendence, is clearly a point of divergence with Marion's saturated phenomenon and my own sense of the hyperbolic in being. It is the nature of this excess or overdeterminacy that is at issue, and the articulation of our being in relation to it, or its being in relation to us, beyond all reductive relationality, beyond even mutually symmetrical relationality.

---

does not subject its possibility to any preliminary determination." He goes on to specify three domains, already noted: first, the painting as spectacle (idol); second, a particular face I love (icon); finally, the theophany. I find it interesting that he singles out Anselm's characterization of God, and I would say that the so-called ontological argument has much to do with the issue of the hyperbolic in immanence. On this see, *God and the Between*, 143–44 and 152–53.

The point is not quite to charge Marion's phenomenology with keeping bad company with Kantian dualism, but rather to suggest that the stress on the transcendental, as point of departure to attain givenness by different reductions, does raise questions about its truth to the between. There is a tilt in transcendental philosophy to prioritize the transcendental ego. Clearly Marion is interested in undoing this within the context of phenomenology itself. I would say there are practices of dialectic which point to this undoing of dualism, or to the undoing of the priority of transcendental subjectivity. One might see Hegel and what happened in German philosophy after Kant to be the first serious coming to terms with instabilities within transcendental philosophy. By contrast, one might find in twentieth-century phenomenology a second sustained effort, and sometimes even something of a doppelgänger of this first effort. To note only one or two points, one might recall the move from transcendental subjectivity to historicity in the case of Heidegger. One might also recall the haunting of philosophy by recalcitrant othernesses, of which Schelling in his earlier "working though" was particularly conscious, something central to recent developments in continental philosophy, even to the not-surprising resurgence of interest in Schelling in some postmodern circles.

When Marion discusses being and appearing in Husserl and Heidegger some of his remarks sound almost Hegelian: "As much appearing, so much being."[9] Hegel's phenomenology is a preparation for his logic, when knowing no longer needs to go beyond itself, and thought can think itself.[10] If there is a phenomenology in my approach it cannot be separated from metaphysics; and rather than Hegel's absolute knowing there is metaxological mindfulness which renews itself in a poverty of thinking, all but the opposite of Hegel's absolute knowing. And yet metaxological mindfulness in its own way can be absolved—released into the fertile poverty of the between, where there is a point to logic but

---

9. *The Visible and the Revealed*, 6.

10. It would be a relevant study to look at how Hegel in his *Science of Logic*, while dealing with the doctrine of essence, distinguishes between *Schein* and *Erscheinung*, the first with the meaning of a more dissembling appearance ("seeming"), the second with the meaning of a necessary appearing of the essence, such that any dualism of appearing and essence proves to be dialectically untenable. This discussion in Hegel is a crucial one where he appears to overcome dualism dialectically but with the outcome that the sense of surplus otherness is dissolved.

in the sense of a *logos* of the *metaxu*. In the transdialectical *metaxu*, *logos* is not a matter of thought thinking itself but thought thinking the other to thought thinking itself, thought indeed singing the other, released to agapeic mindfulness, a release itself agapeic. If there is a *logos* here, there is no complete separation of phenomenology and metaphysics—beyond dualism, beyond dialectic, there is a *logos* of the *metaxu*. Phenomenology moves from the natural attitude to a more transcendental standpoint; Hegel moves from natural consciousness to philosophy as absolute knowing. Metaxological philosophy witnesses a different attitude to the natural attitude and philosophy. Both the latter are in the between, both are ways of wondering, out in the world, in the midst, astonished and perplexed there. Much has to do with recollection in thought of the porosity, with the stress of resultant thought, with the emphasis, the direction of thought. The between is not approached in a dyadic way, nor in a dialectical way: there is a fluidity of interplay between the so-called natural and the philosophical attitudes that is closer to the Socratic-Platonic practice of dialectic.

In any case, I do think the Hegelian dialectic has to be acknowledged and answered and not necessarily in the direction of Kant, but in terms of something about the otherness of the thing in itself as not a mere privative indeterminacy. There is something of surplus otherness, so to say, appearing in the phenomena. Am I right in taking the work of Marion as pointing in some such direction, though not in the terms of an explicitly post-Hegelian thought, but in terms of an immanent exploration of what phenomena as such mean? Of course, in Hegel being is voided.[11] It is a mere indeterminacy, the emptiest of the categories. This is not at all what I intend by being and would rather speak again of overdeterminacy. This again means an intimate strangeness in surplus otherness. The overriding dialectic in Hegel does not do justice to this. One might even talk about the shine on things. In ancient philosophy one might point to the *eidos* as the look of the things, but not a look that we impose on the thing by our look. Its look looks thus and thus to our looking. That is to say, the look communicates something of this intimate strangeness in surplus otherness. It is intimate in the sense of calling us into a participative relation and communication. It is strange, not in the sense of an estranging

---

11. See chap. 1, "The Voiding of Being."

other but a mysterious strangeness that always eludes the domesticating grasp of our determinability and self-determination.

Hegel's dialectic is not fully true to this. I have indeed spoken of the saturated surface, of philosophy being on the surface of things.[12] There is a surplus immediacy that is not to be described in terms of the empty indeterminacy of Hegel.[13] This sense of surplus immediacy is taken up with respect to the claims made by Hegel about sense-certainty in the *Phenomenology*—there we find a drive toward the universal which is not attentive to the saturated phenomenon in Marion's sense. I also refer to art and religious praying as ultimate happenings in which this surplus immediacy is crucial, and again Hegel's account of art and religion does not do justice to them. There is a drive onward toward absolute knowing, conceived in philosophical terms, where the goal is said to be reached when "knowledge no longer needs to go beyond itself," where "appearance becomes identical with essence."[14] There is no more intimate strangeness in surplus otherness. There is nothing surplus any more. (Are there considerations here analogous to the question of the adequacy of intention and intuition in phenomenology?)

In contrast to Hegel, I would say that the more "absolute" standpoint is when knowing knows that more than anything else it must go beyond itself—beyond being at home with itself—beyond its determinability and self-determination, in a poverty of philosophy which just in its poverty is rich in communicative openness to this surplus otherness. This poverty is closer to the richest sense of "being true" about which I will say more in the following chapter. It is not an ignorance, nor yet again the resurrection of inquisitive curiosity set once more on determination and determinability. Nor yet is it the self-determination of cognition that would master being as other, and also its own otherness. This poverty is on the threshold of the overdeterminacy, where its being true knows it does not know, and where a new ontological reverence for the mystery of being as intimately strange comes home to us again.

One can sense a familial intimacy here with what Marion is trying

---

12. See "On the Surface of Things: Transient Life and Beauty in Passing," in Desmond, *The Gift of Beauty and the Passion of Being: On the Threshold between the Aesthetic and the Religious* (Eugene, Ore.: Wipf and Stock, 2018), chap. 2.
13. On this see *The Intimate Strangeness of Being*, chap. 3.
14. *Phenomenology of Spirit*, §80 and §89.

to communicate with the idea of the saturated phenomenon. There is an exodus into a bright darkness in which one is almost nothing, and yet the nothing is not nothing. One can be strangely full of emptiness, where there is a fulfillment in being emptied. One is emptied of false fixations, and of false absolutizations of autonomous knowing. To be full of emptiness is to be filled in emptiness by the passage of mindfulness in the porosity of being. This is a form of mindfulness that itself is more primally porous to what is communicated in the between. I think also of the *interloqué*, the interlocuted: being in an interlocution, addressed before responding in a *passio essendi* more primal and porous than our *conatus essendi*. The interlocuted as respondent interlocutor yet participates in wording the between: locuting the *inter*. To go to school philosophically: a *paideia* in eu-locution, well-wording the between.

At issue with this poverty of knowing is recollection of an *original porosity of being*, neither objective nor subjective, but enabling both, while being more than both, where there is no fixation of the difference of minding and things, where our mindfulness wakes to itself by being woken up by the communication of being in its emphatic otherness. Before we reflectively come to ourselves, in the original porosity of being there is the more primal opening in astonishment, opened to what communicates to it from beyond itself. We do not open ourselves; being opened, we are as an opening. The opening is not indeterminate, not determinate, not self-determining. There is something overdeterminate about it. To understand it, it is important to attend to differences between wonder in the modalities of astonishment, perplexity, and curiosity.[15] All determinate knowing is made possible by it, but it is not yet determinate knowing. The porosity is not a vector of intentionality that goes from subject to object. It is not determined by a univocally fixed objectivity stamping its determinacies on a *tabula rasa*. If it is not determinate objectivity, neither is it indeterminate or self-determining subjectivity. The porosity is prior to univocal objectivity and it is prior to intentionality. In and through it we are given to be in a patience of being more primal than any cognitive or pragmatic endeavor to be. (Once again I sense analogies sympathetic with what is involved with Marion's saturated phenomenon.) This patience entails our being awoken in a not yet determinate

---

15. See chapter 3, above, as well as *The Intimate Strangeness of Being*, chap. 10.

minding that is not full with itself or fulfilled with objects but filled with an openness to what is beyond itself. The porosity suggests what looks like such a paradoxical conjunction of fullness and emptiness: being filled with openness, hence being empty and yet being full.

I would underscore the ontological/metaphysical character of this. The porosity of being is like a no-thing. It is not an indeterminate nothing from which nothing could come to be. It is not determinate negation, for this presupposes beings as already in being and in the process of becoming. If I were to call it an overdeterminate nothing it would be to invoke the paradoxical conjunction of fullness and emptiness. In its irreducibility to indeterminacy, determination, or self-determination, such a no-thing is inseparable from surplus creative power out of which beings come to be beings. In their coming to be there is a patience in their being received into being, yet they are relatively for themselves, and as such embody a conjunction of the passion to be (*passio essendi*) and the endeavor to be (*conatus essendi*). In the twinning of patience and striving, we are the porosity of being become mindful, become willing.

THE IDIOCY OF BEING AND VANITY

I now want to offer a more particular contrast of the four hyperboles of being and the saturated phenomenon. I will first offer a brief description of the particular hyperbole and then proceed to engage with cognate concepts in Marion's thought.

The *first hyperbole* I name as *the idiocy of being*. There is something idiotic about given finite being as given to be, that exceeds all our efforts at the finitization of its determinate thereness and intelligibility. In its given overdeterminacy it manifests a surplus immediacy of being. It shows a sheer "that it is" which shines with an intimate strangeness. The idiocy is this intimate strangeness of its ontological concreteness as exceeding our determination of it in terms of our abstract universals. Finite being happens to be without inherent necessity, and while it might seem to be absurd, I think it should be called rather a *surplus surd*. To describe this surplus surd as the absurd would not be right, for it makes all finite intelligibilities possible. Presupposed by all finite intelligibility, it is not itself a finite intelligibility. The surplus of given being stuns us into mindfulness about what gives it to be at all, as there is no necessity to its being there at all, nor does it explain itself. The ontological patience of finite being makes mindfulness porous to what exceeds finite determination. To be as finite exceeds the terms of finitude itself. In being received as being, finitude is not simply thrown down in the between, but as hyperbolic it is thrown above itself.

There are those who limit, even reject the principle of sufficient reason. (Heidegger has a bone to pick with Leibniz.) One can understand why the idiocy might suggest this limitation, even rejection. The idiocy as this primal ontological givenness is not the outcome of that principle, nor is it possible to make the givenness *qua* given more intelligibly determinate with respect to it. However, this need not mean the rejection of intelligibility. Rather, determinate intelligibility comes to be out of this more original givenness, this inconvertible being given to be of what is. When I say there is an intimate strangeness to it, this is not a mere empty indeterminacy. The rose is without a why, it will be said, and yes, it must be said, but what is the nature of the why at stake here? Clearly it is not a determinate "why" we can specify, or a "why" subject to our self-determining reason. Yes, but givenness *qua* givenness, can be responded to in a plurality of ways, not all of which put the "why" completely out of play. There is a "why" of wondering beyond the "why" of determinate curiosity. This latter might seem more faithfully to serve the principle of sufficient reason but the former as surplus to determinacy opens to the "why" of the overdeterminate givenness as such. This "why it is" is in the hyperbolic dimension. It wonders not about a determinate cause, but about the be-cause in the sense of the cause of the "to be": why being at all?

Where are some of the places in Marion's work that might be relevant here? I wonder if his exploration of vanity is connected with the idiocy of being.[16] One might say yes, though vanity expresses the matter in the mode of the deprivation of wonder, close to boredom. Vanity is when the marvel vanishes from the things as given, perhaps through weary overfamiliarization. The things are just there, idiotic but empty, and we are just there too, oppressed by the idiocy, for the charge of the surplus of the overdeterminate seems now either to have evaporated or become an un-

---

16. *God without Being*, trans. Thomas A. Carlson (Chicago: University of Chicago Press, 1991), 108–38, where Marion also has his sights on *agapē* in reflecting on vanity.

bearable burden. But vanity is only vanity because something more affirmative was once promised, indeed offered, and is still secretly anticipated, but its coming is withheld, or its arrival has been thwarted, and so we are disappointed. Perhaps we have related to the given in such a way that we remake it as a void idiocy—not a mysterious idiocy on the verge of the sacred. Indeed, relative to the latter, one might connect it with the idiocy of the divine in the event of mystic intimacy.[17]

If the idiocy is not determinate, it is also not indeterminate; it is overdeterminate, in excess of the determinate and our self-determination. Nevertheless, it is enabling of determinacy and self-determination. One asks again if this surd character about the givenness *qua* given is simply absurd? I would say our response depends on what ontological attunement marks us as between-beings, marking also what rejoinder we bring to bear on the given. There is an original astonishment in which the surd is communicated as not at all absurd, but an excess of mystery moving all our efforts to surpass the absurd as such. Amazement is porous to its idiotic marvel. If we bring an attunement only of opposing doubt or *a priori* suspicion, or an orientation of demand that being meet our measure, we have set ourselves up in advance for disappointment. In one extreme of estrangement we will treat it as the nauseous (Sartre) rather than as an intimate strangeness. It is then a surd that is absurd, if not repulsive. The *Es gibt* of Heidegger is not to be numbered with this attunement, but there is something about the *il y a* ("there is") of Levinas which is in the same family. I do not deny that we can be struck into the sinking feeling that there is something horrifying about being at all. It is and will be always too much. But horror and marvel are cousins. The surd is a blank idiocy and we blanch. Why do I think of the blank Leviathan, Moby Dick, monster of the deep, and creature of deathless mystery? The monstrous de-monstrates the idiocy of the sacred.[18]

---

17. *God and the Between*, chap. 13.
18. See *The Visible and the Revealed*, 5, where Marion generalizes from the rose to all phenomena as being without "why." I would distinguish different ways of why-ing: one corresponding to a more determinate and determinative curiosity, another answering to the tortured why of erotic perplexity, another again communicating the why-ing of agapeic astonishment. Being may be without a definitive determinate "why" in the first sense, but it is not without the why-ing of the second and the third modes. I think with Heidegger and other self-proclaimed philosophers of finitude, there is at work a postulatory finitism where finitude is considered as the "absolute" horizon in a world said to be without absolutes. Such fin-

I want to say there is a surd not absurd but saturated with qualitative worth and it is communicated in the intimacy of being. All being has this intimacy (true artists have a feel for this), a kind of mute interiority, one might even say. There are no neutral objects. Nausea is revolt fallen from an original astonishment whose porosity is reassembled in the form of visceral recoil, perhaps maturing into defiance. This is not simply a matter of the positive versus the negative. The too-muchness of the overdeterminacy can be heavy with presence, pregnant with a weight we find hard to bear. A touch of it is felt on hearing a song like "Sunday in Savannah":[19] the sulky boredom of a long soundless Sunday afternoon, with the humid air hardly stirring, everything resting in quiet, and nothing happening. But when nothing happens, suddenly one looks up and is lifted by a startling dawning that all this is recalcitrant, massive, dreadful—and yet marvelous and hovering lightly on the threshold of an immense mystery. This is the idiocy of being too. Always already given, and we grow in it, and as it dawns on us, it crushes us, empties us, releases us.[20] The idiocy of the intimate comes forth into the desire of the worthy more explicitly with the erotics of selving, but there is a secret love in the idiotic. Love of the worthy is there in the aesthetics of happening also. I return to the aesthetics and erotics below.

There is a silent "yes," silent but not autistic, more like the silence out of which communication and the music of the word comes, a deeply intimate ontological affirmation that holds us in being. It offers and receives us in being. And this "yes" is not first our "yes." We are affirmed before we affirm—"yessed" before we say "yes." The first ontological "yes" idiotically lives us. It is the communication of the overdeterminate prior to our determinate being as ourselves and prior to our becoming as self-determining. This first "yes," we can "yes" again in our second "yes," in our redoubled "yes," again and again. We can also mutilate this radically intimate love of being. Do we need a (phenomenological) *reduction* to

---

itude is that greater than which none can be conceived, taking over the role of God as defined by Anselm and foregrounded by Marion right at the end of his discussion of the saturated phenomenon. If I am not mistaken, a true thinking through of the meaning of the saturated phenomenon would mean we would have to give up postulatory finitism and again traverse in thought the threshold between finitude and infinity—a metaxological traversal. On postulatory finitism, see my *Is There a Sabbath for Thought?*, chap. 1.

19. See *Is There a Sabbath for Thought?*, 313; see also 37.
20. See *The Intimate Strangeness of Being*.

help us approach the significance of this "yes"? The hyperbole indicates a being *carried up* to it. We often ask "What's up?" and thereby ask about what is going on, about ongoingness in a broad sense and in a more special sense where our particular interest is vested. See "What's up" as referring us to *arising as such*—arising as being and into being. It comes up, and hence we ask "What's up?" We come to ourselves as being in this arising, in this something "being up" as arising. "What's up" is not neutral being, it is not nauseous, it is not an abstract universal, not even the concrete universal. It participates in the intimate universal. We are on the threshold of the mystery of the overdeterminate.

THE AESTHETICS OF HAPPENING, ICONS, IDOLS

The *second hyperbole of being, the aesthetics of happening*, opens up to the replete sensuousness of given being. One might say that our astonishment becomes ontological appreciation of the incarnate glory of the manifest creation which, showing itself sensuously, exceeds finitization. We are native to the material world, and our nativity brims over with ambiguity so rich in suggestion that it is resistant to our soon intervening conceptual domestications. Appreciation of immanence passes a threshold of immanence into a mysterious love of transience that exceeds transience. There is an aesthetic overdeterminacy to finitude, we find ourselves porous on the boundary of finitude and there is communicated a transport before the beauty of things. As if we are moved by a music in things, we are transported into another space of mindfulness hyperbolic to anything we can fix determinately in immanence.

This second hyperbole finds many analogues in Marion's diverse occupation with art and the aesthetic. His important distinction between the icon and the idol is clearly one that is resonant with the hyperbolics of aesthetic happening. Clearly also the sense of the aesthetic here is permeable to sacred significance: it is not merely aesthetic and can never be.[21] The idol takes shape when the looker, in and through the aesthetic spectacle, is returned to himself. One might be dazzled, yes, by

---

21. In addition to *The Idol and Distance: Five Studies*, trans. Thomas A. Carlson (New York: Fordham University Press, 2001). See also *In Excess: Studies of Saturated Phenomena*, chaps. 3 and 5; *The Crossing of the Visible*, trans. James K. A. Smith (Stanford, Calif.: Stanford University Press, 2004).

what is aesthetically happening but there is a circle of self-relation that is traversed. And while one might seem to exceed oneself toward what is other, the idolatrous other is the mirror in which we are really just returned to ourselves. The self-exceeding is no self-exceeding. The icon, by contrast, is the event where there is no closure to a circle of self-relation but the awakening to find oneself breached by being beheld. I do not behold but am beheld. I like to speak of a "beholding from"—in beholding, we are beholden to, and we behold from what is other to us. The look is not just our looking but the look communicates to and with us. I would say that the happening cannot be described in terms of a self-transcending alone, since rather something other communicates with us. If it is self-transcending, the transcending is beyond self because there is an other beyond self that communicates. The happening is more at the level of the *passio essendi*, and its intimacy with the porosity, than at the level of a *conatus essendi* that endeavors for itself in its thrust beyond itself. In one sense, there is a reversal of the intentionality of self-transcending, in another sense not just a reversal but the opening up in us of something prior to self-transcending. In the language I use, the intentionality of the endeavor to be is shown to be subtended by our *passio essendi* and our porosity. And this becomes a receiving welcome for what exceeds itself toward us. There is a sense too in which the communicating other itself becomes porous. Hence there is no mirroring in an idolatrous sense because the other to which we are related, or which is related to us, cannot be thus held for the purposes of a closed circling back to ourselves.

We are on thresholds of passing—passages of a between that is not just between us and ourselves. There is an *agapē* of the aesthetic, as Aristotle seems to suggest (*he tōn aisthēseon agapesis*, in Metaphysics 980a23) when speaking of astonishment (*thaumazein*). I think there is a generalized sense of iconic aesthetics which points in this direction. I recall Plato in the *Timaeus: pasa anankē tonde ton kosmos eikona tines einai*, "it is altogether necessary that the cosmos be a certain eikon" (*Timaeus* 29b). This is a statement where aesthetics and metaphysics also pass over into each other. Truly looked at, all being is iconic; being truly looked at, all being is iconic. Our beholding from the aesthetics of happening participates in being truly looked at, and truly looking.

Again there is the fertile doubleness here of fullness and emptiness.

The significance of "cosmos," for instance, draws our attention to the well-balanced harmony of the whole, but the beauty of the whole is no self-enclosed totality. It not only points beyond itself, but as an "open whole" there is communication to it from beyond itself in terms of the origin of its being thus beautifully an open whole at all. The whole seems to close on itself on a boundary. But an open whole is full for itself but not full of itself. It is paradoxically full as an open between, and hence as porous to what is more than it and its own self-fulfillment. In that sense, it is full with what it cannot contain, and hence is not full but an open space of receiving from what is beyond itself. We catch a glimmer of this in great works of art which have this dense inexhaustibility, and yet at the same time a paradoxical poverty, in which the "too-muchness" and the "almost-nothing" of the aesthetic happening are twinned together.

To return to a perhaps more familiar sense of the aesthetics of happening: there is here a determinacy but it is of such a richness and surplus that it shows the determinate as exceeding itself in its sensuous being there and its becoming. The determinate is more than determinate, and we come to the intimation of this "more" by mindful attention of what is determinately there. There is nothing static about this opening of the determinate to what enables determining. And it is thus not just our self-determination. One might be tempted in such a direction by thinking that the otherness is again a place where we come to ourselves. Is not this somewhat like the idol in Marion? It would then be what Kant calls a *subreption*. A subreption is when we attribute to the object what properly belong to the subject. We are not true when we take the attribution as belonging to the object, because it belongs to us. This is a term Kant uses in connection with the sublime but Kant is here not being true to the sublime as a true manifestation of stunning otherness *qua* other.

I remark briefly on the sublime because it is mentioned (as I noted above) by Marion in connection with Kant and suggested by him as connected with the saturated phenomenon. For me the equivocity of Kant is plain, leading to something that I cannot accept. In Kant the sublime is a subreption (*Critique of Judgment*, §27), attributing to the object what properly is of the subject. In the end this means there is no sublime object or other as such. There is no true sublimity as genuinely other. The whole process by which we are brought low and elevated in the experience of the sublime comes, in the end, to *our being elevated to ourselves* in terms of our superior destiny as moral beings. The essential truth of sublimity is our moral superiority to everything in nature. The entire process wends circuitously around to our moral sublimity—supreme and more than all of nature. I do not think that this is entirely wrong, because there is something sublime about us, but it is not right, however, relative to what is at play, and what it keeps out of play. Most of all it underestimates the *threshold nature of the happening* that is between the aesthetic/ethical and the religious/sacred. Kant moralizes the sublime, and this moralization both weakens the aesthetic power of the happening and interrupts the rupture of the sacred. It is unable or unwilling to grant the breakthrough of the equivocal communication of the sacred.

One of the areas which is fruitful here in connection with both the saturated phenomenon and the hyperboles of beings is certainly the discussion of *aesthetic ideas* in Kant. Marion draws our attention to the importance of these.[22] Ideas for Kant have to do with the unconditional, the maximum. Aesthetic ideas rouse our search after the unconditional—they are representations of imagination that occasion much thought without any determinate thought being adequate to them. They function as setting our seeking in motion in a more than conceptually determinable way. I would note that Kant predominantly puts the issue from the side of *our being impelled to seek* in determinacy beyond determinacy for the finally indeterminable. The otherness of the unconditional as finally indeterminable remains regulative, and Kant frames all this transcendentally. This is one-sided from the point of view of the *metaxu* and the metaphysics of the between. We need a different thinking of the regulative and constitutive ideal.[23] With Kant the very otherness *qua* other is folded back into what it is for us through the circuit of the sublime subreption. A metaxological sense of the sublime is stretched differently between aesthetic finitude and infinity, and least of all is the otherness of the sublime a subreptive detour back to our own confirmed powers of self-determination.

To speak in the language of determination, the aesthetic idea represents the arousing of indeterminable thinking at the edge of determinability, a thinking which might be considered suggestive of the overde-

22. *The Visible and the Revealed*, 32–33.
23. I will pursue this point again in relation to "being truthful" and mystery in the following chapter.

terminate, though this latter insight is not one that Kant voices. Perhaps one reason Kant lacks this insight follows from his sense of infinity as always just heuristic and regulative, and hence as defined predominantly in terms of indeterminacy and the anticipation of the totality of complete determinations of the unconditional (as he understands this). By contrast, the sublime also rouses something indeterminable beyond fixed and finite determinacy, but the indeterminable otherness is brought back to the autonomous self-determination of the self as moral subject, and hence here too the threshold that passes to the overdeterminate is not understood, much less passed through by Kant. If I am not mistaken Marion's saturated phenomenon removes us from the space of (aesthetic) subreption in Kant's sense. In that respect it is close to a metaxological sense of the hyperbole of aesthetic happening. One could ask if Marion's journey in and through phenomenology, and its proximity to transcendental philosophy, can handle the complications, indeed equivocal vacillations, inherent in Kant's treatment. One could ask also of Kant something he never asked himself: Is there an *agapē* of the things of *aesthēsis*?

THE EROTICS OF SELVING AND THE EROTIC PHENOMENON

Our being moved to seek after the maximum, central to Kant's aesthetic idea, brings us to the *third hyperbole of being: the erotics of selving*. We awaken to ourselves as intimately hyperbolic, for we know ourselves as both finite and yet infinitely self-surpassing. We are endowed with transcending power, and yet at the same time we come to realize we do not simply endow ourselves. One could say that the immeasurable passion of our being is self-exceeding, and yet the self-exceeding exceeds also the selving that we are. It might be put this way: the erotics of our selving is hyperbolic to a *conatus essendi* that drives itself to its own most complete self-determination in immanence. Our erotics witnesses to a *passio essendi* that is marked by a primal porosity to what exceeds all determination and finally our own self-determination.

In some ways I hesitate to speak just about "self." I wonder why there is "soul music" but not "self music." Perhaps "soul" is closer than "self" to the *passio essendi*, the intimate idiocy, and the porosity. Perhaps one might even think of "erotic souling," as a longing that belongs in the mystery of the enigmatic porosity. After all, not a little of "soul music" is bound up with the agony and enchantment of eros. Could one see the selving as a crystalizing of (en)souling, itself undergone as the animating principle of life? The erotics of selving shows the soul emerging in the body in articulated form(ing). In this emergence there is a pointing of the selving back to the *poros* and the *penia*, even as, simultaneously, the secret sources of our intimate being emerge more with the carrying energy of the *conatus*. Hence the reference to being engendered and engendering in *co-natus*. That is, in the endeavor to be there is endeavor to *enable being beyond itself,* for *co-natus* puts us in mind of a being "born with," or "birthing with." In erotic generation, there is what comes to one from beyond oneself, and there is the lure toward the beyond of selving, through the lover or the beloved to the children of future time.

We think of "self" as connected with the human self, but I would speak of selving rather than self and this is not confined just to human beings. There is an erotics of being not exclusive to its humanized form. All things selve. I quote from the marvelous poem of Gerard Manley Hopkins, "As Kingfishers Catch Fire, Dragonflies Draw Flame":

> Each mortal thing does one thing and the same:
> Deals out that being indoors each one dwells;
> Selves—goes itself; *myself* it speaks and spells,
> Crying *What I do is me: for that I came.*

If erotics is more than our selving, nevertheless our selving shows it most intimately and most extensively. In the poem, what is foremost is the outering, the uttering of selving in the between. Nevertheless, the selving that outers itself goes infinitely deep, like the well that is bottomless, even though it resounds when stones fall in it and make a strike beyond the rim.

Somewhat differently put, in the finite being, there is an infinite restlessness. In the immanent, there is something more that is not to be contained in immanence. This again is how I invoke the hyperboles of being: happenings in immanence that are not possible fully to determine in terms of immanence. They are thresholds in the immanent between that tell of a porous boundary between the immanent between and something that is more than it. Thus in our erotic selving, we are asked to pay attention to a certain doubleness. As already indicated, we naturally think of eros as self-surpassing, but there is also a mysterious being given to oneself in self-surpassing, and indeed before and beyond self-surpassing. This is not a matter of giving oneself to oneself. It is not a matter of the endeavor to be coming into its own sole sovereignty. Rather all of this is a matter of *endowed enabling*, of being endowed as enabled to be. Something other than self-enabling enables self-enabling.

At the same time that there can be a coming to self in a fuller and fulfilled way, this coming to oneself is in and through the other. There is reciprocity possible here, yes; but this doubleness now here, as between selving and othering, can also tilt toward dangerous equivocity. The self-surpassing endeavor can become intoxicated with its own coming to itself and play down, or pay little or no attention to, or repress even, the way the other gives one to oneself, being thus an enabling other involved in its own way in allowing one's coming to self. Though the selving is never through itself alone, its self-affirmation can come to think of itself as primarily through itself alone. Our being given to be through the gift of the loving other is crucial. Forget it, reject it, mutilate it, and a mutation occurs in erotic selving. I think here of the way the Greeks recognized this essential temptation of eros in distinguishing *eros ouranios* and *eros turannos*. The tyrannical eros flies high on the energy that comes to uttering in one, that takes one out in an exhilaration that can become bewitched with itself. It becomes love loving loving, tempted to close the double metaxological intermediation of self and other into a sovereign and singular self-mediation of the original endowed energy of enabled and enabling "to be."

One of the ways I try to address this matter is to recall the story told in the *Symposium* by Socrates/Diotima of the double parentage of eros in terms of *poros/penia*. Often what is foregrounded is eros as lacking, as *penia*, and as seeking fulfillment and completion. But the parentage of eros in *poros* is just as important. If nothing else, the origin of eros hearkens back to feast of the gods. As we know from this telling, the gods are celebrating the birthday of Apollo, and however it happens, *penia* manages to couple with *poros* drunk with divine nectar: eros is born of their union. (Was this original coupling already not erotic then—eros before eros, before our eros …?) What is intimated by the parentage of *poros*? I take this to open the suggestion that there is a more original porosity in eros, prior to the self-surpassing endeavor to be we associate with the *conatus*. There is a patience of being, perhaps suggested by the metaphor of sleep at the divine feast. The feast is working its way in us, through us, when we are erotically awakened, aroused. Eros has something to do with a divine festivity waking up in the flesh, waking up to itself in the flesh, waking the flesh up to itself as more than flesh.

I see here a certain promise of *agapē* (by contrast with any dualism of eros and *agapē*). At the origins of eros, erotic seeking cannot be disjointed from the surplus festivity of the gods, even if in the scrabble of scarce life we often lose sight of this. Worth noting is that one might think of the poverty too as partaking of a kind of porosity—being nothing, poverty is ready for all things other to itself. Again this readiness, as being nothing, can mutate, carried by the *conatus*, into a power of negation, which in *eros turannos* issues in a taking of all things other. Its indigence, as energized to go beyond itself as indigence, then becomes a grasping at what it would have for itself. In the extreme, it is like a greedy person at the feast of life who takes too much, more than he needs, even for himself. In this taking the festivity of life is turned to spoils. "Being nothing" curdles into a negativity that ever runs the risk of spoiling, despoiling the feast of life. The surplus is no longer of generosity, but the usurping surplus of *pleonexia*—wanting more and more, more than enough, beyond all satisfaction. This usurping surplus is testimony to the infinite restlessness of erotic selving, though in the counterfeit form of tyrannical willing of itself. It parodies origination by endlessly making itself anew as a form of always overtaking eros, greedy because at bottom ungrateful eros.

Marion, one recalls in discussing the saturated phenomenon, mentions "a particular face I love" and refers it to the icon.[24] And of course, he has written strikingly of the erotic phenomenon.[25] There are many admirable analyses in his reflection. He speaks of an erotic reduction, but one might ask: Does the possibility of an *agapeic reduction* make sense? And if not, why not? Is the recurrence to the agapeics of the porosity, in the erotics of selving, to be described as an agapeic phenomenon? Is the language of the phenomenon true to the agapeics of being? I hesitate about the language indebted to phenomenology which suggests breaking with the natural attitude, in the interests of the reduction. Eros is a

---

24. *The Visible and the Revealed*, 47.
25. *The Erotic Phenomenon*, trans. Stephen E. Lewis (Chicago: University of Chicago Press, 2007).

metaxu, as Plato said. It lifts us up, charges and even transfigures the so-called natural attitude, but we come to be charged by eros not through the precise steps of a phenomenological method but by the upsurge of an energy beyond method and reduction. Every method and reduction, *qua* the moving of thinking, is itself moved by an erotic energy. There is an erotics of philosophy, prior to and beyond method, prior to and beyond reduction. There is an erotics of reason.[26] I understand that philosophers do not now frequently speak of love or eros. While Marion is not wrong about this, his claim is much truer of modern rationalists. It is not true of the longer tradition, certainly not the Platonic, and indeed its transformation in Christianity. There is also the fact that *philia* is hugely present in premodern thought. It is somewhat recessed in modernity, for reasons I try to address elsewhere.[27] And there is almost complete silence in the philosophical tradition about love as *agapē*. I have spoken about it, and Marion has been one of the few to raise it for philosophical consideration.

I find it somewhat odd the way Marion begins with the question: Who loves me? This might be understandable in a heartless world, in an ethos neutralized, objectivized, and under the dominion of serviceable disposability. It is understandable also in terms of the egocentric position that is strongly present in our modern orientation to things and others. One recalls the mocking refrain of the detective Kojak: "Who loves ya baby?" Of course, the point is to work through toward something other. I can understand one might offer an archaeology of self-affirming love, passing into and through the *conatus*, attaining a mindfulness of the *passio*, arriving at the open space of the primal porosity. One might discover these to be enabled in, enacted by the happening of self-affirming love, in erotics, *philia*, and agapeics. One might discover all of these to reveal the between-being of all forms of being in love; a between-being which carries with it a fearful equivocity that opens the different forms of love to betrayals and mutilations.

If I compare the matter to Augustine, there is the working of, and then the mindfulness of, the restless heart, and erotics is very much

---

26. See *The Erotic Phenomenon*, 209, where Marion concurs on this important point. See *The Intimate Universal*, chap. 7, "The Erotics of the Intimate Universal."
27. "Tyranny and the Recess of Friendship," in *Amor Amicitiae: On the Love That Is Friendship*, ed. Thomas Kelly and Philipp Rosemann (Leuven: Peeters, 2004), 99–125.

bound up with this restlessness. In all of this there is the matter of the dead ends to which equivocal eros brings us again and again, to existential and religious *aporiai* beyond which we cannot pass on our own power. Then too there is the circling around itself of love in love with love, the collapse in us of the doubleness of love (as between selving and other) into the single self-circling autoerotic closure. There is the purgation of the tyrannical eros which is idolatrous, for idolatry is the self-absolutizing of eros which absolves itself from the absolute as other and circles around itself, even when it circles in the company of others, even the divine other.

The mutation of eros into self-circling will to power involves a certain univocal logic of being number one. I would hold to a certain plurivocal sense of erotics. This is enacted in Plato's *Symposium* in the plurality of speeches of which none is entirely excluded from having something true to say, even though some are more true to eros than others. I cannot agree with the univocal conception of eros at the end of the *Erotic Phenomenon*.[28] Am I mistaken that Marion wants to eroticize *agapē*,[29] whereas I want to recollect the promise of *agapē* in eros? If I demur concerning a dualism of the two, I demur also with a univocalizing, and again plead for a metaxology beyond self-mediating dialectic. In the many forms of love, it is the *different forms of relativity between* self and other that are at issue—from self-affirming love, to *philia*, to eros, to *agapē*.[30]

There is also the infinite restlessness: you have the intimate emergence of the overdeterminate in the human being, or perhaps better put, the mingling of the overdeterminate and the indeterminate. Erotics brings us back to mystery as enacted on the threshold beyond determination and self-determination. *Indeterminate*: an openness that cannot be confined to any one determination or set of determinations, the openness of the indeterminate to determination and self-determination. *Overdeterminate*: more than the indeterminate, because it is not lack that surpasses itself, or seeks beyond itself, but the given energy of being as

---

28. *The Erotic Reduction*, 217: "Love is said and is given in only one, strictly univocal way." On the plurivocity of eros Plato's *Symposium* has hardly been surpassed. Someone like Freud is not in the same class.

29. See ibid., 220–21.

30. On the forms of relativity of different loves and their mutation into different hatreds, see *Is There a Sabbath for Thought?*, chap. 9.

surplus that, though knowing its lack, is energized to seek what as other will enable it to be more than lacking. Erotic selving is already more than lacking in itself in order to be able to address the sense of lacking that emerges in its finitude. While not the absolutely overdeterminate, it participates in this overdeterminacy, in this surplus of affirming being. This surplus is both self-affirming and affirming what is other. The surplus affirming is first affirming in us, before we affirm that already given affirmation of being, and become open to affirming the other whose affirming of us has allowed us to come to ourselves more truly.

This means that the infinite in us is not just in the striving to be, in the *conatus essendi*, unless we do justice to the "co-" of *conatus*, insofar as this recalls us to the source of "being with" in the event of being born to being at all. We need again to recall the *passio* first, and even more the secret working of the infinite in the porosity—not determinate, not self-determining, but more than all determinations and allowing determination and self-determination. The double parentage of eros in the *Symposium* is also a reminder of the unavoidability of paradoxical language, bordering on the contradictory, certainly beyond univocity, and enmeshed in ambiguities that court equivocity. *Penia* and *poros*: all but nothing and yet somehow full, a fertile void; or a fertility that makes void to enable fructifying, a loving that makes a way (as positive) but that makes way to make a way (and so seems almost nothing). It is for reasons like these that I believe there is a promise of the agapeic in the erotic. As I put it above, it is *after* drinking deep at the feast of the gods that *poros* is approached by *penia*—divine intoxication asleep in the coming to be of eros—a divine *agapē*, the sleeping promise of the intoxicated *agapē* in the generation of the erotic.

The feasting of the gods, the secret agapeics of the erotic come forth in the impulse of erotics not only toward engendering but toward immortalizing: to be beyond death. (Miguel Unamuno had a passionate sense of this; whether he made full philosophical sense of this passionate urgency of ultimacy is another thing.) For Marion too: "Love demands eternity because it can never finish telling itself the excess within it of intuition over signification."[31] I am not sure I would quite put it in those terms. The hyperbolics of selving shows erotics to be self-surpassing but

---

31. Ibid., 210.

also passing self—passing on. We see this in generation, this energy of passing, the transience of erotics—and much of the appeal of beauty is bound up with this. But beyond engendering, there is also passing on, and the enigma of death, and perplexity about passing beyond death, struck as we sometimes are by the intimation of the beyond of death, the deathless. Thus erotics is bound up with art and immortalizing. This is not only a matter of leaving something worthy behind one when one is gone, gone into death. There is sought something of a deathlessness in the work itself. Great works destroy our conceit but there is also a promise of eternal rejuvenation, a promise of resurrection. It is no doubt with the beloved other that we know the lovable that we would were saved from death. Marcel has words to the effect that our love of the beloved other entails our desire and hope: you will not die. Love appeals for eternity for the beloved. Saul Bellow ends his book *Ravelstein*, memorializing his friend, celebrating him: "You don't easily give up a creature like Ravelstein to death."[32]

It is in and through religion that the immortalizing of erotics is most universally distributed. Being religious reveals the intimate universality out of which the passion of erotics emerges, and toward which the endeavor of erotics tends, for the divine is there at the origin and at the end. Erotics then spans the extremes. Thus on one side, we are drawn to the archaeological mythos of primordial origin—*in illo tempore*—*fadó*, *fadó*, long, long ago, in a "time" beyond time. Mythic and immemorial, in memory beyond memory, the beyond of time communicates in the "time" of the origin. Then also, on the other side, there are the eschatological myths of a justice beyond the normal distinction we draw between life and death. One recalls the myth of Er. We call to mind the suffering, death, and resurrection of Christ, where creation, Fall, and re-creation converge on the hope of resurrection and flesh beyond death.

I invoked earlier the selving so dear to Hopkins, and now this comes back in the double form of poverty and surplus, almost nothing and more than all things, in his poem "That Nature is a Heraclitean Fire and of the comfort of the Resurrection." Too much and almost nothing:

… Million-fuelèd, nature's bonfire burns on.
But quench her bonniest, dearest to her, her clearest-selvèd spark

---

32. Saul Bellow, *Ravelstein* (New York: Penguin, 2000), 233.

Man, how fast his firedint, his mark on mind, is gone!
Both are in an unfathomable, all is in an enormous dark
Drowned. O pity and indignation! Manshape that shone
Sheer off, disseveral, a star, death blots black out ...

Nothing and then enough, more than enough, too much, more than too much:

... Enough! the Resurrection ... Flesh fade, and mortal trash
Fall to the residuary worm; world's wildfire, leave but ash:
In a flash, at a trumpet crash,
I am all at once what Christ is, since he was what I am, and
This Jack, joke, poor potsherd, patch, matchwood, immortal diamond,
Is immortal diamond.

THE AGAPEICS OF COMMUNITY: DOES MARION REDEEM THE PROMISE?

Finally I turn to the *fourth hyperbole* which I call *the agapeics of community*. Here is a compact statement of some salient features. The hyperbole concerns what one might term the beyond of selving, selving beyond selving which is rather an othering or being other that reveals our relations to others as traversing the *metaxu* in generous receiving and giving. The agapeics manifests the overdeterminacy of a surplus generosity, beyond determinacy, indeterminacy, and self-determination. The surplus is not only in being receptive to the gift of the other but in freeing us to give beyond ourselves to others. This is a giving again which consists in the passing on of goodness itself. Indeed, giving on generously is the agapeic good of the "to be." Once again, beyond determinacy, indeterminacy, and self-determinacy, in the finiteness of our lives together, there is the promise of an overdeterminate generosity beyond finite reckoning. Here we come upon the sense of sacred mystery which calls on our being truthful. In the agapeics of community there passes (on) a surplus good that makes itself available in an absolute porosity. One might speak of an absolved porosity of the *passio essendi* that ethically communicates itself as a *compassio essendi*. This communication takes us to the limit of self-determining ethical life, for in its wording of the between it reveals the overdeterminate incarnation of the holy.

Again I draw attention to a certain doubleness in the agapeics as most fully answering to the communion of surplus and emptying that allows the passage of love to circulate among many. *Surplus*: this clearly refers to the overdeterminacy in the hyperbolic dimension, a going beyond in a living sense, a beyond with reference to our every effort to pin it to this determinacy or that, or to define it exhaustively in terms of our autonomous self-determination; in excess of determinacy and self-determination but it is not merely indeterminate *qua* the living communication of surplus generosity, super-plus generosity. *Emptying*: this refers to the manner in which the surplus opens a space of porosity for what is other to itself to come to be, and to become itself. The emptying makes a way (*poros*) that is there as making way; and as making way, it seems not to be there, but it is there as not there to enable the being there of all that is other to itself.

The doubleness of this togetherness of surplus and emptying seems like an equivocity, but if so it is a saturated equivocity that calls for metaxological intermediation. It is dialectical in one sense, as reminding us of the fact that ultimate significance often must invoke the dual language of opposites, bordering on paradox—a *coincidentia oppositorum* in Cusa's terms. But it is transdialectical insofar as dialectic is tempted to treat the union of opposites as really a way of describing a single, unitary process, an essentially self-mediating, self-determining process. The agapeics is not that, because it most superbly communicates the between and communicates in the between, with all the irreducibility of selving and othering to one inclusive totality. Agapeic communication is a more radical release of communication than a matter of self-communication.

Eros is generally the preferred philosophical focus in the long tradition stretching back to the Greeks. *Agapē* is hugely inflected in the Christian configuration of the ethos of being, and in our understanding of the between, but it is rarely the focus of thematic reflection by philosophers.[33] To put the stress on agapeic being, being agapeic, need not be

---

33. Philosophers have not often addressed themselves to the agapeic. One does think of figures such as Augustine, Bonaventure, Aquinas, Pascal, and the order of charity. One thinks of missed opportunities, such as Nietzsche's bowdlerized version of Christian love. Nor have philosophers always been good witnesses of the holy. Who would one name? I exclude from serious consideration Vattimo's miracle of transubstantiating Nietzschean nihilism into Christian *caritas*. Is Deleuze taking the name of Christ in vain when he refers to Spinoza as "the Christ of the philosophers"? Can one think of Christ, like Spinoza, throwing flies to spiders for cruel fun, for recreation? Re-creation? Glee in death, rather. Spinoza's fun reminds one of the

just to trespass into the sanctum of theology and break the protocols of academic divisions. Agapeic being, or being agapeic, reveals the richest sense of communication of the "to be." To allow that to be woven into the texture of philosophical reflection entirely transforms the meaning of mindfulness, and certainly requires a deep porosity of philosophy itself to religion. In other words, it requires much that the modern ideal of autonomous thinking simply cannot meet, because the boundary has already been sealed, or a spiritual apartheid has been enforced, or perhaps a bargain of collusion has been concluded between theologians and philosophers that keep each apart alone in their designated homelands. No roaming is allowed beyond the borders so defined in the spiritual/academic concordat. However, this collusion or concordat cannot hold indefinitely, not only because we are thinkers in the very passage between zones, but because on whichever side of borders we are there is a surplus always already at work, and this has to do with the *agapē* of being. This is the surplus of the mysterious overdetermination. This is an ontological/metaphysical mystery that is not retracted into itself and for itself but that primally and ultimately communicates itself—it communicates to us of the creative generosity of the good. The communication of this surplus gives being to be, and to be as good. We live our participation in the goodness of being in our own native love of our own "to be" and secret love of the "to be" in a communicative sense more than is singularized in our own unique "to be."

Regarding Marion and *agapē*, he outlines a task in *God without Being*, but does not entirely carry it out, to my knowledge. He seeks to go beyond Heidegger from being to God, Heidegger whom he accuses of a second idolatry, though his own discourse on being is shaped by Heidegger's terms. Marion points to *agapē* as beyond being. And he describes the task as beyond what he deems the double idolatry of Heidegger: "To think God, therefore, outside of ontological difference, outside the question of Being ... what name, what concept, and what sign nevertheless remains feasible? A single one, no doubt, love."[34] Thinking God as *agapē*: "This task, immense and, in a sense, still untouched, requires working

---

wanton gods of Lear. Christ is not just the promise of the *agapē* but the realized incarnation of the promise. He is the redemption of the promise.

34. *God without Being*, 46–47.

love conceptually (and hence, in return, working the concept through love), to the point that its full speculative power can be deployed."[35]

One is heartened by the stress on the agapeic. What if metaxologically the task is to be mindful of the promise of *agapeic being*? We must think what it means to *be* agapeic. I add that this task he proposes not only reflects some of the aims of my work, but it permeates the thinking from the outset. It is not grafted on as if from outside (a "grafting" of theology onto philosophy attributed to Marion by some of his critics). Without a resurrected sense of the agapeics of communication, how venture to think the agapeic being of God? If "God without Being" were to mutate into "Being without God," the hyperboles of being would lose meaning, and one worries about being left with the devalued, indeed void being of modern nihilism rather than the agapeics of being in communication. Being without God sounds less like the gift of creation, in its saturated idiocy and the glory of the aesthetic happening, as a dark gnostic double. How indeed talk of God's *being* as agapeic?

I wondered above if Marion in the *Erotic Phenomenon*, with its univocal understanding of love, is trying to eroticize *agapē* (and indeed friendship), while in a metaxology of the hyperboles of being the point would be more the discernment of the promise of the agapeic in self-affirming love, *philia* and eros, and all of this without any univocalization of love, with a plurivocalization rather. The point would not be a matter of an "either/or" between one kind of love and another, or indeed a dialectical appropriation of one kind to another, but the agapeic aligning of the plural forms of love, each vested after its own kind with the promise of the agapeics of community.

One might refer here to Marion's *Prolegomena to Charity*, of course. This work is indeed prolegomenary, hence preparatory; and yet, in the final pages of this book, he does sketch "some of the features of charity."[36] In the fourth section, he offers a characterization of charity in terms reminiscent of the way a metaxological metaphysics asks us to put it, namely, as surplus generosity making a way by making way.[37] But in the fifth and final section, he claims "it is above all important not to suf-

---

35. Ibid., 47.
36. *Prolegomena to Charity*, trans. Stephen E. Lewis (New York: Fordham University Press, 2002), 164–69.
37. Ibid., 164–68.

fer the influence of what metaphysics has thought about love. For today, in this tradition, love and charity have suffered similar devaluation. Love is reduced to 'making love,' charity to 'doing charity'—words prostituted in the first case, betrayed in the second, each equally submitted to the iron law of 'making or doing,' and thus of objectification."[38] Needless to say, what I mean by metaxological metaphysics cannot be recognized or recognize itself in this claim about "metaphysics." Quite to the contrary, it seeks the signs of the agapeic in the happening of being as the between. Interestingly, Marion cites the "hyperbole" from St. Paul about "knowing the charity of Christ which surpasses all knowledge" (Eph 3:19). Why could not a metaxological metaphysics listen well to St. Paul's great hymn to *agapē* (ἀγάπη), along whose hyperbolic way (ὑπερβολὴν ὁδὸν, 1 Cor 12:31) we are enjoined to go, beyond the best of other great gifts, and though now, in the sometimes dreadful equivocity of immanent finitude, we see things in enigma (ἐν αἰνίγματι, 13:12)?

The more fully worked out view of eros recently in his *The Erotic Phenomenon* has garnered most attention. To repeat a question: could one, should one speak of *The Agapeic Phenomenon*? Would that be the right way to talk about *agapē*? Concerning the divine love I find myself again uneasy with the claim in the *Erotic Phenomenon* about the univocity of love: the love of God is the same as our love.[39] Marion astonishingly claims: "God practices the logic of the erotic reduction as we do, with us, according to the same rite and following the same rhythm as us, to the point where we can even ask ourselves if we do not learn it from him, and no one else. God loves in the same way as we do."[40] The love by which God loves me is the same love by which I love God—Marion does not quite put it this way. But this way of putting it reveals a kind of dialectical univocity that transposes Eckhart's famous claim: the eye by which I see God is the eye by which God sees me; they are one and the same. The same idea is transposed dialectically into speculative thought by Hegel: my understanding of God is God's own self-understanding in me.

Needless to say, in my own work such a claim to univocity is troublingly equivocal—and suspect of shortchanging the essential dissimilitude which is always greater than the similitude when it comes to things

---

38. Ibid., 168.
39. *The Erotic Phenomenon*, 221.
40. Ibid., 222.

divine. In the plurivocity of love (self-affirming, erotic, philial, agapeic) it is crucial to keep in mind *different forms of relativity* between self and other at work in the different loves, for these difference are significant in how we approach the divine mystery. Without this we risk producing an idol of thought rather than placing ourselves in readiness for an iconic communication of the divine. It is just Hegel's lack of finesse in discriminating between these different forms of relativity that leads to a counterfeit double of God. If there is a kind of unity of love, or better put, comm-unity, I have tried to explore this in terms of the promise of the *agapē* in all the different forms of love, including self-affirming self-love. The *agapē* of being is already at work in our own love of our own being. This goes deeper than the self-insistent endeavor to be and when we are pointed back to the *passio essendi* and the primal porosity, we come to realize we are lived, indeed created, by a love surplus to our ontological self-love, always beyond it, and yet also always radically intimate—we are at all only in virtue of this love. Whether we go out, or go in, whether we go down or go up, the surplus mystery of the *agapē* of being meets us. For it is the most radically intimate companioning mystery out of which we live when we believe we have dissolved all mystery. We have not been true to ourselves then, we have not been true to being other than ourselves, we have not been true to mystery.

There is, in my view, a secret reserve of surplus promise in *all* the hyperboles of being, hence also in *all* the forms of love. In self-affirming love, in *philia*, in eros, the promise of the agapeic is given. If there is a plurivocity here it is not a dualism, nor an equivocity that disseminates a merely unrelated and dissolving diversity. There is community, there is communivocity. It will not do to say that *agapē* (or eros as Marion seems to suggest) is the one love that runs through all, as if that were a vindication for univocity. Not at all, for once the nature of *agapē* is understood in relation to the surplus generosity of the overdetermination, it is the releasing plurivocity of its broadcast that is closer to the truth of the matter. This plurivocity reveals the inappropriateness of the univocal insistence. Agapeic love insists thus on nothing, and hence is open and ready for all, with a porosity that is no mere lack but the creative readiness to make a way by making way to allow what is other to come into its own being for itself, as well as its own promise of being agapeic.

Being true to the agapeics of being brings us to the overfull mystery. It is so full it is as if there were nothing there; so full that we are nonplussed by it, super-plus as it is to all determinate expectations and self-determining projections. The way of the *agapē* is to make a way, and to make a way (*poros*) by making way. The way of mystery opens before us as if it there was nothing there, but the divine overdeterminacy is there, just as opening and enabling a passage of communication, a communicative passing. Communicative passage is not just this or that determinacy, not just what our self-determination determines to be there, not also an indeterminacy as lacking of determinacy, but the overdeterminate as surplus fullness itself as making a way, a porosity, a passage. Seeming nothing and more than all, one thinks of a ravishing music that is in its passing, that comes to sound and to pass by, to sound and resound, and to be full of the most heart-touching intimacy when it passes into us, into us as the porosity it newly opens again, that we listen enchanted, and sometimes we do not know if we heard the music or dreamed it, and then it seems hardly to matter whether we dreamed it or were woken by it to a mystery that is as passing into us, passing through us, passing beyond us. We wake to quotidian consciousness with the glow of an enigmatic gratitude.

Finally in relation to the hyperbole of the agapeics, there is a being true to mystery on the threshold of the holy, a being true to the *mysterium tremendum et fascinans*. The holy shakes us on a threshold we cannot absolutely determine and that goes beyond our self-determination. Being true fills us with dread about our own defection from the *agapē* of the holy. Yet we are filled with a longing for intimate redemption by the holy. We are as nothing, we are as an opening and our bones are as water. Being nothing there is a passage of amazement in the idiotic porosity. Being exposed and unsheltered, there is an appeal for the shelter of forgiving goodness, a sanctum for the naked. Reverent wonder and dread go together, there is a kind of holy idiocy, a sacred stupor, whenever the unapproachable is nigh. There is the solicitation that we let ourselves be consecrated as a shelter of love in the unarmed porosity of being.

7 ∞ Being True to Mystery and Metaxological Metaphysics

OPENING

The importance of metaphysics has never lacked for appreciation in the Catholic orientation to philosophy, yet the manners in which metaphysics has been diversely criticized since Kant have left it in a struggling condition. This legacy of criticism has had different aftereffects in both the analytic and the continental ways of doing philosophy. Analytic philosophy in its earlier incarnation was not hospitable to metaphysics, perhaps identifying this with overstated claims of idealistic speculation, against which were expressed the hostilities of positivism and the dismissiveness of more ordinary language philosophy cutting it down to common-sense size. Notable today is that within analytic philosophy a practice of metaphysics is flourishing, though not always to the liking of everyone. With the continental tradition one could not use the word "flourishing" in connection with metaphysics, though admirers of thinkers such as Deleuze and Badiou do not share the more standard antimetaphysical animus common in twentieth-century continental philosophy. Here the influence of Heidegger and his admirers cannot be underestimated. How is this contested place of metaphysics to be approached in light of its important sources in modern thought? How is it to be approached with reference to the longer tradition in the relation of Catholic thought and the need of metaphysics?

After the weakening of the hegemony of Thomistic practices of Scholastic philosophy, in America at least one of the attractions of continental thought was the perception that it remained true to a larger vision of the human condition, as well as being attuned to a variety of important historical and cultural nuances in matters philosophical. Phenomenology, nevertheless, is one continental approach that eschews "metaphysics."

What this means is connected with certain practices of metaphysics, not least among these being a kind of rationalistic Scholasticism, not itself confined to Catholic traditions. As I have argued throughout, one can defend the practice of metaphysics as metaxological as more fruitful, and as revealing the impossibility of avoiding metaphysics, even in the avoidance of metaphysics. I have just contrasted this approach to metaphysics with Jean-Luc Marion's eschewal of "metaphysics" in favor of phenomenology as first philosophy. In some respects, the practice of phenomenology without "metaphysics" reveals a kind of *Kantian flavor* to its understanding of things. But one of the most important sources of the contestation of metaphysics is the negative reaction to the speculative dialectic of *Hegel*. This reaction has significance for the practice of philosophy in America in the twenty-first century by Catholic thinkers.

Interesting here is the willingness of some Catholic philosophers and departments in Catholic universities to engage in dialogue with Hegel, in sometimes sympathetic ways.[1] The Hegelian approach was sympathetically greeted, in part, I hold, as a response to a loss of a sense of the whole, with the weakening of the prestige and centrality of Aristotelian Thomism in Catholic intellectual circles. Analytic philosophy offered nothing comparable, given its own roots in the rejection of Hegelian holism. The issue of the completion and end of metaphysics stems as much from a response to Hegel as it does from Heidegger, and if there is a continuing need for metaphysics, we have to come to terms with that. Metaxological metaphysics tries to address the question as much relative to Hegel as to Heidegger. Metaxological thinking is transdialectical in a sense that does not give up on metaphysics, but develops it in directions capable of a generous hermeneutics of earlier metaphysicians in the Western tradition. Such a metaphysics contributes to being catholic as helping make sense of the intimate universal.

If a major attraction of Hegel to some Catholic thinkers was his philosophizing in light of the whole, a serious issue has always been the openness of Hegel's speculative dialectic to the irreducible difference and *mystery* of God. Hegelian thought seems adamant that there is no such

---

1. One instance: think of the groundbreaking work of Lawrence Stepelevich at Villanova University in inaugurating and editing for many years *The Owl of Minerva*, journal of the Hegel Society of America. This journal continues to be edited by Ardis Collins at Loyola University of Chicago.

thing as irreducible mystery. If we put the matter in terms of the classical formulation of analogy, there is for Hegel no qualitative *dissimilitude* of God to created being, dissimilitude always and ever greater than the similitude. The completion of metaphysics is not unconnected with the view that reason now finally has the full measure of mystery, and hence not only conceptually surpasses religious representation (to speak with Hegel), but also surpasses itself, especially in the form of contemplative *theōria*. A metaxological metaphysics in search of the true always remains porous to mystery in the sense relevant here. In what follows I want to address the relation of being true and mystery, a relation that will also help crystalize reflection on the contemporary unavoidability of metaphysics, even taking into account the forms of critique it has endured since Kant.[2]

Before turning to this, one final remark on a Catholic thinker deserving of being engaged with great respect. I find it to the point that Bernard Lonergan connects metaphysics, myth, and mystery in *Insight*.[3] Mystery seems to be something positive by contrast with myth which, while understandable with the unfolding in humanity of the desire to know, is more easily overtaken by a "counterposition." The matter would ask more attention than I can here offer but it is of relevance that his discussion makes a connection with dialectic and its equivocations. It is relevant to the religious sense of the sacred, and one might worry that his remarks remain too tied to a pejorative sense of the mythic as primitive (he is aware of the tension here). I sense that his discussion of myth and mystery is governed by a teleology of the desire to know that proceeds from the indeterminate to the determinate: the indeterminacy of initial ignorance is overcome by the progressively unfolding desire to know, itself oriented to intelligibility and being, understood as determinable and determinate, and pointing toward a culmination in full determination of both knowing and being.

Below I will connect a somewhat different sense of mystery which

---

2. A relevant story: I recall once being taken aside by a respected Hegelian scholar, hesitant about my responses to Hegel, to be asked confidentially if my criticism of Hegel had anything to do with the fact that I was Catholic. I just laughed and said the answer would have to remain a secret of the confessional box.
3. *Insight: A Study of Human Understanding, Collected Works of Bernard Lonergan* (Toronto: University of Toronto Press, 1992), 3:553–85.

stresses an overdeterminacy that exceeds indeterminacy, determinacy, and self-determination. This view also looks on the desire to know as itself subtended and exceeded by an original ontological porosity of being in which the desire to know comes to be opened, a porosity that is not itself a determinate desire but an enabling source of determinate desire, and indeed of self-determining desire. The porosity of being comes to manifestation in wonder which itself takes form in different modalities, namely, astonishment, perplexity, and curiosity. There is a more original endowing of being than the desire to know itself. What enables, opens the desire to know? There is an opening which itself enables the desire to know as potentially open to all of being. This I speak of in terms of the primal porosity of being. This, in turn, means that there is a patience of being prior to an endeavor to be. The desire to know is already a move to the determination of the porosity, the patience and the endeavor to be. An ontology of the porosity has implications for the meaning of curiosity also, as we saw in a previous investigation. Lonergan might speak of the *pure* desire to know. I think we should talk about the given porosity that opens up the endowed gift of receiving being in the *passio essendi*, and that also endows the desire to know as a determinate endeavor to know. The pure desire to know (as one might amend Lonergan) returns us to the original porosity, now kept properly unclogged in its intimate truthfulness. Such truthfulness that is laid open to truth is an intimate "being true."[4]

The dominant tradition in the West has too rarely, if ever, done justice to this porosity of being. More often it has turned the more original wonder into a determinate curiosity about a determinate something, hence into an initial lack of knowing which, when worked through, leads to the dispelling of the wonder, not to its deepening. We need a more finessed understanding than this. Again, Lonergan's rich account would require a study for itself, and though I would ask for more on the porosity, I will note that his emphasis on self-appropriation does overlap to a degree with what I will discuss below as "being true." The philosopher is called, we all are called to a "being true" to being, and there is an intimate singularity to this which allows no substitution by another. Yes, there is more than "self" in self-appropriation. "Being true" does ask that

---

4. See *The Intimate Strangeness of Being*, chap. 10.

the philosopher be as fully attuned as possible to the overdeterminacy of *other-being* as well as to *self-being*. "Being true" also has to do with, so to say, an *archaeology* of the desire to know in the original ontological porosity, as well as with a teleology of determinate, self-determining, and more than determinate truth. Such a "being true" is more than a "*self*-appropriation" because as metaxological it finds itself in fidelity to an ontological milieu between self and other, more than each and not reducible to one or the other. Indeed, the "self" of self-appropriation comes to be determinate and self-determining out of the original porosity and *passio essendi*. These ideas will make more sense later on.[5]

BEING TRUE, METAPHYSICS, AND MYSTERY

I turn to the question of metaphysics and mystery, mentioned already, and hovering also over the contrast of the hyperboles of being and saturated phenomena. "Mystery" seems to be an important consideration in thinkers considered Catholic—Gabriel Marcel, for instance.[6] Below I will return to his distinction of mystery and problem in the context of different senses of being true. An adequate understanding of the relation of mystery and being true brings us closer to a practice of metaphysics consonant with its original vocation, as well as the contemporary metaxological metaphysics here proposed.

Mystery is often seen by philosophers as an *epistemic nullity*. We are said to invoke mystery when we do not understand, when we cannot understand, when we are unwilling to try to understand. Mystery stalls us on a limit, one on which nothing of epistemic note happens. To grant mystery is to surrender to obscurity, to abdicate the challenge of cognition, whether philosophic or scientific. Knowing and truth in the relevant regard here are often seen in the light of *determinacy and determinability*. If to know is to know something intelligibly, that is, to know it determinately, mystery must be seen negatively in this light of the indi-

---

5. James Marsh has written thoughtfully of my view on this point in relation to Lonergan and the desire to know. *Lonergan in the World: Self-Appropriation, Otherness, and Justice* (Toronto: University of Toronto Press, 2014), 57–65. On another occasion a fuller reflection might be offered on the porosity prior to the desire to know, Lonergan's understanding of the desire to know, and Heidegger's notion of *alētheia*. Some indications of what that reflection might look like are offered below.

6. *The Mystery of Being*, 2 vols. (London: Harvill Press, 1951).

gence of knowing. To know the truth of something is to be related to it in a manner determinable in principle. As supposedly beyond determination and determinability, an appeal to mystery is symptomatic of epistemic emptiness, a concession to indeterminacy that conceals a sterile surrender to ignorance. Mystery perhaps *might* be invoked when a limit of knowing is reached, as a *provisional pause* in the otherwise endless quest for further and more adequate determination, but in itself mystery can claim no respect, much less reverence. I have worries here about Lonergan's approach to mystery: relative to the "known unknown," as he puts it, "there always is the further question" to be asked.[7] But if the kind of further question is essentially oriented to determinability alone, it does not seem easy to avoid this negative sense of mystery.

This general view, I suggest, is not fully true to either truth or mystery. Interestingly, some of the same things so said about *determinability* could be turned in directions that yield quite different perspectives. Thus we might be referred to the "beyond" of determinability, where indeed there is a kind of poverty of knowing, but strangely this poverty is rich with promise—the promise of the *overdeterminacy* of being true, indeed the overdeterminacy of being. In this light, mystery could not be seen as the opposite of truth, except insofar as the latter is too rigidly tied to univocal articulation, tied to clear, precise, and fixed determinacy. The question is whether such a determination of being true is true to being true. Is it true to the overdeterminacy of being which, in the determinacy, communicates of what cannot be made completely determinate, and which exceeds the measure of our self-determination?

I deliberately speak of "being true" to invoke a condition *between* being and truth. One hesitates in speaking of truth with a big *T*, worrying about a potentially misleading substantializing of the true. One need not object to the intimation that there is truth in a superlative sense toward which we are oriented—indeed truth in a hyperbolic sense. But it is a fair question as to whether the superlatively true can be either simply objectified or simply subjectified. There is a certain articulation of "between-being" that is manifested in the human participation in truth. This is something acknowledged, for instance, in Plato's recognition that we do not possess the complete knowing of the god nor are we marked by the

---

7. See *Insight*, 570.

absence of knowing we seem to find in the beast. In between, we know we do not know, otherwise we could not acknowledge our ignorance. But to be able to grant our ignorance is to *know* we do not know, and still this is to know. It is to know especially our desire for the true as an initially unwilled exigency to seek the true not yet now known. This unbidden seeking is not something determinate simply, but opens and enables our attentive mindfulness to all determinate things, a mindfulness in promise that is not exhausted by any determinate limit. It emerges in and out of an original porosity of being, prior to and exceeding any determinate desire to know. Moreover, the unbidden seeking is not defined at the outset by our powers of self-determination. We wake up to ourselves as not-knowing before we know ourselves as desiring to know. There is the event of astonishment that carries into us the emphatic strike of an otherness that yet is intimately inward. The emphatic strike and the intimately inward pass into each other in the *dawning* mindfulness that we do not know and would know—what exactly it is we would know in a determinate sense, we do not know at the outset—and yet we wake up to ourselves as in search.

We search, but yet again we could not search at all did not some secret intimation of what we seek companion our seeking. This companioning testifies to our between-being: we seek, but only because seeking carries a promise of being able to recognize the sought, if the sought is found by us, if perhaps indeed it finds us. Without the promise of this recognition, no knowing would be possible, no seeking would be enabled at all. We are seekers already in some enigmatic communication with what we seek, or it with us. Nor is the seeking only an indeterminate openness, for such an indeterminate openness would be just an opening and nothing more. There would be no seeking as such, no further determination, for any seeking and further determination would always be governed by more than the purely indeterminate. Purely indeterminate seeking would not be able to acknowledge that we had found the truth we sought when it was found. Through indeterminacy alone there will be no passage of seeking that genuinely passes as true seeking. It is not that we must reject the notion of an indeterminate openness; but there is more at play in the indeterminate than the indeterminate. We do not possess the absolute truth; we are not devoid of a relation to the true; we are called to be true, not only to ourselves, but to what as other to us calls us forth into the porous space of middle mindfulness between the seeking and the sought.

Being true: I would say this has to do with a condition of *being*, a condition of being mindful about being. In this there is the call of a certain *fidelity* to what dawns in our waking up to mindfulness, fidelity to what strikes us into waking in its otherness to our self-determination. We do not construct any of this at the outset. It is prior to construction and deconstruction. For every construction and indeed deconstruction presupposes it as enabling them to do their work. In this dawning, there is something intimate, indeed intimated—we might even speak of a *confiding*. There is a kind of *ontological confidentiality* in the happening of being true itself, and a call to a fidelity to, or with ("con"), what communicates itself in the confidence. An extreme skeptic might want to claim that this is all a "confidence trick" and in the end nothing trustworthy at all. But could we even talk at all of any "confidence trick" if there was not already given a space in which the *anterior confidence* was at work? To wake up to a "confidence trick" we must already be in a space of confidence relative to the trustworthiness of waking up at all. The betrayal in the "confidence trick" is derivative from the trustworthiness of an anterior confidence in waking up as an already given promise of being true. The "confidence trick" is a betrayal of the promise of the original confidence in being true.

Of course, we are using the language of *fides*, of faith here: fidelity, confidence, confidentiality. There is a kind of intimate loyalty, or claim of loyalty in the dawning of the mindfulness that we are to be true. This ontological fidelity is something that merits deeper consideration both from the side of we who seek to know, as well as from the side of that which we seek to know. What is true is what remains true, and remaining true signifies a constant "being with": our constancy in the light of what communicates itself as constant; the constancy of what communicates itself as most ultimately reliable, that is, what we can most trust, what is most trustworthy in the happening of being.

In some ways this is to state anew an old truth, namely, that with regard to truth we are dealing with a necessity we cannot entirely escape, though we can misunderstand or distort or betray it. In evading the call to be true we are unable to evade entirely the necessity of being true. At an extreme, the denial of truth is itself, by implication, a claim to be true and so the claim denying truth is untrue, in being itself marked by a certain embrace of truth. While we can here invoke the notion of performative contradiction, there is more at issue than a trick of logic. What we might call the cunning of logic reveals a necessity in being true that yet is also the enabling of the freedom to be true, or untrue. So we find a troubling doubleness: in the release of this freedom, fidelity to the promise of being true can also become betrayal of the promise. Our being true is placed between extremes of fidelity and betrayal, stressed between them, even torn. The fidelity of being true, or its betrayal, has both epistemic and ontological sides: it does entail an attentive mindfulness being true to itself, but it is not a matter of being true only to itself but to being as other to itself. One might say that the true is not simply for us, but it may be for us to transcend ourselves to what is true as it is for itself. There is a certain service of the true in our going toward its otherness, that is, in our openness to what is true in and for itself.

In the language of a certain form of love, and as I have put it elsewhere, being truthful may be an *agapeic service of the true*.[8] We do not have to know the absolute truth for this to be so. We can acknowledge the fact that often we are split creatures, torn between our doubt and our ardor for truth. Even when we know we are other to the truth, we are related to it in its otherness. Truth as other to us thus shows a certain intimacy to us in the very seeking by us of truth as not being in our possession. There might even be a *dispossession* in being true, intensifying as the intimate call of being true comes most deeply home to us. But even in dispossession the relation of "being between" holds. An extreme lack, when intimately minded—and we are as this intimate minding—cannot be called simply a lack and should be more truly named as a longing or a love. We are beyond ourselves in this intimate longing, but the other unknowingly loved cannot be simply beyond, or entirely beyond all knowing. There is a mysterious crisscrossing of the intimate and the beyond,

---

8. See *Being and the Between*, 493. If this agapeic service is understood it takes us in the direction of a different understanding of the porosity of being, different to Heidegger's *alētheia*—the agapeics, as the service of being true, are seeded in the porosity. The porosity is endowed with the promise of being truthful, itself a finite endowed sign of the true, as the overdeterminacy of being true. Our being true is not only ontological in us, but *qua* endowed is already a communication from the more original source of being true: the agapeic origin. Our being true is an opening intimately and immanently into the true as other to our being truthful. Our being truthful is agapeic fidelity to the true origin that endows our being.

an enigmatic interpenetration of the empty and the full, a marriage of dispossession and plenitude.

In a more sober way of putting it, one might say that the true sought in our being true cannot be just an indeterminate regulative ideal or only a determinate constituted reality. Yet it is both regulative and constitutive. It regulates our search and yet it is not something we self-constitute. Our love of the true is regulative as an ideal to which we aspire, but it is also more than just an ideal, because even to be an ideal, hence regulative, there must be an actual bond with the true that is already constitutive and immanently at work. The service of truth we find in our being truthful is enacted in a between space of otherness that is also a sign on our part of an always finite knowing that knows it does not possess the true absolutely. Again, the language of possession might not be entirely the right way to speak of being true. And yet what is not attained by us is *with us* in our desiring of it.

BEING TRUE TO MYSTERY: BETWEEN DETERMINABILITY AND THE OVERDETERMINATE

Being true, like being itself, is said in many senses. In analogy with Aristotle's *to on legetai pollachōs*, I would like to say *to alēthes legetai pollachōs*. The true is said in many senses correlative to the many senses of the "to be," and this has an important bearing on how we stand in relation to mystery. I summarize in broad terms four senses of being and then correlate them with different senses of being true.[9]

First, the *univocal* sense of being stresses the notion of sameness, or unity, indeed sometimes immediate sameness, of mind and being. Correlative to the univocal sense of being is the search for determinate solutions to determinate problems, impelled by specific curiosity. Second, the *equivocal* sense accentuates diversity, perhaps the unmediated difference of being and mind, sometimes to the point of setting them into oppositional otherness which can rouse restless perplexity in the face of troubling ambiguities. Third, the *dialectical* sense emphasizes the mediation of the different in terms of the reintegrating power of a more inclusive unity. In modern dialectic, we find a strong stress on the self-

---

9. For fuller elaboration see *Being and the Between*, chap. 12.

determination of thought and the primary mediation tends to become a complex form of self-mediation. Fourth, the *metaxological* sense gives a *logos* of the *metaxu*, putting the stress on the wording of the between, in light of the intermediated community of being, intermediation more than the self-mediation of the same. It gives articulation to pluralized intermediation(s), beyond the self-determination of the same. The *inter* is shaped plurally such that, in a way, the *logos* of the *metaxu* is closer to ancient practices of dialectic, for instance, Socratic-Platonic dialogue, than to modern, such as Hegel's. The spaces of otherness in the between remain open. In that between there may be disturbing ruptures that shake the self-satisfaction of self-determining thought, which again and again finds itself intruded on by the overdetermined givenness of being. The metaxological is not our construction (though we construct in the *metaxu*) but is at work before we articulate it reflectively in our categories. There is an immediacy to metaxological intermediacy: a pre-objective and pre-subjective community of being which is also trans-objective and trans-subjective. The *metaxu* enables the work of articulation in the univocal, equivocal, and dialectical formations, but if we absolutize any of these, we risk being untrue to the intermediacy of the given ethos of being in its overdeterminacy. A metaxological philosophy does not reject these other three senses, but seeks to bring them into true alignment with their own promise of overdeterminacy, be it in the form of determination, indetermination, or self-determination.

In light of this fourfold, there is a plurivocity of being true which itself could be correlated with the notions of the determinate, the indeterminate, the self-determining, and the overdeterminate. This correlation has implications for how we remain true to mystery. Again in broad outlines, with the univocal sense given its head, truth tends to be defined in terms of determination and determinability; with the insinuation of the equivocal sense, the notion of a fixed truth is open to the flux of a more fluid indeterminacy; when dialectical considerations come to the fore, the search for the true as the immanently coherent emerges, and in the case of modern dialectic the inseparability of truth and self-determination; when metaxological mindfulness emerges, being true comes to be under fidelity to the overdetermination of being as given to be. The plurivocity of being true does not imply a relativism which claims "there is no truth." It does suggest a kind of relativism in the sense that "being in relation" is crucial to our being true. Nevertheless, "being in relation" is inflected in a plurality of ways, none of which is outside the space wherein the call of fidelity to the true is communicated to us as mindful beings. Different modes of being true reveal different, though related, modes of being in relation mindfully to the happening of being.

UNIVOCITY, EQUIVOCITY, BEING TRUE TO MYSTERY

Where univocity is a dominant requirement, in practical common sense, for instance, or empirical science, the notion of truth as a form of *correctness* comes more to the fore, with a dominant stress on determination and determinability. A proposition is true if, given its univocal enunciation, it corresponds one-to-one to a state of affairs, itself conceived as there with a clear-cut, fixed, cut-and-dried status. There is an essential place for determinable truth, obviously, without which we could not find our way around in the midst of things. Yet the terms of the relation of *adequatio* or correspondence are not themselves so easily fixed in a univocal sense, nor indeed is the relation between them, nor indeed is the milieu of being, the between, wherein these terms and their relation come to some determinacy. There is something more than the determinate at work on all these scores, and the hint of a certain indeterminacy is unavoidable, particularly with respect to what enables the dynamism of these terms, and the relation between them. Finally, this needs the invocation of the overdeterminate, not just as the indeterminate but as the too-muchness of the given between of being.[10]

One might correlate determinability with a straightforward "either/or" between the true and the false: the true is what it is in virtue of not being untrue, and between the two there is a pure exclusion at work. But then: a prayer is neither true nor false, as Aristotle says (*On Interpretation* 17a3–4). Yet, one might suggest, there is a being true in praying that seems impossible to fix with determinable univocity: am I, in praying, in

---

10. In addition to classical notions of *adequatio*, see also in analytic philosophy discussions such as those of Hilary Putnam in *Realism with a Human Face* (Cambridge, Mass.: Harvard University Press, 1992) concerning how propositions "hook on" to the world. Or Richard Rorty, say, in *Philosophy and the Mirror of Nature* (Princeton, N.J.: Princeton University Press, 1981), and generally the questioning of foundationalism as claiming to provide us with univocal certainty concerning the *fundamentum concussum* on which the epistemic warrant of all derivative determinations are to be based.

communication with the ultimate, or do I communicate with nothing? Sometimes one cannot answer "yes" or "no," and yet one prays, and there is something right in the praying and in the continuation without determinable certainty, and being before nothing is not entirely unlike being before God. Praying is hyperbolic to propositional univocity.

The equivocal has to be acknowledged, and this not merely in the sense of a problematic ambiguity that must be overcome with a further univocal truth. The equivocal testifies to a doubleness of showing and concealing, to be true to which requires a finesse for ambiguity over which a more imperial univocity is tempted to run roughshod. If we were to use Pascal's terms, being true in the univocal instance calls on the *esprit de géométrie*, whereas being true in relation to equivocal showing and concealing requires the *esprit de finesse*. Of course, there are challenges to the task of being true here. Equivocity may seem so all-pervasive that we are inclined to surrender to despair of ever attaining the true. The reign of the untrue can seem to be installed with an equivocity so dominant as to seem tyrannical, inducing a hopelessness about accession to a more constant truth. Some of the demands made on being true here are reflected in the stress on doubt, local or hyperbolic, even to skepticism about the possibility of attaining truth at all.

Interestingly, there are practices of skeptical thought that, while denying the adequacy of univocal approaches to the most important things, bring us through equivocity to the verge of a sense of mystery. I think of Pascal again. One might also recall Gabriel Marcel's important distinction of problem and mystery as reflecting the difference of a determinable univocity and an equivocity bordering on mystery. A problem can be objectified, a mystery involves us in a participatory way such that it cannot be completely objectified. Because the problem can be objectifiably determined, in principle it admits of a determinate solution. Because mystery cannot be so objectified, we find ourselves implicated in what is at issue; nor does mystery imply a necessarily correlated "solution." The language of the problem and univocal solubility is not appropriate to the mystery. I would stress that the mystery is of *being*—this is why it implicates us in a manner we cannot entirely objectify, or master through self-determining thought. However—and this is not a point really stressed by Marcel—it also implicates the ontological enigma of "objects" too: their being objects, both as objects and as being at all. One would not want to confine mystery only to that wherein we find ourselves implicated. The mystery we are in passes beyond us, in more senses than one—perhaps even in an infinite sense. As I would put it, the overdeterminacy is of the being of both objects and subjects, and of what is more than can be captured in the language of objects and subjects.

Along the same lines one might suggest also that there is no problem of evil; there is the *mysterium iniquitatis*; there is a regard in which the problem of evil is insoluble. There is no problem of God; there is the mystery of the divine; the superlative mystery of God is insoluble. None of this means absurdity that puts an end to thought—quite the opposite. There is an intensification of mindfulness in the face of this problematic insolubility. There is the energizing of mindfulness in the dimension of the hyperbolic, an energizing which is paradoxically a recourse to an old and new poverty of philosophy. One must see mystery in terms of the original marvel of the middle, disclosed in astonishment. But this is not indeterminacy, tied to the teleology of cognition understood as driven forward from an indeterminate perplexity to a determinate solution. This latter is more a modality of curiosity that cognitively might be said to move from the initially more or less determinate articulation of a problem to the progressively determinate articulation and solution of it. Curiosity is driven beyond itself toward an account of the matter at issue as determinate as is possible. For curiosity, the goal is for there to be no marvel, no wonder, no mystery. Indeed this teleology of determinate cognition is inseparable from a secretly working project of self-determination. If we can prove ourselves cognitively on par with, even superior to, the indeterminacy of the initial perplexity, we can prove ourselves to be the measure of all that is problematic, if only in principle—and hence the whole point is to further our own project of self-determination. Not the determinate as such is the point of the project, but our determination of the determinate, and hence our powers of self-determination, as in excess of every determinacy so fixed by us. The teleology of intrusive curiosity is related to Descartes's ambition to become the "master and possessor of nature."

I see the situation here as double: skepticism may be unavoidable in relation to our failures to attain the true, but it may also be our *honest confession* that we do not know for sure. While the first outlook seems an all but negative outcome, the second is not so, because its very honesty is testimonial to the call to be true, immanently at work in our very failure to attain the true. We must be true to the failure not to attain the true, and in being thus true, we remain on the path of being true, and hence there is no complete failure here. In wrestling with the equivocal, there is an angel in the shadows. There is the possibility for the purgation of our porosity to the true. We are called into question by the failure, we call ourselves into question, but all of this means that the exigent call of being true is inextirpable in our seeking. Hence while seeming to be outside the truth, it is revealed immanently to us that the call to be true is intimate to what we are. What is at stake here is not a simple indeterminacy, though there is an indeterminacy. There is the intimate porosity to truth in our being true. And this intimate porosity, while all but nothing, is not nothing. It is the secret agapeics of the overdeterminate truth, that makes a way by making way in a space of porosity where the spirit of being true springs up in us. Being truthful in not possessing the true—the (equivocal) conjunction of the opposites of our lacking and being full are there in that event of not knowing, and knowing we do not know.[11]

When I speak of porosity to the true, it is appropriate to offer a remark or two on Heidegger's discussion of truth as *homoiosis/orthotes* and as *alētheia*. It is especially appropriate with respect to the determinacy of univocal truth and the indeterminacy of equivocal truth/untruth. With regard to the plurivocity of being true, the matter is not just the doublet of determinate truth and an otherwise indeterminate unhiding which is said to be more primordial than propositional truth. Heidegger is not wrong to call attention to a sense of being true that is more primordial than propositional truth, for we must presuppose our already being in a porosity to the true for us to be able to determine this way or that the truth-worthiness of this determinate proposition or that. His doublet of

---

11. Being true to mystery, in relation to the aesthetics of happening: do we need something like John Keats's "negative capability" "which Shakespeare possessed so enormously"? Here is the famous definition: "Negative Capability, that is, when a man is capable of being in uncertainties, mysteries, doubts without any irritable reaching after fact and reason"; see *John Keats*, ed. Elizabeth Cook (Oxford: Oxford University Press, 1990), 370, "Letter to George and Tom Keats," December 21 or 27, 1817. "Negative capability" is somewhere *between* original astonishment and perplexity, suspended in first wonder and touched with the troubled perplexity of doubts and uncertainties; and not yet overtaken by determining curiosity which brings obsession with univocal fact and reason. The perplexity of the poet calls secretly on a wonder before art and more primal, a *prior* porosity opening a metaxological mindfulness that is not hostile to reason or fact but is not univocalizing of them.

propositional truth (kataphatic?) and *alētheia* (apophatic?) is important, but there is more to be said and it is not evident to me that Heidegger always sees or acknowledges what more is at stake in the opening beyond determinable and determinate truths.

There is the fact that his sense of *alētheia* particularly stresses the privative nature of the unconcealing. *To alēthes* is the unhidden, *das Un-verborgene*. *Alētheia* is the privation of hiddenness, *Unverborgenheit*. Heidegger even uses the likeness of a robbery (*ein Raub*) when speaking of the uncovering of truth in *Being and Time* (§29). With respect to the primal porosity of our being true, it is not a matter of an oscillation between determinate and indeterminate. A privative unconcealing is not quite true enough to the overdeterminacy of the mystery as giving the porosity, and enabling our *passio essendi* as itself a *conatus* for the truth. One might venture that in the *conatus* is a kind of ontological "connaturality" between our being true and the true as other to us, and always as overdeterminate (not just indeterminate) in excess of our determination and self-determination. This is agapeic surplus rather than negation of a hiddenness and privative unhiding. Nature loves to hide, yes, Heraclitus is not wrong. But nature hides in being out in the open and being out in the open gives itself as more primordial than hiding or keeping hidden. Being out in the open: the porosity as the between space of communication in which beings come plurivocally to passing.

In a crucial passage, when talking about access to the thing-in-itself of Kant, Schopenhauer says "we ourselves are the thing-in-itself"; a "way from within [*ein Weg von innen*] stands open to us.... It is, so to speak, a subterranean passage [*ein unterirdischer Gang*], a secret alliance, which, as if by treachery [*Verrath*], places us all at once in the fortress that could not be taken by attack from without."[12] Schopenhauer's *Verrath* brings to my mind Heidegger's likening to a robbery of our wresting the truth of *alētheia* from its hiddenness into *Unverborgenheit*. Suspicion of a crime hangs over the event. It would be an interesting question to reflect further on this passage and the language of secure self-enclosure of the thing in itself and our betrayal, but we must stick with the underground that we ourselves are. A robbery and a treachery: a crime, perhaps something stolen; betrayal of what is not one's own, or taking possession of

---

12. *The World as Will and Representation*, 2:195.

what is not one's own; this is not the agapeic service of the true that is truthfulness. Nor, in these ways of speaking, does the true reveal itself in a self-manifestation that gives itself for the "beholding from" of the receiver. There is no ontological generosity of the true as originating its self-communication as given into the keeping of intimate mindfulness. There is an invasion of a sanctuary, or a break-in into the primordial. A robbery is a breaking into the otherwise self-enclosed; it is not waiting reverently for the seemingly closed to open itself up. There is struggle, striving, in wresting something out of the intimate. There is not a being given of the origin to our porosity and patience, and the invitation to mindfulness of its gift. A pious question to Heidegger: How do you get from *Polemos* to *Gelassenheit*, from theft to gift? Answer: the silence of mystery?

In Heidegger, the equiprimordiality of hiding and revealing seems finally to tilt asymmetrically toward a more primal hiddenness. This might be true (to speak theologically), for the hyperbolic God who dwells in light inaccessible, but not quite so, for nature naturing, or nature natured; though this hyperbolic God is nothing but self-revealing, even granting the asymmetrical transcendence of the divine. This God is not the Heideggerian origin. (One thinks of a self-retracting source turned back in to itself in being turned out of itself.) I wonder if some residue of thinking as negativity is at work in our relation to this happening of unhiding, if there is no unhiddenness at all, if we humans do not bring to express manifestation the work of unhiding. Heidegger suggests that there is no truth without the human being. There seems to be a kind of violence in the pursuit of it, as in his interpretation of Plato's Cave, especially in our going up to the surface of the earth, and into the light of the sun. Rather than the benign violence of the beautiful, as one might put it, rather than the sudden porosity and the *passio essendi* that comes to outing in erotic self-surpassing, this is more reminiscent of a willful *conatus essendi* forcing its way to the top, in a *polemos* that has too many traces of *eros turannos*. I do not doubt the equivocity of eros but at times Heidegger seems relatively asleep to this matter. The affirmative sense of the being given of being, in its coming to be, is there in the porosity of being, and hence is not to be defined in terms of the privative or the negative.

Dialectic in Hegelian and post-Hegelian form is shaped by the dyad of determination and indeterminacy, and then by the transformation via negation of indeterminacy into self-determining thinking. Heidegger's sense of the unhidden is set against this last outcome, but there are dyadic elements of the syndrome as a whole at work in his thinking. Hence again my wonder about the dyad determination/determinability and the indeterminate, and a movement back and forth between the two, including a deconstruction of the determinate and the regress to the indeterminate. All of this is without dialectic, such that Heidegger can draw attention to a between space in the middle between these two. And while this between space cannot be univocally determined or dialectically self-determined, there is no pursuit of a wording of the between in the kind of metaxological terms I propose. In the end, one wonders if there is more of a reiterated sense of the play of univocal determination and equivocal indetermination, with a repeated sense of the equivocity of the self-concealing origin, even in its partial determination out in the light of the unhidden. There is nothing of the paradoxical doubleness of the porosity of being which, if it is to be thought as indeterminate at all, must be given the more affirmative name of the overdeterminate: the always more that, when we try to determine or self-determine it, passes beyond us, before us, as if almost nothing, and not ourselves. Full and empty it manifests the kind of saturated equivocity relative to which the metaxological calls for finesse. One thinks again of Heraclitus (so beloved of Heidegger, as indeed of Hegel and Nietzsche) when he says that Zeus is both satiety and famine. I will return to Heraclitus again in the following chapter, just in connection with this saturated equivocity.

DIALECTIC AND BEING TRUE TO MYSTERY

To come back more directly to the fourfold sense of being: if the very notion of truth may be contested in light of the equivocal, the dialectical and metaxological orientations need not shirk the extreme challenge posed by this. The possible ways of developing the promise of truth are plural, and now to take the dialectical way, we are asked to nurture the seed of mediation that already is intimated in the equivocities of being true—intimated in the truthfulness to self and immanent exigency of honesty asked of us, even when we know we do not know the truth. Suppose the true is other to our comprehension, yet we can further this immanent exigency to be true, even while the true as *other* still solicits our attentive listening. The true as other in not incommunicably other, as we learn from dialogical exchange. In the communicative exchange between self and other, there is an interplay with a *being true more than self or other*, and that yet is immanent in the intermediation between them. The interplay of oneself and an other comes to be articulated along lines in which both sides are subject to the truth coming to manifestation in their communication. This is truth in one regard immanent, and in another regard transcendent; though its eventuation happens between them, hence it either subtends or overarches the contributions of the partners in dialogue. Otherwise no true communication takes place, and no communication in the unfolding of being true.

One of the traditional theories of truth that stresses this immanence of the true is the *coherence theory*—not one side, not the other side, but all the sides of the matter, all the way to the whole of the matter, must be taken together, to get the best sense of the truth at issue. There is much to be said for this view. Still, the question for the coherence theory is whether it shortchanges what disrupts coherence, what resists inclusion in a whole marked by immanent relations only. Being true here finally seem to rest fully at home within a frame of things that is immanently inclusive, even all the way to the inclusiveness of the absolute whole. That is to say, the question of a more *heterogeneous truth*, in excess of an immanent holism comes to trouble us here. An immanent holism may not be fully true to the mystery of the overdeterminacy of being. Perhaps indeed the fullness of the whole is not the surplus overfullness of the overdeterminate. It is, of course, deeply perplexing to consider if there is something more than the whole. What more could there possibly be? Is the question itself not enmeshed in self-contradictory equivocities—not local equivocities here or there, but at the level of the whole, where, if anywhere, dialectical thinking holds all equivocities are to be resolved. And yet the intimation that the overdeterminate is not exhausted by an immanent holism refuses to be put to sleep. If one were to put the point theologically, one would have to ask if there is a God beyond the whole, or are all Gods of the whole or within the whole.[13]

While dialectical interplay reveals plural possibilities, there can be the temptation to recur to a kind of inclusive univocity in the face of

---

13. See *God and the Between*, chaps. 11 and 12.

the multiplied equivocities. I find this not only in the coherence theory in general, but see it carried to an extreme in the modern practice of self-mediating dialectic which reaches its consummation in Hegel's way of thinking. There is an interplay of self and other but the other is a medial other and serves the dialectic as bringing thought through every opposition to being to a more ultimate mediation with itself. Hegel speaks of "pure self-recognition in absolute otherness,"[14] and contemporary pluralists eager to make Hegel a more comfortable fellow-traveler with our *Zeitgeist* pounce on the absolute *Anderssein* as evidence of his "openness to otherness." There is no question of this openness but the issue is the form it takes, and how the openness takes form in the relations *between* self and other. In fact, Hegel's *Anderssein* or "being other" is not really absolute otherness, for it is the *pure self-recognition* that governs the entire operation of the relation in-between. The absolute otherness is itself qualified by this, and so is less absolute in its otherness as such than would appear to be the case at first glance. The true is the whole, in Hegel's famous phrase.[15] This is not untrue, but being true, as in the between, is more than the whole. The heterogeneity of the true over the immanent dialectic of being true is at stake in the metaxological understanding.

In this form of dialectic we witness to the self-determination of being true, and the question is if this form corrals the overdetermination of being. Certainly this self-determination could be seen as fulfilling a kind of teleology from indetermination through determination to thinking's desire to be true to itself and its own immanent exigency. Undoubted-

---

14. *Das reine Selbsterkennen im absoluten Anderssein*, in *Phänomenologie des Geistes*, 24; *Phenomenology of Spirit*, §26.

15. *Das Wahre ist das Ganze*, in *Phänomenologie des Geistes*, 21; *Phenomenology of Spirit*, §20: I tend to see Hegel's famous saying as a post-Kantian displacement of the ancient view that the true and the one are convertible. Obviously, in a dialectical holism, the one is no simple univocal unity but an absolute self-mediating whole, short of which there is only conditional truth—unconditional truth is the one whole. Not a simple univocal unity, this whole is marked by a network of internal relations, and our relation to the true is itself always internal too. Outside of this immanent self-coherence nothing is true. Of course, there are limited, finite modes of knowing, but these two are true according to self-coherence which, however in the case of the finite, can never be absolute. As Hegel puts it, the finite does not coincide with its concept. Only in the absolute whole is the non-coincidence overcome. While finite wholes are not fully true, yet they are not fully untrue, because the play of the true and untrue evident in their becoming contributes to the dialectical articulation of the ultimate whole.

ly, this is something appealing in Hegel, but the question persists as to whether in all instances justice is done to the overdeterminacy. Not surprisingly, the mystery is dispelled. Nor is there any reserve of Heideggerian *Verborgenheit*. This form of dialectic is more linked to a teleology of knowing which proceeds from wonder to the dissolution of wonder; not in terms of a determinate truth, but a self-determining "being true," relative to which there is nothing finally other. Wonder at the mystery may, on this view, be granted at the beginning, but at the end this is entirely brought out of its hiddenness, and there is no more wonder, and no more mystery. This is explicitly so in Hegel's understanding of the teleology of art and religion, each privileged with membership of absolute spirit, but it is a membership which in the end is overtaken by the ultimacy of philosophy and its concept, for which there is no mystery, in principle and in the end. Interestingly, Hegel does speak of the mystical as passing beyond the understanding (*Verstand*), but the mystery does not pass beyond Reason (*Vernunft*), for on this truest level, it is perfectly manifest.

METAXOLOGY AND BEING TRUE TO MYSTERY

In the metaxological orientation to truth, we are seeking to do justice to the overdeterminacy of being, beyond determination, indeterminacy, and self-determination. Moreover, the overdeterminacy is at issue with respect to both selving and othering, as well as the between-relations in which and through which they are in communication. Both selving and othering have to be granted their truth and their asking of us that we be true to both. For there is an immanent otherness to selving that is the threshold of the overdeterminate in the intimacy of our singular being. Further, there is the exceeding otherness of the milieu of being in its given thereness which communicates plurivocally of the ontological potencies of the (primal) ethos.[16] A dialectical holism does not seem true enough to the overdeterminacy of selving and othering, and of both together. By contrast, a *logos* of the *metaxu* suggests a community of being true, faithful to the pluralism of relations between self and other. The point could be put from the side of the universal or the particular. The

---

16. In *God and the Between,* when I speak of these plurivocal communications in terms of the hyperboles of being, they serve as thresholds of mystery.

point is evident even when the singular is in revolt against the community. The solicitation of this fidelity is at work even in the corrosion of skepticism or in self-congratulation about one's superior irony. There is always the call of truth—an *ananke* from which we cannot escape, because every escape is within this *ananke* we think we are escaping. This *ananke* witnesses to an already effective community of mind and truth, at work in the mindfulness that tries to be truthful. It would be difficult to make sense of our seeking this or that truth, were we not already in such a reserved community. We are what we are as truth-seekers by virtue of being in this metaxological community of truth. We are truthful by virtue of being able to cooperate faithfully in the work of its truth.

An interesting point is that the *pragmatic notion of truth* (in C.S. Peirce, for instance) in its appeal to the "the long run," *vis-à-vis* the community of inquiry, shares something with the more recent deconstruction of univocal truth, perhaps because both are in the end essentially "Kantian" positions.[17] We can see both as moving beyond a univocal fixation with the present and with what we now determine to be the case. We might fear that the present fixes us to what is, but there is an equivocity in all of this. I would ask: if we appeal to the long run, are we appealing just to the true as a regulative ideal, and if so, is it only a heuristic anticipation we cannot avoid, and yet which never allows us now to say without demur: this is? Truth risks being an always deferred other, then, not entirely different from the indeterminate "to come" we find with deconstruction, or that place "somewhere over the rainbow" about which the song dreams. To cite the White Queen in *Alice Through the Looking Glass*: "The rule is, jam to-morrow, jam yesterday but never jam today.... It's jam every other day: today isn't any other day, you know." Alice objects: "It MUST come sometimes to 'jam today.'" She truthfully answers the White Queen, "It's dreadfully confusing!" Alice is a wise child. We too must ask if there is any sense in which the true is constituted as actu-

---

17. As noted above, Aristotle said that the least number, properly speaking, is two (*Physics* 220a27). To count to one you have to count to two. One thinks of Hegel's counting to three in order to be able to count to one truly. If one is univocity, if two is equivocity, if three is dialectic (becoming one again in self-mediating dialectic), then four is metaxology. As four is beyond the self-mediating one, properly to count to two you have to count to four. Metaxology is not monadic, dyadic, triadic; metaxology is quadratic. One thinks of C.S. Peirce's firstness, secondness, thirdness, but a metaxological sense of secondness would require fourthness beyond dialectical thirdness.

al. I think one has to say that if truth is only what will come to be determined "in the long run," then we risk evacuating it of its claim. In pointing beyond the univocal fixation of the present, and invoking a deferral that will never end, we offer in the latter case a voiding equivocation not only in relation to the true as such, but also in relation to our own being true. Suppose the true were only a regulative ideal toward which we move, or something to come on which we must wait, perhaps in a painful process of infinite deferment, then can we even speak of the true as such an "ideal" at all, and can we make any intelligible sense of the character of our longing and waiting?

Put simply, can any ideal be regulative at all if it is not in some respect *already at work* in our present circumstances, drawing on our seeking, or spurring our transcending, or communicating to us what we now lack, though we long for it. The true has to be already at play now; it cannot be deferred to what will eventually be established, for then it would never eventually be established. Our truthful longing moves us "toward" the true, and in this "toward" the true is already intimate, otherwise there would be no longing at all, and no being truthful, even when we know we do not know the truth. Being truthful points to a constitutive "true," and this is there enigmatically and overdeterminately at work in the between. Once again the overdetermination is not an indeterminacy, and while it may be beyond univocal determination, it is not exhausted by a self-determining process of thought.

One has to raise the doubleness of the equivocal to a higher level of mindful finesse. This is ingredient in what it means to be true to mystery. Thus one might suggest that the true is *both* a regulative ideal (for we never completely possess it, though we might always tend toward it), *and also* constitutive actuality, especially with respect to its already effective being at work intimately in our being truthful. The longing of being truthful is a belonging with the true, belonging to the true, as intimately communicating in and through our self-transcending. The true is constitutive in regard to our being truthful; it is regulative as the unconditional and ultimate, toward which we tend but of which we are never the masters. We are never on a par with truth's transcendence. The double nature of metaxological truth reflects this. This is a position that is neither Kantian nor Hegelian. Kant postulates a regulative ideal with a kind of transcendence—an always deferred completion which cannot explain the present work of the unconditioned. Hegel proposes a constitutive ideal entirely immanent; unconditionally immanent truth without proper reserve, and without true transcendence. And for reasons given above, it cannot be identified with Heideggerian *alētheia* also.

In relation to being true metaxologically, it is not a question of pitting this against the other configurations of being true but more a matter of aligning them with the fuller reserves of the promise of truth diversely at work in each. We can recuperate something of the truth of correspondence in being true metaxologically. Correspondence is not univocal facticity, not idealistic generality, but *truthful responsibility*, a shared honesty of being inseparable from the communication of being true. Nor do we close ourselves off from the sting of skepticism or harden ourselves to all the seductive insinuations of equivocity, or turn our backs on the relative responsibility of self-determining thinking. These too awaken in the unconditional call to be truthful, awaken us to this call, and so partake of the community of being true. Our middle condition comes home to us in a shared metaphysical con-fidence of being. An intermediated condition of being truthful incarnates for human beings an elemental honesty and ultimate metaphysical con-fidence. We come to know ourselves in a community of truth already shared, and shaping us before we shape ourselves. (This is a very Catholic thought, especially too if one's sense of the catholic points toward the *intimate universal*.) Our share of truth, our sharing of truth in being truthful, partakes of what is always more. Once again we do not possess absolute truth, but in honesty we are not devoid of community with it. In the between-beings we are, these extremes of poverty and plenty touch and spark, in the night of mystery, an astonishing asking of us to be truthful. We cannot close back into ourselves out of relation to what is other and beyond us. Quite to the contrary, there can be no such closure, for as between-beings we are beyond ourselves in being ourselves.

In summary, then, there is a plurivocity to being true metaxologically. First, there is the unconditional demand of *truth to self*. This may entail a cruel purgation, as we are often vain, and love the untruth of the half-true. There is an agapeic generosity to self in being true to self—in the end a consent that is not at all cruel. The most intimate cruelty occurs in the way we are the untrue in fighting against the purgation of our clogged porosity of being, porosity to the true. There is something existential about this, and there can also be something confessional about this. It bears on a witness to self, a witness of self—and in community, because before others or another. If God is the ultimate other, sacred confession is the most intimate form of being true to self—in the sight of another. Augustine tried to enact this, finding that one cannot enact it completely, for one forgets, though one can witness to it, with purged porosity, with acknowledged forgetfulness, and with love for the other who attends. There is something merciless here and also something more deeply merciful. Practice the truth with love: this applies to our own self-knowledge also. If we hate ourselves, we are not being true. There is an agapeic consent in being true to self. We find ourselves in being affirmed before we find ourselves and affirm ourselves. Truthfulness to self is a kind of fullness after all, itself enfolded by the fuller fullness of the metaxological community of being. In a way, we are always talking about a love that lives in us—a love of truth alive in us. We may easily tell lies, but we hate to be told lies, as Augustine noted long ago. This testifies to that living love we are—and which we frequently betray—though we hate ourselves to be betrayed, and even this our hate reveals the more primordial love.

We are this living love, not just in virtue of loving ourselves but in virtue of finding ourselves in being loved. There is *the other side* to being metaxologically true that is not and cannot be just our own truth. I do not see this as just an intersubjective acknowledgment of the truth of others, fellow others. That is part of it, to be sure, but more deeply the notion of the very otherness of the true is here at issue. One might even talk of the *transcendence* of truth. The immanently unconditional meets the hyperbolically unconditional. The intimate universal is what is here at stake. It is at stake in confession and witnessing. And there is nothing self-insistent here: there is a call that does not insist but invites; that makes way in making a way; that hollows out a space for spiritual freedom that will hallow truthfulness.

There is a kind of Augustinian suggestiveness to the paradoxical doubleness here: intimate interiorizing of truthfulness is coupled with emphatic accentuation of the transcendence of truth as other. We recollect truth in inwardness, truth thus recollected in being truthful recedes beyond recollection. We face the perplexing enigma of the true as excessive, both intimately and transcendently. Always beyond us, we are always the quest of it, and yet the quest shows that already we are intimate with it. A *metanoia* is required of us: reverse the reversal of defining the true as only for us. Rather it is for us to own that the true is not for us to own; and as so simply not for us, it is so for us. Otherness and interiority interface in the intimate universal.

In being true to mystery we remain true to our constitution as between-beings. The beast does not know it does not know; the god knows it knows; the human being knows it does not know, and thus knows, though it does not know. This last is a complicated double condition: between empty and full, and both empty and full, and neither empty nor full. It seems like something entirely equivocal, even duplicitous, but the question is whether this duplex being is just duplicitous or rather saturated with an equivocity that it must seek to intermediate. One might say: as dialectic raises univocity to a higher power, so metaxology raises equivocity to a higher power. Even then this may mean that the human being will never absolutely dissolve the equivocity through itself—to do so through itself alone would be to reiterate the equivocity. The equivocity is not a duplicity to be replaced by univocity, but a mystery whose excess affirmatively constitutes the condition of between-being as such: a mystery whose intermediation yields an understanding that does not cause the mystery to evaporate but rather allows us to come to know the mystery at depths of wonder that will never be dispelled.

8 ∽ Flux-Gibberish

For and against Heraclitus

OPENING

This reflection is occasioned by an impression gleaned from Aristotle's *Metaphysics*. It is a not a reflection on Heraclitus in the mode of straightforward scholarly or philological study but one inspired by, *companioned* by Heraclitus. In a *companioning approach* the thinker who occasions the reflection is less an object of scholarly research and more one who brings forth connatural thinking in us, as we try to understand him and the matters that engage him. Such a companioning approach has not been uncommon with Heraclitus, as he seems to be just the kind of thinker that calls forth such a response. There is another approach that I call the *ventriloquizing approach* which makes the thinker a medium on whom to project the favored ideas of the interpreter. Companioning can become ventriloquizing, and then the words we have of Heraclitus function like such a medium: Rorschach blots or indeterminate pictures onto which we project ourselves. I have that worry with some of the important interpreters of Heraclitus, at times with Heidegger, for instance, though he might well make claim to epitomize companioning thought with Heraclitus.[1] I will look at aspects of the respective approaches of Hegel and

---

1. A separate study would be needed to do justice to Heidegger's engagement with Heraclitus. In *Early Greek Thinking*, trans. D. F. Krell and F. A. Capuzzi (San Francisco, Calif.: Harper and Row, 1975) Heidegger's rumination on *alētheia* offers some of his best thoughts, with some bearing on the doubleness I take up below (see 113–14). While Heidegger's *Heraclitus Seminar* has a number of well-formulated insights, his reflections in the essay on "Logos" tell us perhaps more about Heidegger than Heraclitus. I have offered some thoughts on the porosity of being which seems to me to enter a space where Heidegger's sense of *alētheia* might be developed in directions not quite the same as Heidegger's. As called to agapeic service of the true, our being truthful does not make us the "wrester" of truth from its hiddenness, or even its thief, but the receiver of it, the beneficiary of its gift. To vary slightly my pious question: How get from robbery to grace?

Nietzsche, both of whom witness to a sense of Heraclitus's companioning presence.[2] And yet here too one senses some element of ventriloquizing, and the voice of Heraclitus comes to sound not entirely unlike the voice of Hegel or of Nietzsche. Admittedly, there may be an inevitable temptation to find in Heraclitus what one brings to him. It may be impossible to avoid ventriloquizing entirely. At the same time, there is something *resistant* in Heraclitus's mode of articulation that makes one diffident in (pro)claiming that now, at last, one is the privileged interpreter to understand him and fully take his philosophical measure. Heraclitus offers us striking thoughts that strike one into thought—thought that opens up philosophical porosity to the deepest perplexities. He can be challenging as a companioning thinker without necessarily being made an object of scholarly research which, of course, is not to gainsay the need to learn from the scholars and philologists.

I will explain presently the impression gleaned from Aristotle, but overall I am interested in the relation of becoming and intelligibility, interested in how the identification of Heraclitus as a thinker of flux has been understood as undermining the stability of intelligibility. Pure flux without stable intelligibility would seem to lead to "flux-gibberish," as I am inclined to call it. In the final analysis becoming would seem to be devoid of an abiding intelligibility, while our efforts to articulate it without falsification would seem to lead to gibberish rather than articulate speech. I think of Socrates in the *Theaetetus* (183a) where he connects the position that all is motion with Protagoras's view of man as the measure: "if all things are in motion, every answer, on whatever subject, is equally correct."[3] If all things are equally correct, all things are equally incorrect (a view that comes alive again and again, in Nietzsche's *Birth of Trag-*

---

2. On ventriloquizing and companioning hermeneutical practices, and indeed also on other possible approaches, specifically with respect to Hegel, see my paper, "Despoiling the Egyptians—Gently: Merold Westphal and Hegel" in *Gazing through a Prism Darkly Reflections on Merold Westphal's Hermeneutical Epistemology*, ed. B. Keith Putt (Bronx, N.Y.: Fordham University Press, 2009), 20–34. The points made there can have application to other thinkers also, Heraclitus included.

3. "Supporters of the theory of forms were led to it by means of Heraclitus's argument concerning truth, in which he holds that whatever is perceived by the senses is in a state of flux. [Accepting that much of his argument these philosophers go on to argue] that if there is to be science our knowledge of anything there must be other entities in nature besides those perceived by the senses, inasmuch as there can be no science of what is in a state of flux." *Metaphysics* 1078b12, as translated in *The Presocratics*, ed. Philip Wheelwright (New York: Macmillan, 1985), 80.

edy, for instance). The threat of flux-gibberish does not seem so far away. I will come again to what I intend by "flux-gibberish" and how this bears on the determinacy and constancy of intelligibility. But if some pervading sense of the flow of becoming must be granted, how does this bear on the constancy of intelligibility? My guiding question: how should one think the flow and the constancy together? And can we look less askance on gibberish and what its equivocal promise communicates? If we have to speak against Heraclitus, do we need also to speak for him, even more for than against him? My reflections will be as much about flux and gibberish as about the inspiring companionship of Heraclitus.

ARISTOTLE'S IRRITATION

Reading Aristotle's *Metaphysics* one can be struck by what seems like an irritated tone in his presentation of thinkers whom one can take to be the defenders of the flux. The irritated tone is ambiguous in that it is not always directly and immediately zoned on the person of Heraclitus himself, but seems to regard those influenced by his doctrines, those Heracliteans who perhaps put stress *only* on flux, followers perhaps not entirely true to the very rich complexity of Heraclitus himself. Heraclitus is indeed mentioned when Aristotle calls the law of contradiction the most certain (*Metaphysics* 1005b20). With regard to such a first axiom, those who demand a demonstration lack education (1006a). The word that Aristotle uses here is *apaideusia*, one who is not the beneficiary of *paideia*, one still a *pais*, a child, an *infans*, without language, perhaps one still babbling, gibbering—I will return to an overlap with Heraclitus's child. In *Metaphysics* IV we sense a certain *exasperation* to his criticism. Those people who demand a reason for everything, claim the right to contradict themselves (1011a). Again Heraclitus is not expressly named but Aristotle refers to those who affirm and deny. The goal seems to be to say both "yes" and "no" (1008a), and perhaps neither "yes" nor "no." Such a thinker thinks and does not think (1008b) and the question is posed: what is the difference between him and a vegetable? Earlier Aristotle had said that here discussion is pointless (1008a30). Again he makes reference to the "professed followers of Heraclitus" as well as Cratylus (1010a), with respect to the indeterminate and the impossibility of true predication.

A remark on Plato's *Cratylus* is not irrelevant here. Most philosophical interest has been focused on the reflection on names and things in the latter part of the dialogue, but in truth there is much in Socrates's earlier etymological concerns in *Cratylus* that is related to my theme of flux-gibberish. What can we say at all, if all is flux? Cratylus himself is said to have been reduced to silence, allowing himself only the gesture of communicating with his raised finger. Aristotle rightly draws our attention to the performative oddness of this. A raised finger, whether index finger or not, indicates. But what? Think of Cratylus as not unlike an ancient Samuel Beckett as trying to back out of words, but the unwording can only be done with words. The silence of the flux is not exactly the gibberish of the flux and yet to speak its silence we must give a sign, must word the unwording.

Undoubtedly too, the context of the *Cratylus* is very Heraclitean, with the stress on running, motion, and so on—even to the metaphor of Socrates himself as a runner in the athletic games who in rushing along cannot quite stay on the racecourse (414b; see also 420d). Even if some of Socrates's etymologies risk being parodies of the Heracliteans, they make lots of sense, given the orientation that is communicated by Socrates's ingenuity. Socrates is both playful and serious in offering his etymologies of the gods. The Loeb translation speaks of these as "facetious" but this has connotations of superciliousness.[4] "Being facetious" does not capture entirely the doubleness of being playful and serious simultaneously. Socrates says: "For the gods too are fond of play" (*philopaísomenes gar kai theoí*, 406c). The word *paidikon* recalls too the word *paideia*: having relation to the child who in being playful is yet serious. Call this doubleness of Socrates a lighthearted Heracliteanism. He vindicates the possibility of a *comic Heraclitus*, by contrast with Heraclitus of lore as "the weeping philosopher." Comedy and *logos* are not simply antithetical, and there is a mordant humor in some of Heraclitus's sayings.

One is tempted to juxtapose Socrates's playfulness to the ponderous seriousness of Heideggerian etymologies. Where is the laughter in Heidegger's thinking? What role has the comic poet in the destiny of Heideggerian *Seyn*? There is nothing analogous to the huge role Plato gives to Aristophanes in the *Symposium*. Notice how again and again Socrates re-

---

4. Plato, *Cratylus*, in *Plato in Twelve Volumes*, trans. H. N. Fowler, Loeb Classical Library (Cambridge, Mass.: Harvard University Press, 1970), 4:81.

fers back to the *archaic* meanings of words as the most true, and the most liable to distortion by additions or deletions over time; notice indeed his contrivance, his *mechanē*, of attributing these distortions to outside influences, the influences of the *barbaroi*. One might see here the comparison of the autochthonous and the allochthonous—almost Heideggerian, did not Socrates's playfulness communicate an explicit disclaimer that we must take all of this with some grain of etymological salt. Yes, perhaps these etymologies might even be true, but we must retain the orientation of the "likely story" in the double sense of likely, meaning likely and unlikely! Still, it is undoubtedly true that many of his philosophical etymologies of the names of the gods (including those of Cronos and Rhea, in 401e–402b) are deeply interesting, even *qua* speculative suggestions, because to one who is attuned to what is on offer there is a deeplying ontological orientation coming through in the playfulness.[5] To do justice to this would require another study.

To return more directly to Aristotle: among the important issues at stake are his commitment to the law of identity and the law of excluded middle. A being is itself and not another thing. It is logically impossible to suppose that the same thing is and is not, as some think Heraclitus said (*Metaphysics* 1005b24). To be is to be determinate, a *tode ti*.[6] If this is the case, our quest for intelligibility will always be marked by a certain predilection for *univocity*. Those who stress the flux will not be interested in letting beings settle into a more or less constant position. Similarly, there will be the temptation to mimic in speech this fluid ontological character in unsettling rhetoric. I am not now judging between Aristotle and these defenders of the flux, merely recounting the impression that grew on me. Thus if these defenders spoke, as it is implied they did, and intelligibility requires some ontological stability, the ensuing position they would embody might be aptly described as "flux-gibberish."

Ostensibly this seems a rather negative and dismissive categorization, but is it so simple? The term certainly will be so dismissive if gibberish is just seen as meaningless discourse, and, of course, gibberish is

---

5. Apropos of Heidegger, see Socrates's etymology of *alētheia* (421b) as connected to the divine motion of the universe, because it is a divine wandering (*theía ale*).

6. "The doctrine of Heraclitus, which says that everything is and is not, seems to make all things true" (*Metaphysics* 1012a). See 1005b: if all true, all is untrue. Heraclitus is named again at 1012a34.

often seen so, and rightly. But the question again: is it so simple? One of the things I want to suggest is that if we look a little bit more closely at the meaning of gibberish, gibberish itself is not just gibberish. And perhaps also "flux-gibberish" might suggest more than just a merely negative and dismissive judgment. There is the hint of dual possibility here. The universal impermanence is not to be gainsaid but neither is a certain perplexing permanence of the universal—perhaps not quite Aristotle's immanent universal but what I call the intimate universal.[7]

I recall how for some deconstructionists, it was flux all the way down, and some critics of deconstruction bridled in a way reminiscent of Aristotle's irritation.[8] Flux-gibberish? Is it fair to say that here we find patterns of thought that would preserve a kind of "radical" indeterminacy that, it seems, do not want to risk "contamination" by commitment to anything more determinate? I overhear in my imagination a conversation with a possible (impossible) deconstructionist like this:

A: The jug is half-full.
B: No, the jug is half-empty.
A: Very well, the jug is half-empty.
B: No, the jug is half-full.
A: Very well, the jug is half-full.
B: You said that before! But the jug is half-empty.
A: You are incorrigible, impossible!
B: Impossible! Yes!
A: But no, No! We can't decide.
B: Half-full, half-empty.
A: Neither half-full, nor half-empty.
B: Not one, not the other.
A: Nothing.
B: [*sighing*] Impossible!

I am put in mind of Hegel's sharp remarks about unbridled skepticism, comparing it to bickering children who love to contradict each oth-

---

7. See my *The Intimate Universal*.
8. See John D. Caputo in his *Radical Hermeneutics* (Bloomington: Indiana University Press, 1988) where it is repeated again and again that it is flux all the way down. The companioning constancy of the *logos* does not always escape mockery: clapped in postmetaphysical stocks for collusion with static being and rotten fruit thrown at it for all the sins of logocentrism.

er.⁹ Skepticism, of course, manifests the negativity of thought, but if it is only negative we are ultimately deprived of an affirmative outcome. Analogously, the above deconstructive oscillation between determinacy and a "certain" indeterminacy is not unimportant for the issue of whether in naming "flux" we are finally naming "anything" or "nothing"; though oddly, this radical indeterminacy seems to have infinitely protean power, and seems just as able to mutate from "nothing" into the superabundance of illimitable excess. And hence one has to wonder if the radical indeterminacy remains so radically indeterminate after all, and that the naming of it is only a *quasi*-naming; and that really we cannot tell if, after all, nothing is named at all. Flux-gibberish again?

This mingling of the negative and positive seems to be the intertwining of two opposites or irreconcilables. The mingling of opposites, or the twining, is often thought to reflect something about the essential character of Heraclitus's own utterances, and I will come to this too a little bit more fully. "Opposition brings concord. Out of discord comes the fairest harmony."¹⁰ I would speak of a certain *saturated equivocity* in this way of speaking, saturated because this seemingly equivocal speech could well be defended as containing deeply affirmative significance. The equivocal speech is often seen as deficient speech by philosophers who put the ideal of univocal precision on a philosophical pedestal. Aristotle has a tendency in this particular direction. And this is perhaps the source of his irritation. Of course, Aristotle is not a mere univocalist, given the fact that he says that being is said in many senses, and given the fact that in addition to the univocal sense, he also speaks of the equivocal and analogical senses. That itself is a large question, and I have said some things on this topic in earlier chapters, but nevertheless the point is this: if there is this saturated equivocity then any simple "yes" or "no," uttered in the mode of univocity, will not do justice to the issue at stake. Again there is a certain sense in which we will have to speak for and against Heraclitus, and say our "yes" and/or "no" almost simultaneously. If this seems to fall into the mold of equivocal utterance too soon, let me say a word or two about the words "flux" and "gibberish" before turning more directly to Heraclitus.

9. *Phenomenology of Spirit* §203; on the importance of skepticism, see §§78–79.
10. τὸ ἀντίξουν συμφέρον καὶ ἐκ τῶν διαφερόντων καλλίστην ἁρμονίαν καὶ πάντα κατ' ἔριν γίνεσθαι (fr. B 8).

WORDING FLUX AND GIBBERISH

I offer a short etymological excursus, mingling, with respect for Socrates, the playful and the serious, and not without due reverence for the gods' high friendship of play. In the word *flux* there is the sense of the fluent (*fluere*) and with this the sense of the labile and the mobile. Flux is often thought of as formless, but this is obviously not so if we think of the connection of flux and reflux: there is a coming and going, we are referred to a recurrence, a pattern. Two examples: the tides come in and go out according to a cyclic pattern, and the circadian rhythm constitutes a temporal pattern ingrained in the body, governing the cycle of waking and sleeping, stubborn to our interventions seeking to alter the pattern of passing from diurnal to nocturnal, nocturnal to diurnal.[11] Or one thinks also of the notion of efflux—flowing out, effluence. One adverts to the notion of influence: flowing in. Flux seems to be a more watery word than a fiery—more Thales's word, and less Heraclitus's word (for whom fire figures notably). Interesting is the word "flush": a rush of wa-

---

11. Here we find constancy in rhythmic recurrence. The circadian rhythm synchronizes us with the daily round of the sun. It falls between 23.8 and 24.8 hours. The sun rises and sets and rises again. This is a very Heraclitean thought: the going up and the going down: one and the same, and yet there is no cease from motion. There is a rhythm of recurrence in the rising and the setting. Circadian rhythm is interesting as an embodiment of the *logos* in the cycle of a recurrent becoming. It is not an intellectual construction. It is immanent in the flesh of the being, and this flesh as living is in communication with rhythms in the cosmos that are not living and potentially mindful in the same sense. The *logos* runs in and through the rhythm. Circadian rhythms have been studied in relation to sleep patterns; for instance, jet lag might be seen as an example of straining the *logos*: though the rhythm is not entirely impervious to influences, it is very difficult to bend it from itself and its own cycle of becoming. Consider how the health of shift workers frequently suffers. Young children go the bed earlier, get up earlier. Older people, from age fifty-five on, recur to the rhythm of the very young; become morning people, the circadian rhythm comes back. In the middle years the energies of the body can shift the patterns of waking and sleeping. But if we are deprived of light, say, by living in a cave, or with someone who is totally blind, the rhythm can be disturbed. Those blind with a little light tend to synchronize with the circadian rhythm. A communication from without resonates with a fleshed clock that is within. The body has its timed being in resonance with the time of nature's cycles, a relevant thought with respect to aging and the timing of the flesh. I take these examples in a Heraclitean spirit: everything runs, but the flux is not formless. A more subtle forming is at work. Not listening to the *logos*, we can override the finer form, say, of the cosmic "clock": our digital clocks, dianoetic machines to measure the passage of time, measuring, however, our projections of univocal instants. In this respect, listening to the circadian rhythm of the flesh is not a matter of "vulgar time." There is recent research suggesting that burns incurred in the day heal quicker than burns incurred in the night; a connection with the low level of night activity is suggested, as if circadian rhythms are in the skin cells themselves.

ter. A flush of the face, in shame, for instance—in the blush, say. "Flush" may be related to "flash," water and fire coming together. We think of a flash flood, the flash of fire and the flush of water together (Heraclitus and Thales). A *royal flush* in poker, the *summum* of card combinations, the highest *run* of the cards, beyond which nothing greater can be gotten; one cannot run or flow or move higher.

Running, of course, reminds one of streaming: *Panta rhei*, Πάντα ῥεῖ, all flows. There is a downside in older age when we suffer from rheumatism: *rheumatizein*, suffer from the flux, from *rheuma* (that which flows), a bodily discharge. Worse in wet weather, it is said according to folk wisdom. Dryness and wetness are not far away in the thinking of Heraclitus. A drunk soul is wet (fr. B 118). *Rheum* and *rhea*, the flow again, as in *diahorrhea*; *logorrhea*, excessive flow of words—already on the threshold of gibberish. (Žižek!) *Rheum*: there is a possible relation to *rhythm*, which marks an unfolding with a recurrent pattern—if there is flux here once again it is not quite formless. There is the story, perhaps apocryphal, that Heraclitus, disgusted with his fellow men, retreated to the mountain and fed on herbs, only then to suffer from dropsy. And to be cured of this— and not before issuing his paradoxical taunt: how do you make a drought out of a rain storm?—Heraclitus is said to have immersed himself in a heap of dung, with the thought that the heat of the dung would evaporate the moisture of the dropsy. Alas, it was Heraclitus himself who evaporated and passed on.[12]

What now of the word *gibberish*? It refers us to a speech that is quick and unintelligible, rapid and inarticulate. It is related perhaps to jabber, to chatter. It was used in the early seventeenth century for the language of rogues and gypsies: outsiders, beyond the law. The language of the stranger or foreigner is gibberish: they gibber-jabber, they gabble. Gibbering is sometimes associated with idiots, madmen; they speak and they do not speak. Think of the "language" of James Joyce's *Finnegans Wake*: English "deconstructed" and "reconstructed" by runs of mongrel punnings, plurivocal in the influx of many other languages, replete with saturated equivocity, perhaps a kind of flux-gibberish for those who would disparage it (his brother Stanislaus thought it "genius gone mad," though Joyce

---

12. From Diogenes Laertius, IX.I; see G.S. Kirk and J.E. Raven, *The Presocratic Philosophers: A Critical History with a Selection of Texts* (Cambridge: Cambridge University Press, 1957), 182.

himself referred to it as a "great joke"). But only recall the moving speaking of Anna Livia Plurabelle, the river Liffey that runs through Dublin, the "Black Pool" (in Irish, *Duibhlinn*) at the end of her journey, as she is about to flow into the arms of the sea; powerfully evocative of the meeting of the waters, riverrun rush home to sea. I think too of the story of the sad man in the tavern who, when asked about his sadness, spoke of his wife's incessant speaking: "She talks and she talks and she talks." And they asked of him: "But what does she say?" His answer: "That she don't say."

Gibberish: a speaking that is not speaking. It speaks to none. Does it give a sign? Heraclitus: the Lord whose oracle is at Delphi neither speaks out nor conceals but gives a sign (fr. B 93). Perhaps slightly surprising, as Apollo is the god of light (among other things, plague included). Of course, the language of oracles is gibberish to scientistically minded philosophers. The language of a Hegel or a Heidegger is gibberish to them. Flux-gibberish: a flash flood of speech that comes forth to communicate but passes by without communicating. Saying everything in a rush, and saying nothing that remains despite this rush. A cascade of sounds seeming to be significant but signifying nothing. Is it idiotic? Idiotic without wisdom? Or can there be an idiot wisdom in it?[13]

There can be an element of threat or menace or fear in gibbering. Think of a child gibbering in fear before a punitive or brutal parent, say; or terror at a ghost, itself gibbering, an apparition of the labile dead that reduces one to jelly, one's bones flowing away like water. Heraclitus, thinker of the double word: Dionysus is also Hades (fr. B 15). The shades of Hades are themselves gibbering shadows, squeaking like bats rather than speaking like humans. There is a late poem of William Butler Yeats in which Cuchulain enters the otherworld, and finds that the dead, weaving shrouds sing, but they "had nor human tunes nor words, / Though all was done in common as before; / They had changed their throats and had the throats of birds."[14] One recalls examples of a horrifying kind of

---

13. The sense of the idiotic is central in my work, for instance, in *The Intimate Universal*, chap. 5. See also "Idiot Wisdom and the Intimate Universal: On Immanence and Transcendence in an Intercultural Perspective," in *Transcendence, Immanence, and Intercultural Philosophy*, ed. Nahum Brown and William Franke (London: Palgrave Macmillan, 2016), 153–81; also *Philosophy and Its Others*, 309–11; *Perplexity and Ultimacy*, chap. 2.

14. W. B. Yeats, *The Poems*, ed. Daniel Albright (London: Everyman, 1990), "Cuchulain Comforted," 379–80. Yeats is very Heraclitean (fr. B 62) when he entertains the thought of dying each other's lives, and living each other's death.

gibbering, such as when William James, speaking of the sick soul, mentions "the *green skinned youth* of black hair" that reduced the observer to horror and "a mass of quivering fear."[15] There is a similar image in Nietzsche: "What I fear, is not the horrible shape behind my chair, but his voice: it is also not the words, but the dreadfully inarticulate and inhuman sound of that shape. Yes, if he only could speak as human beings speak!"[16] Our fear of flux-gibberish is not only logical irritation but here is closer to existential, indeed metaphysical horror.

HERACLITUS AND SATURATED EQUIVOCITY

Here briefly is a picture of Heraclitus in which the above insinuated sense of doubleness is important. Heraclitus has normally been presented as someone who defends the view that everything becomes. On this score, there are many philosophers who have shown deep respect for him, and among them Hegel and Nietzsche can be particularly mentioned in recent centuries. Of course, it is a one-sided picture to think of Heraclitus as stressing only being as becoming, and equally crucial is the doctrine of the *logos* that runs through all things. If there is a stress on becoming, this is not a matter of merely formless flux. To the contrary, truly philosophical attention to *phusis* hears the *logos* that is immanent in all being. We find ourselves witness to a kind of startling doubleness: the conjunction of the fluency of flux with the constancy of form. A process of becoming is not genuinely a process of becoming without those two.

Here are some representative citations where we see something of this doubleness: in one fragment we find the togetherness of the seawater as both pure and polluted, pure for the fish, poison for the human (fr. B 61). The name of the bow is life but its work is death (punning word-play on *bios*: *biós* as bow, *bíos* as life: βιός τῷ τόξῳ ὄνομα βίος ἔργον δὲ θάνατος, fr. B 48). In another, we are minded of how the living and the dead are as changing into each other (fr. B 88). In another again, things are to be taken as a whole and not a whole (fr. B 10). In one more, the doubleness of

---

15. *The Varieties of Religious Experience* (New York: Penguin, 1985), 160.
16. *Werke in Drie Bänden*, ed. Karl Schlecta (München: Carl Hanser Verlag, 1956), 3:148: "Was ich fürchte, ist nichts die schreckliche Gestalt hinter meinem Stuhle, sondern ihre Stimme: auch nicht die Worte, sondern der schauderhaft unartikulierte und unmenschliche Ton jener Gestalt. Ja, wenn sie noch redete, wie Menschen reden!"

descriptions is deemed suitable of God who is both day and night, winter and summer, war and peace, satiety and want (fr. B 67). "It is in changing that things find repose" (fr. B 84a: μεταβάλλον ἀναπαύεται, to offer one instance of Heraclitus's semantic compression). There is the well-loved saying about how things being at variance are in agreement, the harmony being in the bending back, as with the lyre and the bow (fr. B 51: bow and lyre so intimately related to Apollo). To return to the divine again: "one the wise: it is willing and unwilling to be called by the name of Zeus" (fr. B 32). Then further again, immortal mortals, mortals immortal—both together and perhaps as passing into each other, they live each other's death and die in each other's life (fr. B 62). I have already mentioned the double sign of the oracle at Delphi, not I think made enough of by the Nietzscheans: Dionysus is also Hades (fr. B 15). The sacred barley drink separates when it is not stirred (fr. B 125)—for the equipoise of the whole we need the togetherness of opposites of rest and motion, constancy and change.

That sampling should suffice. In many of these fragments we witness the characteristic themes of Heraclitus: not stress on flux simply but on transformation in which there is becoming but also rhythm and recurrent pattern; yes, transformation of one into many, or an opposite into its opposite, but also the togetherness of one and many, of the opposites themselves.[17] One is reminded of James Joyce's pithy phrase: "two thinks at a time." And, strikingly, this togetherness of the opposites, is not simply in different phases of an unfolding, such that the opposites are simply outside of each other. They are not just, so to say, *diachronically strung out but are synchronically superposed*. The *syn* is a between joiner—meaning that it is also the "*dia*" separator as well as a between of transition—the matter is not chronological simply but ontological, I would say. We see also (to borrow a term from quantum theory) the superposition of opposites in relation to the divine.[18] If the Lord whose oracle is at

---

17. Epitomized by fr. B 31: πυρὸς τροπαὶ πρῶτον θάλασσα, θαλάσσης δὲ τὸ μὲν ἥμισυ γῆ, τὸ δὲ ἥμισυ πρηστήρ ... θάλασσα διαχέεται καὶ μετρέεται εἰς τὸν αὐτὸν λόγον ὁκοῖος πρόσθεν ἦν ἢ γενέσθαι γῆ. Kirk and Raven translation: "Fire's turnings: first sea, and of sea the half is earth, the half 'burner' [i.e., lightning or fire] ... <earth> is dispersed as seas, and is measured so as to form the same proportion as existed before it became earth." *The Presocratic Philosophers*, 199. Plodding prose, I agree.

18. The double languages of quantum theory are suggestive relative to the breakdown of the more univocal language of classical mechanics, and the need to think both the corpuscle

Delphi does not communicate in univocal propositions nor conceal but gives a sign, the sign given is marked by a saturated equivocity that can be taken in different ways, just because of this superposition of opposites.

A relevant interpolation: it is important to approach rightly the fact that in all these communications there is a significant inter-animation of *muthos* and *logos*. We do not see the logical as a regnant univocal reason superimpositing itself on equivocal *muthos*. It is *logos*, in one sense emergent from *muthos*, but in another sense nurtured on it, and not as a provisional food that later will be replaced by the truer rational substitute. There is a kind of superposition of *muthos* and *logos*, and hence the saturated equivocity is inherent in, immanent in the *logos* itself. It is constitutive and not provisional. It is not biding its time for the advent of emancipated *logos*. The *logos* is what it is and articulates itself like the oracle at Delphi with signs that themselves resist an entirely univocalizing mastery.

Even though there are jibes by Heraclitus against the religious practices of the day,[19] there is a porosity at work in his thought between *muthos* and *logos*. One senses a univocalization at work in Aristotle that somehow misses the mark when the ultimate principle taken as water or fire or air is treated as an original cause, understood in a more determining univocal sense. The tendency then is toward the loss of the saturated equivocity that comes up from the more mythic root, and that allows these words to be charged with resonances that have been silenced in the determinability of univocal causation. The closing off of the rising up of this root has not happened in Heraclitus. This is not because he is "primitive" in this "Aristotelian" sense. He is primitive in being more in resonance with the original sources, themselves first expressed in myth, and perhaps never entirely leaving the space of the mythic when they are

---

and the wave together: the corpuscle is the staple unit, atomic and reliable, so to say; the wave is the fluent rhythm in which the dynamic indeterminacy and overdeterminacy at the bottom of all things takes form; but constancy and fluidity are both required, perhaps to be thought together in a superposition. In calling for the need of such a double modality of descriptions quantum mechanics does have the appearance, to the more univocalizing mind, of a kind of post-Newtonian flux-gibberish. And yet this seems required by truthfulness to what is. See *Being and the Between*, chap. 3.

19. Bigotry is the sacred disease (fr. B 46); they pray to images as if they were to talk to houses (fr. B 5); their processions and hymns to the phallus would be shameless were they not done in honor of Dionysus (fr. B 15); when defiled, they purify themselves with blood, as if filth were to be washed off with filth (fr. B 5).

meant to communicate these more original sources. *Muthos* and *logos* are communications eventuating in the porosity of being. Close this porosity and *logos* becomes univocal, becomes logic, becomes reason in a more determinate form. If we take the light of the latter as *the* light, the one and only true light, Heraclitus is either more primitive in the undeveloped sense, or more confused in the univocal sense. This is not the meaning of the saturated equivocity.

There is a consequence here too for how we are philosophically to approach the sayings of Heraclitus. There is a certain *performative* dimension to his wording of the thoughts. Performing them they come more dynamically to life. I think of the onomatopoeic quality in the Greek to the famous saying about never stepping into the same river: *Potamoĩsi toĩsin autoĩsin embaínousin, hetera kai hetera hudata epirreĩ*. The fluency of the water is worded, worded as it flows in a speaking enactment that communicates fluid passing.[20] We have to remember the threshold of utterance whereon *logos* is between the oral and the literal, the spoken and the written. We who lack finesse for the enacting *logos* in its *determining* and favor the enacted utterance in its *determinacy* tend also to favor more the ideal of univocal precision in *logos*, in the wording of being, and hence too the fixed proposition. If we are attuned to this threshold of utterance, we understand it cannot be adequate to take Heraclitus only as proposing univocal propositions or theories which we are then to subject to conceptual or logical analysis, that is, subject to the measure of a determinable and univocal precision, for then surely we are going to find that Heraclitus contradicts himself. *Mon Dieu!* This cannot be allowed to stand, and we quickly construct more coherent theories, or perhaps ven-

---

20. ποταμοῖσι τοῖσιν αὐτοῖσιν ἐμβαίνουσιν ἕτερα καὶ ἕτερα ὕδατα ἐπιρρεῖ· καὶ ψυχαὶ δὲ ἀπὸ τῶν ὑγρῶν ἀναθυμιῶνται (fr. B 12). See above my remark about the final flow of the river Liffey, Anna Livia Plurabelle, into the arms of the sea at the end of James Joyce's *Finnegans Wake*—it too is marvelously onomatopoeic. Listen to these lines: "Can't hear with the waters of The chittering waters of Flittering bats, fieldmice hawk talk. Ho! Are you not gone ahome? What Thom Malone? Can't hear with hawk ofbats, all thim liffeying waters of Ho, talk save us! My foos won't moos. I feel as old as yonder elm. A tale told of Shaun or Shem? All Livia's daughtersons. Dark hawks hear us. Night! Night! My ho head halls. I feel as heavy as yonder stone. Tell me of John or Shaun? Who were Shem and Shaun the living sons or daughters of? Night now! Tell me, tell me, tell me, elm! Night night! Telmetale of stem or stone. Beside the rivering waters of, hitherandthithering waters of. Night!" James Joyce, *Finnegans Wake*, ed. Robert-Jan Henkes, Erik Bindervoet, Finn Fordham (Oxford: Oxford University Press, 2012), 215–16.

triloquize a meaning through selected sayings of Heraclitus, a meaning less insolent to our more univocal measures of determinate argumentation. This is something that, for instance, can happen with efforts to interpret the first of Heraclitus's words marking the opening of his book on nature, words themselves insolent toward those who try to understand the *logos* and him.[21]

COMPANIONS OF HERACLITUS: HEGEL AND NIETZSCHE

Nietzsche and Hegel were two philosophers partial to Heraclitus as a companioning thinker, and in them we not find the irritation of the univocal mind with equivocal doubleness. In his little monograph *Philosophy in the Tragic Age of the Greeks*, unfinished and unpublished in his life, Nietzsche tends to offer a fairly simple contrast of being and becoming in his portrait of Heraclitus. He generally sees himself as a bannercarrier for becoming, over and against the mummifying tendencies of the metaphysicians in their sanctification of static being. In *Ecce Homo* Nietzsche suggests even that Zarathustra has been anticipated by Heraclitus. Nietzsche does share with Heraclitus the poetic ability to capture deep insights in an image that is saturated with ambiguity but also pregnant with the promise of significance. When it comes to the more systematic elucidation of what this secret promise is, Nietzsche is not always the most trustworthy guide in wording flux. It is interesting to see Nietzsche's own adherence to Schopenhauer seeping into his early picture of Heraclitus in touches of influence that reflect Schopenhauer's metaphysics of the will, the high solitude of the genius manifested in the pride of Heraclitus, with tragic pessimism not being far from what made Heraclitus "the weeping philosopher." Agon is important for Nietzsche, *polemos* being the father of all things for Heraclitus (fr. B 53). But it is interesting to reflect that Nietzsche in a later work (*Genealogy of Morals*)

---

21. Aristotle, *Rhetoric* 1407b11–18 criticizes Heraclitus for bad grammar in fr. B 1, his opening fragment: "To punctuate Heraclitus is difficult because it is often unclear whether a given word should go with what follows or with what precedes it. When, for instance, at the beginning of his treatise he says, 'Although this logos exists always men are unaware [of it],' it is unclear whether 'always' belongs with 'exists' or with 'are unaware.'" Where Aristotle has a tendency toward univocity, Heraclitus tends toward equivocity, and between the two some misunderstanding is bound to happen. Hegel expresses his agreement with Aristotle's criticism on this point—a surprising lapse in dialectical finesse.

speaks of this crucial antagonism: Plato versus Homer. We are startled to remember that Heraclitus tells us that it is *Homer* who should be thrown out of the lists and beaten with a stick (fr. B 42). Nietzsche did love Heraclitus, but he would not beat Homer with a stick. He would beat Plato. Heraclitus is perhaps more like Plato in his criticism of the anthropomorphic gods, though perhaps in all three, Plato included, the permeability of the poetic and philosophical is a fertile origin of thought.

Hegel, the great systematizer, has something to say on the particular score of being and becoming. He tells us that there is hardly an utterance of Heraclitus that he has not somehow managed to include in his own *Science of Logic*. There is something paradoxical here also, insofar as we think of Hegel, the systematizer, as believing that everything can be brought into the lucid life of the rational concept. How then to pair him with Heraclitus the obscure (*ho scotenos*), pair them as he pairs himself with Heraclitus? Heraclitean obscurity seems the antipodes to the lucidity demanded by Hegel's logical concept. And did not Hegel himself often rail against the obscurity of his own contemporaries, particularly those claiming immediate intuition or romantic imagination as the surest, indeed sacred guide to darkest truth. Heraclitus was called riddler (*ainiktēs*).[22] Consider what Hegel says of the riddling phase of *Geist* which finds expression in the symbolic form of art. Riddles are perplexing and perplexed *beginnings* but the maturing of *Geist* solves all riddles, and attains the lucidity of the rational concept. Here is what Hegel says about the riddle in his discussion of the symbolic form of art: "The riddle still conceals the explicitly known meaning, and the chief thing was still clothing the meaning in related though heterogeneous and far-fetched ways. Allegory, on the other hand, made the clarity of the meaning so very much the sole dominating end that personification and its attributes appear degraded into purely external signs. Now the figurative unites with the clarity of the allegorical with the pleasantry of the riddle."[23]

Symbolic art expresses the spiritual world of the Orient, and there is something of the Orient in Heraclitus, or at least in Hegel's interpretation of him. But one cannot see Hegel quite endorsing the Sybil who, raving, being full of the god, reaches out over a thousand years (fr. B 92).

22. On this see Kirk and Raven, *The Presocratic Philosophers*, 184.
23. G. W. F. Hegel, *Hegel's Aesthetics: Lectures on Fine Art*, trans. T. M. Knox (Oxford: Clarendon Press, 1975), 1:403.

Speaking of the metamorphoses of fire into water, water into earth, and earth again become fluid and fiery (referring, I take it, to Heraclitus's fr. B 31), Hegel says: "These oriental, metaphorical expressions are, however, in Heraclitus not to be taken in their strictly sensuous signification."[24] Hegel holds that the unfolding of spirit will *overcome* the riddle and the oracle. The saturated equivocity, as I am calling it, the riddling, seem at most a promising beginning for Hegel, but the dialectical development of this beginning will drive toward lucid conceptual self-determination. The riddle of the beginning is not seen as promising something other, promising perhaps another sense of beginning (with a half-bow in the direction of Heidegger).

Of course, the affinity between Hegel and Heraclitus has much to do with Hegel's own efforts to offer us a logic of becoming, to think process *qua* process. His speculative dialectic is not fixated on the logic of identity, as everything identical is inseparably related to what is other to itself. In a process of becoming, a being becomes other than itself, indeed becomes itself more fully in becoming other to itself. Flux names an ongoing process of being in which the self-becoming of things unfolds according to an immanent logic. It is not hard to see here the overlap with Heraclitus's emphasis upon the *logos* that runs through things, or the thunderbolt that pilots all things. And all of this with reference to the most common (*koinon*), that is to say, most universal space within which our own truest thinking takes shape. Speculative dialectic is waking up from the sleep of finite thinking.

The contrast of Nietzsche and Hegel helps me state a problem or, perhaps better, an *orientation*. The Nietzschean orientation—and this we see more in his later writings than in the relatively early monograph I mentioned—tends to stress flux at the expense of form. I am thinking, for instance, of Nietzsche's claim in the *Gay Science*: the world is to all eternity chaos. Admittedly, this itself is more ambiguous than just the antithesis of intelligibility and form. In an archaic sense of "chaos," there is contained the meaning of a kind of gap, a gap of which we might think as almost a kind of nothingness, even a kind of between, in which things come to be. Hesiod: out of chaos the order of the gods (theogony) and the

---

24. *Lectures on the History of Philosophy*, trans. E. S. Haldane (London: Kegan Paul, Trench, Trübner and Co., 1892), 1:289.

order of the cosmos (cosmogony) comes to be. Nevertheless, in Nietzsche there is a tendency to attribute this form to us, as somehow imposing our own values and intelligibilities on the flux otherwise devoid of them, and simply marked by a will to power that resists our full anthropomorphization. "Nature is always worthless—but one has at some time given, donated worth to it, and *we* were those givers and donators! We human beings have first created the world that pertains to human beings!"[25] Such worthless nature is a modern reconfiguration of given becoming, not the *phusis* that loves to hide. I see here elements of an inheritance from Kantian epistemology in which the constructive powers of the human knower are stressed, such that without our contribution to the shaping of flux there is no stability to be found there, even though we no sooner contribute intelligibility than we become amnesiac about our own contribution, and take it simply to be there for itself.

Hegel, on the surface, seems to be an heir of Kant in the same direction who would but differ in emphasis, insofar as he does stress the dynamic and active contribution of the knowing subject. Nevertheless, granting our contribution, what we know, in fact, are the things themselves, and there is an enigmatic sense in which our contribution contributes nothing, beyond its openness to the intelligibility that shows itself in the process of becoming as such. I think that this more "realistic" understanding of Hegelian "idealism" can be put in the same family as the Aristotelian view of the identity of the knower and the known. That aside, the important point to make here is that we find an acknowledgment of a certain kind of indeterminacy in the nature of things, but because we are also in quest of intelligibility, we have to make the move

---

25. *The Gay Science*, trans. Walter Kaufmann (New York: Randon House, 1974), §301: "die Natur ist immer wertlos: sondern dem hat man einen Wert einmal gegeben, geschenkt, und *wir* waren diese Gebenden und Schenkenden! Wir erst haben die Welt, *die den Menschen etwas angeht*, geschaffen." *Friedrich Nietzsche: Werke in Drei Bänden*, ed. Karl Schlechta (München: Carl Hanser Verlag, 1959), 2:177. There is no given worth to the "to be" as such. Think, by contrast, of Gerard Manley Hopkins: "That nature is a Heraclitean fire ..." Nietzsche's view, just stated, seems to me to be a very modern orientation to nature, not at all resonant of the charge of *phusis*, communicated in the saturated equivocity of Heraclitus's wording of naturing. What a chasm separates the view that nature loves to hide (φύσις κρύπτεσθαι φιλεῖ, fr. B 123) from nature as always worthless! Nietzsche stresses Heraclitus as a student of Anaximander in *Philosophy in the Tragic Age of the Greeks*, trans. Marianne Cowan (Washington, D.C.: Regnery, 1996), 50. But his insinuation there is of a Schopenhauerian pathos, made congruent with the "wisdom" of the Silenus that "it is good *not* to be."

from indeterminacy as such to something more determinate. Hegel's dialectical sense of the development of a process of becoming answers to this passage from indeterminacy to determination.

Nietzsche has no such dialectical sense, and if I am not mistaken he tends to think that the determination is a superimposition on our part on what in itself is, by its very nature (if one could say that) indeterminate. It is not surprising that Nietzsche would have hermeneutical successors in some of the practitioners of deconstruction, to name just them. One has the impression, now and then, when reading Derrida, that the ghost of Aristotle turns in his grave and utters a wordless communication from beyond death: flux-gibberish. The companioning constancy of the *logos* is not honored highly enough. If the picture above is correct which portrays the doubleness in Heraclitus, in which flux and *logos* are in the state of superposition, to borrow again the apposite notion from quantum theory, then charges of logocentrism are themselves parasitic upon lack of attention to the double languages that are required to do justice to just such a superposition.

To sum up here with respect to the indeterminate and the determinate: if Nietzsche sees the chaos of the indeterminate, it may be chaos giving rise to form, and yet he seems to see determinations from the standpoint of our imposition of form on flux. We make determinate what in itself is indeterminate. This may be a widespread epistemological and ontological orientation today, but it is not Heraclitus. The doubleness there has an ontological, one might say even, theological resonance to it. The mythic language of Zeus needs to be taken seriously, as seriously as the language of the *logos*. *Muthos* and *logos*, for all the strain of their difference, belong to a family in which the true names of the ultimate are sought. Admittedly, there is a recurrence to myth in Nietzsche, often in opposition to what he sees as the superficiality of *logos* in the philosophical tradition since Socrates. I sense that Heraclitus speaks from somewhere else again, and I will say a bit more about that later.

HEGEL'S ENDORSEMENT OF HERACLITUS
AND ARISTOTLE

There is something about Hegel as a Heraclitean that, by contrast to Nietzsche, could be said to be more fully true to Heraclitus, and this on

For and against Heraclitus   271

both fronts of the flux and of *logos*. One representative citation from Hegel on Heraclitus which offers a sort of overview of the issues at stake:

> If we put aside the Ionics, who did not understand the Absolute as Thought, and the Pythagoreans likewise, we have the pure Being of the Eleatics, and the dialectic which denies all finite relationships. Thought to the latter is the process of such manifestations; the world in itself is the apparent, and pure Being alone the true. The dialectic of Zeno thus lays hold of the determinations which rest in the content itself, but it may, in so far, also be called subjective dialectic, inasmuch as it rests in the contemplative subject, and the one, without this movement of the dialectic, is abstract identity. The next step from the existence of the dialectic as movement in the subject, is that it must necessarily itself become objective. If Aristotle blames Thales for doing away with motion, because change cannot be understood from Being, and likewise misses the actual in the Pythagorean numbers and Platonic Ideas, taken as the substances of the things which participate in them, Heraclitus at least understands the absolute as just this process of the dialectic. The dialectic is thus three-fold: (α) the external dialectic, a reasoning which goes over and over again without ever reaching the soul of the thing; (β) immanent dialectic of the object, but falling within the contemplation of the subject; (γ) the objectivity of Heraclitus which takes the dialectic itself as principle. The advance requisite and made by Heraclitus is the progression from Being as the first immediate thought, to the category of Becoming as the second. This is the first concrete, the Absolute, as in it the unity of opposites. Thus with Heraclitus the philosophic Idea is to be met with in its speculative form; the reasoning of Parmenides and Zeno is abstract understanding. Heraclitus was thus universally esteemed a deep philosopher and even was decried as such. Here we see land; there is no proposition of Heraclitus which I have not adopted in my Logic.[26]

One might speak here of Hegel's sense of the beginning of a process of becoming in terms of indeterminacy. Being is said by Hegel to be the sheerly indeterminate, as lacking all determination. And yet it is not for that reason the really first concrete thought. While the indeterminate is acknowledged by him, one might say this is never mere flux devoid of form. Quite to the contrary, here we come upon the very impetus to determinacy, suggesting that sheer flux rather reveals itself as a process of forming, which when more fully developed turns out to be a process of

---

26. *Lectures on the History of Philosophy*, 1:278–79.

self-forming. This is inherent in his very ontology of the indeterminate as such: at the outset merely implicit but as the process more fully unfolds itself, it shows itself as becoming, via the negation of being, and becoming more explicitly logical to the end. But it would seem, in a way not always clear, that the *logos* is at work from the outset.

I should point out that there are many passages in Hegel's *Phenomenology of Spirit* and *Science of Logic* that, on initial reading, certainly would seem to again cause Aristotle's ghost to turn toward the light and the judgment: flux-gibberish.[27] Recall, however, Hegel's endorsement of Aristotle's criticism of the grammatical ambiguity of Heraclitus's formulation (*Rhetoric* 1407b11–18): Aristotle and Hegel are joined together in their philosophical desire for determinacy and do not see that grammatical ambiguity might be redolent of the saturated equivocity, itself full with overdetermined ontological significance. That said, it would be unfair to Aristotle not to grant that his view of becoming is very sophisticated *vis-à-vis* the matter of holding together flux and the constancy of intelligibility. For that matter, Aristotle and Hegel are blood brothers here. There are extraordinary passages in the *Phenomenology of Spirit*, for instance, where Hegel is, so to say, offering conceptual mimeses of fluctuations between sameness and otherness that ask of his readers energetic participation in the very unfolding of the process itself. This can never be truly described from an external point of view uttered in neutrally indicative propositions. This is part of the truth of what Hegel calls the speculative proposition.[28] It is also true of his description of life, an

---

27. See when thought "runs to and fro" causing its terms to "spin … round and round in their whirling circle" (*Phenomenology of Spirit*, §131). "Argumentation is reflection into the empty 'I,' the vanity of its own knowing" (§59). Running to and fro might remind one of Joyce's "hitherandtithering waters" but recall also my claim (in chapter 3) that the modalities of wonder are not a three-layered cake but that there is fluctuation and permeability in tune with the original porosity of the wonder itself.

28. The speculative proposition: "The general nature of the judgment or proposition, which involves the distinction of Subject and Predicate, is destroyed by the speculative proposition, and the proposition of identity which the former becomes contains the counter-thrust against that subject-predicate relationship.—This conflict between the general form of a proposition and the unity of the Notion which destroys it is similar to the conflict that occurs in rhythm between metre and accent. Rhythm results from the floating center and the unification of the two. So, too, in the philosophical proposition the identification of Subject and Predicate is not meant to destroy the difference between them, which the form of the proposition expresses; their unity, rather, is meant to emerge as a harmony. The form of the proposition is the appearance of the determinate sense, or the accent that distinguishes its fulfillment; but that

extraordinary effort to mimic in conceptual terms the energetic pulsation of the living process itself as a simple infinity. Hegel: "[A] simple infinity, or the absolute Notion [Concept], [which] may be called the simple essence of life ... whose omnipresence is neither disturbed nor interrupted by any difference, but rather is itself every difference, as also their supersession; it pulsates within itself but does not move, inwardly vibrates, yet is at rest. It is self-identical, for the differences are tautological; they are differences that are none."²⁹

All this granted, the movement from the indeterminate toward the more determinate, while serving to show the forming unfolding of the logic of process, is oriented in Hegel's way of thinking toward *self-determination*. Indeterminacy determines itself in the determinate and so always is the promise of a more complete self-determination. I mention this because Hegel and Nietzsche do not entirely diverge as descendants of Kant. Strangely even in Nietzsche, what above I call the double descriptions is subtended by a monism of will to power, and the most explicit characterization of this in Nietzsche is *self-affirming*. Self-affirming will to power is not quite the rational self-determination of Hegel but it is not entirely other to it. The monism of absolute *Geist* that thinks itself in mimicry of Aristotle's thought thinking itself is not entirely strange to *the will that wills itself* as the flux comes to full self-affirming utterance. *Hen to pan* can be applied to *Wille* as much as to *Vernunft*. Hegel and Nietzsche are very exotic univocalists, and both of them are not entirely devoid of that same tendency to be found in Aristotle in response to Heraclitean doubleness, interpreted as an equivocity that runs away from stable intelligibility in claiming that all things run.³⁰

---

the predicate expresses the Substance, and that the Subject itself falls into the universal, this is the *unity* in which the accent dies away." *Phenomenology of Spirit*, §38.

29. Ibid., §162.

30. This might not seem evident with Nietzsche but if one reads him as finally being defined by a monism of will to power, then the surface of plurality, even in his later thought, will not be the last word. Noteworthy is the intrusion of Schopenhauer's metaphysics of the will in the picture of Heraclitus in *Philosophy in the Tragic Age of the Greeks*. While Hegel endorses Aristotle's claim from the *Rhetoric* of grammatical obscurity with respect to the placing of words in Heraclitus, and seems to put it down generally to the limitations of Heraclitus "the obscure," Heidegger's sense of the unconcealing that also conceals, conceals even itself in the event of unconcealing, is closer to what is more intimately at stake in Heraclitus. See note 35 below.

THE OVERDETERMINACY OF BEING AND
THE FLUENT COSMOS

Hen kai pan was the motto of the youthful Hegel, Schelling, and Hölderlin for their "Church invisible." And of course, there is a kind of "monism" in Heraclitus: "It is wise to agree all things are one" (*hen panta einai*, fr. B 50). How to think of this? The response I want to suggest is to consider the doubleness differently, taking note of the reserve of communication: just so in terms of the *overdeterminacy* that is neither the indeterminate, the determinate, nor the self-determinate. What I am calling the saturated equivocity of Heraclitus's discourse is his entry into the space of the overdeterminate, and out of that space his effort to speak the superposition of seeming opposites that calls for utterance there. There is a oneness to it: "Wisdom is one thing. It is to know the thought by which all things are steered through all things."[31] Yet there is a doubleness to it, even in the oneness: "Wisdom is one, it is willing and not willing to be called by the name of Zeus."[32] Is this flux-gibberish, and yet not flux-gibberish, both all at once: dark enigma and sober lucidity together?

Suppose we grant the fluent sense of the cosmos, the universal impermanence. Fluency cannot be a matter of determinacy only. If it were, the cosmos would be the collection of static constants, a collection itself static. How one would move from one to the other, how the one moves to the other, would be hard to make intelligible. That we do move, and that beings move, sometimes move themselves, indicates a passage *between* determinations, and this passage between cannot itself just be another determination. Between determinations there is a between of transition, and one of the reasons we often have recourse to the idea of indeterminacy is to make sense of the passage between one determination and another. Where orientation to the happening of process has a univocal character, we will fixate on the determinacies but we cannot make sense of the *passage between* determinacies. If we insist on univocity, this passage between will count for nothing, precisely because it cannot be made univocal.

This is one of the reasons why the idea of the indeterminate is often

---

31. Fr. B 41: εἶναι γὰρ ἓν τὸ σοφόν, ἐπίστασθαι γνώμην, ὁτέη ἐκυβέρνησε πάντα διὰ πάντων.
32. Fr. B 32: ἓν τὸ σοφὸν μοῦνον λέγεσθαι οὐκ ἐθέλει καὶ ἐθέλει Ζηνὸς ὄνομα.

seen in an entirely negative light: it is the absence of determinacy and hence also the absence of univocal intelligibility. In response, what can now happen is that while we seem to save the intelligibility of determinacies, it is at the cost of sacrificing the intelligibility of the passage between determinacies. I take it that Heraclitus understood all of this. But he does not *explain* to us what we are to understand. Like the Lord whose oracle is at Delphi he does not speak out or conceal, but gives a sign. That is to say, in the fragments that are extant we see his penetration of the matter, but we do not see from the fragments how it might be made intelligible in a more systematically articulated way. He sees the thing but does not give us a theory of the thing or a theory of how we see the thing. What we have of his work is not in the business of theory in that respect. This is one of the reasons why his writing is saturated with striking images; the images themselves are saturated with significance that resist an exhaustive univocal determination. The practice of his writing itself embodies a sense of the needed space between determinations, perhaps porosity between determinations needed to account for passage between one determination and another. This porosity perhaps goes a way to making some sense of why opposites are not juxtaposed but superposed. A univocalist might say: superposition means just to pile determinations on top of each other, making it needful to disentangle them from each other, but I do not think this is the best way to understand either the matter itself or Heraclitus.

Why not just assent to the Hegelian response? This acknowledges the indeterminacy, it acknowledges the flow, it acknowledges the necessity of determination, and it seems to connect them all in the more inclusive process of the self-determination of the *logos*. The reason I am diffident about this as the most adequate response is that it stresses the indeterminate as a starting point, in itself lacking in determination that then, just because of this lack, is necessitated to determinacy and self-determination. My worry is that this is not at all the *archē* in the sense implied by the articulations of Heraclitus. This and the saturated sense of the equivocal require something analogous to the superposition of two opposed ways of talking. Hegelian dialectic comes very close to this but my point is rather that if the originating source of determinate articulation is not to be described in the language of indeterminacy, then we have to rethink the matter. The equivocity has to be looked at differently.

I think we need this notion of overdeterminacy, referring here to a sense of what exceeds all determination; what exceeds also the logic of self-determination; what exceeds also the idea of the indeterminate, particularly insofar as that tends toward the too negative, even empty, idea of a merely indefinite origin; exceeds perhaps also the kind of univocal *logos* with which many philosophers are most at home. If there is a saturated equivocity here perhaps it is pointing toward a poetic-mythic *logos*, not the opposite of philosophical *logos*, but emerging out of a source of articulation itself marked by a kind of "too-muchness" for all our finite determination of things. Overdeterminacy and hiddenness are twinned: rising and setting (see fr. B 16) do not offer univocal manifestation, or indeed dialectically exhaustive manifestation. Hegel does not get properly the togetherness of *muthos* and *logos*, nor dwell mindfully enough on the threshold between the two. He offers a teleology of logical self-determination, via a becoming of the indeterminate through its own determinations. More remains in reserve, even as it communicates itself. To name the threshold and to be mindful of the togetherness we need the overdeterminacy.

Given the highly poetic resonance of Heraclitus's writings, one might think here of great works of art as offering such an articulation that is not illogical, that is not alogical either, and that yet exceeds determinate logics of univocity, as well as self-determining logics of dialectic of which Hegel offers perhaps the greatest expression. There is an abiding inexhaustibility, a source enabling of infinite astonishment, an origin out of which finite articulations emerge but which itself exceeds all finite articulations, and indeed any articulation claiming to be self-infinitized (as I understand Hegel's characteristic mode of articulation to be). I am speaking of the excess or "too-muchness," but in line with the saturated equivocity, one could equally refer to the sense of emptiness. This might equally be seen as hyperbolic in this sense that it could not be articulated in the language of an indeterminacy marked by the mere absence of determination. I think one might speak here again, with suitable qualification, of the indeterminacy in a more affirmative sense and not merely in this negative sense.

It is for reasons just implied that I prefer to distinguish the indeterminate, even in this affirmative sense, from the overdeterminate, insofar as our characteristic ways of thinking will tend to link up the indeterminate with the logic of determination or self-determination. The "too muchness" that is also at the same time an emptiness refers us to a more original space of porosity in which everything flows and out of which everything comes to determinate articulation, sometimes in cyclical ways that reveal recurrent constancies in the very process of flowing itself, sometimes in terms of eruptions of novelty that communicate surprising newness to a process of unfolding. That original porosity is very hard to talk about because it is nothing in particular, and hence we are inclined to think of it in terms of the merely negative indeterminacy. But it is not to be described really as nothing in particular, because in this approach our focus upon determinacy takes away from the "too-muchness" as such, again a "too-muchness" that, paradoxically, is an emptiness out of which beings come to be.[33]

I think the distinction between *becoming* and *coming to be* is needed here. The orientations that we looked at above in Nietzsche and Hegel primarily stressed a poetics of becoming with the first, and with the second a speculative logic of becoming, leading to self-becoming. Coming to be is something more original than becoming, more original than self-becoming, insofar as everything that becomes must first be and come to be, before it becomes itself or something other. If becoming cannot be exhausted by the beings that become, in a more original and radical sense coming to be cannot be so reduced, as it is presupposed by every process of (self-)becoming, presupposed also by the things as they become, indeed as they participate in being at all.

The language of flux points to this but it is not enough; and the language of flux with the immanent constancy of recurrent intelligibility may not be enough either. Is the porosity of being of which I speak here to be approached in a *subtractive* way? We take away what stands in the way, and then one has a way, a *poros*—the process is no longer stalled by an aporia, an impasse with no way forward. If you take away what bars the way, you open a path. Is this a porosity? Suggestive though this is, I would not put it this way. If the porosity is subtractive only, then the priority of that from which one subtracts remains. How then to speak of a prior porosity?

Think of *to apeiron*: why and how speak of it at all? (Remember Her-

---

33. On this porosity, see most recently *The Intimate Universal*, chap. 5.

aclitus is held to be a disciple of Anaximander.) We know it was an ancient anxiety that all would dissolve in the fog of the indefinite; only the boundary or the *peras* allows us to speak intelligibly, to avoid gibberish. Intelligibility is defined by boundary. The subtractive way would say: take away the *peras*, and you have *to apeiron*. But then the subtractive way leads to the indeterminate as the indefinite rather than the affirmative indeterminate as the overdeterminate. If the boundary relative to the overdeterminate is made fluid, it is within an anterior openness in which something flows through the openness. But this flow will be possible only if there is an energy that is not just the medium of porosity through which it might flow. The porosity is the between through which this other energy can flow. If we speak again of coming to be, must there be an even more original energy that itself enables the creation of the porosity? Can we think of any flow or flux without such an original energy? If so, the subtractive strategy cannot be the last word. That there is flow means there is more than *to apeiron* as the indeterminate, the indefinite, the lacking of determination. This is where the thought of the overdeterminate must come in, even if we go to the extreme of the subtractive indeterminate. The latter is in the end essentially negative, a voiding of the determinate. But then the question comes back as to how the determinate comes to be, comes to be determinate; how the limited comes to be from the unlimited; the finite from the infinite. Once again we need a language that is more than the indeterminate.

These are hard questions, but suffice it here to say that I cannot find either in Nietzsche or Hegel an adequate sense of the more original coming to be. In both, I suspect, it can be traced to a certain weakness with respect to ontological astonishment before the "that it is" of things. Needless to say, I might speak with Schelling here, or indeed with either Leibniz or Heidegger, in respect of the great question: Why is there something rather than nothing, why being at all and not nothing? What I am calling ontological astonishment is very close to the sense of the marvel that finds its hospitable home in the religious myth, and in which the poet can also participate, offering us an image in which we can contemplate the memory of the gift of the marvel. It seems to me one of the reasons why we find Heraclitus so inviting is precisely because we sense the fermentation, the gestation of that sense of ontological astonishment in his startling, paradoxical utterances.

For and against Heraclitus   279

Consider this: "The sun ... is new every day" (ὁ ἥλιος ... [καθάπερ ὁ Ἡράκλειτός φησι,] νέος ἐφ' ἡμέρῃ ἐστίν, fr. B 6). This might seem to be bland and unsurprising. The sun rises, the sun sets: the diurnal upcoming becoming the nocturnal downgoing. How everyday![34] But if the newness of the day is taken as striking us into metaphysical mindfulness, there could be seen to be expressed in the utterance the ontological astonishment. The day returns: amazement at the light, always old, ever new—welcome return of the trusted coupled with shining surprise out of the sea of the unexpected. The night comes on: trepidation at the impending darkness, perhaps peace settling on the encircling stillness. There is marvel at the intimate strangeness of being at all. "How can anyone hide from that which never sets?" (fr. B 16).[35] This, I suggest, is not an empirical description, not a theory, but is like an exclamation of amazement, as when the child points to the moon and murmurs: Moon! You might say this murmuring is related to gibber(ing) but as idiotic the question is whether it reveals a source of intimate engagement, an *idiot wisdom*.[36]

The point might be connected to Heraclitus's image of time as a child playing draughts (fr. B 52), and I will return to the child and gibberish one more time, but this invocation of the child is again something easily turned into bland platitude. But if ontological astonishment is at work in it, we are talking about something other again. The sudden precipitation of ontological astonishment reopens the original porosity. This is a

---

34. We have this fragment from Aristotle's *Meteorologica* 355a13, suggesting for him, I would say, a context less of ontological astonishment as determinable causality.

35. "The sun is new every day." How compare to the privative alpha in Heidegger's *a-lētheia*? This might seem like the privative infinite, but there is more at play, if the unconcealing has to be wrested from the concealed (in the earlier Heidegger, certainly). This is *not* my point about an original giving of porosity. The original opening of the porosity is an endowing, offered to us, not wrested from the concealed. Recalling again how Heidegger uses the likeness of a robbery (*ein Raub*, in *Being and Time* §29), one is put in mind of Prometheus stealing the fire of the gods, and Zeus as the jealous god who would otherwise keep it from mortals. Theft is not the original gift; in truth, theft comes after the gift given. The primal porosity is not an oscillation between the determinate and indeterminate, not a privative unconcealing of the determinate out of the indeterminate. There is the overdeterminacy of the origin in giving the porosity. This is agapeic surplus rather than negation of a hiddenness. Nature loves to hide. It hides in its agapeic surplus that gives way in making a way, hides in being out of the way, out in the open fluency of the porous between. "How could anyone hide from that which never sets?"

36. See Desmond, "Idiot Wisdom and the Intimate Universal," 153–81; also *Philosophy and Its Others*, 309–11.

reason why the poetic compression of Heraclitus calls to mind the Zen compression of the *koan*. The thunderbolt may pilot all things but when it strikes, we may find ourselves saying with Yeats: "Blackout; Heaven blazing into the head: / Tragedy wrought to its uttermost."[37] When mindfulness is porous to the overdeterminate, there is no (determinate) thought, and there is too much thought; and when one tries to state this (re)doubled condition, one stammers to get it all out. The wording risks becoming a kind of stuttering. If one can catch one's breath the wording might flow out. There is an overload of significance that can look idiotic; when (st)uttered the overdeterminacy looks idiotic.

And Heraclitus's obscurity? We might now see this not as due to a dearth of intelligibility but rather to excess of intelligibility, excess hyperbolic to determinate and self-determining intelligibility. There is a light that blinds us, there is a night that arouses perplexity that is more ultimate than the certainties of determinate day. Heraclitus invites us into that night and into that light.

LISTENING TO WORDING THE BETWEEN

And what then again of flux-gibberish? What again of Aristotle's irritation? Did not Aristotle after all acknowledge at the beginning of the metaphysics that the human being is marked by wonder, and that this too is the *archē* which is the originating source of all quests for knowledge? That is true. But I find it interesting that later and fairly soon in the *Metaphysics*, and confirmed generally by the orientation of his think-

---

37. *The Poems*, 341, from the poem "Lapis Lazuli." For James Joyce's take on the thunderbolt, hear: "bababadalgharaghtakamminarronnkonnbronntonnerronntuonnthunntrovarrhounawnskawntoohoohoordenenthurnuk!"—a word near the opening of *Finnegans Wake*, 3: thunderbolt or flux-gibberish, or a gibberish word answering to the thunder? This hundred-letter word, meant to signify a thunderclap, comes in the third paragraph, just after "The fall(baba ...)"; and after the famous opening, "riverrun, past Eve and Adams, from swerve of shore to bend of bay, brings us by a commodius vicus of recirculation back to Howth Castle and Environs." In the book the thunderclap sounds ten times, each clap being a different hundred-letter word, though the last clap is made up of 101 letters, in all 1,001 letters, thought to recall the 1,001 Arabian Nights, and to signify the commodious vicus (Vico) of recirculation (cyclic history). Suppose, though, there is no circle, no line: no right side of history, not in the past, not in the present, not in the future, but above: above history, in relation to the superior, time's other, do we find the right side? See Eric McLuhan, *The Role of Thunder in Finnegans Wake* (Toronto: University of Toronto Press, 1997), x–xi; he connects the work with Mennipean satire, and the thunderclaps are not at all gibberish.

ing overall, the coming of wonder moves from an initial indeterminate opening toward a kind of closure of wonder. Wonder has to be made more determinate and precise in order to pose a properly formulated question, again in a determinate respect. By these means we make progress toward an answer that itself will be marked by the appropriate determinacy, responding to the initial wonder, responding in such a way that in the answer the originating wonder is dispelled. That he uses the example of the geometrical problem to illustrate this teleology of wonder is instructive. The logic of determination governs the unfolding of the initial opening, which now seems to have more of the character of an indeterminacy of ignorance, which is overcome in the knowing that determinately answers the question put more precisely and properly.

The enigmatic sayings of Heraclitus are (bad) flux-gibberish only, if this is always what it means to give an answer, or to give a *logos*. If, however, these sayings are generated out of an intimate dwelling with the overdeterminacy, marked by the porosity of never-to-be-dispelled ontological astonishment, this cannot be the last word on the matter. To see it from this orientation is to require a shift in the meaning of originating wonder, and indeed in the sense of what it means to answer that wonder. It may well then be that the family relation between marveling in myth and the desire to know (of which Aristotle takes note) is of deeper significance than the supersessionist view of philosophical logic that has been the main inheritance of the history of philosophy.

Listening to the *logos* means reopening the porosity to the original space where the word takes form: a kind of birthing in us, a con-natus, something is being born in the soul, but it is not a self-birthing simply, it is not a work of art giving birth to itself. The birthing of the working of art is as much *received* in the promise of inspiration and carried out in the faithful work that redeems the promise, in work that is not work, as the lifting energy of the companioning power is with it. Like the runner who suddenly has the wind behind him, though were he to look he would see nothing and feel nothing there, for, in a slight shift of metaphor, the lifting wind is a second wind that is his own and never his own and that carries him into a new space of moving along the way. Or to reverse the metaphor, it may be that only in moving fast into the wind and against the wind, that one gets lift, like those birds who can only take off when they first run against the opposing wind. They are caught by the wind, as they catch the wind, and carried up above, they settle on the serene air, forget its lift and think only their own wings keep them up.

I have said just a few words about the fluency of the world and much more could be said, of course. But what about gibberish? It is instructive to call to mind again the origin of the word in terms of its etymology, mentioned at the outset. Gibberish is still a form of speaking, it is a *logos*, though to the hearer it is an unintelligible *logos* relative to logical *logos*. Is this a function of the gibberish itself, or is a function of our being unable to hear the *logos* in the gibberish? As I pointed out above, there are various words that are involved in the etymologies like gaggle, gabble. One might also think of babble: a babbling brook, say, singing the flux-gibberish of nature, of the stream of life. Babbling brooks often generate bad poetry, of course. To recall, the famous saying of Heraclitus that one cannot step into the same river twice has, in the Greek, an onomatopoeic character to it: the words, orally announced, mimic the babbling of a brook. I can only make one point here and it is the following and it bears upon that rich sense of the origin of articulation already mentioned. I am thinking of the babble of children, origins of our own access into the space of the word, into the space of our being able to word the between. The image of the child is very appropriate given Heraclitus's image of the kingly power: "Time is a child playing draughts, the kingly power is a child's" (αἰὼν παῖς ἐστι παίζων, πεττεύων· παιδὸς ἡ βασιληίη, fr. B 52). It is an image much loved by many, including Nietzsche in the famous opening discourse of Zarathustra on the "Three Metamorphoses." In Nietzsche the child is an image of innocent creation: destruction and recreation to infinity but constituting the cycle of the whole.

That aspect of it I will leave to one side, beyond noting in Nietzsche the stress on the self-propelling wheel (*ein aus sich rollendes Rad*),[38] a stress perhaps suitable to (self)becoming but not to the shining surprise of more original coming to be. I will make a suggestion that I do not think is made often, if it ever is. The child is first an infant, *infans*, without words, and then it begins to babble; the babble is gibberish, it is a struggle for determination and early on it ends mostly in indeterminate results, but the babbling is the intimate becoming of the power of word-

---

38. "Unschuld ist das Kind und Vergessen, ein Neubeginnen, ein Spiel, ein aus sich rollendes Rad, eine erste Bewegung, ein heiliges Ja-sagen." *Werke in Drie Bänden*, ed. K. Schlecta, 2:294.

ing of the child. We adults later listen to the babbling of children, and we try to divine in the babble what the child is trying to communicate. (We adults can be speechless, *infans*, with surprise!) The babble in due course takes on form, and becomes more intelligible to the hearer or to the interlocutor with the child. Babbling is on the way to wording, gibberish on the way to *logos*. But now consider this: will the babble ever take articulate communicative form if the child is not in the first instance *spoken to*? The playing of the child with words, its wording of its being in the between, is *not the child playing simply with itself*. There is another speaking to it. If there were not this wording of another, say, the communication of the mother that woos the infant into words, what is latent in the play of babble would not unfold truly, and the child would never enter the cosmos of communication, in a fuller sense. The child plays with itself, but this seems to me to be an incomplete image if we forget that without *the other playing with the child*, then worlds, like words, do not take on the constancy of form that we do find in the cosmos that communicates. This sense of being spoken to before one speaks seems to me to correspond to the difference between coming to be and becoming. The child becomes, it does not come to be as giving its own being to itself, and yet it comes to be. In the gibberish of the flux the communication of coming to be is prior to the becoming of both the gibberish and the flux. And it is because of this that the flux is flux and not flux, the gibberish is gibberish and not gibberish.

Selected Bibliography

Aquinas, Thomas. *Commentary on Aristotle's Metaphysics*. Translated by John P. Rowan. Revised edition. South Bend, Ind.: Dumb Ox Press, 1995.

Badiou, Alain. *Being and Event*. Translated by O. Feltham. London: Continuum, 2005.

Balthasar, Hans Urs von. *The Glory of the Lord: A Theological Aesthetics, Volume One: Seeing the Form*. Translated by E. Leivà-Merikakis. San Francisco, Calif.: Ignatius Press, 1982.

Ball, Philip. *Curiosity: How Science Became Interested in Everything*. Chicago: University of Chicago Press, 2013.

Barth, Karl. *Church Dogmatics* I/1. Translated by G. W. Bromiley. Revised edition. Edinburgh: T and T Clark, 1975.

Bellow, Saul. *Ravelstein*. New York: Penguin, 2000.

Betz, John. "Beyond the Sublime: The Aesthetics of the Analogy of Being (Part One)." *Modern Theology* 21, no. 3 (July 2005): 367–411.

———. Beyond the Sublime: The Aesthetics of the Analogy of Being (Part Two)." *Modern Theology* 22, no. 1 (January 2006): 1–50.

Brandom, Robert. *Reasoning, Representing, and Discursive Commitment*. Cambridge, Mass.: Harvard University Press, 1994.

Burke, Edmund. *A Philosophical Enquiry into the Origin of Our Ideas of the Sublime and the Beautiful*. Edited by Adam Phillips. Oxford: Oxford University Press, 1990.

Burrell, David. *Analogy and Philosophical Language*. New Haven, Conn.: Yale University Press, 1973.

Caputo, John D. *Radical Hermeneutics*. Bloomington: Indiana University Press, 1988.

Clarke, W. Norris. *Explorations in Metaphysics*. Notre Dame, Ind.: University of Notre Dame Press, 1994.

Coleridge, Samuel Taylor. *Samuel Taylor Coleridge, The Major Works*. Edited by H. J. Jackson. Oxford: Oxford University Press, 2000.

Crews, Frederick. *Freud: The Making of an Illusion*. London: Profile Books, 2017.

de Boer, Karin. *On Hegel: The Sway of the Negative*. New York: Palgrave Macmillan, 2010.

Deleuze, Gilles. *Nietzsche and Philosophy*. Translated by Hugh Tomlinson. New York: Columbia University Press, 1983.

Deleuze, G., and F. Guattari. *What Is Philosophy?* Translated by H. Tomlinson and G. Burchell. New York: Columbia University Press, 1984.

Desmond, William, ed. *Hegel and His Critics: Philosophy in the Aftermath of Hegel*. Albany: State University of New York Press, 1989.

———. *Philosophy and Its Others: Ways of Being and Mind*. Albany: State University of New York Press, 1990.

———. *Being and the Between*. Albany: State University of New York Press, 1995.

———. *Perplexity and Ultimacy: Metaphysical Thoughts from the Middle*. Albany: State University of New York Press, 1995.

———. "The Solitudes of Philosophy." In *Loneliness*, edited by Lee Rouner, 63–78. Notre Dame, Ind.: University of Notre Dame Press, 1998.

———. *Ethics and the Between*. Albany: State University of New York Press, 2001.

———. *Hegel's God: A Counterfeit Double?* Aldershot: Ashgate, 2003.

———. *Art, Origins, Otherness: Between Art and Philosophy*. Albany: State University of New York Press, 2003.

———. "Tyranny and the Recess of Friendship." In *Amor Amicitiae: On the Love that Is Friendship*, edited by Thomas Kelly and Philipp Rosemann, 99–125. Leuven: Peeters, 2004.

———. *Is There a Sabbath for Thought? Between Religion and Philosophy*. New York: Fordham University Press, 2005.

———. *God and the Between*. Oxford: Blackwell, 2008.

———. "Despoiling the Egyptians – Gently: Merold Westphal and Hegel." In *Gazing Through a Prism Darkly: Reflections on Merold Westphal's Hermeneutical Epistemology*, edited by B. Keith Putt, 20–34. Bronx, N.Y.: Fordham University Press, 2009.

———. *The Intimate Strangeness of Being: Metaphysics after Dialectic*. Washington, D.C.: The Catholic University of America Press, 2012.

———. "Wording the Between." In *The William Desmond Reader*, edited by Christopher Simpson, 195–227. Albany: State University of New York Press, 2012.

———. "The Potencies of the Ethical." In *An Ethics of/for the Future*, edited by Mary Shanahan, 62–75. Cambridge: Cambridge Scholars Publishing, 2014.

———. "Idiot Wisdom and the Intimate Universal: On Immanence and Transcendence in an Intercultural Perspective." In *Transcendence, Immanence, and Intercultural Philosophy*, edited by Nahum Brown and William Franke, 153–81. London: Palgrave Macmillan, 2016.

———. *The Gift of Beauty and the Passion of Being: On the Threshold between the Aesthetic and the Religious*. Eugene, Ore.: Wipf and Stock, 2018.

Diels, Hermann. *Die Fragmente der Vorsokratiker*. Edited by Walther Kranz. Sixth edition, revised. Berlin: Weidmann, 1952.

Drury, M. O'Connor. *The Danger of Words and Writings on Wittgenstein*. Edited by D. Berman, M. Fitzgerald, and J. Hayes. Bristol: Thoemmes, 1996.

Foucault, Michel. *The Archaeology of Knowledge*. Translated by A. M. Sheridan Smith. New York: Harper and Row, 1976.
Gilson, Etienne. *History of Christian Philosophy in the Middle Ages*. New York: Sheed and Ward, 1955.
Gonzales, Philip. *Reimagining the Analogia Entis: The Future of Erich Przywara's Christian Vision*. Grand Rapids, Mich.: Eerdmans, 2019.
Hadot, Pierre. *Philosophy as a Way of Life*. Translated by Michael Chase. Oxford: Blackwell, 1995.
———. *What Is Ancient Philosophy?* Translated by Michael Chase. Cambridge, Mass.: Belknap Press of Harvard University Press, 2002.
Hart, David Bentley. *The Beauty of the Infinite: The Aesthetics of Christian Truth*. Grand Rapids, Mich.: Eerdmans, 2003.
Hegel, G. W. F. *Lectures on the History of Philosophy*. Translated by E. S. Haldane. London: Kegan Paul, Trench, Trübner and Co., 1892.
———. *Phänomenologie des Geistes*. Hamburg: Felix Meiner, 1952.
———. *Science of Logic*. Translated by A. V. Miller. New York: Humanities Press, 1969.
———. *Hegel's Aesthetics: Lectures on Fine Art*. Translated by T. M. Knox. Oxford: Clarendon Press, 1975.
———. *Phenomenology of Spirit*. Translated by A. V. Miller. Oxford: Clarendon Press, 1977.
———. *The Encyclopaedia Logic: Part 1 of the Encyclopaedia of Philosophical Science with the Zusätze*. Translated by T. F. Geraets, W. A. Suchting, and H. S. Harris. Indianapolis, Ind.: Hackett, 1991.
Heidegger, Martin. *Early Greek Thinking*. Translated by D. F. Krell and F. A. Capuzzi. San Francisco, Calif.: Harper and Row, 1975.
———. *Schelling's Treatise on the Essence of Human Freedom*. Translated by J. Stambaugh. Athens: Ohio University Press, 1985.
———. *Aristotle's Metaphysics Θ 1–3. On the Essence and Force of Actuality*. Translated by W. Brogan and P. Warnek. Bloomington: Indiana University Press, 1995.
———. *Being and Time*. Translated by Joan Stambaugh. Revised with a foreword by D. J. Schmidt. Albany: State University of New York Press, 2010.
Herari, Yuval Noah. *Homo Deus: A Brief History of Tomorrow*. London: Harvill Secker, 2015.
Hylton, Peter. *Russell, Idealism, and the Origins of Analytical Philosophy*. Oxford: Clarendon Press, 1990.
James, William. *The Varieties of Religious Experience*. New York: Penguin, 1985.
Jaspers, Karl. *Philosophy*. 3 vols. Translated by E. B. Ashton. Chicago: University of Chicago Press, 1969–71.
Joyce, James. *Finnegans Wake*. Edited by Robert-Jan Henkes, Erik Bindervoet, and Finn Fordham. Oxford: Oxford University Press, 2012.
Kant, Immanuel. *Prolegomena to Any Future Metaphysics*. Translated by Paul Carus. Indianapolis, Ind.: Hackett, 1977.

———. *Critique of Pure Reason*. Translated and edited by Paul Guyer et al. Cambridge: Cambridge University Press, 1989.

———. *Opus Postumum*. Translated and edited by Eckhart Förster and Michael Rosen. Cambridge: Cambridge University Press, 1993.

———. "The Conflict of the Faculties (1796)." In *Religion and Rational Theology*, translated and edited by A. W. Wood and G. Di Giovanni. Cambridge: Cambridge University Press, 1996.

———. *Critique of Practical Reason*. Translated and edited by Mary Gregor. Cambridge: Cambridge University Press, 1997.

———. *Groundwork of a Metaphysics of Morals*. Translated and edited by Mary Gregor. Cambridge: Cambridge University Press, 1997.

———. *Critique of the Power of Judgment*. Edited by Paul Guyer. Translated by Eric Matthews. Cambridge: Cambridge University Press, 2000.

Keats, John. *John Keats*. Edited by Elizabeth Cook. Oxford: Oxford University Press, 1990.

Kirk, G. S., and J. E. Raven. *The Presocratic Philosophers: A Critical History with a Selection of Texts*. Cambridge: Cambridge University Press, 1957.

Levinas, Emmanuel. *De l'existence à l'existant*. Paris: Fontaine, 1947.

———. *Totality and Infinity*. Translated by A. Lingis. Pittsburgh, Penn.: Duquesne University Press, 1968.

———. *Existence and Existents*. Translated by A. Lingis. The Hague: Nijhoff, 1978.

Locke, John. *An Essay Concerning Human Understanding*. Edited by Roger Woolhouse. Harmondsworth: Penguin, 1997.

Lonergan, Bernard. *Insight: A Study of Human Understanding, Collected Works of Bernard Lonergan, vol. 3*. Toronto: University of Toronto Press, 1992.

MacDowell, John. *Mind and World*. Cambridge, Mass.: Harvard University Press, 1994.

Malabou, Catherine. *The Future of Hegel: Plasticity, Temporality and Dialectic*. Translated by L. During. London: Routledge, 2005.

Marcel, Gabriel. *The Mystery of Being*. 2 vols. Translated by G. S. Fraser. London: Harvill Press, 1951.

Marion, Jean-Luc. *God without Being*. Translated by Thomas A. Carlson. Chicago: University of Chicago Press, 1991.

———. "The Final Appeal of the Subject." In *Deconstructive Subjectivities*, edited by Simon Critchley and Peter Dews. Albany: State University of New York Press, 1996.

———. *The Idol and Distance: Five Studies*. Translated by Thomas A. Carlson. New York: Fordham University Press, 2001.

———. *In Excess: Studies of Saturated Phenomena*. Translated by R. Horner and V. Berraud. New York: Fordham University Press, 2002.

———. *Prolegomena to Charity*. Translated by Stephen E. Lewis. New York: Fordham University Press, 2002.

———. *The Crossing of the Visible*. Translated by James K. A. Smith. Stanford, Calif.: Stanford University Press, 2004.

———. *The Erotic Phenomenon.* Translated by Stephen E. Lewis. Chicago: University of Chicago Press, 2007.
———. *The Visible and the Revealed.* Translated by C. M. Gschwandtner et al. New York: Fordham University Press, 2008.
Maritain, Jacques. *A Preface to Metaphysics.* New York: Sheed and Ward, 1948.
Marsh, James. *Lonergan in the World: Self-Appropriation, Otherness, and Justice.* Toronto: University of Toronto Press, 2014.
McFague, Sally. *Metaphorical Theology.* Minneapolis, Minn.: Fortress Press, 1997.
McInerny, Ralph. *The Logic of Analogy.* The Hague: Martinus Nijhoff, 1961.
McLuhan, Eric. *The Role of Thunder in Finnegans Wake.* Toronto: University of Toronto Press, 1997.
Merleau-Ponty, Maurice. *Signs.* Translated by H. and P. Dreyfus. Evanston, Ill.: Northwestern University Press, 1964.
Nietzsche, Friedrich. *Der Wille zur Macht.* Leipzig: Kröner Verlag, 1930.
———. *Werke in Drie Bänden.* Edited by Karl Schlecta. München: Carl Hanser Verlag, 1956.
———. *Thus Spoke Zarathustra.* Translated by R. J. Hollingdale. Harmondsworth: Penguin, 1961.
———. *Twilight of the Idols and the Anti-Christ.* Translated by R. J. Hollingdale. Harmondsworth: Penguin, 1968.
———. *The Will to Power.* Translated by W. Kaufmann and R. J. Hollingdale. New York: Vintage, 1969.
———. *The Gay Science.* Translated by Walter Kaufmann. New York: Random House, 1974.
———. *Philosophy in the Tragic Age of the Greeks.* Translated by Marianne Cowan. Washington, D.C.: Regnery, 1996.
Pieper, Josef. *The Silence of St. Thomas: Three Essays.* Third edition. Translated by John Murray and Daniel O Connor. South Bend, Ind.: St. Augustine's Press, 1999.
———. *Scholasticism: Personalities and Problems of Medieval Philosophy.* Translated by Richard and Clara Winston. South Bend, Ind.: St. Augustine's Press, 2001.
Pippin, Gladden J. "Directing Philosophy: Aquinas, Studiousness, and Modern Curiosity." *Review of Metaphysics* 68, no. 2 (December 2014): 313–46.
Preston, Aaron, ed. *Analytic Philosophy: An Interpretive History.* New York: Routledge, 2017.
Przywara, Erich. *Analogia Entis.* In *Schriften,* vol. 3. Einsiedeln: Johannes Verlag, 1962.
———. *Analogia Entis: Metaphysics: Original Structure and Universal Rhythm.* Translated by John R. Betz and David Bentley Hart. Grand Rapids, Mich.: Eerdmans, 2014.
Putnam, Hilary. *Realism with a Human Face.* Cambridge, Mass.: Harvard University Press, 1992.
Rorty, Richard. *Philosophy and the Mirror of Nature.* Princeton, N.J.: Princeton University Press, 1981.

Schelling, F. W. J. *The Grounding of Positive Philosophy: The Berlin Lectures.* Translated by Bruce Matthews. Albany: State University of New York Press, 2008.
Schopenhauer, Arthur. *Sämtliche Werke.* Edited by Wolfgang Frhr. von Lohneysen. Darmstadt: Wissenschaftliche Buchgesellschaft, 1968.
———. *The World as Will and Representation.* 2 vols. Translated by E. F. J. Payne. New York: Dover, 1966.
Stein, Edith. *Finite and Eternal Being.* Translated by K. F. Reinhardt. Washington, D.C.: ICS Publications, 2002.
Tracy, David. *The Analogical Imagination.* New York: Cross Roads, 1981.
Weiss, Paul. *Being and Other Realities.* Chicago: Open Court, 1995.
Wheelwright, Philip, ed. *The Presocratics.* New York: Macmillan, 1985.
Whitehead, A. N. *Process and Reality: An Essay in Cosmology.* Edited by D. R. Griffin and D. W. Sherburne. New York: The Free Press, 1978.
———. *Science and the Modern World.* New York: Macmillan, 1925.
———. "Immortality." In *The Philosophy of Alfred North Whitehead*, second edition, edited by P. A. Schilpp, 682–700. New York: Tudor Publishing, 1951.
Wittgenstein, Ludwig. *Philosophical Investigations.* Translated by G. E. M. Anscombe. Oxford: Blackwell, 1953.
Wordsworth, William. *William Wordsworth.* Edited by Stephen Gill. Oxford: Oxford University Press, 1984.
Yeats, W. B. *The Poems.* Edited by Daniel Albright. London: Everyman, 1990.

Index

Abelard, 127
Absolute knowing, 79, 115, 199–201
Adorno, Theodor, 51n3, 151
Aesthetics of happening, 9, 29, 36, 53, 67, 206–09, 240
Agapeic origin, 95, 234n8
Agapeic service, 68; of truth, 234, 24, 252n1
Agapeics of community, 78, 214--7, 219–25, 240
Analogy, 9–10, 22, 49–95, 127n1, 195, 228, 235. *See also* hyperbole; metaphor; symbol
Anaximander, 269n25, 278
Anselm, St., 198n8, 206n18
Anti-Christ and analogy, 54, 168
Aquinas, St. Thomas, 18n1, 21, 28, 36, 49–50, 54–55, 71, 88, 91, 93–94, 117n11, 126–28, 134, 198n8, 220n33
Aristophanes, 255
Aristotle, 1, 2, 5, 15, 20–21, 32, 49, 53n4, 54, 72, 83, 89–90, 93n36, 110, 114, 126, 134, 143, 145–46, 157, 164, 181, 189, 194, 196n4, 237, 247n17, 252–58, 264, 266n21, 270–73, 279–81
Art, 4, 88, 171, 181–82, 185, 206
Astonishment, 4,5, 8 12, 17, 25, 33, 36, 40, 47, 96–125, 134, 139, 154, 159, 189, 202, 205–8, 229–32, 239–40, 276–78, 281. *See also* curiosity, perplexity, wonder
Atheism, 78, 83
Augustine, St. 36, 55, 117n11, 215, 220n33, 250
Autonomy, 23, 26–27, 32–34, 41, 44, 60, 63–64, 66, 73, 75, 79, 84, 90, 123, 169, 190
Badiou, Alain, 19n1, 28, 226

Barth, Karl, 54, 55
Bataille, George, 80, 149n14
Baumgarten, Alexander Gottlieb, 28, 128
Beauty, 69–70, 90n31, 207, 209, 218. *See also* sublime
Beckett, Samuel, 255
Bellow, Saul, 218
Benedict XVI, Pope, 49
Bewitchment of the age, 32; of equivocity, 115; of philosophers, 139, 165
Bonaventure, St., 220n33
Brandom, Robert, 154
Burke, Edmund, 112n9

Caputo, John, 257n8
Carnap, Rudolf, 42
Catholicism, 51–52, 54, 126, 128, 176, 184, 226–28, 230, 249
Child/childhood, 63, 91, 118, 166, 181, 212, 247, 254–55, 257, 259, 261, 278; and Heraclitus, 282–83
Christ, 44, 57, 151, 168, 218, 220n33, 223.
Christianity, 6, 19, 49, 52, 57, 85, 87, 92–93, 153n19, 215, 220
Cogito, 167
Coleridge, Samuel Taylor, 53n4, 108n7
Collins, Ardis, 227n1
Comedy and *logos*, 255
Community, 68, 93, 113, 126, 132, 171, 180, 219–25, 236, 246–47, 249–50. *See also* agapeic service; metaxological
Comte, Auguste, 4, 42
Compassio essendi, 219. *See also passio essendi*
Conatus essendi, 68, 90, 100, 117, 159, 187,

Conatus essendi (cont.)
202–3, 208, 211, 217, 242. *See also passio essendi*
Counterfeit/counterfeit double, 11, 76, 96–97, 119n13, 121, 169, 224
Crews, Frederick, 98n2
Cusanus, Nicolaus, 220
Curiosity, 8, 10–12, 96–125, 133–36, 139, 201–4, 229, 235, 239–40. *See also* astonishment, perplexity, wonder

De Boer, Karin, 151n16
Deleuze, Gilles, 19n1, 44, 51n3, 57, 90, 149n14, 151, 168, 220n33
Derrida, Jacques, 1, 51, 151, 270
Descartes, René, 25, 27, 33, 57, 63, 134, 141, 167, 171, 197, 239
Dialectic/dialectical, 6, 9, 11–14, 18, 21–22, 32, 35, 38–45, 47, 53–54, 57, 65–66, 74–79, 84, 86, 88–94, 98, 100, 103–4, 126–59, 162–63, 167, 169–70, 173–74, 177, 189, 191, 198–201, 216, 220, 222n3, 237–78, 235–36, 243–47, 251, 266n21, 268, 270–71, 275–76. *See also* univocity, equivocity, metaxological
Dickens, Charles, 117n11, 181
Dionysus/Dionysian, 44, 85, 87, 114, 139, 152
Dostoevsky, Fyodor, 80, 83, 114, 139

Earth, 29, 68, 76, 80, 86n27, 108n7, 111, 122, 124, 178, 242, 263n17, 268
Eckhart, Meister 223
Eden, 123
Enlightenment, 37, 51–52, 61–62, 65–67, 78, 86, 126, 137, 167
Equivocal/equivocity, 3, 6, 8–9, 12, 14, 17–18, 21, 22–27, 30, 33–35, 39, 42, 44–46, 49, 52, 49–95, 96, 100, 102, 113, 190–21, 130–33, 135, 137, 139, 142–45, 149–55, 157–78, 162, 164, 166, 169, 171, 174, 188, 191, 198, 205–11, 213, 215–17, 220, 223–24, 235–38, 240, 242–45, 247–49, 251, 254, 259, 262, 264–66, 268, 272–76. *See also* univocity, metaxological, dialectic
Erotics, 95, 126, 206, 211–18. *See also* eros

Eros, 44, 48, 98, 151, 167, 189, 212–17, 220, 222–24, 242. *See also* agapeic service

Faith, 37, 59, 75, 82, 86, 90, 127; faithful thought, 178, 182, 246–47. *See also* fidelity and trust
Feuerbach, Ludwig, 41, 78
Fichte, Johann Gottlieb, 58, 148, 167, 198
Fidelity, 7, 9, 11, 24–25, 18, 54, 82, 88–89, 179, 181–82, 230, 233–34, 236–37, 247. *See also* faith and trust
Finesse, *esprit de finesse*, 7, 9, 12, 24, 27–28, 30, 40, 45–46, 52–53, 56–58, 60–61, 66, 66–67, 71–72, 90, 121, 130, 133, 139, 152, 159, 161, 164, 167, 172–76, 188, 224, 229, 238, 243, 248, 265–66
Finite/finitude, 9, 11, 13–14, 22–23, 35, 44, 48, 50, 53–54, 57, 59, 65, 67–68, 71, 73–75, 80–81, 87, 89, 92–95, 113, 119n13, 122, 139, 164, 168–70, 180, 187, 191–92, 195, 197, 203–7, 210–12, 214, 217, 219, 223, 235, 245n15, 268, 271, 278. *See also* infinite/infinity
Flood of words, 260–61
Foucault, Michel, 149n14
Freud, Sigmund, 98, 216n28

Genius, 53n4, 260, 266
Gilson, Etienne, 127n3
God-man, 41, 76
Gonzales, Philip, 54n7
Gratitude, 185, 187–88, 191, 225

Habermas, Jürgen, 1
Hades, 178, 261, 263
Hadot, Pierre, 127, 128n5
Heaven, 68, 121, 160, 280
Hegel, G. W. F. 1, 8–11, 13, 15, 18, 19n1, 28, 35, 37–47, 51–52, 59, 71, 74–83, 86–87, 89, 91, 93, 95, 101, 104–5, 115, 118–19, 121, 138, 143–44, 146–56, 159, 163, 165–69, 172–73, 179, 182, 184, 186, 189, 191–92, 198–207, 223–24, 227–28, 236, 242–43, 245–49, 252–53, 257, 261–62, 266–78

Heidegger, Martin, 1, 5, 12, 14–15, 18, 20, 28, 32, 35, 42, 44, 46–47, 51n3, 52, 54, 55, 86n27, 100–01, 106, 120, 128–29, 138, 140, 153, 165, 193, 196, 199, 204–05, 221, 226–27, 230n5, 234n8, 240–43, 249, 252, 255–56, 261, 273, 278, 279n35
Hell, 81
Heraclitus, 15, 142, 145, 241, 243, 252–80
Hesiod, 268
Higgins, Paul, 45n22
Herod, 185
Hobbes, Thomas, 66
Homer, 267
Hölderlin, Johann Christian Friedrich, 86n27, 153, 274
Hume, David, 30, 32, 61, 62, 67
Hyperboles of being/hyperbolic, 13–15, 36, 41, 47, 54–55, 59, 65, 68, 79, 83, 88, 90, 92–95, 104, 119n13, 130, 164, 168–72, 180, 185, 190, chapter 6, 230–31, 238–39, 242, 250, 276, 280. *See also* analogy

Idiot/idiocy of being, 87, 178, 203–6, 211, 222, 225, 260–61, 279–80
Indeterminacy, 8, 10–11, 14, 17–18, 20, 28, 39–40, 42, 46–47, 68, 71, 75, 78, 92, 97, 102–5, 112, 115, 118–19, 135, 147, 173, 200–5, 210–11, 216, 219–20, 225, 228–29, 231–32, 235–37, 239–43, 245–48, 252, 254, 257–58, 264, 269–82. *See also* overdeterminacy
Infinite/infinity, 9, 11, 13, 54, 59, 64, 68, 74–75, 89, 96–97, 107, 120–22, 124–25, 168–69, 191–92, 197, 206, 210–12, 214, 216–17, 239, 248, 258, 273, 276, 278–79, 282. *See also* finite/finitude
Irish Philosophy, 128, 139, 156, 176, 184, 261

Jaspers, Karl, 18n1
James, William, 262
Job, 129
Joyce, James, 107, 181, 260, 263, 265n20, 272n27, 280n37

Kant, Immanuel, 1, 6, 8, 9, 18, 19n1, 28, 30–40, 42, 45n22, 58, 69–74, 76–83, 87, 101, 110, 114–15, 128, 143, 147–53, 159, 165, 167–69, 194, 197, 198–200, 209–11, 226–28, 241, 245n15, 247–48, 269, 273
Keats, John, 240n11
Kelly, Luke, 158
Kierkegaard, Søren, 42, 44, 114, 151, 153, 183

Laugh/laughter, 1, 9, 156, 189, 228n2, 255. *See also* comedy
Leibniz, Gottfried Wilhelm, 27, 63, 204, 278
Levinas, Emmanuel, 46, 87, 88, 205
Locke, John, 126n1
Lonergan, Bernard, 228–29, 230n5, 231
Lyotard, Francois, 81

MacDowell, John, 154
McEvoy, James, 128n4
Malabou, Catherine, 151n16
Marcel, Gabriel, 18n1, 218, 230, 238
Marion, J-L, 1, chapter 6
Maritain, Jacques, 18n1
Marsh, James, 230n5
Marx, Karl, 41–44, 72, 78, 98, 143, 149, 151, 153n19, 184
Mencken, H.L. 98
Mercier, Désiré, 128
Metaxological, 2, 5, 7, 9, 12–16, 21–22, 35, 45, 47, 51n3, 53, 78, 88–92, 95, 100, 103–4, 133, 148, 150, 153–57, 163, 169–72, 175, 182–83, 186, 190, 192, 194, 198–200, 206, 210–11, 213, 216, 220, 222–23, chapter 7. *See also* univocity; equivocity; dialectic
Moby Dick, 205
Monotheism, 26
Moses, 160
Music, 156, 165, 206, 207, 211–12, 225. *See also* song

Negation/negativity, 10–11, 19, 32, 39–41, 45, 78–79, chapter 3, 169, 189, 203, 214, 227, 240, 242–43, 252, 258, 278, 279

Nietzsche, Friedrich, 4, 6, 15, 19, 41–44, 46, 80–82, 85–88, 91, 98–99, 101, 114, 116, 138, 149n14, 151, 153, 165–66, 168–69, 220n33, 243, 253, 262, 266–70, 277–78, 282
Nihilism, 85–86, 156n24, 220n33

O'Mahony, Brendan, 128n4
Overdeterminacy/overdeterminate, 8, 11, 17–18, 28, 31, 37, 39, 41–42, 46–48, 58, 71, 92, 97, 102–4, 106, 108, 112–13, 116, 118–20, 125, 135, 139, 150, 171, 173, 196, 198, 200–7, 211, 216–17, 219–21, 224–25, 229–31, 234–37, 239–46, 248, 264, 274, 276, 278–81. *See also* indeterminacy

Parmenides, 144, 157, 158, 271
Pascal, Blaise, 27, 37, 58, 72, 167, 173, 174, 220n33, 238
Passio essendi, 68, 90, 109, 122, 159, 171, 187–89, 201–3, 208, 211, 215, 217–19, 224, 229–30, 241–42. *See also compassion essendi; conatus essendi;* porosity of being
Paul, St. 95, 180n6, 223
Peace, 114, 167, 178, 263, 279
Perplexity, 8, 11–12, 16, 17, 20–21, 48, 50, 54, 62, 96, 105, 111–16, 118–19, 121, 123, 127, 134–36, 138–39, 141, 154, 164, 182, 202, 205, 218, 229, 235, 239–40, 261, 280. *See also* astonishment; curiosity; wonder
Plato, Platonism, 4–6, 13, 15, 19–20, 27, 31–32, 43–44, 54, 57, 67, 72, 80, 88, 92–93, 110, 114, 134, 137, 143, 144n12, 145, 150–51, 153, 157–59, 160, 160–63, 172n5, 194, 200, 215–16, 236, 242, 254–55, 267, 271
Pieper, Josef, 127
Plurivocity, 2–3, 8–9, 12, 17–21, 28, 32, 45–46, 49–50, 52, 54–55, 58, 61–63, 68, 77, 82–83, 86, 90–91, 101, 127, 127, 137, 148, 150, 152, 157, 160–61, 163, 170, 184, 188, 190, 192–94, 216, 222, 224, 236, 240–41, 246, 249, 260
Poet/poetics, 12–13, 53n4, 82, 86n27, 100, 153, 155, 160–92, 255, 266–67, 276–78, 280, 282

Porosity of being, 14, 15, 22–26, 29–30, 34, 36, 40, 43, 47–48, 55–56, 58–59, 68, 75, 81–83, 88, 92, 95, 99–101, 106–13, 117–20, 122–25, 139, 150, 159, 161, 164, 171–74, 182–84, 186–88, 191–92, 195–96, 200, 202–3, 206, 208, 211–15, 217, 219–21, 224–25, 229–30, 232, 234, 240–43, 249–50, 252–53, 264–65, 272, 275, 277–79, 281. *See also passio essendi*
Posthumous porosity, 122
Postulatory finitism, 13, 35, 44, 48, 65, 73, 80–81, 168–70, 191–92, 206n18
Prayer, 74, 237
Prometheus, 279n35
Przywara, Erich, 54
Purgatory, 81
Putnam, Hilary, 237n10

Romantic/Romanticism, 61–62, 65–67, 86, 119n13, 167, 267
Rorty, Richard, 138, 154–55, 156n24, 237n10

Sartre, Jean-Paul, 205
Saturated phenomenon, 13–15, 47, 84, 169, chapter 6
Schelling, Friedrich Wilhelm Joseph von, 38, 45, 153n19, 198, 199, 274, 278
Scotus, Duns, 59
Schopenhauer, Arthur, 3, 19, 41, 44, 80, 101, 165, 166, 241, 266, 269, 273n30
Scientism, 65, chapter 3, 155–56
Serviceable disposability, 123, 125, 215
Shakespeare, William, 85, 176, 260n11
Shestov, Lev, 51
Skepticism, 7, 28, 31–32, 35, 57, 61, 67, 73, 115, 238–39, 247, 249, 257–58
Socrates/Socratic, 15, 93, 139, 143, 150, 157, 158, 162, 200, 213, 236, 253, 255–56, 259, 270
Song, 158, 179–82, 186n6, 200, 206, 247, 282. *See also* music
Spinoza, Baruch, 27, 35, 44–45, 57–58, 66, 74–75, 86–87, 93, 151, 153, 168–69, 174, 220n33
Stein, Edith, 18n1, 54

Stepelevich, Lawrence, 227n1
Sublime, 66, 81–82, 112n9, 197, 209–11. *See also* beauty
System/systematics, 3–8, 12–13, 18, 27, 33, 38, 40, 42–44, 46–47, 52, 54, 77–78, 90, 100–1, 104, 128, 130, 133, 146, 148–55, 266–67, 275

Thales, 19, 259, 260, 271
Totalitarianism, 44
Transcendence, self-/transcendence as other, 13, 20, 33, 35, 41–44, 53, 55, 58–59, 61–62, 65–68, 70–71, 74, 76, 78, 80, 82–83, 87–94, 113, 122–23, 148, 150–51, 153, 163–64, 168–70, 180, 183, 186–87, 191–92, 196, 198, 242, 248–50, 261
True, being, 2, 4, 9, 13–15, 21, 46–48, 58, 85–86, 104, 106, 115, 120–21, 175, 180–84, 186n8, 193n1, 201, 206, 214, 216, 224–25, chapter 7, 252, 256, 264, 270–71
Trust, 34, 144, 157, 176, 233, 266

Ultimacy, urgency of, 186, 217
Univocal/univocity, 2, 5–6, 8–12, 14, 17–19, 21–32, 34–37, 39, 41, 44–47, 49–69, 71–78, 82, 84, 86–87, 90–95, 97, 100–03, 106, 114, 116, 118, 120–21, 124, 127, 131–37, 140–47, 152, 155–58, 160–63, 166–67, 170, 173–74, 188–91, 194, 202, 216–17, 222–24, 231, 235–38, 240, 243–45, 247–49, 251, 256, 258–59, 263–66, 273–76. *See also* equivocity; dialectic; metaxological

Vattimo, Gianni, 220n33
Vico Giambattista, 72n17, 162, 181, 289n37

Weiss, Paul, 18n1
Whitehead, A. N., 18n1, 60
Will-to-power, 44, 73, 79–80, 86, 101, 122, 124–25, 138–39, 145–46, 169, 188, 216, 269, 273
Wittgenstein, Ludwig, 91n34, 136, 139, 140, 154–57
Whole, the, 22, 24–25, 32, 37–39, 46, 55, 58–60, 62, 65, 67, 71, 74–75, 82, 84, 86–87, 96–97, 104, 115, 118–19, 121–24, 134, 136, 140–45, 148, 161, 165, 168, 171–73, 180–81, 185, 209, 227, 239, 243–45, 262–63, 276, 282
Wolff, Christian, 20, 40, 128
Wonder, 10–11, 24–25, 46, 84, 89, 92, chapter 3, 124, 130, 185, 200, 202, 204, 211, 225, 229, 239–40, 246, 251, 272n27, 280–81. *See also* astonishment; curiosity; perplexity
Wooing 82, 121
Wordsworth, William, 108n7, 135

Yeats, William Butler, 261, 280

Zen, 280
Zeno, 143–45, 148, 158, 271
Zero, return to, 47, 192
Žižek, Slovoj, 260

The Voiding of Being: The Doing and Undoing of Metaphysics in Modernity was designed and typeset in Minion by Kachergis Book Design of Pittsboro, North Carolina. It was printed on 60-pound Maple Eggshell Cream B18 and bound by Maple Press of York, Pennsylvania.

www.ingramcontent.com/pod-product-compliance
Lightning Source LLC
Chambersburg PA
CBHW022037290426
44109CB00014B/889